The Origins of the Shīʿa

The Sunnī-Shīʿa schism is often framed as a dispute over the identity of the successor to Muḥammad. In reality, however, this fracture only materialized a century later in the important southern Iraqī city of Kūfa (present-day Najaf). This book explores the birth and development of Shīʿī identity. Through a critical analysis of legal texts, whose provenance has only recently been confirmed, the study shows how the early Shīʿa carved out independent religious and social identities through specific ritual practices and within separate sacred spaces. In this way, the book addresses two seminal controversies pertaining to early Islam, namely the dating of Shīʿī identity, and the means by which the Shīʿa differentiated themselves from mainstream Kūfan society. This is an important, original, and path-breaking book that marks a significant development in the study of the early Islamic world.

Najam Haider is an Assistant Professor of Religion at Barnard College in New York City.

Cambridge Studies in Islamic Civilization

Published titles are listed at the back of the book.

The Origins of the Shīʿa

Identity, Ritual, and Sacred Space in Eighth-Century Kūfa

NAJAM HAIDER
Barnard College, Columbia University

CAMBRIDGE
UNIVERSITY PRESS

CAMBRIDGE
UNIVERSITY PRESS

32 Avenue of the Americas, New York NY 10013-2473, USA

Cambridge University Press is part of the University of Cambridge.

It furthers the University's mission by disseminating knowledge in the pursuit of education, learning and research at the highest international levels of excellence.

www.cambridge.org
Information on this title: www.cambridge.org/9781107424951

First published 2011
First paperback edition 2014

A catalogue record for this publication is available from the British Library

Library of Congress Cataloguing in Publication data
Haider, Najam Iftikhar, 1974–
The origins of the Shi'a : identity, ritual, and sacred space in eighth-century Kūfa / Najam Haider.
p. cm. – (Cambridge studies in Islamic civilization)
Includes bibliographical references and index.
ISBN 978-1-107-01071-0 (hardback)
1. Shi'ah – Iraq – Kufah – History. 2. Kufah (Iraq) – Religion.
3. Shi'ah – History. I. Title. II. Series.
BP192.7.K75H35 2011
297.8′20956747–dc22 2011008815

ISBN 978-1-107-01071-0 Hardback
ISBN 978-1-107-42495-1 Paperback

Additional resources for this publication at http://www.cambridge.org/9781107010710

To my parents,
Hasan and Khurshid

Contents

List of Maps and Tables — *page* x
Acknowledgments — xi
Note on Transliteration and Dates — xiii
List of Abbreviations — xv

PART ONE NARRATIVES AND METHODS

1. Kūfa and the Classical Narratives of Early Shīʿism — 3
2. Confronting the Source Barrier: A New Methodology — 24

PART TWO CASE STUDIES

3. In the Name of God: The *Basmala* — 57
4. Curses and Invocations: The *Qunūt* in the Ritual Prayer — 95
5. Drinking Matters: The Islamic Debate over Prohibition — 138

PART THREE THE EMERGENCE OF SHĪʿISM

6. Dating Sectarianism: Early Zaydism and the Politics of Perpetual Revolution — 189
7. The Problem of the Ambiguous Transmitter: Ritual and the Allocation of Identity — 215
8. The Mosque and the Procession: Sacred Spaces and the Construction of Community — 231
9. Conclusion — 249

Bibliography — 255
Index — 269

Maps and Tables

MAPS

1. The Middle East in the early Muslim period *page* xvii
2. Kūfa in the 1st/7th and early 2nd/8th centuries 233

TABLES

1.1. A Timeline of Kūfa in the 1st/7th and 2nd/8th Centuries 7
2.1. Sunnī Sources 35
2.2. Imāmī Sources 36
2.3. Zaydī Sources 37
3.1. A Summary of the Juristic Treatment of the *Basmala* 79
3.2. The Kūfan Traditions (*Basmala*) 81
3.3. Authorities Cited (*Basmala*) 83
3.4a. Single Transmitters (*Basmala*) 87
3.4b. Shared Links (*Basmala*) 88
3.5. Narrative Style (*Basmala*) 92
4.1. A Summary of the Juristic Treatment of the *Qunūt* 119
4.2. The Kūfan Traditions (*Qunūt*) 122
4.3. Authorities Cited (*Qunūt*) 124
4.4a. Single Transmitters (*Qunūt*) 128
4.4b. Shared Links (*Qunūt*) 129
4.5. Narrative Style (*Qunūt*) 135
5.1. A Summary of the Juristic Treatment of Prohibition 164
5.2. The Kūfan Traditions (Prohibition) 166
5.3. Authorities Cited (Prohibition) 171
5.4a. Single Transmitters (Prohibition) 177
5.4b. Shared Links (Prohibition) 178
5.5. Narrative Style (Prohibition) 182
8.1. The Mosques of Kūfa 236

Acknowledgments

First and foremost, I would like to thank Michael Cook and Hossein Modarressi for their guidance and encouragement over the course of the last decade. I could not have asked for better teachers or mentors. Michael Cook was the advisor for my PhD dissertation, which was completed in the department of Near Eastern Studies at Princeton University and provides much of the material for the first part of this book. The word "advisor," however, does not speak to the countless occasions on which he went beyond the call of duty in providing guidance, encouragement, and, when necessary, criticism. Many of the ideas in the final part of the book crystallized during a series of conversations with Hossein Modarressi, to whom I am greatly indebted for his advice, exceeding patience, and consistent support.

Much of the research for this book was conducted in Yemen. In this regard, I owe a significant debt to Bernard Haykel who, in the spring of 2003, was gracious enough to introduce me to the principles of Zaydī Shīʿism and provided valuable contacts with Zaydī intellectual circles in Ṣanʿāʾ. I am also grateful to him for serving as a primary reader and informal advisor for my PhD dissertation, as well as for his counsel and help throughout the years. Special mention must be made of Ahmad Ishaq and the Imam Zayd Bin Ali Cultural Foundation for their assistance in facilitating access to both sources and scholars. Their heroic efforts at preserving the Zaydī cultural and religious heritage in the face of relentless government pressure deserve far more attention than they have received to this point.

In the course of completing this book, I have benefited from interactions with a number of people. Among my teachers, I must thank Gene

Garthwaite, Andras Hamori, Shaun Marmon, James Piscatori, Chase Robinson, and Avram Udovitch. I am indebted to Teresa Bernheimer, Tariq al-Jamil, Maher Jarrar, William McCants, David Powers, Intisar Rabb, Sayeed Rahman, Behnam Sadeghi, Justin Stearns, and Mairaj Syed for their feedback at various stages of this project. I have also profited from conversations with Paul Heck and Felicitas Opwis at Georgetown University as well as the jarring outside perspective of Janardhan Iyengar at Franklin and Marshall College. Many of the ideas in the latter part of the book were refined during an intensive seminar on ʿAlids led by Kazuo Morimoto at Princeton University in the spring of 2010. I would like to give special thanks to Wilferd Madelung for his seminal work on the study of early Shīʿism, which has inspired a generation of scholars, and for his insightful comments on my dissertation that helped shape the structure and content of this book. I am also grateful to Andrew Newman for carefully reading through the entire manuscript, as well as the anonymous readers chosen by Cambridge University Press, whose suggestions undoubtedly strengthened the overall argument. Thanks as well to Marigold Acland and the editors at the Press for their support in the publication process.

Finally, I would like to express my gratitude to the numerous traditional scholars in Yemen, Syria, and Iraq who took the time to sit down with a rather clueless graduate student from the United States and patiently explain the nuances of classical Arabic legal and historical texts. These centers of learning continue to preserve a long-standing tradition of scholarship that is too often underappreciated in the academy. Their generosity humbled me on a number of occasions and contributed significantly to the completion of this project.

I conclude as one often does in the course of acknowledgments by sincerely crediting my teachers, colleagues, and friends for the merits of this book while taking full and exclusive responsibility for any errors or misinterpretations.

Note on Transliteration and Dates

The system of transliteration employed in rendering Arabic names, technical terms, and other phrases into Latin characters is essentially the same as that utilized in most contemporaneous academic journals (e.g., *International Journal of Middle Eastern Studies* or *Islamic Law and Society*). The primary exceptions to this strict transliteration are certain well-established locations that are referred to by their common names. Most prominent among these are the cities of Mecca and Medina and the geographical regions of Syria, Yemen, Iraq, and Iran. The final *tāʾ marbuṭa* is only indicated in transliteration when in a conjunctive form where it is audibly pronounced. Thus, I use *basmala* instead of *basmalah* but write out *Ḥilyat al-ʿulamāʾ*.

Dates are given according to the Ḥijrī and Gregorian calendar (e.g., 122/740). Death dates are provided at the first mention of each historical figure in the main text. Within the footnotes, death dates are offered in cases where they are relevant to the argument. For death dates of authors found exclusively in the footnotes, see the bibliography.

Abbreviations

HERESIOGRAPHIES

FBQ	Ibn Ṭāhir al-Baghdādī, *al-Farq bayn al-firaq*
FQ	al-Nawbakhtī, *Firaq al-shīʿa*
KM	al-Qummī, *Kitāb al-maqālāt*
MIm	al-Nāshiʾ al-Akbar, *Masāʾil al-imāma*
MIs	al-Ashʿarī, *Maqālāt al-islāmiyyīn*
MN	al-Shahristānī, *al-Milal waʾl-niḥal*

LEGAL AND HISTORICAL WORKS

Akhbār	Aḥmad b. Sahl al-Rāzī, *Akhbār Fakhkh*
Débuts	van Arendonk, *Les débuts de l'imāmat zaidite au Yémen*
DIQ	Madelung, *Der Imam al-Qāsim*
Ifāda	al-Nāṭiq biʾl-Ḥaqq, *al-Ifāda*
Maqātil	al-Iṣbahānī, *Maqātil al-Ṭālibiyyīn*
Maṣābīḥ I	Aḥmad b. Ibrāhīm, *al-Maṣābīḥ*
Maṣābīḥ II	ʿAlī b. Bilāl, *al-Maṣābīḥ*
Mughnī I	Ibn Qudāma, *al-Mughnī* (1986)
Mughnī II	Ibn Qudāma, *al-Mughnī* (1996)

COLLECTIONS OF *ḤADĪTH* AND TRADITIONS

Sunnī

KAS I	al-Shaybānī, *Kitāb al-āthār* (1965)
KAS II	al-Shaybānī, *al-Āthār* (1998)

MAR	'Abd al-Razzāq, *Muṣannaf fī 'l-ḥadīth*
MIAS	Ibn Abī Shayba, *Muṣannaf*
SAD	Abū Dāwūd, *Sunan*
SB	al-Bukhārī, *Jāmi' al-ṣaḥīḥ*
SIM	Ibn Māja, *Sunan*
SKB	al-Bayhaqī, *al-Sunan al-kubrā*
SM	Muslim b. al-Ḥajjāj, *Jāmi' al-ṣaḥīḥ*
SN I	al-Nasā'ī, *Sunan* (1930)
SN II	al-Nasā'ī, *Sunan* (1991)
SN III	al-Nasā'ī, *Sunan* (2001)
ST	al-Tirmidhī, *Sunan*

Imāmī

BM	al-Barqī, *al-Maḥāsin*
KK	al-Kulaynī, *al-Kāfī*
ṬI	al-Ṭūsī, *al-Istibṣār*
ṬT	al-Ṭūsī, *Tahdhīb al-aḥkām*
WS	al-Ḥurr al-'Āmilī, *Wasā'il al-shī'a*

Zaydī

AA	Aḥmad b. 'Īsā, *Amālī*

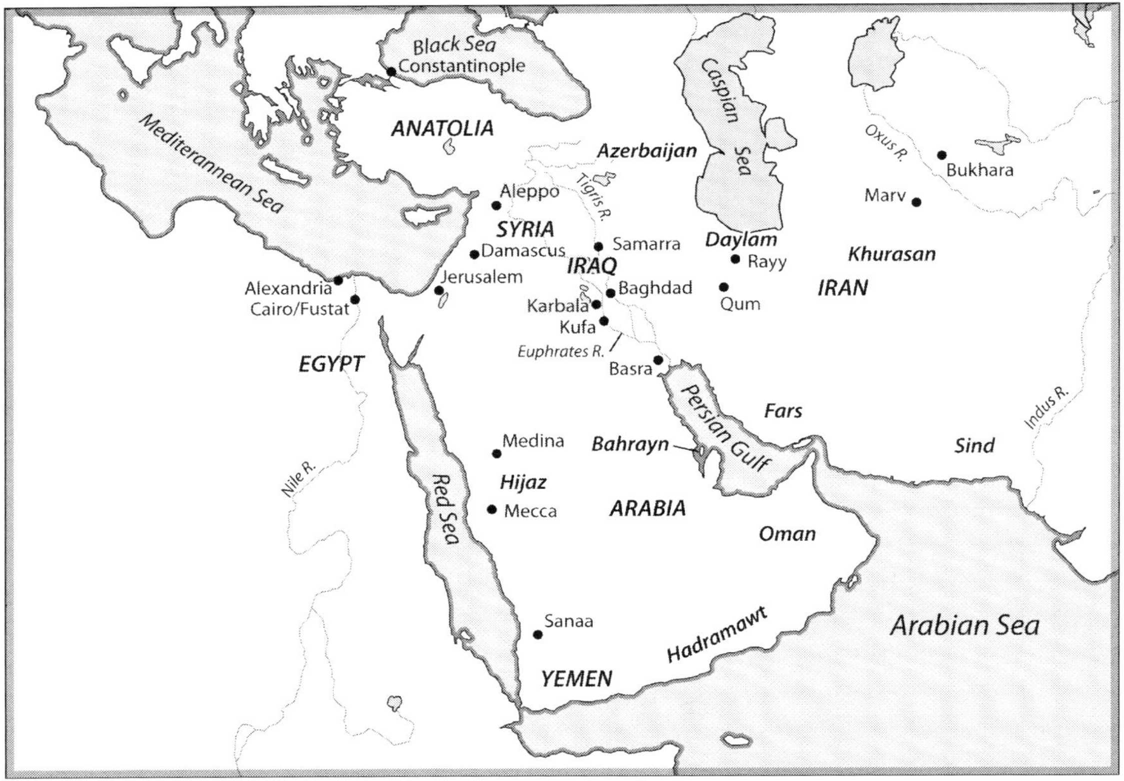

MAP 1. The Middle East in the early Muslim period.

PART ONE

NARRATIVES AND METHODS

1

Kūfa and the Classical Narratives of Early Shī'ism

Kūfa, located on the banks of the Euphrates River in southern Iraq, was founded by Sa'd b. Abī Waqqāṣ (d. 55/675) following the Muslim victory over the Sassanian army at Qādisiyya in the year 17/638.[1] Originally intended to house Arab tribesmen in seclusion from subject populations, the settlement also served as a base for future conquests in northern Mesopotamia and Iran. In the 1st/7th century, Kūfa witnessed dramatic urban growth accompanied by a well-documented rise in tension that pitted early-comers, who had participated in the initial conquests, against tribal elites (*ashrāf*) and late-comers (*rawādif*), who clamored for a larger portion of the state's newfound wealth.[2] The early-comers had profited from the policies of Abū Bakr (d. 13/635) and especially

[1] My synopsis of the history of Kūfa draws heavily on *EI*², s.v. Kūfa (Djait) and *idem*, *Kūfa*. The former offers a succinct timeline of important political developments, whereas the latter focuses primarily on the city's architectural and demographic transformation over the first two centuries. Other references are noted in the footnotes that follow.

[2] In the following section, I use the term "early-comer" to refer to figures who had taken part in the initial battles in Iraq and whose social status was predicated first and foremost on their conversion to Islam as opposed to their tribal standing. This is not to say that all early-comers lacked tribal credentials; there are numerous examples of individuals from distinguished tribal backgrounds who converted early and participated in the conquests. In referring to these latter figures, however, I use the term "tribal elite" (*ashrāf*). This decision results partly from a desire to avoid unwieldy terms such as "tribal elite early-comer" and partly from the fact that their social identity and loyalties were primarily predicated on their lineage. For a more detailed breakdown of the subtleties of these categories, see Hinds, "Alignments," 348–53 and 357, and Hodgson, *Venture*, 1:197–211. For a very general survey of Iraqi political history in the 1st/7th and 2nd/8th centuries, see Kennedy, *Prophet*, especially chapters 4 and 5. For a discussion of the composition, influx, and settlement of the *rawādif*, see Donner, *Conquests*, 226–36.

'Umar (d. 23/644) who allotted economic benefits and political posts primarily on the basis of Islamic precedence (*sābiqa*).[3] When 'Uthmān became caliph in 23/644, however, the early-comers were politically and economically marginalized and replaced by tribal elites who could command (or purchase) the loyalty of their fellow tribesmen.[4] Over the next decade, Kūfa witnessed a substantial influx of late-arriving tribesmen,[5] the establishment of financial procedures that favored the tribal elites,[6] and a halt in territorial expansion on the two Kūfan fronts of Azerbaijan and Rayy.[7] The volatile environment that resulted from these factors contributed to Uthmān's murder at the hands of Egyptian early-comers in 35/656 and facilitated 'Alī's (d. 40/661) subsequent assumption of the caliphate.[8]

The same political alignments that destabilized Kūfa in the first half of the 1st/7th century persisted into the Umayyad period. Mu'āwiya (rl. 41–60/661–80) confirmed the authority of the tribal elites[9] and essentially ruled through their auspices, further undermining the political position of the early-comers and accelerating their general economic disempowerment.[10] Over the next century, it was clan leaders with significant wealth and tribal status who dominated Kūfa with the backing of the Umayyad caliphs in Syria and their governors in Iraq (see Table 1.1).[11] The early-comers continued to clamor for a socio-political order based on Islamic precedence, which they expected would restore their economic rights.[12]

[3] Madelung, *Succession*, 57–77.

[4] Hinds, "Alignments," 355–67 (for the marginalization of early-comers without tribal credentials) and 353 (for the relations between tribal elites and late-comers). See also Kennedy, *Prophet*, 73–4.

[5] Hinds, "Alignments," 352–3.

[6] *Ibid.*, 359–60.

[7] *Ibid.*, 355–6.

[8] For more on the factors that led to 'Uthmān's demise, see Hinds, "Murder," 450–69.

[9] Hinds notes that the tribal elites were the least enthusiastic of 'Alī's supporters at Ṣiffīn and among the quickest to accept Mu'āwiya's offer of arbitration (Hinds, "Alignments," 363 and 366). See also, *idem*, "The Ṣiffīn Arbitration Agreement," 93–113.

[10] Hinds, "Alignments," 348 and 357. For more on Kūfa during Mu'āwiya's caliphate, see Kennedy, *Prophet*, 84–6.

[11] Hinds characterizes the arrangement as one in which "tribal leaders were supposed to support, and were in turn supported by the government. The pre-Islamic clan organization was the essential basis, but in the changed environment of a central government and the garrison towns of Kūfa and Baṣra" (Hinds, "Alignments," 347).

[12] Hinds identifies the *qurrā'* as a specific division among the early-comers and mentions their splintering into a number of movements, including the Shī'a and the Kharijites (Hinds, "Alignments," 347–8 and 358–65). For more on the usage of the term *qurrā'* and its contested meaning, see *EI*[2], s.v. Qurrā (Nagel). See also, Kennedy, *Prophet*, 78–80.

They were joined by a growing non-Arab Muslim (*mawālī*)[13] population that felt systematically discriminated against by Umayyad fiscal policies. The resulting coalition coalesced behind the political claims of the descendants of ʿAlī.[14] The reasons for the particular prominence of the ʿAlids ranged from a belief in the superiority of their knowledge by virtue of their descent from the Prophet (i.e., the early Shīʿa) to a fond remembrance of ʿAlī's support of early-comer rights and his decision to make Kūfa the caliphal capital.[15]

The dominance of the tribal elites in Kūfa was reinforced in the civil strife that erupted between Mu'āwiya's death in 60/680 and ʿAbd al-Malik b. Marwān's (rl. 65–86/685–705) restoration of Umayyad power in 73/692.[16] They were seminal in obstructing al-Ḥusayn b. ʿAlī's efforts to raise military support and played a central role in his massacre at Karbalā' in 61/680.[17] They were also instrumental in suppressing the rebellion of Mukhtār b. Abī ʿUbayd (d. 67/687), who seized control of Kūfa in 66/685 with a coalition of early-comers and *mawālī*.[18] While these upheavals confirmed the political status quo in Kūfa, they also signaled an important transformation in the nature of the opposition. With the establishment of Marwānid authority, there emerged a cohesive movement of the "piety-minded" that united a myriad of groups with grievances against the Umayyad state behind a universalist vision of an Islamic society.[19]

13 In the context of the Umayyad and early ʿAbbāsid period, the term *mawla* (pl. *mawālī*) was applied to clients of Arab tribes who often, though not necessarily, embraced Islam. Crone notes that *walā'* was a means of integrating non-Arabs into a tribal Arab social structure. The *mawālī* referred to in this section had all converted to Islam and were, therefore, theoretically on an equal societal footing with Arab Muslims. In reality, however, they were subject to severe discrimination, especially in the arena of taxation. For more on the term and its evolution, see *EI*², s.v. Mawla (Crone).

14 The one exception to this rule was the Kharijites who had explicitly rejected ʿAlī in the aftermath of the Battle of Ṣiffīn. See Hinds, "Alignments," 363–7.

15 Hodgson, *Venture*, 1:216–7 and 258–9.

16 For a general history of this period, see Kennedy, *Prophet*, 92–8.

17 *Ibid.*, 89–90.

18 Hodgson, Venture, 1:222; Kennedy, *Prophet*, 94–6.

19 Hodgson characterizes the "piety-minded" in the following manner: "I refer here to the 'Piety-minded' element as a general term to cover all the shifting groups opposed to Marwānid rule, or at least critical of current Muslim life, so far as their opposition embodied itself in idealistic religious attitudes. I am speaking, of course, primarily of the religious specialists, later called *'ulamā'*, who provided much of the leadership.... Only gradually did the social element that we designate as the 'Piety-minded' resolve itself later into sharply differentiated Sunnī and Shīʿī ʿulamā'" (Hodgson, *Venture*, 1:250 and 1:272–6). It should be noted that Hodgson considered the Kharijites an integral part of the broader movement of the piety-minded. See also footnote 28 in this chapter.

It was al-Ḥajjāj b. Yūsuf al-Thaqafī, the Umayyad governor of Iraq from 75/694 until his death in 95/714, who ultimately broke the power of the tribal elites in Kūfa. He did this by imposing a set of thoroughly unpopular and antagonistic policies that included long military campaigns and a reduction in army stipends. These measures sparked a rebellion in 82/701 led by ʿAbd al-Raḥmān b. Muḥammad b. al-Ashʿath b. Qays al-Kindī (d. 83/702), one the most prominent and powerful of the *ashrāf*.[20] After order was restored in 83/702, al-Ḥajjāj fundamentally transformed the administrative basis for the Umayyad governance of Iraq. The central pillar in this reorganization involved the demilitarization of the region through the disbanding of the armies of Kūfa and Baṣra and the establishment of a permanent Syrian garrison at Wāsiṭ.[21] Subsequent Umayyad governors, including Khālid b. ʿAbd Allāh al-Qasrī (gov. 105–120/724–38) and Yūsuf b. ʿUmar al-Thaqafī (gov. 121–6/738–44), relied exclusively on Syrian soldiers to quell unrest in the region. It was these forces that suppressed the rebellions that erupted behind Zayd b. ʿAlī in 122/740[22] and ʿAbd Allāh b. Muʿāwiya in 127/744.[23] Al-Ḥajjāj's changes created a political power vacuum at the highest echelons of Kūfan society, which was ultimately filled by pietist groups.

The establishment of the ʿAbbāsid dynasty in 132/750 marked a decisive turning point in the fortunes of Kūfa. Initially, the city retained its importance, serving as the ʿAbbāsid capital during the caliphate of al-Saffāḥ (rl. 132–6/749–50) and the early reign of al-Manṣūr (rl. 136–58/754–75).[24] This prominence, however, was short-lived and, after the foundation of Baghdād in 145/762, Kūfa experienced a steady and permanent political decline.[25] This was due in part to the location of the new capital, close enough to allow the ʿAbbāsids to crush any rebellions in Kūfa (e.g., that of Ibrāhīm b. ʿAbd Allāh – d. 145/763) but distant enough to shield them from the political intrigues and ʿAlid sympathies of its population.[26] Although the ʿAbbāsid caliphs continued to appoint prominent members of the ruling family to the governorship of Kūfa (and Iraq as a whole), the significance of the post became more symbolic than actual.[27] The foundation of the dynasty's power had shifted east and

[20] Hodgson, *Venture*, 1:245; Kennedy, *Prophet*, 100–2.
[21] Hodgson, *Venture*, 1:245; Hinds, "Alignments," 347; *EI*², s.v. Kūfa (Djait)
[22] Kennedy, *Prophet*, 111–12. For an analysis of ʿAlid revolts in Kūfa beginning with that of Zayd b. ʿAlī, see Chapter 6.
[23] Hodgson, *Venture*, 1:273; *EI*², s.v. ʿAbd Allāh b. Muʿāwiya (Zettersteen).
[24] Kennedy, *Prophet*, 130.
[25] *Ibid.*, 135–6.
[26] Hodgson, *Venture*, 1:287.
[27] Kennedy, *Prophet*, 129.

TABLE 1.1. *A Timeline of Kūfa in the 1st/7th and 2nd/8th Centuries*

Period	Caliph/Ruler	Important Governors	Notable Events
The First Four Caliphs (17–40/638–61)	ʿUmar (17–23/638–44)	Saʿd b. Abī Waqqāṣ Al-Mughīra b. Shuʿba ʿAmmār b. Yāsir	The city is founded by Saʿd b. Abī Waqqāṣ in 17/638 (the fourth year of ʿUmar's reign).
	ʿUthmān (23–35/644–56)	Al-Walīd b. ʿUqba Saʿīd b. al-ʿĀṣ Abū Mūsā al-Ashʿarī	Both al-Walīd and Saʿīd were strongly opposed by Kūfan early-comers, who demanded the appointment of Abū Mūsā in 34/655.
	ʿAlī (35–40/656–61)		Kūfa served as the caliphal capital.
Sufyānid Umayyads (41–64/661–83)	Muʿāwiya (41–60/661–80)	Ziyād b. Abīhi	(**Turning Point #1**) Ziyād was the most prominent of Mu'āwiya's appointments, but power was generally exercised through the tribal *ashrāf*.
	Yazīd b. Muʿāwiya (60–4/680–3)	ʿUbayd Allāh b. Ziyād b. Abīhi	*Massacre of al-Ḥusayn b. ʿAlī at Karbalā' in 61/680
Period of Instability and Civil Strife (60–72/680–91)	Mukhtār b. Abī ʿUbayd (66–7/685–6)		Kūfa was Mukhtār's capital after he consolidated power in 66/685. Mukhtār claimed to be fighting in the name of Muḥammad b. al-Ḥanafiyya (d. 80–1/701) and garnered the support of many early-comers and *mawālī*. He was defeated by an army led by the Kūfan *ashrāf*.
	ʿAbd Allāh b. Zubayr (67–72/686–91)	Muṣʿab b. al-Zubayr	Muṣʿab was defeated by an Umayyad army led by ʿAbd al-Malik b. Marwān in 72/691 at Dayr al-Jāthaliq.

(continued)

TABLE 1.1 *(continued)*

Period	Caliph/Ruler	Important Governors	Notable Events
Marwānid Umayyads (72–126/691–744)	ʿAbd al-Malik b. Marwān (72–86/691–705)	Al-Ḥajjāj b. Yūsuf al-Thaqafī	Al-Ashʿath b. Qays al-Kindī rebelled in 82/701. After al-Kindī's defeat in 83/702, al-Ḥajjāj disbanded the army of Kūfa and replaced it with a Syrian garrison stationed in the newly constructed city of Wāsiṭ. (**Turning Point #2**) The failure of the rebellion marked the definitive end of the dominance of the *ashrāf* in Kūfa.
	Al-Walīd (I) b. ʿAbd al-Malik (85–96/705–25)		
	Sulaymān b. ʿAbd al-Malik (96–9/715–17)	Yazīd b. al-Muhallab	
	ʿUmar b. ʿAbd al-Azīz (99–101/717–20)	ʿAbd al-Ḥamīd b. ʿAbd al-Raḥmān b. Zayd	
	Yazīd (II) b. ʿAbd al-Malik (101–5/720–4)	Maslama b. ʿAbd al-Malik ʿUmar b. Hubayra al-Fazārī	
	Hishām b. ʿAbd al-Malik (105–25/724–43)	Khālid b. ʿAbd Allāh al-Qasrī Yūsuf b. ʿUmar al-Thaqafī	*Zayd b. ʿAlī rebelled and was killed in 122/740 by the forces of Yūsuf b. ʿUmar al-Thaqafī.
Period of Instability and Civil Strife (125–32/743–49)	Al-Walīd (II) b. Yazīd (II) (125–6/743–4)	Yūsuf b. ʿUmar al-Thaqafī	*Yaḥyā b. Zayd killed in Khurāsān in 125/743.
	Yazīd (III) b. al-Walīd (126/744)	ʿAbd Allāh b. ʿUmar b. ʿAbd al-ʿAzīz	

	Chaos (126–30/744–8)		The city was severely divided with two primary power brokers, the Kharijite leader al-Ḍaḥḥāk b. Qays and the ʿAlid rebel ʿAbd Allāh b. Muʿāwiya. ʿAbd Allāh b. Muʿāwiya rebelled in 127/744. After his defeat in 129/746–7, he fled to Khurāsān where he was imprisoned and executed by Abū Muslim.
	Marwān (II) b. Muḥammad (al-Ḥimār) (130–2/748–9)	Yazīd b. ʿUmar al-Fazārī	
ʿAbbāsids (132–93/749–809)	Al-Saffāḥ (132–6/749–54)		Kūfa served as ʿAbbāsid capital from 132/749 to 145/762.
	Al-Manṣūr (136–58/754–75)	The official governor from 132/749 until 147/764 was ʿĪsā b. Mūsā, first cousin to both al-Saffāḥ and al-Manṣūr.	*Muḥammad al-Nafs al-Zakiyya and Ibrāhīm b. ʿAbd Allāh led an unsuccessful rebellion in the Ḥijāz and Iraq in 145/763. (**Turning Point #3**) While the ʿAbbāsids continued to appoint governors after their move to Baghdād, the post lost much of its political and military importance.
	Al-Mahdī (158–69/775–85)		*News of the death of ʿĪsā b. Zayd, who spent nearly twenty-three years in hiding, reached al-Mahdī in 168/785.
	Al-Hādī (169–70/785–6)		*Rebellion erupted in Medina during the pilgrimage of 169/786 under the leadership of Ṣāḥib Fakhkh al-Ḥusayn b. ʿAlī
	Al-Rashīd (170–93/786–809)		*Idrīs b. ʿAbd Allāh was sent to North Africa by his brother where he laid the foundations for the Idrīsid dynasty before being poisoned by an ʿAbbāsid agent in 175/791. *Yaḥyā b. ʿAbd Allāh rebelled in Daylam in 176/792. He was granted a pardon and continued agitating until his execution in 189–805.

Note: The rebellions denoted by an asterisk are discussed in greater detail in Chapter 6. For a complete listing of the governors/administrators of Kūfa into the reign of al-Muʿtazz (rl. 247–52/861–6), see the chapter entitled "Rulers (*wulāt*) of Kūfa" in al-Burāqī's *Tārīkh*.

the most important governorship was now that of Khurāsān. In spite of these changes, Kūfa remained a potential source of unrest through the 2nd/8th and 3rd/9th centuries, with a population notably partial toward and responsive to ʿAlid political claims.

In addition to its political and military importance, Kūfa was home to a range of diverse religious currents,[28] many of which exerted considerable influence on the development of Islamic law and theology.[29] These included two seminal streams of early proto-Sunnī[30] jurisprudence, namely the traditionists and the *ahl al-ra'y*.[31] The traditionists emphasized the unique authority of texts that preserved the opinions of the Prophet, his Companions, and their Successors in the articulation of Islamic law. As the strength of the movement grew through the 2nd/8th century, it provided a strong impetus for the systematic gathering of traditions that ultimately led to the canonical collections of al-Bukhārī (d. 256/870) and Muslim (d. 261/875). The *ahl al-ra'y*, by contrast, predicated legal decisions on personal discretion (or sound judgment) and did not feel bound to previous opinions, even those that could be traced back to the Prophet. The conflict between the traditionists and the *ahl al-ra'y* persisted through the 2nd/8th century, culminating with al-Shāfiʿī's (d. 204/820) efforts at subordinating the rationalism of the *ahl al-ra'y* to the textualism of the traditionist movement. Subsequent centuries saw the rise of systematic Sunnī law schools that increasingly affirmed al-Shāfiʿī's approach and bound the use of rationality by the constraints of traditionism. But the traditionist victory was not absolute. Many legal opinions ascribed to the *ahl al-ra'y* were preserved by the Ḥanafīs who supported them with textual evidence.[32]

[28] These currents were collectively identified earlier as the "piety-minded." They devoted themselves to working out the implications of a society predicated on the Qur'ān and developing a mode of living that adhered to broad Islamic principles. They were united in advocating a broadly conceived Islamic society, but they disagreed over its core principles and building blocks. For the program of the piety-minded, see Hodgson, *Venture*, 1:252–67. See also, footnote 19 in this chapter.

[29] For a description of the intellectual landscape of early Kūfa, see Ibn al-Muqaffaʿ, *Risālat*, 315–18.

[30] The term "proto-Sunnī" is used to refer to a stage before Sunnism had acquired a coherent and distinct doctrinal definition. In other words, "proto-Sunnī" is utilized in the sense of "relating to the earliest manifestations of the sect which we today refer to as the Sunnīs."

[31] The following discussion of Kūfan legal currents draws primarily on Schacht's *Origins*.

[32] Christopher Melchert proposes an alternative narrative that rejects the connection between the Ḥanafīs and Kūfa. Specifically, he claims that Ḥanafism developed in Baghdād, while traditionism was firmly entrenched in Kūfa. It was only when a group of Mālikī Baṣrans began asserting a link to Medina that Baghdādī Ḥanafīs responded by

The central focus of this book, however, lies not in these streams of proto-Sunnism, but rather in the myriad of Shīʿī groups that reportedly first emerged in Kūfa in the early 2nd/8th century. These sects have been the subject of numerous modern studies that examine the formative stages of Shīʿism primarily through the lens of (a) rival historical claims regarding Muḥammad's succession and (b) theology.[33] In such an analytic framework, the notion of Imāmate (*imāma*) holds a particular significance as Shīʿī groups differed over the identity of the legitimate heir to the Prophet, as well as the scope and nature of his authority.

The implications of these differences for the emergence of Imāmī and Zaydī Shīʿism will be discussed in greater detail later. For now, it is important to note that most studies that utilize a historical or theological approach in examining early Shīʿism must contend with the problematic nature of the source material, primarily the absence of Arabic historical chronicles from the entirety of the 1st/7th and most of the 2nd/8th century. One strategy for overcoming this obstacle involves the use of alternative sources of information such as coins, tombstones, or archaeological inscriptions. Given the scarcity of such artifacts, however, scholars are often compelled to rely on written materials that postdate the events they purport to describe by decades or even centuries. In these cases, regardless of the quality and exactitude of the analysis, questions persist regarding the validity of the conclusions. To what extent are the sources projecting the values/mores of a subsequent generation onto events from an earlier generation? Did these sources have access to reliable information or are their historical narratives primarily conjectural in nature? Unfortunately, these problems are not easily managed. They require either the discovery of new historical sources or the development of new approaches to those materials currently available. This book opts for the latter and proposes a novel method for the analysis of the extant sources.

The last thirty years have witnessed a fundamental transformation in the broad textual landscape for the study of early Islam. We now have

ascribing their origins to Kūfa. In making this argument, Melchert rejects the assumption that there was a fundamental legal rift between Iraq (through its use of *ra'y*) and the Ḥijāz (through its affirmation of traditions). See Melchert, "Ḥanafism," 318–47 and *idem*, *Formation*. Nurit Tsafrir depicts 2nd/8th century Kūfa as split between traditionists and the *ahl al-ra'y*, but she also emphasizes the multiplicity within both currents. The traditionists were organized in circles surrounding famous personalities such as Sufyān al-Thawrī and Ḥafṣ b. Ghiyāth. The *ahl al-ra'y* were divided among proponents of the teachings of Abū Ḥanīfa or Ibn Abī Layla. See Tsafrir, *History*, 17–27.

[33] It may reasonably be argued that these two elements were so closely intertwined in the first few centuries that any distinction between them is largely artificial.

access to a corpus of texts whose compilation can confidently be placed in the early 2nd/8th century. These were not "discovered" by chance in a small mosque in some Middle Eastern country; rather they were "uncovered" through the work of a number of scholars who meticulously examined the structure of *ḥadīth*[34] (tradition) collections to demonstrate their early provenance. The specifics of this research is discussed in greater detail in Chapter 2, but its importance is self-evident. The availability of a large group of texts contemporaneous with (possibly) the late 1st/7th century opens up countless possibilities for the study and, perhaps, reconstruction of early Muslim society. From the perspective of a historian, the primary drawback to these sources lies in their focus on legal issues or ritual as opposed to concrete historical events such as dynastic successions or rebellions.

In this book, I propose a methodological approach through which such seemingly ahistorical (and primarily legal/ritual) sources are mined for historical information. Specifically, I use these sources to examine one of the key controversies in the study of the early Islamic period: the birth and development of Shīʿī sectarian identity[35] in 2nd/8th century Kūfa. The remainder of this initial chapter outlines the established narratives (subsequently referred to as "the classical narratives") for early Shīʿism put forward by both premodern and modern scholars and drawn primarily from heresiographical works.[36] In spite of a few minor discrepancies, these narratives exhibit a remarkable degree of consensus regarding the crystallization of Imāmī and Zaydī Shīʿī identities. The particulars of the

[34] In the course of this study, I use the term *ḥadīth* (tradition) to refer to texts that purport to record the opinions/views of authority figures from the first two Islamic centuries. In other words, the term encompasses texts that cite the Prophet as well as those that cite the Companions, or 1st/7th- and 2nd/8th-century jurists (commonly referred to as *āthār*).

[35] When I speak of "identity," I am not referring to a fully developed sectarian group or a formal law school. I am primarily concerned with the point at which particular groups of Muslims (i.e., Imāmīs, Zaydīs, traditionists, the *ahl al-ra'y*) began to perceive themselves as "unique" or "different," often on the basis of a common ritual practice. This initial act of community–building is the prerequisite for the creation of a sect or school of law.

[36] The shortcomings of this genre are well known. Heresiographers were primarily concerned with explaining the disunity of the larger Muslim community. They tried to depict a religious landscape in accordance with traditions that predicted the community's fragmentation into seventy-three sects. The resulting narrative demarcated groups on the basis of distinct doctrinal and theological beliefs. In reality, however, sects are rarely characterized by such a degree of internal coherence. As Josef van Ess observes, "we must never forget that [sects] owe their names mainly to the need for systematizing felt by the heresiographers and that these names are not necessarily a reflection of social or historical reality" ("The Kāmilīya," 216). For traditions dealing with the proliferation of sects, see *FBF*, 23–5; al-Dārimī, *Sunan*, 2:690–1; and *ST*, 7:296–7.

approach utilized in evaluating the veracity of these narratives is discussed further in Chapter 2.

SHĪʿISM UNITED

Beginning in the 2nd/8th century, Kūfa was beset by a series of ʿAlid-led uprisings against the Umayyad and ʿAbbāsid caliphs. These revolts reflected the city's centrality to the political aspirations of multiple streams of early Shīʿism.[37] As varieties of Shīʿism spread to other parts of the Muslim world (particularly Iran), Kūfa maintained its preeminent status as the birthplace of the larger movement.[38] This was best exemplified by the fact that the operational leadership of the ʿAbbāsid missionary network (*daʿwa*) remained firmly entrenched in the city even as it focused its propaganda on the far-off province of Khurāsān. According to the classical narrative (see below), Zayd b. ʿAlī's rebellion in 122/740 signaled a decisive turning point in the history of the broader Kūfan Shīʿī community. Specifically, it provided the impetus for the creation of a distinctly militant (Zaydī) Shīʿism that stood in sharp contrast to the politically passive (Imāmī) Shīʿism fostered by the ʿAlids, Muḥammad al-Bāqir (d. 117/735) and Jaʿfar al-Ṣādiq (d. 148/765). Before examining the purported details and consequences of this split, however, a few words about the general contours of Kūfan Shīʿism are in order.

The two core beliefs that united all the early Kūfan Shīʿa were the conviction that ʿAlī was the rightful successor to the Prophet and the acceptance of the institution of the Imāmate.[39] Within this broad umbrella, there was potential for considerable variation. Disputes arose concerning the nature of ʿAlī's claims, with some Shīʿa asserting that the Prophet had made a clear public declaration regarding succession after his death, and others acknowledging only an implicit designation. This issue had profound implications for the status of those Companions who had actively

[37] They also garnered widespread support among other pietist groups. The disintegration of this coalition and the increased political marginalization of the Zaydī Shīʿa are discussed in Chapter 6.

[38] Kūfa's importance in the larger Imāmī movement derived from its role in transmitting the opinions of the Imāms (prior to the *ghayba*) from Medina (and later Baghdād and Sāmarrāʾ) to cities further east (*EI*², s.v. Kūfa (Djait)). In his comparative study of Kūfan and Qummī *ḥadīth* collections, Newman argues that Imāmīs in Qumm defined themselves in conscious opposition to their Kūfan counterparts. But this seems to have occurred after the *ghayba* and, in any case, implicitly attests to an earlier Kūfan preeminence. See Newman, *The Formative Period*.

[39] For a broad overview of early Shīʿism, see *EI*², s.v. Shīʿa (Madelung).

opposed 'Alī (see below). The doctrine of the Imāmate produced even greater divisions, coalescing around two poles: the nature of the Imām's authority and the method of his "selection."[40] Although a comprehensive examination of these issues lies outside the scope of this study, they will feature prominently in the course of our discussion of the origin narrative of Zaydism. At this point, it suffices to note that early Shī'ī groups were primarily distinguished based on their support of a specific descendant of the Prophet as the legitimate Imām.[41]

Imāmī Shī'ism

The Imāmīs[42] traced the Imāmate exclusively through a line of Ḥusaynid 'Alids and appeared to first materialize around the figures of al-Bāqir and al-Ṣādiq in the early 2nd/8th century. The vast majority of early Imāmīs lived in Kūfa and could only communicate with their Medinan Imāms through a correspondence mediated by merchants, travelers, and pilgrims.[43] Regardless, it appears that al-Bāqir and al-Ṣādiq managed to maintain close ties with their followers and regularly provided religious guidance on issues of ritual and doctrine. The history of the Imāmīs prior to al-Bāqir is more difficult to decipher with any degree of confidence and it remains unclear whether a community of self-identified Imāmīs frequented Zayn al-'Abidīn 'Alī b. al-Ḥusayn al-Sajjād (d. 94/712). The heresiographical sources are of little help in clarifying the situation in this earlier period as they focus chiefly on extremist sects of a highly millenary character.[44]

[40] There are numerous studies on the Imāmate, which focus on issues ranging from the Imām's qualifications to the scope of his authority. For closer examinations of the Imāmate from a variety of perspectives, see Donaldson, *Shi'ite Religion*, 137–41, 395–6; Amir-Moezzi, *The Divine Guide*; Kohlberg, "Community"; and Modarressi, *Crisis*. For more general discussions of the Imāmate, see *EI*[2], s.v. Imāma (Madelung) and Calder, "Significance," 253–64. The possible conflation of the terms Imām and Caliph is discussed by Crone and Hinds in *God's Caliph*.

[41] Crone, *God's Rule*, 99–100 (on the Zaydīs) and 111–12 (on the Imāmīs).

[42] There is a considerable problem in terminology when dealing with the early Shī'ī community. I follow Kohlberg's formulation, using "Imāmī" to denote "the earliest manifestation of the sect that we today refer to as the Imāmī-Twelvers." As discussed later, in the 2nd/8th century, this term included those sects (e.g., the Wāqifiyya) who had not yet broken off to form independent groups and should not be taken as referring *exclusively* to the antecedents of the modern Imāmī-Twelver community. See Kohlberg, "Imāmiyya," 521–34 and *idem*, "Early Attestations," 343–57.

[43] Modarressi notes that "the Ḥijāz, generally speaking, was never a Shī'ite land. Some reports suggest that during the late Umayyad period, only four Shī'ītes lived in Mecca and fewer that twenty in Mecca and Medina combined" (*Tradition*, 39 footnote 1).

[44] See, for example, the table of contents in *MIs*. For the doctrinal beliefs and historicity of these early sects, see Tucker, *Mahdis and Millenarians*.

The Imāmī community in the early 2nd/8th century was characterized by tensions between factions that held disparate, if not contradictory, views regarding the scope of the Imām's knowledge and the nature of his relationship to God. The general confusion that resulted from this diversity allowed for the proliferation of extremist (*ghulāt*) ideas. Given such an environment, it is not surprising that al-Bāqir and (especially) al-Ṣādiq devoted considerable efforts to limiting the influence of Shīʿī extremists[45] while articulating the distinctive tenets of what would become Imāmī Shīʿism. Differences in opinion, however, persisted and became entangled with the question of succession as exemplified by countless instances in which followers tested potential Imāms or strongly questioned their actions. The period following the death of al-Ṣādiq witnessed a series of splits with the emergence of the Ismāʿīlīs and the Nāwūsīs in 148/765 and the Wāqifīs in 184/800. The heresiographers frame these divisions as departures from a normative "Imāmiyya."[46] In other words, they define the Imāmīs primarily in negative terms in opposition to those groups that had broken away to form independent sects.

Most modern studies affirm the centrality of al-Bāqir and al-Ṣādiq in the creation of a distinct Imāmī Shīʿī identity. In doing so, they draw primarily on theological works and predicate their arguments on assumptions about the development of theological doctrines. Much of the foundation for this mode of analysis was laid by Marshall Hodgson[47] and developed in the careful and erudite studies of Wilferd Madelung[48]

[45] This point is made by Hodgson, "Sectarian," 9–12 and *EI*², s.v. Shīʿa (Madelung). See also, Modarressi, *Crisis*.

[46] Kohlberg notes that the name "Imāmiyya" (in combination with "Qaṭʿiyya") was used in reference to the generality of those Shīʿa who held to the Ḥusaynid line eventually affirmed by the modern-day Ithnā ʿAshariyya (Twelvers) ("Imāmiyya," 531). Although subsequently ascribed a normative authority, there is no indication that the line of Imāms revered by the Twelvers was supported by a majority (or even a plurality) of the early Shīʿa.

[47] Hodgson, "Sectarian," 1–13 and *EI*², s.v. Jaʿfar al-Ṣādiq (*idem*). Hodgson highlights the growth in stature of the figure of the Imām in the late 1st/7th and early 2nd/8th century as both a legal and a theological authority. Specifically, he examines the difficulties al-Ṣādiq faced in controlling the flow of extremist (*ghulāt*) ideas among his followers in Kūfa but emphasizes the importance of these same ideas in the development of a distinct Shīʿī identity. This approach is in sharp contrast to that of earlier scholars who concentrated almost exclusively on the issue of succession. See, for example, Donaldson, *Shiʿite Religion*.

[48] *EI*², s.v. Imāma (Madelung), Shīʿa (*idem*); *idem*, *Succession*; and *DIQ*. Madelung focuses primarily on the role of theological and political disputes in shaping early Shīʿism. A similar approach informs Josef van Ess's *Theologie* which presents a detailed analysis of a multiplicity of Shīʿī Kūfan theological circles (see e.g., 1:387–93 on the school of

and Etan Kohlberg.[49] A similar view informs the work of Maria Dakake, who emphasizes the importance of *walāya* (charismatic allegiance or – alternatively – attachment) in the creation of an early 2nd/8th century Shīʿī identity.[50] By contrast, sharply differing perspectives are articulated by Amir-Moezzi,[51] who concentrates on the mystical and esoteric aspects of Imāmī Shīʿism, and Hossein Modarressi,[52] who highlights its deep-rooted rationalist tendencies. Buckley focuses specifically on the figure of al-Ṣādiq, detailing his development of (a) a coherent doctrine of the Imāmate and (b) a concrete ritual and legal edifice in the political aftermath of the ʿAbbāsid revolution.[53]

We are left with a somewhat nebulous portrait of early Imāmī Shīʿism. Both premodern and modern scholars affirm the existence of a contingent of early Shīʿa associated with al-Bāqir and al-Ṣādiq, but there is a great deal of ambiguity regarding the point at which they coalesced into a coherent Imāmī "community" distinguishable from broader Kūfan society. There is a general scholarly consensus that the Imāmīs existed as a discreet sectarian group in Kūfa by – at the very latest – the Imāmate of Mūsā al-Kāẓim (d. 184/800).[54] Although this provides us a *terminus ante quem*, it tells us little about the contours of the community in the early or mid-2nd/8th century under the guidance of al-Bāqir and al-Ṣādiq. We are even less certain of the situation in the late 1st/7th century during the purported Imāmate of al-Sajjād. The central question remains the following: At which point did the Imāmīs constitute an insular community with distinctive practices that set them apart from a vague overarching Kūfan Shīʿism? In this book, I tackle this question through an analysis of the internal structure and form of Imāmī legal traditions. In Chapters 7–8, I

al-Ṣādiq's companion Hishām b. al-Ḥakam) and an examination of important controversies associated with the Imāmate (see e.g., 1:377–82 on the designation of the Imām along with his infallibility; 1:274–78 on his political responsibilities; and 1:278–85 on his knowledge).

49 Kohlberg, "Community," 25–53.

50 See Dakake, *Charismatic*. A similar perspective emphasizing the early importance of *walāya* is found in Eliash, "Genesis," 265–77.

51 See Amir-Moezzi, *The Divine Guide*.

52 See Modarressi, *Crisis* and *idem*, *Tradition*.

53 See Buckley, "Origins," 165–84 and *idem*, "Jaʿfar al-Ṣādiq," 37–58.

54 Crone explicitly places the emergence of Imāmī Shīʿism in the lifetime of al-Kāẓim (Crone, *God's Rule*, 114–15), whereas Hodgson (Hodgson, "Sectarian," 13) and Madelung (,*EI*², s.v. "Shīʿa,") prefer that of al-Ṣādiq without offering a specific date. The earliest dating comes from Modarressi who suggests that the Imāmīs were an "independent political, legal, and theological school" by 132/749 (Modarressi, *Crisis*, 4). This implies that differentiation may have taken place *before* 132/749, possibly during the lifetime of al-Bāqir.

go one step further by addressing the issue of *how* (i.e., the mechanisms through which) the Imāmīs may have carved out an independent identity for themselves.

Zaydī Shīʿism

An examination of the beginnings of Zaydism requires considerably more detail than that of Imāmism. This is because most primary sources (predominantly heresiographies) trace the roots of Zaydism to a specific moment (122/740) and identify its initial adherents as two discrete groups of Kūfan Shīʿa. On the other hand, as mentioned earlier, discussions of Imāmism often concentrate on schisms in which the Imāmīs function as a narrative baseline with little information about the movement's initial coalescence. Much of the classical narrative of early Imāmism rests on the school's own sources (both historical and legal) in addition to heresiographical texts. By contrast, although Zaydī sources discuss failed ʿAlīd rebellions and include discussions of law and theology, their portrayal of their own origins appears strongly indebted to the narrative found in the heresiographical literature.

There is a broad scholarly consensus that Zaydism was a product of the merging of two streams of Kūfan Shīʿism – the Jārūdiyya and the Batriyya[55] – around the revolt of Zayd b. ʿAlī in 122/740.[56] Zaydīs were united in the belief that the Imāmate was the common property of all the descendants of ʿAlī through his sons, al-Ḥasan and al-Ḥusayn.[57] Any qualified[58] candidate could claim the Imāmate by calling others to his cause and rising up in military rebellion against an oppressive ruler.[59] Members of the Muslim community were religiously obligated to respond to his summons and support his efforts at establishing political rule.[60] The Zaydīs often contrasted their activist stance with the political quietism of

[55] As discussed below, the Sulaymānīs were theologically very similar to the Batrīs and appeared to have only crystallized in the later decades of the 2nd/8th century.

[56] The overview of the divisions between the Batriyya and the Jārūdiyya that follows is based on *EI²*, s.v. Zaydiyya (Madelung); *EI²* supplement, s.v. Batriyya (*idem*); and his classical work on the subject, *DIQ*, 44–51. The primary sources for this narrative are six heresiographical works that will be examined in greater detail later. The heresiographical perspective on these divisions is also summarized by al-Masʿūdī in *al-Murūj*, 3:207–8.

[57] *KM*, 71; *FS*, 54–5; *MIm*, 42; *MIs*, 141; *FBF*, 41; *MN*, 1:154 and 159.

[58] As will become clear later, they differed regarding the necessary qualifications for a legitimate Imām.

[59] *KM*, 71; *FS*, 54–5; *MIm*, 42; *FBF*, 41.

[60] *KM* 71; *FS*, 54–5; *MIm*, 42; *MN*, 1:154.

the Imāmīs, whose Imāms they derided for remaining safely concealed in the comfort of their homes.[61]

Below this veneer of unity, however, Zaydism was rent by disputes concerning the two central Shīʿī beliefs identified earlier: the nature of ʿAlī's appointment as successor and the scope of the Imām's authority. The first division involved the status of early Companions who had (a) supported the selection of Abū Bakr (and then ʿUmar) despite ʿAlī's rightful claim or (b) taken up arms against ʿAlī during the first civil war (*fitna*). The second centered on the knowledge and legal authority of the family of the Prophet.[62] A Zaydī's stance on these issues effectively identified him as a Jārūdī or a Batrī.

The Jārūdīs[63] (eponymously linked to Abū al-Jārūd Ziyād b. al-Mundhir – d. mid-2nd/8th century) believed that ʿAlī, al-Ḥasan (d. 49/669), and al-Ḥusayn had clearly and publicly been designated as Imāms either directly by the Prophet or by their immediate predecessors.[64] Given that there was no ambiguity regarding their right to rule, anyone who actively supported rival claims was guilty of disbelief (*kufr*).[65] This had the practical consequence of relegating Abū Bakr, ʿUmar, ʿUthmān, and those Companions who fought ʿAlī in the first civil war (e.g., Ṭalḥa – d. 35/656, al-Zubayr – d. 35/656, and ʿĀʾisha – d. 58/678) to the status of nonbelievers and apostates. In terms of legal authority, the Jārūdīs believed that every descendant of ʿAlī (through Fāṭima – d. 10/632)[66] possessed identical religious knowledge regardless of age or seniority.[67] Some even went as far as to excommunicate those who refused to accept the fundamental equality between the religious (particularly legal) knowledge of an old

[61] *MIm*, 42. Some heresiographers claim that the Jārūdīs consider these false Imāms and their followers as nonbelievers. For this view, see *KM* 71, 75; *FS*, 54–5.

[62] Bayhoum-Daou has argued that the method for the transmission of knowledge was a central issue of debate for the early Zaydīs ("Hishām b. al-Ḥakam," 99). The Imāmīs struggled with the same issue when faced with Imāms who had not reached the age of legal majority beginning with Muḥammad al-Jawād (d. 220/835). For more on the Imāmī case, see the first section of Modarressi's *Crisis*.

[63] *DIQ*, 47–9 and 51.

[64] *FS*, 21; *MIm*, 42; *MIs*, 141; *FBF*, 41; *MN*, 1:158. For Abū al-Jārūd, see Chapters 6 and 7.

[65] *KM* 71; *FS*, 21; *MIm*, 42; *MIs*, 141; *FBF*, 41–2; *MN*, 1:158.

[66] Madelung identifies a group known as the Ṭālibiyya, which extended this general qualifications to include all the descendants of Abū Ṭālib and survived into the 4th/10th century (*EI²*, s.v. Zaydiyya (Madelung)).

[67] *KM* 72; *FS*, 55; *MIm*, 43. There may have been an additional split between a group, led by Fuḍayl b. al-Zubayr al-Rassān, that believed that only Imāms were repositories of knowledge and another, led by Abū Khālid al-Wāsiṭī (also known as al-Kūfī), that extended this privilege to all ʿAlids (*MN*, 1:159).

'Alid scholar and an 'Alid newborn.[68] In cases where an Imām *appeared* to lack the proper scholarly credentials, the Jārūdīs argued that, should the need arise, God would make the required knowledge "sprout in [his] heart as a seed sprouts in the rain."[69] This belief meant that Jārūdīs did not need to rely on legal methods like *ijtihād* or *ra'y*, because any 'Alid could issue an authoritative opinion.[70]

The Batrīs[71] agreed with the Jārūdīs regarding 'Alī's political claims but felt his designation had been implicit rather than explicit.[72] Furthermore, they argued that 'Alī had acquiesced to the community's election of Abū Bakr and 'Umar by taking the oath of allegiance and refusing to rebel.[73] If 'Alī was satisfied with the leadership choices of the Muslim community, then there could be no justification for accusations of disbelief against the first generation of Muslims. In holding this view, the Batrīs also accepted the doctrine that a "less worthy" candidate could become Imām despite the presence of a "superior" candidate.[74] As for 'Uthmān, the Batrīs (like many non-Shī'ī groups) divided his reign into two halves, rejecting the last six years because of his apparent nepotism.[75] Although there are indications that some Batrīs refused to pass judgment on 'Uthmān altogether, this appears to have been a minority position.[76] Most Batrīs also condemned (but fell short of excommunicating) Ṭalḥa, al-Zubayr, and 'Ā'isha for their armed opposition to 'Alī in the Battle of the Camel.[77] Unlike the Jārūdīs, the Batrīs diffused legal authority among the entire Muslim scholarly community, thereby permitting potential Imāms to study with famous traditionists.[78] Given that knowledge was learned rather than divinely inspired, candidates for the Imāmate had to demonstrate a mastery of the law and legal devices such as *ijtihād* and *ra'y*.[79] The Batrī affirmation of the first two caliphs and their doctrine of

[68] *KM* 72; *FS*, 55.
[69] *KM* 72; *FS*, 55; *MIm*, 43.
[70] *KM* 72; *FS*, 55–6; *MIs*, 149.
[71] *DIQ*, 49–50.
[72] *KM* 73–4; *FS*, 20–1; *MIs*, 144; *FBF*, 42–3.
[73] *KM* 73–4; *FS*, 20; *MIm*, 43; *MIs*, 144; *MN*, 1:161.
[74] *KM* 73–4; *MN*, 1:161.
[75] *KM* 73–4, *FS*, 57; *MIm*, 43–4; *MIs*, 144.
[76] For examples of withholding judgment, see *MIs*, 144; *FBF*, 43; *MN*, 1:161. For examples of refutation, see *KM* 73–4; *FS*, 57.
[77] *KM* 73–4; *FS*, 57.
[78] *KM* 73–4; *FS*, 56–7; *MIs*, 149.
[79] In this respect, the Batrīs were different from the Kūfan traditionists who did not allow reason-based arguments and insisted on textual evidence. See *EI*², s.v. Ahl al-Ḥadīth (Schacht); *KM* 73; *FS*, 56–7; *MIm*, 44; *MN*, 1:162.

knowledge placed them firmly within the boundaries of a larger Kūfan proto-Sunnism. Their classification as "Shīʿī" was based on their belief that (a) ʿAlī was the Prophet's successor, and (b) legitimate political authority was thereafter limited to his descendants.

Some sources mention the Sulaymānīs (eponymously linked to Sulaymān b. Jarīr[80] – d. late 2nd/8th century) as a third theological division within Zaydism, which held a modified Batrī position on the key issues identified above.[81] In terms of the succession, they agreed with both the Jārūdīs and the Batrīs that ʿAlī was the best candidate for the Imāmate after the Prophet, but sided with the Batrīs in affirming the Imāmate of the "less worthy."[82] In the election of Abū Bakr, the community had acted in error by overlooking the Prophet's *implicit* designation of ʿAlī as his successor.[83] This mistake, however, was not tantamount to disbelief; it was simply an error in independent judgment (*ijtihād*).[84] In making this argument, the Sulaymānīs rejected both the Jārūdī position that most Companions had apostatized and the Batrī view that Abū Bakr's election was not a mistake. With respect to ʿAlī's opponents in the first civil war (as well as ʿUthmān), the Sulaymānīs aligned with the Jārūdīs in labeling them apostates and nonbelievers.[85] On the issue of knowledge, the Sulaymānīs agreed with the Batrīs that legal authority was diffused among the entire Muslim community.[86]

Even though the heresiographers list these three groups as distinct Zaydī sects, there was a significant theological overlap between the Batrīs and the Sulaymānīs that set them apart from the Jārūdīs. At the heart of this difference was the Jārūdī doctrine of *rajʿa* (return from the dead),[87] which was apparent as early as 145/763 in splinter groups that

[80] There is very little historical information regarding Sulaymān b. Jarīr al-Raqqī. He was active in the middle and late 2nd/8th century and is often described solely in theological terms in the heresiographical literature. As will be discussed in Chapter 6, he is also linked by both Zaydī and non-Zaydī sources to the murder (by poison) of Idrīs b. ʿAbd Allāh in 175/792 (*DIQ*, 61–6).

[81] As a whole, it appears that the Sulaymānīs emerged much later than the Jārūdīs and Batrīs at the end of 2nd/8th century. They seem to have been a general offshoot of Batrism and – in subsequent chapters – will be treated as part and parcel of the Batriyya. They are discussed here in the interests of elaborating the various theological positions ascribed to early Zaydīs.

[82] *MIm*, 44; *MIs*, 143; *FBF*, 42; *MN*, 1:159–60.

[83] *MIm*, 44; *MIs*, 143; *FBF*, 42.

[84] *MIm*, 44; *MIs*, 143; *FBF*, 43; *MN*, 1:159–60.

[85] *MIm*, 44; *MIs*, 143; *FBF*, 43; *MN*, 1:160.

[86] *MIm*, 44–5; *FBF*, 42.

[87] *MIs*, 141–2; *FBF*, 42; *MN*, 1:159. See also, *DIQ*, 56–7.

anticipated the return of al-Nafs al-Zakiyya (d. 145/763).[88] Both the Batrīs and Sulaymānīs categorically rejected *raj'a* and accused its proponents of disbelief.[89] The theological divide between the two camps was also evident in their interactions with the Imāmīs. Although the heresiographies do not mention any debates between individual Jārūdīs and Imāmīs, the Batrīs and Sulaymānīs were known to confront the Imāmīs regarding *taqiyya* (cautionary dissimulation) and *badā'* (change in the course of future events).[90] In a typical example, al-Bāqir was challenged by one his Kūfan followers (i.e., 'Umar b. Riyāḥ – fl. 2nd/8th century) for giving contradictory answers to the same question in different years. When pressed for the reason, al-Bāqir ascribed his initial answer to *taqiyya*. This did not satisfy 'Umar who claimed that there had been no external threat when he had first asked his question. He proceeded to spread the tale among his close associates, many of whom purportedly joined him in converting to Batrī Zaydism.[91] The most famous example of *badā'* involved the early death of Ismā'īl b. Ja'far, who had allegedly been designated by his father al-Ṣādiq as the next Imām. The heresiographers claim that al-Ṣādiq's characterization of the incident as an example of God's *badā'* prompted many of his Companions to defect to the Batriyya.[92] The fact that there are no corresponding examples involving Jārūdīs suggests a degree of theological polarization, with the Imāmīs/Jārūdīs on one side and the Batrīs/Sulaymānīs on the other.

During the course of the 3rd/9th century, "the Batriyya quickly disintegrated as the Kūfan traditionist school was absorbed into Sunnism, while, within the Zaydiyya, the Jārūdī views concerning the Imāmate prevailed and Zaydī *fiqh* was elaborated on the basis of the doctrine of the family of the Prophet."[93] The depiction of early Zaydism presented above is a sociologically believable and smooth account of two groups (treating the Batrīs and Sulaymānīs as a single unit) coming together through the energy of one man's personal charisma. But how much credence can be given to a narrative drawn from heresiographical sources? Can we find evidence for both the initial creation of the sect and its eventual evolution in the contemporaneous sources? These questions are at the heart of the analysis of Zaydī traditions in Chapters 3 through 5.

88 *MIs*, 141; *MN*, 159.
89 *MIs*, 144.
90 *KM* 78–9; *FS*, 64–6; *MN*, 1:160.
91 *KM* 75; *FS*, 59–60.
92 *KM* 77–8; *FS*, 62.
93 *EI*² supplement, s.v. Batriyya (Madelung); *DIQ*, 44.

SUMMARY AND STRUCTURE

This book focuses on two important narratives that purport to describe the birth and development of Imāmī and Zaydī Shīʿism. The first maintains that the contours of a distinct Imāmī identity materialized in the early 2nd/8th century (if not earlier) around the figures of al-Bāqir and al-Ṣādiq. If this view is indeed correct, then an analysis of Imāmī sources from the early 2nd/8th century should reflect this independence. The second contends that Zaydism was born through the merging of two disparate Shīʿī theological groups (i.e., the Jārūdīs and the Batrīs) around the 122/740 revolt of Zayd b. ʿAlī. It then claims that the two groups engaged in an internal struggle for control of the movement, from which the Jārūdīs emerged triumphant. We expect to find evidence for both of these claims in Zaydī traditions from the 2nd/8th century.

Chapter 2 proposes a methodological approach with the potential to evaluate the veracity of the narratives described above. It begins with a survey of scholarly debates on the nature of the extant source material, including a number of recent works, which make a compelling case for the dating of traditions to the early 2nd/8th century (or even earlier). The chapter concludes by outlining the basic parameters of a method for mining traditions for historical information pertinent to early sectarianism.

The second part of the book tests the narratives delineated in Chapter 1 based on the approach developed in Chapter 2. This is done through three case studies that center on important issues of ritual and dietary law. Chapter 3 focuses on the recitation of the phrase "In the name of God, the Beneficent the Merciful" (i.e., the *basmala*) at the start of prayer, whereas Chapter 4 centers on the inclusion of an invocation or curse within the daily prayer (i.e., the *qunūt*). Chapter 5 tackles the prohibition of alcoholic drinks, an issue that aroused considerable controversy in Kūfa. Each case study starts with a legal survey that examines the views and methods of representative jurists from six major premodern legal schools (i.e., Ḥanafīs, Mālikīs, Shāfiʿīs, Ḥanbalīs, Imāmīs, and Zaydīs). It then proceeds to an analysis of the traditions and an evaluation of the degree to which the results agree with the classical narratives. Overall, there is significant support for the existence of an independent Imāmī identity in the early 2nd/8th century, but also a clear need for a revision of our understanding of early Zaydism.

The third and final part of the book addresses core questions regarding the dating of (the *when*) and mechanism for (the *how*) the emergence of Shīʿism. Chapter 6 articulates a new timeline for Zaydī Shīʿism that aligns with the results of the three case studies and finds significant support in the historical sources. Specifically, it highlights how an extended period of covert activity and successive political failures contributed to the crystallization of Zaydī identity. Chapters 7 and 8 utilize a sociological framework to examine the means through which early Shīʿī groups (specifically the Imāmīs) expressed an independent communal identity. Chapter 7 argues for the seminal importance of observable ritual practice. In some instances, the most skew of theological views were overlooked in individuals who adhered to an acceptable form of the daily prayer or ablution. Chapter 8 focuses on the growing demarcation of "sacred spaces" (mainly mosques, but also shrines) where the Imāmī Shīʿa would gather and perform rituals in a distinctive manner. In time, these spaces acquired an independent charisma and were transformed into important centers of pilgrimage.

2

Confronting the Source Barrier

A New Methodology

Every study of early Shīʿism is fundamentally hampered by a lack of contemporaneous historical sources. Very few chronicles can verifiably be dated to the start of the 2nd/8th century, leaving scholars with a myriad of sources from subsequent centuries, which claim an unverifiable reliance on earlier written materials.[1] The degree to which these have been manipulated or altered to fit polemical agendas remains an open question. In the case of heresiographies, for example, it is likely that historical materials were recrafted to fit a particular theological worldview in which one sect was saved and seventy-one (or seventy-two, or seventy-three) were destined for Hell. Faced with such a dilemma, many historians have concluded that substantive research into early Islam is not possible without the discovery of new sources or developments in fields such as archeology or numismatics. This chapter argues for the dating of an entire category of (albeit nonhistorical) sources to the early 2nd/8th century and offers an avenue for utilizing these texts to derive historical information. The first section summarizes important recent scholarship that places ritual law traditions in as early as the late 1st/7th century. The second section lays out the methodology employed in Chapters 3 through 5.

THE SEARCH FOR EARLY SOURCES

In the second volume of his seminal 1889 work, *Muhammedanishe Studien*, Ignaz Goldziher expressed severe skepticism about the entirety

[1] Ibn Isḥāq's (d. 151/768) *Sīra* is the earliest known surviving historical chronicle, but even this text was actually redacted and edited by Ibn Hishām (d. 219/834).

of the *ḥadīth* literature.[2] He argued that political and polemical factors led to a proliferation of fabrication, which made it virtually impossible to derive any factual information from the multitude of seemingly historical traditions preserved in the major collections.[3] In the decades that followed, scholars explored the implications of Goldziher's work for a variety of fields, from early Islamic historiography to the origins and development of Islamic law. They generally adhered to one of two positions with respect to the sources. The first was grounded in a thoroughgoing skepticism that rejected the entirety of the Muslim tradition as the product of a back projection of expectations onto the life of the Prophet.[4] The second affirmed the general utility of the traditions as historical sources while attempting to sift out those reports that appeared to reflect later bias or polemical debates.[5] The two sides have followed parallel tracks through the last century, with little progress toward a resolution of this fundamental epistemological disagreement.[6] Skeptics consider traditions as fabrications unless proven otherwise, whereas their opponents assume veracity in the absence of proof of forgery.[7]

The scholars in each of these camps tend to focus on either the content (*matn*) or the transmission history (via the *isnād* or chain of transmission) of a given piece of information.[8] While Goldziher's work was

[2] The following discussion of the controversies surrounding early Islamic sources is not meant to be exhaustive. For those interested in a detailed study of the topic complete with a survey of the current state of the field, see Motzki, "Dating," 204–53 and *idem*, "Authenticity," 211–58. In the section that follows, I concentrate on those scholars and methods that are particularly pertinent for my work, though the general framework is indebted to Motzki.

[3] Goldziher, *Muslim Studies*, vol. 2. Goldziher explicitly articulates this point on 2:19 and then discusses the process of fabrication in chapters 3 through 5. See 2:89ff, 2:126ff, and 2:145ff.

[4] According to Schoeler (*Biography*, 3–4), the early advocates of this position included Leone Caetani and Henri Lammens. For more recent examples, see Wansbrough's *The Sectarian Milieu* or Crone's *Meccan Trade*.

[5] Schoeler identifies the early advocates of this position as Theodor Nöldeke and Carl Becker (Schoeler, *Biography*, 3–4). For a typical example of this approach, see Watt, *Muhammad*.

[6] For an exchange between Serjeant and Crone, which exemplifies the occasionally hostile relationship between the two camps, see Serjeant, "Meccan Trade," 472–86 along with Crone's response, "Serjeant," 216–40.

[7] A number of varied studies address the differences between these two camps. In addition to Motzki ("Dating"), a few of the more interesting include Schoeler, *Biography*, 3–19; Hallaq, "Authenticity," 75–90; Robinson, *Islamic Historiography*; and Donner, *Narratives*.

[8] In the discussion that follows, I emphasize arguments that generally, though not exclusively, focus on the *isnād* as opposed to the *matn*. This is a result of my particular interest in arguing that written sources were circulated during the early 2nd/8th century in good faith by their compilers.

grounded in a critique of content, the scholar most associated with a skeptical engagement of both content and *isnād*s is Joseph Schacht. In *The Origins of Muhammadan Jurisprudence*, Schacht utilized content criticism to propose a timeline for the development of Islamic law, which relied on his assessment of the sophistication of specific legal doctrines or texts.[9] He also devoted a small chapter to the issue of *isnād*s, highlighting their tendency to "grow backward" and "spread."[10] Schacht described "backward growth" as the false projecting of "doctrines back to higher authorities" beginning with the Successors but culminating in the exponential growth of traditions ascribed to the Prophet.[11] He characterized the "spread" of *isnād*s as the "creation of additional authorities or transmitters for the same doctrine or tradition."[12] In spite of these problems, Schacht suggested that *isnād*s might conceivably be utilized for the dating of traditions. The relevant passage is important enough to quote at length:

> These results regarding the growth of *isnād*s enable us to envisage the case in which a tradition was put into circulation by a traditionist whom we may call NN, or by a person who used his name, at a certain time. The tradition would normally be taken over by one or several transmitters, and the lower, real part of the *isnād* would branch out into several strands. The original promoter NN would have provided his tradition with an *isnād* reaching back to an authority such as a Companion or the Prophet, and this higher, fictitious part of the *isnād* would often acquire additional branches by the creation of improvements which would take their place beside the original chain of transmitters, or by the process which we have described as spread of *isnād*s. But NN would remain the (lowest) common link in the several strands of *isnād*s.... Whether this happened to the lower or to the higher part of the *isnād* or to both, the existence of a significant common link (NN) in all or most *isnād*s of a given tradition would be a strong indication in favor of its having originated in the time of NN.[13]

Most scholars continue to refer to the NN, identified by Schacht as the originator of a given tradition, as the "common link." Schacht's method for dating traditions was fundamentally transformed by G. H. A. Juynboll who proposed the general rule that the greater the number of independent chains of transmission that emerged from a common

[9] Schacht, *Origins*, 176–89.
[10] *Ibid.*, 163–75.
[11] *Ibid.*, 165.
[12] *Ibid.*, 166. Michael Cook explores the implications of the tendency of *isnād*s to spread in *Early Muslim Dogma*, 107–16.
[13] *Ibid.*, 171–2.

link, the greater the probability that the transmission reflected a historical reality.[14] He actualized his approach through the production of schemata that tracked every *isnād* for a given tradition and then identified common links or "bundles" of transmission.[15] Single strands of *isnād*s were removed and the creation of the tradition was then ascribed to the earliest common link.[16] Both Schacht and Juynboll concluded that the creation and circulation of traditions proliferated in the early to mid-2nd/8th century, with the former explicitly characterizing the first half of the 2nd/8th century as the start of the "literary period."[17]

The ambiguous use of the term "literary period" justifies some discussion at this point as it hints at a dispute that was related to the issue of dating traditions, namely the interaction between the oral and the written in the transmission of knowledge. If it could be shown that scholars in the 2nd/8th or even the 1st/7th century were largely working with written sources, this would make the wholesale forging of traditions a far more complicated and difficult process. There would remain the possibility of faulty transmission or minor additions/deletions to a given text, but large-scale fabrication of works in such an environment would be unlikely. This point is central to the methodology of the present study, which (as will become clear below) assumes not the "authenticity"[18] of traditions, but rather their faithful collection and transmission in the early 2nd/8th century.

14 This had the practical effect of reducing many of the authorities that Schacht would have considered common links into "seemingly" common links falsely added to *isnād*s by later transmitters. Juynboll demonstrates his approach in "Methods," 343–83; "Notes," 287–314, especially 290–8; and "Early Islamic Society," 151–94. For his discussion of the historicity of a given transfer of information between two transmitters, see Juynboll, "Methods," 352–3. Cook questions the validity of dating on the basis of the common link owing, in large part, to the potential spread of *isnād*s (*Early Muslim Dogma*, 107–16). He also highlights some of the shortcomings of the common link through a study of eschatological traditions that are datable on external grounds ("Eschatology," 23–47).

15 Juynboll, "Methods," 351–2.

16 *Ibid.*, 353–4. Juynboll refined his views over time by accounting for the possibility of "diving" (bypassing a common link to cite a higher authority) and developing additional tools such as partial and inverted partial common links.

17 Schacht, *Origins*, 176. Juynboll is slightly more optimistic than Schacht, noting that the oldest common links "cannot possibly be visualized as starting to bring sayings into circulation *before* the year 80/699" (Juynboll, "Methods," 354). Note that Goldziher asserted that traditions were likely recorded in written form from a very early date (*Muslim Studies*, 2:22ff). Lucas comes to a similar conclusion about the beginnings of the *isnād* through a fundamentally different approach (*Constructive*, 347).

18 Authenticity in the sense of a verification of the ascription of an act or statement to an early authority figure.

The modern scholar most commonly associated with the view in favor of the early circulation of written texts is Fuat Sezgin. In his *Geschichte des arabischen Schrifttums*, Sezgin proposed a method through which written works could be reconstructed by comparing the chains of transmission in a given collection.[19] His analytic criterion were, however, quite expansive, and he treated repeated ascriptions to a specific transmitter as evidence for his authorship of a written work.[20] Sezgin essentially argued for the production and circulation of actual books among scholars as early as the middle of the 1st/7th century.[21] At the heart of his approach was the clearly articulated assumption that *isnād*s often denoted either authorship or authorized transmission of a known text.[22]

Sezgin was criticized from a variety of perspectives, the most substantive of which focused on his claims for the circulation of formal written works authorized by individual authors. In this regard, the work of Schoeler and Motzki provided a particularly important corrective in that it problematized the terms "author" and "book" while confirming the early presence of written materials.[23] Schoeler offered a revised understanding of the transition from oral to written transmission and explored how the gradual shift from notebooks and lecture notes to official "published" books led to minor changes in the wording of given traditions.[24] In a similar vein, Motzki suggested that Sezgin had identified "compilers" who might make use of a variety of written and oral techniques, as opposed to authors and their alleged books.[25] He also presented his own method for utilizing *isnād*s to uncover early sources, which was based on a firmer analytic foundation.

Before discussing Motzki's work, however, some of the more recent efforts at dating individual traditions should be mentioned. Many of these focus both on the content and the chain of transmission in a

19 Sezgin, *Geschichte*, 1:53–84 and specifically 80–4. See also, Abbott, *Studies*, vols. 1–2 and especially 2:5–32.

20 Sezgin, *Geschichte*, 1:70ff.

21 *Ibid.*, 1:81 and 70

22 *Ibid.*, 1:70ff.

23 For Motzki, see *Origins*. For Schoeler, see *The Oral and the Written* and *idem*, *Genesis*. For Schoeler's critique of Sezgin, see Schoeler, *Genesis*, 5–9.

24 Schoeler, *Genesis*, 1–6; *idem*, The *Oral and the Written*, 112ff; and *idem*, *Biography*, 114–5. Cook offers a different view of the early controversy surrounding orality versus written sources in "Opponents," 437–530. He concludes that "traditionist literature preserves substantially authentic materials from the second half of the second century; if handled carefully, it can tell us a good deal about the first half of the second century" (Cook, "Opponents," 489). See also, Azmi, *Studies*, 18–27.

25 Motzki, "Dating," 246 and *idem*, "Author," 171–201.

multilayered attempt at identifying the provenance of a given tradition. Both Zaman and Schoeler, for example, combine an analysis of common links with a literary comparison of the text of a given tradition.[26] Schoeler's results claim to push the frontier of historically verifiable traditions as far back as the late 1st/7th and early 2nd/8th century.[27] Behnam Sadeghi, while methodologically similar to Schoeler and Motzki in some respects, proposes a number of new approaches that utilize the geographical associations of transmitters or emphasize the stylistic characteristics of a given text. In recent articles, he has demonstrated the effectiveness of his methods for both dating individual traditions[28] and establishing the authorship of disputed early works.[29] These developments have produced results that are, at times, quite compelling, but it remains to be seen whether they will garner the opposition of a skeptical school of historians that rejects the veracity of noncontemporaneous reports about the events of the first two centuries and demands independent documentary verification of each and every tradition through nonliterary sources (e.g., archeological evidence, numismatics, etc). In the end, the debate between the two sides remains largely unresolved.

The authenticity of traditions ascribed to 1st/7th-century authorities, however, is somewhat ancillary to the approach employed in this work, which is predicated primarily on the premise that texts were transmitted faithfully (for the most part) and without large-scale fabrication *in the early 2nd/8th century*. The strongest evidence for this claim is offered by Harald Motzki in his *Origins of Islamic Jurisprudence*, which, as previously mentioned, refines and complicates Sezgin's early efforts at reconstructing early sources.[30] Specifically, Motzki attempts to corroborate the veracity of the ascriptions in a given *isnād*. He does this by analyzing the internal structure of one section of ʿAbd al-Razzāq's (d. 211/827)

[26] For Zaman, see his unpublished doctoral dissertation entitled *The Evolution of a Ḥadīth* and *idem*, "The Science of *Rijāl*," 1–34. With regard to literary analysis, Schoeler acknowledges a significant debt to the pioneering work of Albrecht Noth (Schoeler, *Biography*, 4ff and 114ff). For Noth, see *The Early Arabic Historical Tradition*.

[27] Schoeler acknowledges that the same basic method (dubbed *isnād-cum-matn*) was simultaneously developed by Motzki (Schoeler, *Biography*, 146 footnote 176). Both have authored studies that employ this approach to derive historical information pertaining to the biography of the Prophet. For Motzki, see *Biography* and *idem*, "The Prophet and the Cat," 18–83.

[28] Sadeghi, "The Traveling Tradition," 203–42.

[29] Sadeghi, "Authenticity," 291–319. For his work on the authorship and dating of the Qur'ān, see *idem*, "Chronology"; and *idem* and Uwe Bergmann, "Codex," 343–436.

[30] Motzki, *Origins*. The ideas in the monograph are spelled out more succinctly in his introduction to *Ḥadīth* and "*Muṣannaf*," 1–21.

Muṣannaf, a large ḥadīth collection, compiled in the early 3rd/9th century, that contains traditions referencing a range of legal authorities including (but not limited to) the Prophet and his Companions.

Motzki begins by identifying the four jurists 'Abd al-Razzāq cites as the direct sources for a vast majority of his traditions, namely Ma'mar b. Rāshid (d. 153/770), Sufyān al-Thawrī (d. 161/778), Ibn Jurayj (d. 150/767), and Sufyān b. 'Uyayna (d. 198/814).[31] He then tackles the issue of whether these ascriptions are real or forged. Did 'Abd al-Razzāq simply attach sound chains of transmission to anonymous and/or fictional traditions or did he actually get his information from his stated sources? To answer this question, Motzki investigates the structure and organization of the material attributed to each jurist. Specifically, he assumes that if 'Abd al-Razzāq fabricated his traditions, then there would be no substantive differences between the corpora of each source. In other words, the characteristics of the traditions taken from Sufyān al-Thawrī would be indistinguishable from those of Ma'mar b. Rāshid because they were "created" by the same author (i.e., 'Abd al-Razzāq). To craft forgeries in which each corpus of traditions ascribed to a particular informant is idiosyncratic in terms of subject matter, manner of presentation, and style (to name but a few characteristics) would be incredibly difficult. Put simply, if groups of traditions associated with each jurist have a unique voice/style, this suggests that 'Abd al-Razzāq faithfully recorded the opinions of each author (perhaps from written works). If, by contrast, groups of traditions linked to each authority are fundamentally similar, fabrication remains a real possibility.

To test this premise, Motzki creates four subsets of traditions (organized around the four primary informants) and investigates the internal structure[32] of each. His analysis reveals that every corpus is unique in terms of style, purported method of transmission, and citation of authority figures. In other words, each of 'Abd al-Razzāq's direct sources transmits a grouping of traditions with a distinctive profile of stylistic preferences, content, and form. This result constitutes strong evidence that 'Abd al-Razzāq was, in fact, accurately relating information from his informants rather than fabricating it.[33] This process places possible

[31] Motzki, "*Muṣannaf*," 3–4.

[32] Motzki focuses on the following characteristics: the use of *ra'y* (personal discretion), the nature of the relationship between narrator and source, the citation of authorities, the use of complete versus partial *isnād*s, and transmission terminology.

[33] Motzki, "*Muṣannaf*," 7–8.

forgery of the texts to – at the very earliest – the generation of ʿAbd al-Razzāq's sources (i.e., the mid-2nd/8th century).

Motzki then applies this same method a second time to the four subgroupings of traditions transmitted by each of ʿAbd al-Razzāq's sources. Once again, he finds that the structural features and idiosyncrasies of these accounts suggest veracious transmission. In this manner, Motzki reaches as far back as ʿAṭāʾ b. Abī Rabāḥ (d. 115/733), finding no evidence for systematic forgery.[34] He argues persuasively that these results confirm the existence of written traditions in the early 2nd/8th century that were used as raw materials for subsequent larger collections.[35] It is likely that ʿAbd al-Razzāq was consulting small written collections ascribed to (or possibly acquired from) his primary informants in the course of his own authorship. By the late 3rd/9th century, these smaller compilations no longer served a purpose and disappeared.[36]

Motzki's research effectively argues for the circulation and largely faithful transmission of traditions in the early 2nd/8th century, the period generally associated with the formation of Kūfan sectarian identities.[37] His larger work also strongly suggests that written[38] sources in the 2nd/8th century were transmitted in subsequent collections[39] with an eye toward accuracy; they were not simply inventions connected to stock chains of transmission.[40] Other studies have verified the provenance of important

[34] *Ibid.*, 8.

[35] For Motzki's arguments in favor of written sources, see footnote 27 in this chapter.

[36] Motzki, "*Muṣannaf*," 1.

[37] The extant Sunnī collections preserve the legacy of the traditionist movement along with dimmer echoes of the *ahl al-raʾy*, who increasingly justified their positions on a textual basis. See Chapter 1.

[38] It is worth reemphasizing that Motzki (and Schoeler) do not conceive of these written materials as formal books but rather as different kinds of memory aids or lecture notes.

[39] Whereas Motzki focuses on the *Muṣannaf* of ʿAbd al-Razzāq, his conclusions are suggestive for other collections such as those of Ibn Abī Shayba and al-Bayhaqī, because mass fabrication would become increasingly more difficult with the passage of time. For a detailed analysis of Ibn Abī Shayba's work, see Scott Lucas, "Legal *Ḥadīth*," 283–314. Although Lucas' article is not focused on the issue of authenticity, he offers an argument against the wholesale fabrication of traditions by Ibn Abī Shayba ("*Legal Ḥadīth*," 308, and, especially, footnote 105)

[40] The actual form and nature of these written sources remains an issue of debate. Whereas Schoeler asserts that the impetus for works organized in the manner of a *muṣannaf* emerged in the early 2nd/8th century, he also notes that the societal norm was to transmit knowledge in public through audition, without the use of any written materials. Though these texts may have enjoyed a degree of fluidity, they were ultimately bound by lecture notes or memory aids that were kept at home (Schoeler, *Genesis*, 5). Of particular importance is the fact that traditions were transmitted in a mixed oral-written form, allowing

2nd/8th-century Sunnī collections such as the *Muwaṭṭaʾ* of Mālik b. Anas (d. 179/795) and the *Kitāb al-āthār* of Muḥammad al-Shaybānī (d. 189/804–5).[41] There have also been careful studies that have demonstrated the dependence of canonical Sunnī works such as the *Ṣaḥīḥ* of al-Bukhārī[42] on a corpus of earlier written texts.[43]

Whereas Motzki focuses primarily on the Sunnī *ḥadīth* literature, research into Imāmī collections has yielded similar results. Etan Kohlberg and Hossein Modarressi have exerted considerable effort toward identifying and salvaging the earliest layer of Imāmī legal literature.[44] They argue that Imāmī traditions were initially preserved in *uṣūl* (sing. *aṣl*),[45] which were "personal notebooks of materials received through oral transmission" from one of the Imāms.[46] In *Tradition and Survival*, Modarressi highlights the written nature of these works by citing instances where later authors corrected mistakes in traditions by referring back to the original text of an *aṣl*.[47] He also partially reconstructs many of these early sources, taking chains of transmission that end with a specific author and correlating them with references to written works in the premodern bibliographical literature.[48] In doing so, Modarressi pushes the horizon

for the possibility of some changes in the text in the course of transmission but arguing against the thesis of wholesale fabrication.

[41] There is extensive scholarship on the dating of the *Muwaṭṭaʾ*. See, for example, Calder, *Studies*, 20–38; Dutton, *Origins*; Hallaq, "Dating," 47–65; El Shamsy, *Tradition*, 33–46; and Motzki, "The Prophet and the Cat." Sadeghi discusses both the *Muwaṭṭaʾ* and the *Kitāb al-āthār* ("Authenticity").

[42] Al-Bukhārī's *Ṣaḥīḥ* is the only collection other than ʿAbd al-Razzāq to be analyzed in a systematic manner on par with Motzki's work on the *Muṣannaf*. See Sezgin, *Buhārî'nin*.

[43] For numerous examples of this tendency, see Azmi, *Studies*, 293–300. There is an immense volume of scholarship that discusses the structure, compilation, and evolution (in terms of authoritativeness) of the Sunnī canonical and noncanonical collections. The following list is not exhaustive but highlights some of the most useful studies: Lucas, *Constructive*; *idem*, "Divorce," 325–68, which compares the compilation techniques and legal approaches embedded in five of the canonical and one of the noncanonical Sunnī collections; *idem*, "Legal Principles," 289–324; Melchert, "Abū Dāwūd al-Sijistānī," 9–44 and especially 22–34, where he examines the internal structure of the *Sunan* through a comparison with other major collections; *idem*, "Aḥmad ibn Ḥanbal," 32–51, which contrasts the *Musnad* with the major Sunnī canonical collections; Brown, "Ibn Mājah,"; and *idem*, *Canonization*.

[44] See Modarressi, *Tradition* and Kohlberg, "*Al-Uṣūl*," 128–66.

[45] The most common terms for these notebooks were *ʿaṣl* and *kitāb*, but the sources also refers to them as *juzʾ*, *nuskha*, and *ṣaḥīfa* (Modarressi, *Tradition*, xiv). See also, Azmi, *Studies*, 28–30.

[46] Modarressi, *Tradition*, xiv.

[47] Modarressi offers both Sunnī and Imāmī examples of this process in footnotes 13 and 14 on page xv of the introduction to *Tradition*. See also, Azmi, *Studies*, 293–300.

[48] Modarressi, *Tradition*, xv.

for written Shīʿī works back into the early 2nd/8th century.[49] After the rise of the large Imāmī collections (e.g., al-Kulaynī's *al-Kāfī*), "the original *uṣūl* became dispensable from a practical point of view," so that only thirteen identifiable examples were known to al-Majlisī (d. 1110/1699) in the 12th/17th century.[50] Many of the *uṣūl* are no longer extant, but it is reasonable to conclude that the recording of written Imāmī traditions was relatively common in the early to mid-2nd/8th century.[51]

As opposed to the Sunnīs and the Imāmīs, the earliest extant layers of Zaydī texts consist primarily of problematic[52] legal and theological tracts. In fact, the first and most important Zaydī collection of traditions (i.e., Aḥmad b. ʿĪsā's *Amālī*) was only compiled in the mid-3rd/9th century.[53] No scholar has applied Motzki's method of structural analysis to the *Amālī*, and there have been no attempts at ascertaining its component parts in the manner of Kohlberg and Modarressi. Despite the lack of research, it is possible to offer some tentative assumptions based on parallels with other sectarian communities. Specifically, the Sunnī and Imāmī cases suggest that the practice of recording traditions was widespread in early 2nd/8th-century Kūfa; even the *ahl al-ra'y* were using texts to support their legal positions.[54] It stands to reason that the Zaydīs – or at least

[49] Modarressi's conclusions align with those of Motzki (and, to a lesser extent, Sezgin) in demonstrating the potential for the reconstruction of early works through their citations in subsequent sources.

[50] Kohlberg, "*al-Uṣūl*," 129. In the first volume of *Tradition*, Modarressi (like Motzki in the Sunnī context) attempts to uncover the broad outlines of numerous early Imāmī works including the *uṣūl*.

[51] Kohlberg notes that most *aṣl* authors were disciples of al-Ṣādiq (Kohlberg, "*Al-Uṣūl*" 129). Modarressi attributes a number of *uṣūl* works to disciples of Muḥammad al-Bāqir in the early 2nd/8th century (Modarressi, *Tradition*, 39–127 on Kūfan Shīʿism in the Umayyad Period). Buckley dates these sources to the lifetime of al-Ṣādiq contemporaneous with the growth of written materials among proto-Sunnī traditionists ("Origins," 165–84).

[52] Problematic in the sense that modern scholars doubt their attribution to early Zaydī authorities. The most striking examples are works ascribed to Zayd b. ʿAlī, the eponymous founder of the school, including *al-Musnad* and several theological treatises. Madelung notes that these texts are "too disparate in style and doctrinal positions to be the work of a single author and may mostly be seen to represent currents in the early Kūfan Zaydiyya" (*EI*², s.v. Zayd b. ʿAlī [Madelung]).

[53] Aḥmad b. ʿĪsā b. Zayd b. ʿAlī, one of the leaders of the Kūfan Zaydī community in the mid/late 3rd/9th century, is described as a strong Jārūdī. For more on Aḥmad b. ʿĪsā from a Zaydī perspective, see the biographical appendix of al-Ṣanʿānī's *Kitāb raʾb al-ṣadʿ*, 3:1681. See also footnote 122 in Chapter 6 of this volume.

[54] Schacht observes that the *ahl al-ra'y* would sometimes cite texts but adopt positions that went against those texts (Schacht, *Origins*, 73–7). See also, Lucas, "Legal *Ḥadīth*," 310–4 and *idem*, "Divorce," 362–5.

their Batrī constituents[55] – were engaged in a similar intellectual project. In the absence of information to the contrary, we can reasonably conclude that the traditions contained in the *Amālī* are drawn from previous Zaydī written works from the early or mid-2nd/8th century.

Advances in *ḥadīth* studies over the last few decades have created new possibilities for the study of early Islam. We now possess a corpus of written texts datable to the early 2nd/8th century contemporaneous with events (e.g., Zayd b. 'Alī's revolt in 122/740) and important figures (e.g., al-Bāqir and al-Ṣādiq) seminal to the formation of sectarian identity.[56] Some of the material found in these collections focuses on political watersheds, military rebellions, or controversies at the heart of important theological polemics, which complicates their utility in historical research. At the same time, they also include large numbers of traditions concerned with issues of ritual law such as the proper methods for ablution and prayer, the rites of pilgrimage, and dietary restrictions that, as Lucas has recently shown, appear less prone to forgery or fabrication.[57] The next section presents an approach for using these legal and seemingly nonhistorical texts to test the sectarian narratives detailed in Chapter 1. In doing so, it avoids the use of traditions that purport to describe historical facts in favor of legal traditions focusing on ritual.

METHODOLOGY

Based on the survey of the previous section, it is possible to assert with considerable confidence that ritual law traditions were recorded without wholesale fabrication in the early 2nd/8th-century Muslim world.[58] In the case studies that follow in Chapters 3, 4, and 5, a cross section of these

[55] As noted in the previous chapter, the Batrīs were part of the Kūfan traditionist milieu, which means they were recording traditions in the early 2nd/8th century. The fact that the Imāmīs were compiling *uṣūl* suggests that the Jārūdīs might have been doing the same. The general idea here is that the compilation and recording of traditions was a common and widespread practice in 2nd/8th-century Kūfa. The element unique to traditionists was their demand that every legal ruling be based on a clear text.

[56] For these narratives, see Chapter 1.

[57] See Lucas, "Divorce," 364–5 and *idem*, "Legal *Ḥadīth*," 307–14 where he argues against systematic forgery by demonstrating the overall paucity of Prophetic traditions in the canonical collections, as well as, the tendency of some of the earliest collectors ascribed a traditionist perspective to cite non-Prophetic authorities in matters of law.

[58] This is not to say that there were no forgeries, but that the burden of proof with respect to these texts falls on those who claim fabrication. Moreover, as will be argued later, a few cases of fabrication do not invalidate the general methodology employed in this book. The reliance on large numbers of traditions should effectively neutralize any fabricated outliers.

TABLE 2.1. *Sunnī Sources*

Author/Compiler	Work
Mālik b. Anas (d. 179/795)	*Al-Muwaṭṭa'*
Muḥammad b. al-Ḥasan al-Shaybānī (d. 189/804–5)	*Kitāb al-āthār*
Sulaymān b. Dāwūd al-Ṭayālisī (d. 203/819–20)	*Musnad*
ʻAbd al-Razzāq al-Ṣanʻānī (d. 211/837)	*Muṣannaf*
Ibn Abī Shayba (d. 235/849)	*Muṣannaf*
Al-Dārimī (d. 255/869)	*Sunan*
*Al-Bukhārī (d. 256/870)	*Jāmiʻ al-ṣaḥīḥ*
*Muslim b. al-Ḥajjāj (d. 261/875)	*Jāmiʻ al-ṣaḥīḥ*
*Ibn Māja (d. 273/887)	*Sunan*
*Abū Dāwūd (d. 275/889)	*Sunan*
*Al-Tirmidhī (d. 279/892)	*Jāmiʻ al-ṣaḥīḥ*
*Aḥmad b. Shuʻayb al-Nasā'ī (d. 303/915)	*Sunan*
Aḥmad b. al-Ḥusayn al-Bayhaqī (d. 458/1066)	*al-Sunan al-kubrā*

* Denotes the six canonical collections. See the bibliography for full references for all these works.

texts taken from canonical and noncanonical Sunnī, Imāmī, and Zaydī collections are subjected to a series of analyses designed to ascertain when different sectarian groups began developing independent identities.

The preparatory step in this process is the actual gathering of traditions associated with each community. For the Sunnīs, traditions are drawn from the sources listed in Table 2.1, which include the six canonical collections as well as a number of noncanonical works.[59] The most

[59] For background on the organization and structure of these works, see footnotes 39 and 41–43 in this chapter.

TABLE 2.2. *Imāmī Sources*

Author/Compiler	Work
Aḥmad b. Muḥammad al-Barqī (d. 273/887–8)	*al-Maḥāsin*
*Muḥammad b. Mas'ūd al-'Ayyāshī (d. 320/922)	*Tafsīr*
Muḥammad b. Ya'qūb al-Kulaynī (d. 329/941)	*Uṣūl min al-Kāfī*
*Ibn Furāt (d. 4th/10th century)	*Tafsīr*
Muḥammad b. al-Ḥasan al-Ṭūsī (d. 460/1067)	*al-Istibṣār* *Tahdhīb al-aḥkām*
Muḥammad b. al-Ḥasan al-Ḥurr al-'Āmilī (d. 1104/1693)	*Wasā'il al-shī'a*
Al-Majlisī (d.1111/1699)	*Biḥār al-anwār*
Ḥusayn Taqī al-Nūrī al-Ṭabrisī (d. 1320/1902)	*Mustadrak al-Wasā'il*

* Denotes Imāmī *tafsīr* works that extensively cite traditions. See the bibliography for full references for all these works.

glaring omission from this list of sources is the *Musnad* of Aḥmad ibn Ḥanbal (d. 241/855), which, though referenced in the course of the analysis, is not utilized for the purposes of raw data. Its exclusion derives partly from the difficulty of salvaging pertinent texts and partly from the fact that its numerical contribution to the analysis would be minimal (as a result of overlap with other cited works) in comparison to that of, for example, 'Abd al-Razzāq or Ibn Abī Shayba (d. 235/849).[60] By contrast, the inclusion of al-Bayhaqī, whose work is quite late as compared to other collections, is based on his tendency to preserve unique chains of transmission not found elsewhere. In a very limited number of instances, I have also made use of singular traditions found in Ibn 'Abd al-Barr's (d. 463/1070) *al-Istidhkār*.

The Imāmīs do not consider any collection of traditions as "canonical" in a sense analogous to the six Sunnī works cited above. Bearing this in mind, the Imāmī collections utilized in this study are drawn from the sources recorded in Table 2.2.

[60] Melchert notes that the *Musnad* is very repetitive and does not contain an abundance of legal materials (Melchert, "Ahmad ibn Ḥanbal," 45).

TABLE 2.3. *Zaydī Sources*

Author/Compiler	Work
Zayd b. ʿAlī (d. 122/740)	*Musnad*
Aḥmad b. ʿĪsā b. Zayd (d. 247/862)	*Amālī* (preserved in al-Ṣanʿānī's *Kitāb ra'b al-ṣadʿ*)
Abū Ṭālib Yaḥyā b. al-Ḥusayn (d. 469/1077)	*Amālī* (preserved in Jaʿfar b. Aḥmad's *Taysīr al-maṭālib*)
Badr al-Dīn al-Ḥusayn b. Muḥammad (d. 661/1223)	*Shifā' al-uwām*

The collections of al-Ḥurr al-ʿAmilī (d. 1104/1693), al-Majlisī, and al-Ṭabrisī (d. 1320/1902) stand out among the Imāmī sources for their late dating. Any study of Imāmī literature, however, would be incomplete without al-Ḥurr al-ʿAmilī's *Wasā'il*, which includes traditions cited by al-Kulaynī (d. 329/941) and al-Ṭūsī but adds significant additional materials sometimes taken from *uṣūl* or other texts that are no longer extant. The works of al-Majlisī and al-Ṭabrisī are of far less importance to this study and are mentioned only because they provide a handful of rare but important traditions. In general, however, al-Majlisī's massive compendium is avoided as he simply compiled all available traditions with little to no assessment of accuracy or reliability. Al-Ṭabrisī's work, in the end, contributes only 9 of the nearly 230 traditions utilized in Chapters 3 through 5.

There are significantly fewer sources available for Zaydī traditions.[61] Those of greatest importance are listed in Table 2.3.

The *Musnad* of Zayd b. ʿAlī is a derivative collection composed of traditions taken from a juristic work that is ascribed to him but which is more likely a reflection of trends in early Kūfan Zaydism.[62] The first verifiable collection of Zaydī *ḥadīth* – and the source central to the case studies that follow – is the *Amālī* of Aḥmad b. ʿĪsā (d. 247/862), a grandson of Zayd b. ʿAlī, who spent much of his life on the run from the ʿAbbāsids.[63] There is a rare edition of the work entitled *Kitāb al-ʿulūm al-shahīr bi-Amālī Aḥmad b. ʿĪsā* (no date or place of publication), but

[61] For a general overview of the Zaydī *ḥadīth* literature, see al-ʿIzzī, *ʿUlūm al-ḥadīth*.

[62] *DIQ*, 54–7 and *EI*², s.v. Zayd b. ʿAlī (*idem*).

[63] The Amālī was first written down by Muḥammad b. Manṣūr al-Murādī (d. 290/903), who obtained the traditions either directly from Aḥmad or from one of his two sons, ʿAlī and Muḥammad. For more on the text, see *DIQ*, 82–3.

the entirety of the text is also preserved in ʿAlī b. Ismāʿīl al-Ṣanʿānī's modern commentary entitled *Kitāb ra'b al-ṣad*ʿ. The only extant *ḥadīth* collection from the Caspian branch of the Zaydīs is the *Amālī* of Abū Ṭālib al-Nāṭiq bi'l-Ḥaqq Yaḥyā b. al-Ḥusayn (d. 424/1033)[64] preserved by Jaʿfar b. Aḥmad (d. 572/1177) in his *Taysīr al-maṭālib*. The work's uniqueness in comparison to other Zaydī collections stems from its inclusion of nearly complete chains of transmission often stretching back to the Prophet or prominent early Imāms. The most important Zaydī collection from the late premodern period is Sharaf al-Dīn Ḥusayn b. Muḥammad's (d. 661/1263–4) *Shifā' al-uwām* which preserves a significant number of Prophetic traditions but whose primary intent is to articulate differences of opinion between the Hādawīs and the Nāṣirīs,[65] the two most important Zaydī schools of law.[66] The notable exclusion of Muḥammad b. ʿAlī al-ʿAlawī's (d. 445/1053) unpublished (but forthcoming) *al-Jāmiʿ al-kāfī* derives from its minimal citation of authorities from the first two centuries. The *Jāmiʿ* is not a *ḥadīth* collection in the classical Sunnī (or even Imāmī) sense as it focuses instead on organizing the opinions[67] of four Zaydī Imāms[68] from the late 3rd/9th century in an easily accessible form.[69]

Having compiled all the traditions on a given issue from the collections associated with each sectarian community, we are ready to proceed to the analysis, which consists of two steps. The first involves the filtering of Kūfan traditions from the larger undifferentiated mass of accounts. The second consists of a three-tiered comparison of the internal structure of Kūfan texts associated with each sectarian community.

[64] For more on Abū Ṭālib al-Nāṭiq bi'l-Ḥaqq, see *DIQ*, 133–4, 172–82.

[65] For the origins of and differences between the Hādawī and Nāṣirī Zaydīs, see *EI*², s.v. Zaydiyya (Madelung).

[66] The text often begins with traditions that cite the Prophet or ʿAlī to establish the broader parameters of a particular legal issue. It then proceeds to articulate the Yemenī Hādawī stance through Qāsim b. Ibrāhīm al-Rassī (d. 246/860) or his grandson al-Hādī (d. 297/910), and the Caspian Nāṣirī view through al-Nāṣir li'l-Ḥaqq Ḥasan b. ʿAlī al-Uṭrūsh (d. 304/917) or al-Mu'ayyad bi-Allāh Aḥmad b. al-Ḥusayn (d. 411/1020). Al-Shawkānī's *Wabl al-ghamām* is a commentary on the *Shifā*ʾ that attempts to refute many of its legal rulings on the basis of the canonical Sunnī ḥadīth collections.

[67] Madelung has used the final section – devoted to theological issues – to argue against the attribution of a developed Muʿtazilism to al-Qāsim b. Ibrāhīm. For more on this, see *DIQ*, 80 and, "Imām al-Qāsim b. Ibrāhīm," 39–48.

[68] Al-Qāsim b. Ibrāhīm b. Ismāʿīl al-Rassī, Aḥmad b. ʿĪsā b. Zayd b. ʿAlī, Ḥasan b. Yaḥyā b. Ḥusayn b. Zayd b. ʿAlī b. al-Ḥusayn (d. 260/874), and Muḥammad b. Manṣūr al-Murādī.

[69] Muḥammad b. ʿAlī al-ʿAlawī, *al-Jāmiʿ*, 1:1–2. For more on this work, see Madelung, "Imām al-Qāsim b. Ibrāhīm."

GEOGRAPHY

Every large *ḥadīth* collection includes traditions from a variety of urban locations, reflecting the breadth of an author's pursuit of religious knowledge. In most cases, compilers would travel far and wide to find teachers who had preserved unique accounts or were renowned for their possession of the shortest and most direct chains of transmission from a prominent authority. This study is particularly interested in Kūfa due to its integral importance in the classical narratives of early Shī'ism. It is necessary, therefore, to distinguish texts circulating in Kūfa from those of other centers of learning such as Baṣra, Mecca, Medina, or Damascus.

The key to such a differentiation lies in a text's chain of transmission, which purports to describe its "travel history" beginning with a prominent authority figure and ending with the author of a given work. We start by investigating the biographical literature for each individual in a given chain of transmission with a particular interest in his/her geographical affiliation. Indeed, geography was one of the key concerns of biographers who often evaluated the likelihood that one individual had transmitted from another based on whether they had resided in the same city for an extended time. On the basis of this information, it is possible to determine the city where a given tradition was in circulation at the start (and into the middle) of the 2nd/8th century. For example, a chain of transmission might begin with an authority figure in Medina (e.g., the Prophet), proceed to Baṣra through a Companion (e.g., Anas b. Mālik – d. 91 or 93/709 or 711), and circulate among Baṣran jurists (e.g., 'Āṣim b. Sulaymān – d. 141 or 143/759 or 761) before being recorded by a Yemeni scholar (e.g., 'Abd al-Razzāq).[70] Such a tradition would be classified as Baṣran because a majority of its transmitters (especially those in the late 1st/7th and 2nd/8th centuries) lived in Baṣra. Similarly, it is reasonable to assert that an account circulating among 2nd/8th-century Kūfan transmitters contained an opinion prevalent within Kūfa at the time.

It is possible to dispute the accuracy of the transmission histories of traditions. In fact, a number of modern scholars have emphasized the *isnād*'s

[70] For this tradition, see *MAR*, 3:29 – 4977. In this (and subsequent) citations of legal traditions, I offer volume and page number (e.g., volume 3 and page 29) along with the specific number assigned to a given tradition by the compiler/author (e.g., the tradition is designated by the number 4977). In Chapters 7 and 8, by contrast, I often refer to traditions or groups of traditions drawn from historical and other (nonlegal) genres where numbering is either nonexistent or nonessential. In these cases, the references are limited to volume and page numbers.

vulnerability to manipulation through the skillful work of a forger or the honest temptation to validate a praiseworthy practice in the eyes of the larger community.[71] These objections must be answered by those who argue for the veracity of *entire* chains of transmission. In this study, by contrast, we can bypass the issue of forgery on four grounds. First, given that we are primarily interested in the early 2nd/8th century, we only have to focus on those transmitters who lived in the 2nd/8th century rather than delving into the more controversial realm of the 1st/7th century.[72] Second, as noted in the previous section of this chapter, traditions were being recorded in written collections in the early 2nd/8th century. This makes it likely that transmission involved a written component (i.e., notebooks, etc.) in addition to the classical method of oral recitation and memorization, rendering forgery far more difficult (though not impossible). Third, even forged traditions may be accurately identified with a given city. If a Baṣran scholar was fabricating traditions, he would likely rely on Baṣran transmitters, because the citation of Kūfan transmitters would provoke a response from Kūfan scholars acquainted with the individuals.[73] The use of Baṣrans to support a Baṣran position would be the safest bet for acceptance. Finally, the sheer number of traditions used in this study minimizes the impact of forged outliers with geographically misplaced chains of transmissions. In conclusion, it is quite sensible to assume that, by focusing on transmitters from the early to mid-2nd/8th century, we can place a particular tradition (or groups of traditions) in a specific city.

[71] Cook, for example, has argued that an analysis of common links overlooks the possibility that a forger might simply attach a sound *isnād* to a falsified text (Cook, *Early Muslim Dogma*, 107–12). See also, Schacht's *Origins*, 27–30 and *EI*², s.v. Ahl al-Ḥadīth (*idem*), along with Goldziher's *Muslim Studies*, vol. 2, especially 27–164.

[72] Put differently, if the transmission history of a text is valid for the late 1st/7th and 2nd/8th century (as argued by Motzki, Kohlberg, and Modarressi), then – at the very minimum – the chain of transmission tells us where a tradition was circulating in this period. A tradition circulated by 2nd/8th century Baṣrans invoking the authority of the Prophet may not be ascribable to Muḥammad but it likely reflects the common ritual practice of Baṣra.

[73] The counterargument may be made that a Baṣran would forge traditions with Kūfan transmitters in order to discredit the Kūfan legal position. These would function as "rogue" traditions with perfectly sound chains of transmission and prominent Kūfan authorities articulating views at odds with Kūfan practice. In such a case, we would expect to find very clear contradictions between the views ascribed to identical Kūfan legal authorities. In the three subsequent case studies, however, one of the most striking results is the general coherence of views ascribed to these authorities. In many instances, we even find Kūfan authorities articulating a Kūfan position (in direct opposition to the Baṣran view) preserved in a Baṣran line of transmission. This attests eloquently to the veracity of some *isnād*s.

This conclusion opens up numerous potential avenues for research. Once traditions are grouped on the basis of geography, it may be possible to reconstruct the local ritual practice of important Muslim urban centers (i.e., Mecca, Medina, Kūfa, and Baṣra).[74] For example, if a sufficiently large number of Medinan traditions support a given practice (e.g., the wiping of the feet for ablution), this provides strong evidence for its widespread acceptance among the broader Medinan population. The reconstruction of a city's ritual practices may, in turn, provide significant insight into its overarching values and/or ethical mores. The choice of a set of rituals may reflect a particular view of, for example, gender in a period for which we have virtually no other contemporaneous sources.[75] This geographical mode of analysis may also speak to the transition from localized ritual practice to the rise of the formal law school (*madhhab*).[76] Specifically, it may complicate some standard assumptions about the geographical origins of certain law schools. In the case of the recitation of the *basmala* at the start of prayer, for example, it appears that (surprisingly) the Mālikī position is almost exclusively predicated on Baṣran as opposed to Medinan textual evidence.[77]

These research possibilities, however, lie outside the scope of this study, which is primarily interested in utilizing Kūfan traditions to analyze Shīʿī communal identity in the early 2nd/8th century. The process detailed earlier provides the raw material required for the comparisons that follow. In subsequent chapters, the designation of traditions as 2nd/8th-century Kūfan is the product of an often unstated geographical analysis of the *isnād*s of accounts drawn from the Sunnī, Imāmī, and Zaydī collections.

Structure

The analysis begins by identifying every Kūfan tradition from the 2nd/8th century with either a unique content (*matn*) or a distinctive chain of

[74] Kūfa is of special importance in this regard as it possessed a unique ritual diversity in the 2nd/8th century. By contrast, Baṣra, Mecca, and (to a lesser extent) Medina were almost exclusively associated with a single, internally cohesive ritual practice on a variety of issues.

[75] For a representative example of this tendency, see Halevi's *Muhammad's Grave* which identifies a particular pietist orientation at the core of Iraqi traditions on burial and funeral processions.

[76] For the growth and development of the formal law school, see Hallaq, *Origins*.

[77] For more on the *basmala*, see Chapter 3.

transmission.[78] It should also be noted that a majority of traditions that have survived into the modern period are of Kūfan provenance and, on some issues, they outnumber the combined total of all other cities. This is particularly relevant as the structural comparisons discussed below require the presence of large numbers of traditions. These texts are grouped on the basis of the sectarian community that recorded them in a canonical or noncanonical work,[79] and then each corpus is compared with respect to its (1) use of legal authorities, (2) chains of transmission, and (3) narrative style/literary form. The specifics of this process are elaborated as follows.

Legal Authorities. The first comparison centers on the use of authority figures to validate a legal opinion or ritual practice. While all the sectarian groups acknowledge the unquestionable stature of the Prophet, they differ significantly regarding his Companions and Successors. Sunnī schools of law confer a blanket authority on the entire generation of the Prophet's Companions. In so doing, they (theoretically) refuse to differentiate between a member of the Prophet's household (e.g., 'Alī) and a reformed enemy (e.g., Abū Sufyān – d. 32/653). This equity even extends to figures who took up arms against each other in the first civil war, with the conflict framed as a political disagreement with no bearing on religious credentials.

The Imāmī and (later) Zaydī Shī'a, by contrast, restrict authority to the Prophet's family and descendants.[80] In fact, the rejection of traditions narrated by certain Companions is a fundamental characteristic of Imāmī traditions. This category of suspect early figures includes those known to have opposed 'Alī's leadership claims after the death of the Prophet (e.g., Abū Bakr, 'Umar), as well as those who took up arms against him (e.g., Ṭalḥa, al-Zubayr). In contrast to the Imāmī emphasis on a singular genetic

[78] As explained in greater detail earlier, we are primarily concerned with the circulation of texts in 2nd/8th-century Kūfa as opposed to the veracity of entire chains of transmission. Even if a tradition is forged, we can confidently place it in Kūfa as a legal proof text forwarded by a specific sectarian group.

[79] In this section, substantive legal opinion is of secondary importance relative to the degree of overlap between the Sunnī, Imāmī, and Zaydī texts. It is not surprising that the legal rulings preserved by each sectarian group reflect its distinctive practice. In the case of Sunnī texts, this includes a range of views that eventually crystallized into the Ḥanafī and Shāfi'ī positions. The Imāmīs and Zaydīs also generally forward singular ritual practices that persist into the modern period.

[80] For Imāmī views of the Companions, see Kohlberg, "Ṣaḥāba," 143–75. For Zaydī views of the Companions, see Kohlberg, "Companions," 91–8.

line, the (later) Zaydīs situate religious authority among the entirety of 'Alī's descendants through either al-Ḥasan or al-Ḥusayn.[81]

A comparison of the use of authority figures between the three sectarian traditions can help determine when each community began developing an independent identity. In the early period, we expect to find numerous common authorities in the mold of the Prophet. This represents a time when sectarian groups were in their earliest stages and still functioned primarily in concert with the broader Muslim population. Once these groups coalesced into defined insular communities, however, they began citing a set of authorities who represented their particular political (and religious) perspective. Thus, the prominence of Sa'īd b. Jubayr's (d. 95/713) legal rulings in both Zaydī and Sunnī traditions indicates a degree of overlap between the two groups in the late 1st/7th century, whereas the lack of any shared authorities after the early 2nd/8th century supports differentiation.

This method may be criticized by arguing that a community could (and often did) rewrite its early history to fit subsequent theological developments. In such a scenario, the Imāmīs who accord exclusive legal authority to a single genetic line of Imāms could have sifted out traditions that invoked non-Imām authority figures, leaving the impression that such accounts never existed at all. This contingency cannot be overlooked, but it should be viewed in the broader analytic context of this study. Specifically, this first comparison does not exist in a vacuum; rather it is part of a three-step process in which the second and third comparisons are much less prone to historical rewriting or alteration. The value of a general agreement in the results of all three comparisons outweighs the potential problems associated with the first alone.

The Composition of Isnāds – Transmitters and Shared Links. The second comparison focuses on chains of transmission, examining the extent to which different sects utilized the same individuals for the preservation of legal knowledge.[82] This is done in two steps. The first is concerned with

[81] The Zaydī stance changed as the religious community experienced a gradual process of "Sunnification." For details of this change, see Cook, *Commanding Right*, 247–51. For Shawkanī's role in the Sunnification process, see Haykel, *Revival*.

[82] In the following analysis, the sectarian allegiances of specific transmitters are not as important as the degree to which sects rely on identical *isnād*s and common transmitters. Sa'īd b. Jubayr's appearance in the Sunnī and Zaydī traditions, for example, is far more significant than his status as a 'Sunnī' or 'Zaydī' because it suggests a link between the two communities.

singular figures upheld as reliable transmitters by multiple sectarian traditions. The second is interested in extended "shared links" consisting of two or more common transmitters.

The common use of single transmitters suggests that two (or more) communities considered the same figure trustworthy. The overlap of a series of two or more transmitters (shared links), by contrast, holds greater significance as it reflects an overt agreement regarding an individual's scholarly associations and (by extension) communal loyalties. The point after which a sectarian group begins relying on completely unique sets of transmitters and distinct chains of transmission (roughly) intimates the development of an independent group identity. Specifically, it suggests an internal cohesiveness and insularity embodied by the demand that an individual unambiguously affirm his communal loyalties.

A few examples can help better illustrate the notions of (1) shared single transmitters and (2) shared links. Let us begin by looking at the following two chains of transmission taken from Sunnī and Zaydī traditions regarding the *basmala*:

Sunnī Tradition[83]	Zaydī Tradition[84]
ʿUqba b. Makram b. ʿUqba (d. 234/849)	Muḥammad b. ʿAlāʾ b. Kurayb (d. 247–8/861–2)
‖	‖
Yūnus b. Bukayr b. Wāṣil (d. 199/814)	Yūnus b. Bukayr b. Wāṣil (d. 199/814)
‖	‖
Misʿar b. Kidām b. Ẓuhayr (d. 153–5/770–2)	Yūnus b. ʿAmr b. ʿAbd Allāh (d. 159/775)
‖	‖
Muḥammad b. Qays (d. 125–6/743–4)	Ḥusayn b. ʿAlī b. Ḥusayn b. ʿAlī b. Abī Ṭālib (d. 157/774)
‖	‖
Abū Hurayra (d. 58/678)	ʿAmr b. Shuraḥbīl (d. 68/688)
‖	‖
Muḥammad (d. 11/632)	Muḥammad (d. 11/632)

Here we find a common transmitter (Yūnus b. Bukayr – d. 199/814) mentioned in one Sunnī and one Zaydī tradition, both of which ultimately invoke the authority of the Prophet. It is important to note that Yūnus b. Bukayr does not narrate to or from identical individuals. In the Sunnī tradition, he relates from Misʿar b. Kidām b. Ẓuhayr and is quoted by ʿUqba b. Makram b. ʿUqba, whereas in the Zaydī tradition he cites Yūnus b. ʿAmr b. ʿAbd Allāh and is transmitted by Muḥammad b. ʿAlāʾ b. Kurayb.

[83] *SKB*, 2:69–2397.
[84] *AA*, 1:255–357.

While the common citation of Yūnus b. Bukayr by Sunnīs and Zaydīs is significant, the fact that he occurs in wholly independent chains in each text diminishes the overarching importance of the connection. The link might be the product of conflicting claims over his loyalty as opposed to any substantive overlap between Sunnīs and Zaydīs.

A similar dynamic is evident in the citation of Muḥammad al-Bāqir in Sunnī and Imāmī collections. The implication of his appearance in the *isnāds* of both groups is reduced by differences in the individuals he is portrayed as transmitting to and from. The Sunnīs associate him with standard traditionist figures (e.g., Bassām b. 'Abd Allāh – d. 148/765), whereas the Imāmīs link him to distinctly Shī'ī personalities (e.g., Fuḍayl b. Yasār – d. 148/766). Similarly to the case of Yūnus b. Bukayr, this difference reflects a disagreement over al-Bāqir's academic affiliations as well as his religious (and even political) loyalties. In general, single links of this kind do not offer clear evidence for an intersection between communities. At most, they suggest permeable barriers that allowed individuals to navigate between multiple sectarian identities. They should, therefore, be approached with caution albeit with the understanding that (1) a large number of such commonalities might ultimately support an overlap between groups, while (2) a paucity might indicate separation.

A more significant sign of overlap between sectarian communities is found in strings of common transmitters or shared links. These directly allow us to infer the point at which groups may have differentiated into independent entities. The following Sunnī and Zaydī chains of transmission provide a typical example of a shared link:

Sunnī Tradition[85]	Zaydī Tradition[86]
	Muḥammad b. Yazīd b. Muḥammad b. Kathīr (d. 248/862)
	‖
Khallād b. Khālid (d. 220/835)	'Amr b. Ḥammād b. Ṭalḥa (d. 222 or 228/837 or 843)
‖	‖
Asbāṭ b. Naṣr (d. 180/796)	Asbāṭ b. Naṣr (d. 180/796)
‖	‖
Ismā'īl b. 'Abd al-Raḥmān b. Abī Karīma (d. 127/745)	Ismā'īl b. 'Abd al-Raḥmān b. Abī Karīma (d. 127/745)
‖	‖
'Abd al-Khayr b. Yazīd (d. late 1st/7th century)	'Abd al-Khayr b. Yazīd (d. late 1st/7th century)
‖	‖
'Alī b. Abī Ṭālib (d. 40/661)	'Alī b. Abī Ṭālib (d. 40/661)

85 *SKB*, 2:66–2388.
86 *AA*, 1:258–365.

As opposed to single common links, the chains presented here share a long series of transmitters that begin with ʿAlī and extend through the entirety of the 1st/7th and into the latter part of the 2nd/8th century. They only diverge after Asbāṭ b. Naṣr, with the Sunnī tradition continuing through Khallād b. Khālid and the Zaydī tradition proceeding via ʿAmr b. Ḥammād. It is significant to note that all of the figures prior to and including Asbāt appear in numerous Sunnī and Zaydī chains of transmissions in addition to this isolated example. This supports an overlap between the communities reflected in their shared approval of a common pool of transmitters through the early 2nd/8th century. The correlation disappears dramatically after Asbāṭ as both Khallād and ʿAmr are mentioned exclusively in Sunnī and Zaydī chains. Put simply, the shared link suggests a divergence of the two sectarian groups at some point in the middle of the 2nd/8th century. By the end of the century, the two groups were relying on distinctive transmitters, indicating (perhaps) the crystallization of insular communal identities.

Narrative Style. The third comparison concerns the narrative style of a tradition's content as opposed to its transmission. This is the most subjective of our comparisons as it rests on the stylistic choices a community makes in presenting information rather than the information itself. These choices may embody norms for the production and circulation of religious knowledge, or they may simply result from a group's attempts at distinguishing itself from rival communities.

Two outcomes are possible in this final comparison. (1) There may be no substantive differences in the literary forms used by each sectarian group for preserving information. For example, two or more communities may convey knowledge through a series of exchanges between a questioner and an authority and only alter the names of individuals to suit sectarian tastes. The shared use of a particular style (or styles) would suggest that the traditions of each group were drawn from a common pool of narrative forms. It would also diminish the possibility that a clearly demarcated boundary separated rival communities. (2) Alternatively, the comparison may show that different sectarian groups utilized distinctive styles or – more importantly – increased their reliance on particular narrative forms after a specific point in time.[87] This would provide evidence

[87] This is not the same as saying that groups exclusively used one style. The *distribution* of styles is the most important factor in this comparison.

for a group's independence and reflect a conscious effort at differentiating itself from broader Kūfan society.

Chapters 3, 4, and 5 include traditions that adhere to one of eight primary narrative styles/forms: (1) question/answer statements, (2) eyewitness accounts, (3) direct quotes of legal positions, (4) exemplary statements, (5) sign/list traditions, (6) written correspondence, (7) exegesis, and (8) biblical stories. Representative examples of each together with a discussion of their potential ambiguities are offered below.

QUESTION/ANSWER. The first narrative style is a question-and-answer dialogue wherein a disciple/student asks an authority about an issue and generally receives a curt definitive judgment.[88] The answer is not accompanied by any supporting evidence or reasoning. In a typical example, the Kūfan Imāmī Muʿāwiya b. ʿAmmār (d. 175/791) recounts meeting al-Ṣādiq on a visit to Medina:

> I asked Abū ʿAbd Allāh [al-Ṣādiq], "If I rise for the prayer, do I recite the *basmala* as part of the *Fātiḥa* of the Qur'ān?" He said, "Yes." Then I asked, "If I recite the *Fātiḥa* of the Qur'ān [outside of prayer], do I recite the *basmala* as part of the chapter?" He said, "Yes."[89]

The validity of this response is a direct consequence of the Imām's stature. He is the direct source of knowledge and offers no discursive explanation beyond the judgment itself. This is in stark contrast to other question/answer traditions in which prominent figures from early Islam serve as conduits for religious knowledge. Such is the case in the following exchange narrated by a Meccan transmitter, Ibn Abī Najīḥ (d. 132/750):

> I asked Sālim b. ʿAbd Allāh b. ʿUmar (d. 105/723), "Did ʿUmar b. al-Khaṭṭāb perform the *qunūt* in the morning prayer?" He said, "It is only [an act] that the people invented (*aḥdathahu*) afterwards."[90]

Here, Sālim is merely relaying information that originates (and is legitimized) by a Sunnī figure of unassailable authority (i.e., ʿUmar). The Imāmī sources contain similar examples as when Fuḍayl b. Yasār asks al-Bāqir about the permissibility of *nabīdh* (date wine). The Imām replies that "God, Mighty and Exalted, prohibited it [*nabīdh*]

[88] Motzki's analysis focuses exclusively on dicta and responsa, whereas I include numerous additional narrative types.

[89] *KK*, 3:312–3–1.

[90] *MAR*, 3:28–4969.

specifically while the Messenger of God prohibited all intoxicating drinks."[91] Regardless of these epistemological nuances, however, each account is structured around a proposed question followed by a clear and precise answer.

EYEWITNESS ACCOUNTS. The second narrative form consists of eyewitness reports in which an informant directly observes an authority figure perform an act with a bearing on ritual practice. The critical element in these reports is the actual observation, attested through the use of phrases such as "I prayed" or "I heard." The Kūfan Sa'īd b. 'Abd al-Raḥmān b. Abzā (d. late 1st/7th century), for example, narrates the following tradition:

> My father ['Abd al-Raḥmān b. Abzā – d. mid to late 1st/7th century] prayed behind 'Umar and heard him audibly recite the *basmala*.[92]

'Abd al-Raḥmān unambiguously takes part in the prayer in question, ruling out the possibility that the information was obtained through a third source. The tradition also elevates his status by linking him to 'Umar, an important and influential legal authority, through the act of prayer itself. The Imāmīs offer parallel examples such as the following account narrated by Ṣafwān b. Mihrān b. al-Mughīra (d. mid-2nd/8th century):

> I prayed behind Abū 'Abd Allāh [al-Ṣādiq] daily and he would perform the *qunūt* in every prayer regardless of whether the recitation was audible or inaudible.[93]

Once again, the credibility of the account is predicated to a large degree on the actual observation of an authority in action.

The case of the daily prayer is unique in that eyewitnesses were aware of when and where the ritual would be performed on a daily basis. They merely showed up at the appropriate venue at the proper time and were privy to the information in question. The situation is more complicated with other aspects of practice (such as dietary law), where the generation of a report depends on a confluence of circumstances. In the case of intoxicants, for example, there may only be a handful of instances when an authority figure explicitly accepts or refuses a particular drink. One

91 *KK*, 6:408–5.
92 *AA*, 1:255–356.
93 *KK*, 3:339–2; *ṬI*, 1:65–494; *WS*, 6:261–7903.

of the most famous such cases is narrated by ʿUqba b. Thaʿlaba b. ʿAmr (d. 42/662):

> The Prophet was thirsty as he circled the Ka'aba and called for a drink. *Nabīdh* (date wine) was brought forth from the watering place. He smelled it and furrowed his brows. Then he said, "Bring me a portion of water from *Zamzam*." He poured it in and drank it. A man asked him, "Was not this prohibited, O' Messenger of God?" He said, "No."[94]

In other instances, transmitters are placed in the audience for public speeches or among worshippers listening to Friday prayer sermons. This was likely the case in the following tradition related by ʿAbd Allāh b. ʿUmar (d. 73/692):

> ʿUmar ascended the pulpit and said, "The prohibition of *khamr* – which is derived from five substances: grapes, dates, honey, wheat, and barley – was divinely revealed. *Khamr* is that which confuses the intellect."[95]

While this account might also constitute a direct legal opinion (the third narrative style), it is included among eyewitness reports because of its contextual clarity. Put simply, there is no doubt regarding the fact that an informant directly observed the action or speech conveyed in the tradition.

DIRECT QUOTES OF LEGAL OPINIONS. The third narrative style includes exemplary statements from authority figures but without any indication of how this information was obtained. These are not prompted by questions (from inquisitive students) and do not reference other authorities. Rather, they are clear and concise opinions such as the one expressed by al-Bāqir where he states: "Every prayer in which the recitation is audible contains a *qunūt*."[96]

The transmitter for this statement is Abū Jārūd, but he plays no active role in soliciting the information. It is unclear whether he asked a question, observed a speech, attended a lecture, or was simply conveyed the opinion by an intermediate party. A similar dynamic is found in a Sunnī tradition where Saʿīd b. Jubayr ascribes the view that "the prayer recitation should begin with the *basmala*"[97] to ʿAbd Allāh b. ʿAbbās (d. 68/688), with no further commentary.

94 *SN III*, 5:114–5193; *SKB*, 8:527–17438.
95 *SB*, 1099–5581.
96 *AA*, 1:288–415.
97 *SKB*, 2:71–2405.

EXEMPLARY STATEMENTS. Although exemplary statements are quite similar to direct quotes in their brevity and lack of context, they explicitly associate specific practices to a given authority. Whereas a direct quote ascribes a clear statement to an authority, an exemplary statement simply associates a ritual law position with an authority. For example, a Zaydī tradition quotes al-Bāqir as asserting that "the Messenger of God would audibly recite the *basmala*."[98] In this instance, the main authority figure is the Prophet, but he is not being questioned or quoted. It is possible that he is being observed but this is not made clear by the text itself, which simply connects the practice of the *basmala* to the example of the Prophet. A range of early authorities are cited in a similar manner. In one Zaydī tradition, 'Abd al-Raḥmān b. Ma'qil b. Muqarrin (d. 80/699) states:"'Alī would perform the *qunūt* in the *maghrib* prayer, cursing men by their names."[99]

Perhaps 'Abd al-Raḥmān had observed this personally. The text, however, offers no information to support that assumption. Instead, we are simply told that the practices in question (i.e., the *qunūt* in the sunset prayer and cursing) were endorsed by a figure of the stature of 'Alī whose behavior was worthy of imitation.

WRITTEN CORRESPONDENCE. The category of written correspondence is related to direct quotes and exemplary statement in terms of content, quoting the opinions of legal authorities, or the examples of important historical figures. It differs due to its emphasis on a material exchange of information through the medium of letters or formal petitions. In such accounts, it is not necessary for the first informant and the authority to have met in person or studied in the same city. Rather, reliability is predicated on the existence of an original written document containing both the initial question and the subsequent answer as embodied in the following Imāmī tradition:

> I ['Alī b. Muḥammad b. Sulaymān (d. mid 3rd/9th century)] wrote to the Jurist [al-Hādī (d. 254/868)] asking him about the *qunūt*. He wrote, "If there is an urgent necessity [due to fear of harm] (*idha kānat ḍarūra shadīda*), then do not raise your hands and say the *basmala* three times."[100]

The use of the verb "to write" clearly establishes that this information was obtained from al-Hādī through some form of written communication.

[98] *AA*, 1:243–315.
[99] *Ibid.*, 1:288–417.
[100] *WS*, 6:274–7948 and 6:282–7974.

SIGN/LIST TRADITIONS. The sixth narrative form involves long lists that bring together seemingly disparate legal issues in a single tradition. These texts may simply be a means of collating larger packets of information into an accessible form, or they may result from the combining of two (or more) texts into a single account. In a typical example, the Kūfan jurist Ibrāhīm al-Nakhaʿī (d. 96/714) gathers together those elements of the ritual prayer that a leader should recite silently:

There are four [parts of the prayer] recited silently by the *Imām*: the *basmala*, the *istiʿādha*, the *Âmīn*, and when he says "God listens to him who praises Him," he says [silently], "Praise for you, our Lord."[101]

List/sign accounts may also play a more sectarian role as evident in an Imāmī tradition that explicitly associates a series of (seemingly unrelated) ritual practices with Shīʿī identity including "the performance of fifty-one daily prayer cycles, the audible *basmala*, the *qunūt* before the *rakʿaʿ*,[102] the prostration of gratitude (*sajdat al-shukr*), and the wearing of a ring on the right hand."[103] These accounts are united by their use of the list as the central axis for conveying information.

EXEGESIS AND BIBLICAL STORIES. The final two narrative styles are fairly straightforward. Exegetical traditions legitimize legal positions through the use of Qur'ānic verses, whereas biblical accounts offer explanations grounded in the example of previous prophets and communities. In the case of intoxicants, a number of accounts begin with Q5:90[104] and offer commentary similar to the following:

The Prophet recited [Q5:90] from the pulpit. Abū Wahb al-Jayshānī arose and asked him about beer (*mizr*). He [the Prophet] said, "What is beer?" He [Abu

[101] *MAR*, 2:57–2598. All four elements mentioned here are parts of the prayer. The first will be discussed in Chapter 3. The second (*istiʿādha*) is the uttering of the statement "God protect me from accursed Satan" prior to start of the recitation in the prayer. The third (*āmīn*) refers to saying "Amen" after the end of the first recitation in the prayer. The fourth references the step in prayer when a supplicant stands up straight right before prostrating on the ground (*sujūd*).

[102] This refers to the step in the prayer after recitation when a supplicant bends over and places the palms of his hands on his knees.

[103] This tradition is taken from al-Majlisī, *Biḥār*, 85:84–28. As discussed in this chapter, I generally avoid al-Majlisī's compendium of traditions as he simply compiled all available texts with little to no critical discernment. The *sajdat al-shukr* refers to a special prostration of gratitude that the Shīʿa would perform at the completion of every mandatory prayer. See, for example, *KK*, 3:326–18 and 3:344–20.

[104] Q5:90 – O' you who believe! *Khamr* and games of chance and idols and divining arrows are only an infamy of Satan's handiwork. Leave it aside so that you may succeed.

Wahb] responded, "It is something made from wheat." The Prophet said, "All intoxicants are prohibited."[105]

The Prophet's final statement expands the scope of Q5:90 beyond grape wine to include intoxicants of all varieties. Biblical stories related to intoxicants generally center on Noah's experience with grapes after the flood:

> Noah was ordered to cultivate plants. When he wanted to plant grapes, Iblīs – who was by his side – said, "This tree is for me." Noah said, "You lie." Iblīs said, "So what part of it is mine?" Noah said, "Two-thirds is yours." On this basis, *ṭilā'* [made from] a third [of the grape] was made good.[106]

Here the prohibition of wine is projected back to the time of Noah who is aware of the problematic nature of grape-based drinks. The narrator (in this case al-Bāqir) then connects the story to an issue of contemporary importance to the 2nd/8th century Imāmī community, namely the legal status of *ṭilā'*.

EMERGING IDENTITIES

This chapter began with a discussion of recent scholarship that confidently dates traditions to the early 2nd/8th century. Unfortunately, these accounts are primarily concerned with matters of ritual as opposed to religious or political developments that would be of particular interest to historians of the early period. Given this gap between the available source material and the goals of modern scholars, there is a particular need for the development of techniques that would allow for the derivation of historical information from these seemingly ahistorical texts.

This chapter details one such potential approach that centers on the structure and form of large groupings of accounts. First, traditions are sorted on the basis of geography to identify those in circulation in 2nd/8th century Kūfa, the birthplace of multiple Shī'ī communities. Second, these Kūfan texts are subjected to a three-tier comparison centered on their use of authority figures, chains of transmission, and narrative styles. It is argued that a sectarian group's reliance on insular and distinct personalities and literary styles reflects the potential emergence of an independent identity. In other words, a community differentiates itself by demanding

105 *SKB*, 8:507–17365.

106 *WS*, 25:286–31922. *Ṭilā'* is a fermented drink made after boiling away two-thirds of the volume of grape juice. It will be discussed in greater detail in Chapter 5.

the unambiguous loyalty of its members (as exemplified by its appropriation of specific authorities and transmitters) and asserting a type of intellectual confidence (as evident in its use of distinctive narrative forms).

Chapters 3 through 5 apply this comparative methodology to three case studies in ritual law: the *basmala*, the *qunūt*, and the prohibition of intoxicants. Each begins with a legal survey of a given issue from the perspective of four Sunnī (Mālikī, Ḥanafī, Shāfiʿī, and Ḥanbalī) and two Shīʿī (Imāmī and Zaydī) schools of law. This is followed by the three comparative analyses described earlier. It should be noted that this approach cannot specify an exact date for the crystallization of sectarian identities. Rather, it can help provide a general time frame for their emergence. This, in turn, allows us to evaluate the reliability of the narratives preserved in noncontemporaneous historical and heresiographical sources (discussed in Chapter 1) that (1) date an independent Imāmī community to the early 2nd/8th century and (2) claim Zaydism emerged in the early 2nd/8th century through the merging of two disparate strains of Shīʿism (Batrism and Jārūdism).

PART TWO

CASE STUDIES

3

In the Name of God

The Basmala

How did the Prophet pray? At first glance, we may assume that this question is easy to answer. After all, the daily prayer is one of the cornerstones of Islamic orthopraxy and such information should be preserved within the Islamic *ḥadīth* literature. In many cases, traditions do, in fact, depict the prayers of the Prophet and other prominent early legal authorities. These accounts, however, are often contradictory, with contrasting descriptions of some prayer steps and disagreements regarding the inclusion of others. This diversity has been codified in the legal positions of the four Sunnī and two Shī'ī legal schools considered in the present study. Some of the most prominent and visible differences (e.g., the placement of the hands) are not counted among the fundamental components of the prayer.[1] Recitation (*qirā'a*), by contrast, is of critical importance, with mistakes carrying serious religious consequences and possibly invalidating the prayer as a whole. It is not surprising, therefore, that jurists devote entire sections to the recitation, addressing questions of structure and selection. Which chapters (*sing. sūra*/ *pl. suwar*) of the Qur'ān should be recited during the first two prayer cycles? Is it necessary to recite an entire chapter, or are fragments of chapters sufficient? Should these Qur'ānic passages be uttered aloud or whispered?

This chapter focuses on a related issue, namely the necessity of prefacing recitation with the formula, "In the name of God, the Beneficent the

[1] The prayer is organized around "cycles" of required actions and utterances. A different number of cycles are necessary for each of the five daily prayers: the dawn (*fajr*) prayer includes two cycles, the noon (*ẓuhr*), afternoon (*'aṣr*), and night (*ishā'*) prayers include four cycles, and the sunset (*maghrib*) prayer includes three cycles. For a summary of the required steps of the daily prayer, see Tabbarah, *Spirit*, 129–36.

Merciful" (subsequently referred to as the *basmala*).[2] It is divided into two sections. The first provides juristic context regarding the debate over the *basmala* by examining the views of six of the major Sunnī and Shīʿī law schools (i.e., the Ḥanafīs, Mālikīs, Shāfiʿīs, Ḥanbalīs, Imāmīs, and Zaydīs). The second applies the methodological approach described in Chapter 2 to Kūfan traditions pertaining to the *basmala* drawn from the Sunnī and Shīʿī *ḥadīth* collections. The chapter concludes by exploring the implications of our results for the validity of the classical narratives of early Shīʿism.

THE JURISTIC CONTEXT

The juristic debate over the status of the *basmala* involves two issues. The first concerns the verse's relationship to the Qur'ānic text. Although there is a general consensus that the phrase occurs in Q27:30 as an integral part of the revelation, jurists differ on its status at the head of individual chapters.[3] Some maintain that this initial *basmala* is the first verse of every *sūra*, whereas others contend that it simply marks the end of one *sūra* and the start of the next. The second contentious issue centers on the use of the *basmala* in the daily prayer. Specifically, should it be part of the recitation and, if so, should it be uttered audibly or silently? A jurist's position on the first issue dictates, to a large degree, his approach to the second. If the *basmala* is affirmed as the first verse of the *Fātiḥa* (Q1), then it is difficult to justify its exclusion from the prayer. The question then is no longer its recitation, but rather the *manner* of its recitation (audible vs. silent). If, by contrast, the *basmala* is not considered part of the *Fātiḥa*, then the jurist has a free hand in dealing with matters such as inclusion or audible/silent recitation.

In the section that follows, I explore the central legal strategies employed by the six selected law schools in their discussions of the *basmala*. This is not intended as an exhaustive survey of each of the schools,

[2] The Islamic legal tradition has generated a vast corpus of work dealing with the recitation of the *basmala* in the context of prayer. In the remainder of the chapter, any mention of the "issue of the *basmala*" refers specifically to the recitation of the *basmala* at the start of the *Fātiḥa* in the first cycle of the five daily prayers. Other issues discussed by the jurists include: the recitation of the *basmala* before the second Qur'ānic selection in each of the first two prayer cycles, the recitation of the *basmala* if the worshipper's second selection spans two *sūra*s, and the recitation of the *basmala* in the second and subsequent prayer cycles.

[3] The *basmala* is quoted in Q27:30 ("It is from Sulaymān, and it is, 'In the name of Allāh, the Beneficent, the Merciful'"). This is accepted by every legal school.

but rather as a broad summary of their methods of argumentation and the positions they ultimately came to favor. In actuality, there was a significant degree of latitude within individual schools so that a creative jurist had the ability to articulate wholly unique arguments.

The Ḥanafīs

Although the Ḥanafīs do not include the initial *basmala* in the Qur'ānic text, they recite it silently at the start of the ritual prayer. Many Ḥanafī jurists mention this opinion in brief descriptions of ritual without providing much in the way of supporting textual evidence.[4] More detailed discussions are found in (1) comprehensive juristic tracts that cite traditions from the Prophet (among other early authorities)[5] and (2) exegetical works that explore the legal consequences of specific Qur'ānic passages. The latter are particularly important given the centrality of historical arguments regarding the compilation of the Qur'ānic text in the school's treatment of the *basmala*.

In *Aḥkām al-Qur'ān*, Aḥmad b. 'Alī al-Jaṣṣāṣ (d. 371/982) articulates a typical Ḥanafī approach to the *basmala* rooted primarily in Qur'ānic arguments.[6] He begins by noting that the *basmala* was not originally placed at the start of every chapter.[7] It is widely accepted that, prior to the revelation of Q27:30, the Prophet prefaced each *sūra* with "In the name of your Lord," a phrase drawn from the very first revelation (i.e., Q96:1).[8] Thus, the position of the *basmala* at the head of Qur'ānic chapters was a late development and merely reflected the personal preference of some of the Companions. Had the initial *basmala* been an integral

[4] For representative examples, see al-Ṭaḥāwī, *Mukhtaṣar*, 26; al-Qudūrī, *Mukhtaṣar*, 27.

[5] The earliest such work is *KAS I*, 152–3. Al-Shaybānī offers a series of traditions that support the silent *basmala*, but he does not address the verse's Qur'ānic status, offer logical arguments, or acknowledge contradictory textual evidence.

[6] al-Jaṣṣāṣ, *Aḥkām*, 1:8 and 1:13–15. For a slightly different argument forwarded two centuries later by al-Marghīnānī, see *al-Hidāya*, a commentary on al-Qudūrī's *Mukhtaṣar*. The discussion starts with a summary of the case for the audible *basmala*, which focuses on a paraphrased Prophetic tradition and an opinion (ascribed to al-Shāfi'ī) in favor of the practice in audible prayer cycles. Al-Marghīnānī rejects this argument, interpreting accounts in which the Prophet performs the audible *basmala* as indicative of his role as a teacher. In other words, Muḥammad only used the audible *basmala* in an educational capacity to reaffirm the formula's insertion at the start of the prayer recitation; he did not intend this as a general endorsement of its audible recitation. The section ends with a series of traditions narrated by Anas b. Mālik, which report that the Prophet "did not audibly recite the *basmala*" (*al-Hidāya*, 1:120).

[7] al-Jaṣṣāṣ, *Aḥkām*, 1:8. See also, al-Dānī, *al-Bayān*, 231.

[8] Q96:1 – "Recite in the name of your Lord Who created."

part of each chapter, the Prophet would have uttered it from the start of his mission. The fact that he only adopted the convention of reciting it at a later point in his life constitutes strong evidence against its Qur'ānic status. Although al-Jaṣṣāṣ considers this historical line of reasoning as sufficient to justify the Ḥanafī position, he acknowledges the opposing views of rival law schools and attributes them to regional differences. The Kūfans are described as strong supporters for the initial *basmala*'s inclusion in the Qur'ān, whereas the Baṣrans are characterized as proponents of exclusion.[9]

Al-Jaṣṣāṣ next turns to the issue of the recitation in the daily prayer, affirming the Ḥanafī stance in favor of the silent *basmala*. This view generated considerable criticism from opposing law schools that accused the Ḥanafīs of internal inconsistency.[10] The Shāfiʿīs (and, to a lesser extent, the Mālikīs) pointed to the Ḥanafī practice of uttering one verse of the *Fātiḥa* (i.e., the *basmala*) silently while reciting the remaining verses audibly.[11] Al-Jaṣṣāṣ answers this accusation with the reasonable observation that, from the perspective of the Ḥanafīs, there is no contradiction in a silent *basmala* and an audible *Fātiḥa*. Given that the verse and the chapter are independent textual entities, the manner of reciting one has no direct bearing on the other. Al-Jaṣṣāṣ also quotes a wide array of traditions that advocate both the silent and the audible *basmala*. The credibility of the latter, however, is called into question on the basis of a series of (1) rational arguments and (2) internal contradictions.[12] He concludes that the preponderance of reliable evidence supports the silent *basmala* at the start of recitation.

Al-Jaṣṣāṣ's discussion of the *basmala* is paralleled in a number of Ḥanafī exegetical works that serve to emphasize the school's concern with maintaining the integrity of (their own vision of) the Qur'ānic text.[13] Abū al-Layth al-Samarqandī (d. 393/1002?), for example, relates interpretations of Q15:87[14] (a verse also routinely invoked by other schools) that

[9] al-Jaṣṣāṣ, *Aḥkām*, 1:8; al-Dānī, *al-Bayān*, 231.

[10] Imāmī polemics against the Ḥanafīs, for example, focus on the discrepancy between the school's inclusion of the *basmala* in the prayer and its exclusion from the Qur'ān. This is discussed in greater detail later in the chapter.

[11] This is specific to the morning and evening prayers in which the recitation for the first two cycles is audible.

[12] al-Jaṣṣāṣ, *Aḥkām*, 1:13–15.

[13] Of course, al-Jaṣṣāṣ is part of the exegetical tradition in that his *Aḥkām* is structured in the manner of a Qur'ānic commentary.

[14] A majority of both Sunnī and Shīʿī exegetes hold that Q15:87 ("And We have bestowed upon you the seven Oft-repeated [*sabʿan min al-mathānī*] and the Glorious Qur'ān")

clearly differentiate the *basmala* from the *Fātiḥa*.[15] His gloss of the opening chapter omits the verse altogether without even discussing its potential relationship to the Qur'ānic text. Maḥmūd b. 'Umar al-Zamakhsharī (d. 538/1144), by contrast, follows al-Jaṣṣāṣ in his claim that the initial *basmala* merely signifies the end of one chapter and the start of the next.[16] Even non-Ḥanafī exegetical works acknowledge the centrality of the Qur'ān to Ḥanafī legal discourse on the *basmala*.[17]

Overall, the Ḥanafī position rests on (1) historical arguments regarding the Qur'ānic text and (2) traditions that endorse the silent *basmala*. The first are used to justify the rejection of the Qur'ānic status of the initial *basmala* whereas the second allow for its incorporation into a package of formulaic invocations uttered between the opening of the prayer and the start of recitation. As will become evident later in the chapter, the Ḥanafīs were criticized by the Mālikīs for allowing a non-Qur'ānic phrase to be used in the recitation and by the Shāfi'īs for their dismissal of traditions favoring the audible *basmala*.

The Mālikīs

Mālikī jurists agree with the Ḥanafīs that the initial *basmala* is not part of the *Fātiḥa*, but rather than reciting it silently at the start of prayer, they excise it altogether and begin recitation with the verse, "Praise be to God,

refers to the *Fātiḥa*. In his *Tafsīr*, al-Ṭabarī offers three different interpretations. First, he says that it may refer to the seven longest *sūra*s of the Qur'ān which are often repeated because they contain parables and narrative warnings. Second, he links the verse to the *Fātiḥa*. Third, he states that the verse could refer to seven of the positive qualities of the Qur'ān. Al-Ṭabarī accepts the second view as the correct one (al-Ṭabarī, *Tafsīr*, 4:646–48). Al-Qurṭubī adds that the verse might refer to the Qur'ān as a whole which may be divided into seven sections (*al-Jāmi'*, 10:54–5). In the end, he too accepts the standard interpretation that it refers to the *Fātiḥa*. In fact, most Sunnī and Shī'ī exegetes affirm this view. For a representative Sunnī example, see Fakhr al-Dīn al-Rāzī's *al-Tafsīr*, 19:206–10. For Shī'ī examples, see al-Ṭabrisī's *Jawāmi'*, 1:801–3 and *Majma'* (1997), 6:146–8. These works explicitly discuss the issue, but there are also many legal texts that simply assume the interpretation and refer to the *Fātiḥa* as the "seven oft-repeated verses." In fact, every jurist cited in this study implicitly or explicitly accepts the view that the *Fātiḥa* must have seven verses on the basis of Q15:87. Since the Shāfi'īs count the *basmala* as a verse in the *Fātiḥa* and the Mālikīs do not (below), the two schools divide the remaining verses differently to meet the requirement of seven. Rubin summarizes these possibilities, but his conclusion regarding the earliest interpretation is unconvincing ("Exegesis," 141–56).

15 al-Samarqandī, *Tafsīr*, 2:224–5.

16 al-Zamakhsharī, *al-Kashshāf*, 1:25.

17 See, for example, Ibn Kathīr, *Tafsīr* (1966), 1:31.

Master of the Worlds" (Q1:2).[18] They rely on two lines of reasoning to support this view. The first is grounded in textual evidence (i.e., traditions dealing with the structure of the Qur'ānic text and the form of the daily prayer), whereas the second is predicated on the living tradition of Medina (*'amal*).[19]

The earliest articulation of the textual argument is found in the *Muwaṭṭa'* of Mālik b. Anas, the eponymous founder of the Mālikī law school.[20] Mālik quotes two accounts that depict the Prophet and the first three caliphs as beginning the prayer recitation with Q1:2. A third tradition praises the *Fātiḥa* as an especially blessed Qur'ānic chapter (linking it to Q15:87[21]) but does not include the *basmala* as one of its verses. A similar approach informs Saḥnūn's[22] (d. 240/855) *al-Mudawwana al-kubrā*, which relates two reports that the Prophet "began the recitation with 'Praise be to God, Master of the Worlds,'"[23] and a third that claims the first three caliphs "did not recite the *basmala* when they began the prayer."[24] Cognizant of the potential for ambiguity, Saḥnūn notes that the *basmala* (in these cases) was recited "neither silently to oneself nor audibly."[25] Most subsequent Mālikī discussions of the issue cite the traditions recorded by Mālik and Saḥnūn as clear and definitive evidence for the Prophet's original practice.

Over time, the scope of the Mālikī textual argument expanded beyond the prayer recitation to encompass the relationship between the *basmala*

[18] I am using the Kūfan numbering system standard today in most of the Islamic world. The Medinan numbering system – which is preserved by the Mālikīs – would consider this verse Q1:1 rather than Q1:2.

[19] For a comprehensive discussion of the origins and development of Medinan *'amal* as well as a critique of its utility a source of law, see El Shamsy, *Tradition*, 10–14 and 33–46. See also, Dutton, "Sunna," 1–31, specifically 5–14. The textual argument is "first" in the sense that it was the first view explicitly articulated by Mālikī jurists in their legal works. As El Shamsy shows, however, the "second" argument based on *'amal* was the dominant line of reasoning in Mālikī legal discourse (*Tradition*, 42–3).

[20] Mālik b. Anas, *al-Muwaṭṭa' (riwāyat Suwayd b. Sa'īd)* (1994), 85–6. The versions of the text transmitted by Muḥammad al-Shaybānī [*al-Muwaṭṭa'* (*riwāyah Muḥammad al-Shaybānī*) (2003), 60] and Yaḥyā b. Yaḥyā al-Laythī [(1996), 1:136] espouse a fundamentally identical position through their use of 'the dialogue tradition' discussed later in the chapter. A similar tradition-laden discussion is found in Saḥnūn, *Mudawwana*, 1:186.

[21] For interpretations of this verse, see footnote 14 of this chapter.

[22] Saḥnūn, *Mudawwana*, 1:186. Saḥnūn was a jurist from Qayrawān who played an important role in the spread of Mālikism in North Africa and Spain in the 3rd/9th century. For more on Saḥnūn, see *EI*², s.v. Saḥnūn (M. Talbi).

[23] See *SIM*, 1:267 and *SKB*, 2:75. In the second tradition, the first three caliphs are cited alongside the Prophet.

[24] See Mālik b. Anas, *al-Muwaṭṭa'*, (1994), 85.

[25] Saḥnūn, *Mudawwana*, 1:186.

and the Qur'ānic text. In his *al-Istidhkār*, for example, the 5th/11th century jurist Ibn 'Abd al-Barr offers a series of explanations for the *basmala*'s presence in the earliest written copies of the Qur'ān.[26] He then quotes numerous variants of a report (not mentioned by Mālik or Saḥnūn) in which Muḥammad describes a "dialogue" (subsequently referred to as "the dialogue tradition") that occurs during the ritual prayer between God and a worshipper wherein each verse of the *Fātiḥa* is framed as a formulaic response to a specific divine question.[27] In these traditions, the Prophet does not count the *basmala* as part of the *Fātiḥa* but still enumerates seven verses (as required in the exegesis of Q15:87) by placing a "verse stop" between the words *alayhim* and *ghayr* in Q1:7. This is the numbering convention that was associated with the Qur'ānic reading of Medina, Syria,[28] and Baṣra in contrast to that of Kūfa and Mecca, which counted the *basmala* as a verse.[29] Ibn 'Abd al-Barr concludes that there is no sound basis for including the *basmala* in the *Fātiḥa* given that the chapter already contains seven clearly demarcated verses.[30] As opposed to the traditions recorded by Mālik and Saḥnūn, Ibn 'Abd al-Barr considers the dialogue tradition as the strongest and most conclusive evidence for the validity of the Mālikī stance.[31]

A second (and more foundational) Mālikī line of reasoning for the *basmala*'s exclusion from the *Fātiḥa* emphasizes the living tradition of Medina. Mālik himself does not explicitly invoke this argument, but it is significant to note that he relies almost exclusively on reports narrated and preserved by Baṣran chains of transmission.[32] Dutton explains this curious fact with the claim that "there were no *ḥadith*s on these matters

[26] Ibn 'Abd al-Barr, *Istidhkār*, 2:154.

[27] *SM*, 1:296 – 38 and 1:297 – 40 and 41. Mālik cites this tradition in the versions of the *Muwaṭṭa'* transmitted by Yaḥyā b. Yaḥyā al-Laythī and Muḥammad al-Shaybānī but only in the course of discussing the audibility or silence of a supplicant's recitation in a group prayer. See Mālik b. Anas, *al-Muwaṭṭa'*, (1996), 1:136 and *idem*, *al-Muwaṭṭa'*, (2003), 60.

[28] For the Syrian text, see Spitaler, *Die Verszählung*, 31 (table 1).

[29] Kūfan and Meccan readers counted the *basmala* as the first verse and did not include the division between *alayhim* and *ghayr*. The controversy over the counting of verses is mentioned by al-Qurṭubī (*al-Jāmi'*, 1:91–107) and al-Ṭabrisī (*Jawāmi'*, 1:15–6). In his *Bayān*, al-Dānī focuses on the issue of counting verses in general, while succinctly summarizing the differences with respect to the *Fātiḥa* (*al-Bayān*, 231).

[30] Ibn 'Abd al-Barr, *Istidhkār*, 2:172–3.

[31] For Ibn 'Abd al-Barr's preference for the dialogue tradition, see *Istidhkār*, 2:154. For examples of other arguments and traditions, both in favor of and against the Mālikī view, see Ibn 'Abd al-Barr, *Istidhkār*, 2:173–4 and 179–82.

[32] El Shamsy sees the establishment of the normative authority of *'amal* as the driving force in the composition of the *Muwaṭṭa'* (*Tradition*, 31–2 and 42–3).

in Medina because there was no need for them."[33] In other words, the Baṣran texts supplied independent verification for a practice (the omission of the *basmala*) that was so broadly accepted in Medina that it did not merit the circulation of any traditions at all. While it may be true that the Medinans of Mālik's time did not recite the *basmala*, there were certainly Medinan accounts in circulation that supported its recitation.[34] Mālik was undoubtedly aware of the contradictory textual evidence but preferred the Baṣran accounts precisely because they aligned with Medinan practice *during his lifetime*. El Shamsy highlights this tendency, emphasizing Mālik's belief that normative authority was embedded not in reports about the sayings of the Prophet but in the practice of the Medinan community as a whole.[35] The apparent disparity between Medinan practice and Medinan traditions created an opening for competing schools to question the very integrity of Medinan *'amal* as a source of law.[36]

A number of Mālikī jurists forward a line of reasoning that falls back on the normative authority of Medinan living practice to reconcile contradictions in the textual evidence.[37] In *Kitāb al-nawādir wa'l-ziyādāt*, for example, Ibn Abī Zayd[38] (d. 386/996) alludes to reports in which various early authorities recite the *basmala* either audibly or silently in

[33] Dutton, "Sunna," 19 footnote 68. In *Origins*, Dutton reiterates this point, writing that the *basmala* was one of a number of practices "that were not recorded initially in the form of *ḥadīth* but were nevertheless known generally amongst the people and understood to have originated in the time of the Prophet. Other practices, however, although recorded in authentic *ḥadīth*s ... were not acted upon by their transmitters because they did not represent the *sunna*. In other words, they were either exceptional instances or earlier judgments that had later been changed, or otherwise minority opinions that held little weight, and which, even though they derived from the Prophet, were nevertheless outweighed by other judgments also deriving from the Prophet" (Dutton, *Origins*, 45).

[34] Some examples of Medinan traditions that generally support an audible *basmala* include *MAR*, 2:59, and *MIAS*, 1:361. For Medinan accounts of Mu'āwiya's visit to the holy cities that favor the audible *basmala*, see al-Shāfi'ī, *Umm*, 1:212–3 and *SKB*, 2:72.

[35] El Shamsy, *Tradition*, 42–3.

[36] El Shamsy points out that this avenue for criticizing Mālik was pioneered by his students, Muḥammad al-Shaybānī and al-Shāfi'ī (*Ibid*., 48–54). The latter articulated this position most clearly in the chapter of the *Umm* concerning his differences of opinions with Mālik.

[37] El Shamsy highlights the centrality of this tendency in Mālikī legal discourse (*Tradition*, 37–46 and specifically 42–3). By contrast, Dutton argues that *'amal* was always more authoritative that textual evidence ("Sunna," 8).

[38] A prominent Mālikī-Ash'arī jurist from Qayrawān, pivotal in the spread of Mālikism in North Africa. For a detailed study of his life, see Sayeed Rahman's unpublished doctoral dissertation entitled *The Legal and Theological Thought of Ibn Abi Zayd al-Qayrawani*.

the prayer.[39] He notes, however, that these accounts are contradicted by equally valid traditions arguing for the omission of the *basmala*.[40] Given this confused situation, Ibn Abī Zayd concludes that the textual evidence has to be pushed aside in favor of Medinan *'amal*, which rejects the *basmala* in the prayer and considers it an extraneous marker signifying the end of one chapter and the start of the next.[41] A similar argument is put forward by Abū Bakr ibn al-'Arabī (d. 542/1148) [42] who, faced with deep contradictions in the textual tradition, cites the living tradition of Medina as the best indicator of proper practice and the strongest proof for the validity of the Mālikī view.[43]

The Mālikīs hold that the *basmala* should not be recited at the start of the *Fātiḥa* in the first cycle of compulsory prayers. They make extensive use of textual arguments grounded in the Medinan/Syrian/Baṣran Qur'ānic recitation,[44] the exegesis of Q15:87, and the dialogue tradition. When faced with opposing traditions forwarded by other law schools (e.g., the Shāfi'īs below), Mālikī jurists employ one of two strategies. They either characterize them as weak and unreliable (e.g., Ibn 'Abd al-Barr, al-Qurṭubī[45] – d. 671/1273) or dismiss them on the basis of the normative authority of Medinan *'amal* (e.g., Ibn Abī Zayd, Ibn al-'Arabī).

39 Ibn Abī Zayd, *al-Nawādir*, 1:172–3. Although Ibn Abī Zayd refers to the opinions of legal authorities and implies a familiarity with the textual tradition, he does not quote them in detail.

40 *Ibid.*, 1:172.

41 *Ibid.*, 1:173. Whether the omission of the *basmala* did, in fact, reflect the *'amal* of Medina was called into question by a number of Shāfi'ī and Zaydī jurists (see later in the chapter). Sectarian attacks against the Sunnīs assailed the Mālikī position that the *basmala* was inserted into the text of the Qur'ān by the Companions or employed by the Prophet himself to divide *sūras*. In particular, Shī'ī polemics accused the Sunnīs of compromising the integrity of the text by allowing for the possibility of human intervention.

42 A prolific Mālikī scholar from Seville in al-Andalūs. See *EI*², s.v. Ibn al-'Arabī (J. Robson).

43 Ibn al-'Arabī, *Aḥkām*, 1:18–19.

44 This recitation is still seen in the standard Warsh Qur'ānic text prevalent in Northern Africa.

45 Al-Qurṭubī recounts three opinions regarding the *basmala*: (1) it is the first verse of every *sūra* (the Shāfi'īs); (2) it is foreign to the Qur'ān except in the case of Q27:30 (the Mālikīs); and (3) it is the initial verse of the *Fātiḥa* but excluded from subsequent *sūras*. The second position (attributed to Mālik b. Anas) is considered most authoritative based (counterintuitively) on the persistent disagreement among scholars. Specifically, al-Qurṭubī argues that the Qur'ānic text must be verified by certain (*qaṭ'ī*) knowledge and multiple lines of transmission (*tawātur*). If there is no consensus that a certain verse or phrase is part of the Qur'ān, then it cannot be considered an integral part of the text. This argument is then supplemented by an interpretation of the dialogue tradition reminiscent of Ibn 'Abd al-Barr (al-Qurṭubī, *al-Jāmi'*, 1:93–4).

Given their view that the initial *basmala* is external to the *Fātiḥa*, there is no reason for Mālikīs to include it in the prayer or address the question of its audible or silent recitation.[46]

The Shāfiʿīs

In contrast to the Ḥanafīs and the Mālikīs, Shāfiʿī jurists uphold the *basmala* as the first verse of the *Fātiḥa* and recite it audibly in audible prayer cycles and silently in silent ones. Their arguments attempt to navigate the space between a large mass of contradictory traditions. Oppositional proof texts are either interpreted in a manner that supports the Shāfiʿī view or dismissed through a close criticism of their chains of transmission.

A typical Shāfiʿī treatment[47] of the *basmala* is found in ʿAlī b. Muḥammad al-Māwardī's (d. 450/1058) *al-Ḥāwī al-kabīr*.[48] The pertinent section begins with an affirmation of the *basmala* as the first verse of almost every chapter of the Qur'ān (the exception being *sūrat al-barā'a* – Q9) but with the caveat that this view is not based on conclusive textual evidence.[49] In practical terms, this means that the issue remains open for debate and oppositional views may be articulated without fear of excommunication. Al-Māwardī then summarizes three arguments for the *basmala*'s exclusion from the text of the Qur'ān. First, he mentions a tradition in which the Prophet and the first two caliphs begin their prayer recitation with Q1:2.[50] This account, he explains, is utilized by the

[46] For a Mālikī analysis of the issue in which the *basmala*'s recitation is permitted but deemed reprehensible (*makrūh*), see Ibn al-Munayyir al-Iskandarī's commentary in the text of al-Zamakhsharī's *al-Kashshāf*, 1:22–45.

[47] The issue was also discussed by Muḥammad b. Idrīs al-Shāfiʿī in his *Kitāb al-umm*. Many of al-Māwardī's proofs were – in fact – drawn from al-Shāfiʿī including (1) Prophetic traditions that uphold the *basmala* in the prayer and (2) the gloss of texts that state recitation began with "Praise be to God, Master of the Worlds" as referring to an early name for the *Fātiḥa*. The school's general concern with strictly upholding the integrity of the text of the Qur'ān is reflected in the final sections of al-Shāfiʿī's discussion where he emphasizes that the *Fātiḥa* (along with every other *sūra*) must be recited from beginning to end with every letter in the place in which it was originally revealed by God. The order of the verses cannot be changed, a forgotten verse cannot be recited out of order, and no verses from different *sūra*s may be arbitrarily inserted at the discretion of the individual (*al-Umm*, 1:210–4).

[48] al-Māwardī, *al-Ḥāwī*, 2:104–9. The *Ḥāwī* is a commentary on Ismāʿīl b. Yaḥyā al-Muzanī's *Mukhtaṣar*. Al-Muzanī, a pupil of Shāfiʿī, spent most of his life in Egypt and is regarded as one of the most important early Shāfiʿī jurists. He is noted for his independent views (*EI*², s.v. al-Shāfiʿī (Heffening)). Similar discussions of the *basmala* are also found in al-Nawawī, *Majmūʿ*, 2:290–313 and al-Shīrāzī, *al-Muhadhdhab*, 1:242–3.

[49] al-Māwardī, *al-Ḥāwī*, 2:105.

[50] *Ibid.*, 2:105.

Ḥanafīs and the Mālikīs together with Q96:1 to contend that the *basmala* was not originally a part of the Qur'ān. When God revealed Q96:1 (the first revelation), instead of commanding the Prophet to recite the *basmala*, he ordered him to recite "In the name of your Lord."[51] If God had intended each chapter to begin with the *basmala*, then why did he not reveal it at the start of the first revelation? Second, Māwardī recounts the argument[52] that the text of the Qur'ān must be based on consensus so that any disagreements over a verse immediately exclude it from the Qur'ānic text.[53] Third, he mentions a line of reasoning (ascribed to the Ḥanafīs and Mālikīs) centered on the number of verses in particular Qur'ānic chapters.[54] The advocates of this position contend that counting the initial *basmala* as a part of each chapter would contradict the consensus that Q112, for example, consists of only four verses.[55]

After laying out these oppositional arguments, al-Māwardī articulates the Shāfi'ī position. He begins by citing seven Prophetic traditions that confirm the *basmala*'s place in the *Fātiḥa*.[56] He also mentions a series of historical accounts that depict the initial compilation of the Qur'ān. Specifically, he claims that 'Uthmān's Qur'ān had the *basmala* at the start of every chapter and asserts that its eventual acceptance in the wider Muslim world constituted a consensus in favor of its Qur'ānic status.[57] Turning to the arguments of rival schools (see last paragraph), al-Māwardī explains that traditions claiming that recitation began with "Praise be to God, Master of the worlds" were simply identifying the *Fātiḥa*.[58] They were not meant to be taken literally.[59] He acknowledges that the *basmala* was not present in the first stages of revelation, but dismisses the relevance of this point as many aspects of Islam were added late in the Prophet's life.[60] Finally, he notes that the numbering of verses is a fluid process so that the *basmala* may not have been initially counted among

[51] *Ibid.*, 2:105.
[52] See footnote 45 in this chapter.
[53] *Ibid.*, 2:105.
[54] *Ibid.*, 2:105.
[55] *Ibid.*, 2:105.
[56] *Ibid.*, 2:105–6.
[57] Al-Māwardī acknowledges the counterargument that the *basmala* was only used in early Qur'ānic manuscripts to demarcate different *sūras*, but responds that, if the verse was written within the text, then it must have been considered a part of the text (*Ibid.*, 2:105–7).
[58] In other words, the *Fātiḥa* was initially designated by the phrase, "Praise be to God, Master of the Worlds." For more on this issue, see Jeffery, *Materials*.
[59] al-Māwardī, *al-Ḥāwī*, 2:108.
[60] *Ibid.*, 2:108.

the verses of a *sūra*, or it may have originally been joined to the verse that followed it in the text.[61]

In terms of recitation, al-Māwardī (like the other Shāfiʿī jurists) has little trouble in arguing for the audible *basmala* in audible prayers (i.e., *fajr, maghrib, ʿishāʾ*) and the silent *basmala* in silent prayers (i.e., *ẓuhr, ʿaṣr*). First, he quotes three traditions that depict the Prophet as performing either the audible or the silent *basmala*.[62] He then observes that the simplest way to reconcile these seemingly contradictory texts is by differentiating between prayers based on the nature of their recitation.[63] This conclusion flows naturally from the Shāfiʿī inclusion of the *basmala* in the Qur'ān, which may explain why so few Shāfiʿī jurists felt compelled to address the issue in detail.

The Shāfiʿīs argue that the *basmala* must be recited at the start of the *Fātiḥa* in the compulsory prayers because it is an integral part of the Qurʿānic text. As such, there should be no difference between the recitation of the *basmala* and the rest of the *Fātiḥa*. The entire chapter is recited audibly and silently depending on the prayer and the cycle in question.[64] The Shāfiʿī jurists consciously position themselves in opposition to the Mālikīs and strongly criticize their exclusion of the initial *basmala* from the text of the Qur'ān.[65]

The Ḥanbalīs

For the three Sunnī law schools considered so far, discussions of the initial *basmala* are grounded primarily in ascertaining its relationship to the

[61] *Ibid.*, 2:108. The same reasoning is utilized against the argument that the exegesis of Q15:87 necessarily excludes the *basmala* from the *Fātiḥa* in order to keep the number of verses in the chapter at seven. Al-Māwardī observes that there are various acceptable verse combinations which can be applied to reach the required number, and no consensus as to which of these is valid. For more, see footnote 29 in this chapter.

[62] *Ibid.*, 2:108–9.

[63] *Ibid.*, 2:109.

[64] For a minority Shāfiʿī opinion that upholds the silent *basmala* in all prayers, see al-Baghawī, *Sharḥ*, 2:237–40.

[65] In addition to al-Māwardī's strategy of reinterpreting seemingly pro-Mālikī traditions, some Shāfiʿīs attack Mālikī claims to represent Medinan *ʿamal*. This is done through the use of one of Shāfiʿī's traditions (not mentioned by al-Māwardī), which records an episode during Muʿāwiya's caliphate when he was taken to task by the Medinan population for idiosyncrasies in his prayer including the omission of the *basmala* (al-Shāfiʿī, *al-Umm*, 1:210). Al-Nawawī, for example, references this account as proof that the *Anṣār* and the *Muhājirūn* in Medina originally recited the *basmala* at the start of every *sūra* (including the *Fātiḥa*) in the compulsory prayer. He concludes that Medinan practice at the time of the Prophet differed from Medinan practice at the time of Mālik and could only be ascertained on the basis of textual evidence (al-Nawawī, *Majmūʿ*, 2:300).

Qur'ānic text. If the *basmala* is the first verse of the *Fātiḥa* (the Shāfi'ī view), then its inclusion in the prayer and the manner of its recitation is self-evident. If, by contrast, it is only a marker used to divide chapters (the Ḥanafī and Mālikī view), then its integration into the prayer is problematic. Ḥanbalī discussions of the *basmala* lack the clarity of this logic as they attempt to navigate apparent contradictions in the views ascribed to the school's eponymous founder, Aḥmad ibn Ḥanbal.

The parameters of the Ḥanbalī position are established through works that preserve a multitude of Ibn Ḥanbal's responses to questions dealing with matters of ritual law and doctrine. Although these question-and-answer exchanges rarely contain explicit textual evidence, they implicitly reference the large corpus of traditions that circulated among traditionists. When questioned about the *basmala*, Ibn Ḥanbal affirms its place in the Qur'ān at the start of every *sūra*[66] and agrees with the Ḥanafīs that it should be recited silently in both audible and silent prayer cycles.[67] But there is a problem of consistency here.[68] As opposed to the Ḥanafīs who incorporate the *basmala* into a silent invocation at the start of the prayer recitation, the Ḥanbalīs (or at least Ibn Ḥanbal) believe it is part of the *Fātiḥa*. How then is it justified to recite one part of the *Fātiḥa* silently and another audibly? Ibn Ḥanbal does not appear to deal with this matter directly in any of his responses.

A possible solution to this dilemma (and one that garnered significant support among Ḥanbalī jurists) is offered by Abū Ya'lā Muḥammad b. al-Ḥusayn (d. 458/1065), who writes:

> The *basmala* is part of a verse from *Sūrat al-Naml* [Q27] and a complete verse in and of itself; it is neither a verse from the *Fātiḥa* of the Book nor a complete verse from any other *sūra*.[69]

In other words, the introductory *basmala* is an independent, free-standing Qur'ānic verse unaffiliated with individual chapters. This permits a silent recitation of the *basmala* in every prayer cycle without leaving the school open to accusations of inconsistency. Whereas the entire *Fātiḥa* is recited audibly in audible prayer cycles and silently in silent prayer cycles, the *basmala* is a separate textual unit whose recitation (silent) is governed

[66] Virtually identical information on this issue is preserved in Aḥmad ibn Ḥanbal, *Masā'il* (Medina 2004), 2:535–6 and Aḥmad ibn Ḥanbal, *Masā'il* (1999), 112–13.

[67] Ibn Ḥanbal, *Masā'il* (Medina 2004), 2:536; Ibn Ḥanbal, *Masā'il* (1999), 112–13.

[68] For a similar discussion of the issue in a standard Ḥanbalī *fiqh* manual, see al-Khiraqī, *Mukhtaṣar*, 20.

[69] Abū Ya'lā, *al-Jāmi' al-ṣaghīr*, 39.

by a different set of rules. Such a position effectively resolves many of the contradictions ascribed to Ibn Ḥanbal and allows the school to both (1) accept the initial *basmala* as Qur'ānic and (2) differentiate its recitation (always silent) from that of the *Fātiḥa*.

The most detailed and systematic Ḥanbalī analysis of the issue is articulated by Ibn Qudāma (d. 620/1223) in his *Mughnī*.[70] The discussion begins by affirming that the recitation of the *Fātiḥa* is obligatory in the prayer.[71] This is followed by a series of traditions that either (1) unambiguously reject the audible *basmala* or (2) depict the Prophet reciting the *basmala* (albeit without commenting on the nature of his recitation).[72] Ibn Qudāma concludes that the silent *basmala* best reconciles the apparent contradiction between accounts in which Companions do not hear the Prophet recite the *basmala* and those in which he instructs them to include the phrase in the prayer.[73] In dealing with opposition proof-texts, Ibn Qudāma offers two varieties of criticism. The first includes rhetorical arguments rooted in the meaning of the Arabic verbal root, < q – r – ’ >, which (he claims) can refer to either audible or silent recitation.[74] The second consists of a standard critique of the chains of transmission attached to traditions that support the audible *basmala*.[75]

In a reversal from the juristic literature of the other Sunnī law schools, Ibn Qudāma only turns to the *basmala*'s relationship to the Qur'ānic text *after* discussing its role in the prayer. The analysis here is brief and centers primarily on the dialogue tradition (previously mentioned), which is interpreted as conclusive evidence against the *basmala*'s inclusion in the *Fātiḥa*. This does not, however, definitively rule out integrating the phrase into the prayer recitation.[76] In the end, Ibn Qudāma acknowledges the deep uncertainty surrounding the issue and even concedes that Aḥmad ibn Ḥanbal's views on the matter are contradictory.[77] His central concern in this section, however, is the confirmation of the *basmala*'s use in the prayer rather than its place in the Qur'ān.

Ḥanbalī jurists focus primarily on the question of the *basmala's* audible or silent recitation. This is in stark contrast to Mālikī and Shāfiʿī scholars who treat recitation as a secondary consequence of the dispute

[70] *Mughnī II*, 2:30–4.
[71] *Ibid.*, 2:30.
[72] *Ibid.*, 2:31. For the traditions he cites, see *SKB*, 2:65–6 and 68; and *SN I*, 1:133–4.
[73] *Ibid.*, 2:31.
[74] *Ibid.*, 2:32–3.
[75] *Ibid.*, 2:32–3.
[76] *Ibid.*, 2:32.
[77] *Ibid.*, 2:33–4. Writing in the 6th/12th century, Abū Yaʿlā Muḥammad b. Muḥammad b. al-Ḥusayn does not address this issue in his *Kitāb al-tamām*.

over the verse's place in the Qur'ānic text. The majority Ḥanbalī position holds that the *basmala* is an independent, free-standing Qur'ānic verse separate from the *Fātiḥa*.[78] For proof, the Ḥanbalīs quote a broad range of traditions and argue that their legal reasoning is best able to reconcile any apparent contradictions.

The Imāmīs

The Imāmīs universally affirm the initial *basmala*'s Qur'ānic standing and generally (though not unanimously) endorse its audible recitation in the prayer. Imāmī legal works focus almost exclusively on the issue of recitation, leaving the discussion over the *basmala*'s inclusion (or omission) from the *Fātiḥa* to the purview of *ikhtilāf*[79] and exegetical works. In the section that follows, we examine two works of the famous Imāmī jurist Muḥammad b. al-Ḥasan al-Ṭūsī (d. 460/1067), one a formal juristic tract and the other a typical *ikhtilāf* manual. The section concludes with a brief survey of Imāmī exegetical works that articulate creative interpretations of Q17:46[80] and Q15:87 to support the audible *basmala*.

In *al-Nihāya*, al-Ṭūsī confirms the *basmala*'s place in the Qur'ānic text and advocates its audible recitation.[81] He first broaches the issue in his description of the prayer, stating that the *basmala* is compulsory before the *Fātiḥa* and the *sūra* (of the worshipper's choosing) that directly follows it in the first two prayer cycles.[82] He then asserts that the second recitation in supererogatory prayers (which need not be a complete *sūra*) "should begin at the spot of the [worshipper's] choosing" rather than with the *basmala*.[83] The implication here is that the *basmala* is the first verse of every Qur'ānic chapter. Even though al-Ṭūsī

[78] Whereas the Ḥanbalī legal texts selected above generally limit their discussions to the issue of prayer, the exegetic literature (both Ḥanbalī and non-Ḥanbalī) elaborates the school's views in a more direct manner. The 8th/14th century exegete, Ibn Kathīr, though a Shāfi'ī by law, shared a traditionalist theology with the Ḥanbalīs. This may have influenced his gloss of the *Fātiḥa* which begins with a summary of the possible links between the *basmala* and the Qur'ān, and concludes with the general Ḥanbalī assertion that "it is an independent verse at the start of every *sūra* [but] not part of it" (Ibn Kathīr, *Tafsīr* (1966), 1:30).

[79] These were works that laid out the positions of multiple schools of law on a given issue. They were expressly designed to defend the views of an author's school against the attacks of rivals/opponents.

[80] Q17:46 – "And We place veils upon their hearts lest they should understand it, and a deafness in their ears. And when you make mention of your Lord alone in the Qur'ān, they turn their backs in aversion".

[81] al-Ṭūsī, *al-Nihāya*, 1:302–3.

[82] *Ibid.*, 1:303.

[83] *Ibid.*, 1:303.

advocates the audible *basmala* in every prayer, he considers it recommended (as opposed to mandatory) and allows worshippers (in certain cases) to whisper it in a voice that is neither completely silent nor audible to surrounding observers.[84] This may have been a concession to help Imāmīs avoid persecution at the hands of Ḥanafīs who performed the silent *basmala* in all prayers.[85]

A more detailed examination of the *basmala*'s relationship to the Qur'ānic text is found in al-Ṭūsī's *al-Khilāf*, a work detailing differences between the Imāmī Shī'a and their Sunnī rivals. The section begins with a defense of the Imāmī position that the *basmala* is the opening verse of every *sūra* (including the *Fātiḥa*) on the basis of the "consensus of the school,"[86] a Prophetic tradition narrated by Umm Salama (d. 59–60/679–80),[87] and two Imāmī traditions drawing on the authority of al-Bāqir[88] and al-Ṣādiq.[89] Turning to recitation, al-Ṭūsī claims that the audible *basmala* is only obligatory in audible prayer cycles. In silent prayer cycles, it is recommended (*mustaḥabb*), but the worshiper may choose to recite it silently.[90] Proof for this opinion is drawn from Imāmī juristic consensus together with a tradition on the authority of al-Ṣādiq.[91]

Throughout his discussion, al-Ṭūsī quotes the opinions of prominent Sunnī jurists including the founders of the Mālikī, Shāfi'ī, Ḥanbalī, and Ḥanafī legal schools. In so doing, he situates the Imāmīs in the broader legal landscape and (occasionally) attacks the opinions of rival law schools. His primary targets are the Ḥanafīs for their exclusion of the *basmala* from the Qur'ān at the start of each chapter. In one instance, he criticizes 'Ubayd Allāh b. al-Ḥusayn al-Karkhī (d. 340/951), a prominent Ḥanafī from Baghdād, for his assertion that the *basmala* is a free-standing verse at the start of every *sūra* where it is found in the 'Uthmānic Qur'ānic text.[92] Al-Ṭūsī observes that this directly contradicts the opinion of Abū

84 *Ibid.*, 1:303.
85 For a similar rationale from the Zaydīs, see al-'Alawī, *al-Jāmi'*, 2:53.
86 al-Ṭūsī, *Khilāf*, 1:328–30.
87 A similar tradition is found in al-Shīrāzī, *al-Muhadhdhab*, 1:243 and *SKB*, 2:65 – 2383 and 2:66 – 2385.
88 For this tradition, see *TI*, 1:356–7 – 3; *WS*, 6:58 – 7341; *KK*, 3:313 – 2.
89 For this tradition, see *TT*, 2:69 – 19; *TI*, 1:356–7 – 2; *WS*, 6:58 – 7340; *KK*, 3:312 – 1.
90 al-Ṭūsī, *Khilāf*, 1:331.
91 *Ibid.*, 1:332. For this tradition, see *TT*, 2:68 – 14; *WS*, 6:57 – 7336 and 6:134 – 7543; *TI*, 1:358 – 1; *KK*, 3:315 – 20; al-Ṭabrisī, *Mustadrak*, 4:186 – 4494.
92 *Ibid.*, 1:330. The entire passage citing al-Karkhī and his disagreement with Abū Ḥanīfa is also found in al-Qaffāl's *Ḥilyat*, 2:103. The interesting point here is not that al-Ṭūsī was drawing on Sunnī sources – that much is expected in an *ikhtilāf* work – but rather that he was selectively quoting to highlight their internal contradictions.

Ḥanīfa (d. 150/767) who "did not consider it a verse from the *Fātiḥa* or from any other *sūra*."[93]

The most distinctive Imāmī argument regarding the *basmala* is found in the school's exegetical works. Imāmī interpretations of verses such as Q15:87 or the *Fātiḥa* are similar to those of their Sunnī counterparts with little in the way of substantive disagreements.[94] In the case of Q17:46, however, Imāmī exegetes forward a strikingly different gloss that explicitly supports the audible *basmala*. Specifically, they claim that the verse was revealed as a rebuke against the Meccan polytheists who would turn their backs whenever Muḥammad mentioned the name of God (i.e., the *basmala*) in the daily prayers.[95] This story only makes sense if the Prophet recited the *basmala* loud enough to be heard by a large crowd. Muḥammad b. Mas'ūd al-'Ayyāshī (d. early 4th/10th century) advocates the audible *basmala* on the basis of this interpretation of Q17:46 together with two additional Imāmī traditions.[96] Faḍl b. al-Ḥasan al-Ṭabrisī (d. 548/1153) offers a similar commentary on Q17:46, emphasizing its legal implication for the prayer recitation.[97] Muḥammad b. al-Ḥasan al-Shaybānī (fl. 7th/13th century), by contrast, incorporates Q17:46 in his exegesis of Q15:87 to create a fluid argument in favor of both the *basmala*'s inclusion in the *Fātiḥa* and its audible recitation.[98] Sunnī exegetes, by contrast, interpret Q17:46 as a reference to the Prophet's public proclamations of the first half of the *shahāda* ("There is no god but God"). Not a single Sunnī commentary even alludes to the Imāmī interpretation.[99]

Overall, the Imāmīs are committed to the *basmala*'s inclusion in the *Fātiḥa* and its audible recitation in the daily prayer.[100] Three genres of

[93] *Ibid.*, 1:329. This confusion in the Ḥanafī position was addressed in the first section of this chapter.

[94] For Imāmī exegetic discussions of the *Fātiḥa* and Q15:87, see al-'Ayyāshī, *Tafsīr* (2000), 1:99–100 and 2:437–8; al-Qummī, *Tafsīr*, 1:377; and al-Ṭabrisī, *Majma'* (1997), 1:23–30.

[95] al-'Ayyāshī, *Tafsīr* (2000), 3:55.

[96] For the first of these traditions, see also al-Majlisī, *Biḥār*, 82:24 – 74. For the second tradition, see *ṬT*, 2:290 – 18.

[97] al-Ṭabrisī, *Majma'* (1997), 6:293–4.

[98] al-Shaybānī, *Nahj*, 1:69.

[99] For some Sunnī interpretations of the verse, see al-Ṭabarī, *Tafsīr*, 5:79–80; Ibn Kathīr, *Tafsīr* (1966), 9:21–3; al-Zamakhsharī, *al-Kashshāf*, 2:671; Fakhr al-Dīn al-Rāzī, *Tafsīr*, 20:223; and al-Qurṭubī, *al-Jāmi'*, 10:271.

[100] For the minority opinion that the *basmala*'s recitation should vary in accordance with the overall recitation (i.e., audibly in audible cycles and silent in silent cycles), see al-Shalmaghānī, *Fiqh al-Riḍā*, 104–5 and Ibn Idrīs, *al-Sarā'ir*, 1:217. Although al-Muḥaqqiq al-Ḥillī endorses the audible *basmala*, he concedes that, in silent cycles, it is recommended (*masnūn*) rather than obligatory (*farḍ*) (*Sharā'i'*, 1:64).

Imāmī literature directly address the issue. The first consists of juristic works that assume the *basmala*'s place at the start of every chapter in the Qur'ān and focus their energies on determining its proper manner of recitation in prayer.[101] The second is comprised of *ikhtilāf* works that provide textual and logical arguments to defend the school's opinion in the broader legal landscape.[102] The third includes exegetical works that affirm the *basmala*'s Qur'ānic status through a distinctive interpretation of Q17:46.

The Zaydīs

Unlike the five law schools considered to this point, no single analytic cord binds together Zaydī discussions of the *basmala*. The school (as a whole) upholds the *basmala* as an integral verse in the *Fātiḥa*, but disagreements abound regarding the manner of its recitation in prayer. It is difficult to identify one jurist to represent the general tenor of the school's legal discourse, which includes approaches ranging from rational critiques and polemical arguments to minimalist legal descriptions and brief, unsupported personal opinions. This being the case, the discussion that follows focuses on two jurists who present arguments in favor of (1) the audible/silent *basmala* depending on prayer cycle (the majority opinion) and (2) the audible *basmala* in all prayer cycles (the minority opinion).

The majority Zaydī view is best articulated by Sharaf al-Dīn Ḥusayn b. Muḥammad in *Shifā' al-uwām*.[103] The pertinent section opens with a series of traditions and juristic opinions (mostly from Imāms) that unanimously require a worshipper to include the *Fātiḥa* and (at least) three additional Qur'ānic verses in the prayer recitation.[104] Sharaf al-Dīn then asserts a school consensus on the audibility of the morning and evening prayers (*fajr*, *maghrib*, *'ishā'*) and the silence of the afternoon prayers (*ẓuhr*, *'aṣr*).[105] At this point, he turns to the *basmala*, quoting a series of Prophetic traditions narrated by Abū Hurayra (d. 58/678), Umm Salama, and 'Abd Allāh b. 'Abbās in which the verse is

101 Other juristic works that support the audible recitation include *KK*, 3:312–15 (bearing in mind that this is technically a collection of traditions); al-Ḥalabī, *al-Kāfī*, 117–8; Ibn Bābawayh, *al-Faqīh*, 1:300–5. Many Imāmī works do not discuss the *basmala* in detail including Ibn Bābawayh's *Hidāya* and al-Sharīf al-Murtaḍā's *al-Intiṣār* and *Masā'il al-nāṣiriyyāt*.

102 For a further example, see Ibn al-Muṭahhar, *Tadhkirat*, 3:133.

103 Sharaf al-Dīn, *Shifā'*, 1:272–6.

104 *Ibid.*, 1:272–3.

105 *Ibid.*, 1:273–4.

identified as an essential part of the *Fātiḥa*.[106] With respect to recitation, Sharaf al-Dīn notes that all Zaydī jurists believed that the *basmala* should be audible in audible prayers and silent in silent prayers.[107] He considers this the most reasonable approach given the lack of any substantive justification for singling out an individual verse of the *Fātiḥa* for special treatment.[108]

Although Sharaf al-Dīn does not offer any traditions to support his view on the manner of recitation (the consensus of the school is apparently sufficient), he does address contradictory evidence used by other schools to affirm the audible *basmala* in every prayer (e.g., the Imāmīs). His response consists of three arguments. First, he claims that the Prophet sometimes recited the *basmala* aloud to announce the start of a group prayer to a large (and noisy) congregation.[109] This supports the *basmala*'s inclusion in the *Fātiḥa*, but it does not have a legal bearing on recitation. Second, he observes that the sources do not identify the prayers in which the Prophet performed an audible *basmala*.[110] It is possible, therefore, that the audible *basmala* was only recited in audible prayers. Finally, he interprets traditions in which the Prophet instructs a worshipper to recite the *basmala* as affirmations of its place at the start of the prayer and the *Fātiḥa*.[111] He argues that these instructions were not meant as a general endorsement of the audible *basmala* in all prayers.

The most prominent proponent of the Zaydī minority view is the eponymous founder of the Hādawī law school, al-Hādī ilā'l-Ḥaqq (d. 297/910), whose opinions are recorded in *Kitāb al-aḥkām* in the form of legal polemics and in Muḥammad b. Sulaymān al-Kūfī's (d. early 4th/10th century) *Kitāb al-muntakhab* as a series of conversations. The former begins with the declaration that, "in our opinion, there is no prayer for one who does not audibly recite the *basmala*."[112] Al-Hādī asserts that the *basmala* is the first verse of every Qur'ānic *sūra* and argues that "it is not permissible (for the *basmala*) to be dropped."[113] With respect to

106 *Ibid.*, 1:274.
107 *Ibid.*, 1:274–5.
108 *Ibid.*, 1:275.
109 *Ibid.*, 1:275.
110 *Ibid.*, 1:276.
111 *Ibid.*, 1:276.
112 In this text, al-Hādī seems to adopt the Jārūdī view that the *basmala* must be audibly recited in all prayer cycles. The Batriyya held that the recitation should be silent in prayer cycles where the recitation was silent (al-Hādī *Aḥkām*, 2:105). For a summary of the differences between the Jārūdiyya and the Batriyya with respect to the *basmala*, see *EI*[2] supplement, s.v. Batriyya (Madelung) and Chapter 1 in this volume.
113 al-Hādī, *al-Aḥkām*, 2:105.

recitation, al-Hādī implicitly criticizes the Ḥanafī belief that the *basmala* should be recited silently even when the remainder of the *Fātiḥa* is audible. He argues that such an inconsistency constitutes a flaw in both the *Fātiḥa* and the prayer.[114] Moreover, as the first verse of the first *sūra* of the Qur'ān and as a fundamental statement of the unity of God, the *basmala* should occupy pride of place in public proclamations and audible recitation.[115] Turning to the claim that the *basmala* is not a part of the *Fātiḥa*, al-Hādī's criticism of the Ḥanafīs is even more explicit. This view, he states, does not allow for the *basmala* to be recited in the prayer since it would constitute a human addition (*ziyāda*).[116] The section ends with two traditions. The first cites 'Alī's opinion that deviation from the audible *basmala* invalidates the prayer. The second has the Prophet identifying the devil as the party responsible for the *basmala*'s omission.

Al-Hādī's discussion of the *basmala* in *Kitāb al-muntakhab* is prompted by a question from Muḥammad b. Sulaymān al-Kūfī who asks him about the proper prayer recitation. He answers, "[Begin] with the audible recitation of (the *basmala*) [in] a prayer in which the recitation is audible."[117] He does not address the *basmala* for prayer cycles where the recitation is silent. When pressed for proof, al-Hādī quotes three Qur'ānic verses (Q96:1, Q24:36, and Q2:114), the latter two of which are never mentioned by Sunnī or Imāmī jurists in their discussions of the issue.[118] The first and second are interpreted as commands for audible recitation, while the third is framed as a condemnation of those who forbid audible recitation.[119] Al-Hādī also offers a standard commentary of Q15:87 in which the *basmala* is counted as the first of the *Fātiḥa*'s seven verses.[120]

Al-Hādī then launches into a polemic against those who "reject His name and pronounce it silently."[121] The obvious targets are (once again) the Ḥanafīs and, to a lesser extent, the Shāfi'īs. Al-Hādī notes that, in prayers where the recitation is audible, the Ḥanafīs recite Q1:3 (the

114 *Ibid.*, 2:105.
115 *Ibid.*, 2:105.
116 *Ibid.*, 2:105. As mentioned previously, the only schools that do not consider the *basmala* a verse of the *Fātiḥa* are the Mālikīs and Ḥanafīs. Of these, only the Ḥanafīs recite the *basmala* in the daily prayer.
117 al-Kūfī, *al-Muntakhab*, 39–40.
118 For Q96:1, see footnote 8 in this chapter. Q24:36 – "In houses, which Allāh has permitted to be raised to honor; for the celebration, in them, of His name." Q2:114 – "And who is more unjust than he who forbids that in places for the worship of Allāh, His name should be celebrated?"
119 al-Kūfī, *al-Muntakhab*, 39.
120 *Ibid.*, 39.
121 *Ibid.*, 39.

Beneficent, the Merciful) aloud but only silently whisper the *basmala*. By doing so, they are proudly proclaiming one part of the *basmala* (the Beneficent, the Merciful) while diminishing another (In the name of God). The audible recitation of this latter phrase, however, is explicitly ordered by both Q96:1 and Q24:36.[122] At this point, al-Hādī concedes the existence of traditions in which the Prophet appears to recite the *basmala* silently. Rather than countering these with other traditions (the standard approach of Sunnī and Imāmī jurists alike), he rejects them for their implication that the Prophet disobeyed a direct command from God (Q96:1). Specifically, he asks, "How could he [the Prophet] recite silently that [the *basmala*] whose public proclamation God has confirmed?"[123] Turning to the issue of consistency in recitation, al-Hādī observes that uttering the second verse of the *Fātiḥa* silently in an audible prayer cycle would invalidate the prayer and constitute disbelief (*kufr*).[124] How then could it be permitted to recite the first verse (the *basmala*) silently and the remainder aloud? Al-Hādī urges his hypothetical opponents to consider these arguments and not be guided by idle whims and blind imitation.[125]

Despite a general Zaydī consensus that the *basmala* is a verse at the start of every *sūra*, the issue of recitation within the prayer remains divisive. Most Zaydī scholars (e.g., Sharaf al-Dīn, Yaḥyā b. Ḥamza[126] – d. 749/1348) argue that the *basmala* should be recited audibly in audible prayer cycles and silently in silent prayer cycles in agreement with the Shāfiʿīs.[127] A vocal minority (e.g., al-Hādī, al-Sharafī[128] – d. 1062/1652), by contrast, affirm the Imāmī view that it should always be recited audibly. Faced with these clear divisions within the school, some prominent Zaydī jurists simply relate both positions without expressing a clear preference.[129]

122 *Ibid.*, 39–40.
123 *Ibid.*, 40.
124 *Ibid.*, 40.
125 *Ibid.*, 40. Al-Hādī concludes with two traditions which corroborate the *basmala*'s inclusion in the Qur'ānic text. The first quotes the Prophet as saying that the revelation of the *basmala* denoted the end of one *sūra* and the start of the next. The second is a statement by 'Ā'isha, which states that the devil stole the *basmala* from the people. These traditions support al-Hādī's views but they are of secondary importance as compared with his rational arguments and his unique interpretations of the Qur'ān.
126 al-Mu'ayyad bi-Allāh Yaḥyā b. Ḥamza, *al-Intiṣār*, 3:238–59.
127 This view is implicitly endorsed by al-Nāṭiq bi'l-Ḥaqq in *al-Taḥrīr*, 1:88. Al-Mu'ayyad bi-Allāh Aḥmad b. al-Ḥusayn, by contrast, appears to avoid the issue of silent prayer cycles altogether in *al-Tajrīd*, 62.
128 al-Sharafī, *al-Maṣābīḥ*, 1:146–59.
129 See al-'Alawī, *al-Jāmi'*, 2:52–4; Ibn Miftāḥ, *Sharḥ al-Azhār*, 2:219–27; and Ibn al-Murtaḍā, *al-Baḥr*, 2:244–9.

The Legal Landscape

Table 3.1 summarizes the differences among the six selected law schools regarding the *basmala*'s (1) relationship to the Qur'ān and (2) recitation in the ritual prayer.[130] The Ḥanafīs and the Mālikīs are distinguished by their belief that the *basmala* is not part of the Qur'ān at the start of individual chapters. They argue that the phrase originally signified the end of one chapter and the start of the next. The Ḥanafīs still allow the *basmala* to be recited silently in the ritual prayer as part of a standard invocation inserted between the initial *takbīr* (reciting the phrase "God is the Greatest") and the Qur'ānic recitation. The Mālikīs, by contrast, consider the *basmala* an extraneous insertion into the prayer structure and consider its inclusion reprehensible (*makrūh*). The other law schools accept the *basmala* as a Qur'ānic verse at the beginning of each chapter (with one exception – *sūrat al-barā'a*). The Ḥanbalīs are singular in their belief that it is a free-standing verse between individual chapters, a position that enables them to follow the Ḥanafīs in reciting it silently, even in prayers where the remainder of the recitation is audible. In particular, they argue that the *basmala* is subject to different recitation rules from the *Fātiḥa* because it functions as an independent piece of text. The Shāfi'īs believe that the *basmala* is a part of the *Fātiḥa* and should, therefore, be recited

[130] The Ismā'īlī position matches that of the Imāmīs by affirming the *basmala*'s Qur'ānic status and making its audible recitation mandatory in every prayer (Qāḍī Nu'mān, *Da'ā'im*, 1:160). The Ẓāhirīs (as represented by Ibn Ḥazm) maintain that the relationship of the *basmala* to the Qur'ān is an open question, with both sides in possession of strong proof texts. Because there is no clear way to prove the validity of one view over the other, both are equally acceptable as long as a consistency is maintained. In other words, an individual (i.e., a Shāfi'ī) who believes that the *basmala* is part of the Qur'ān *must* recite it in the prayer, whereas one who does not hold this view may choose to include it (i.e., a Ḥanafī) or not (i.e., a Mālikī). Although Ibn Ḥazm does not take a position on the *basmala*'s place in the Qur'ānic text, he does interpret the textual evidence as strong proof for the silent recitation of the *basmala* at the start of prayer (Ibn Ḥazm, *al-Muḥallā*, 2:280–84). The Ibāḍīs adopt a stance virtually identical to that of the Shāfi'īs. They consider the *basmala* the first verse in every Qur'ānic chapter on the basis of Q15:87, the opinions of early Companions, and the consensus of the school. The acceptance of the *basmala*'s Qur'ānic status then drives them to treat it in the same manner as the rest of the *Fātiḥa*. The verse is recited audibly in audible prayers and silently in silent prayers (al-Shammākhī, *Kitāb al-īḍāḥ*, 1:478–80). For a substantively similar Ibāḍī argument backed by a wide array of textual and logical arguments, see al-Rustāqī, *Manhaj*, 4:138–40. The school of Sufyān al-Thawrī, often associated with Kūfan traditionism, favors the silent *basmala*, but it is not clear whether any distinctions are made between audible and silent prayers. For more on Sufyān al-Thawrī, see *EI*², s.v. Sufyān al-Thawrī (H. P. Raddatz) and al-Mizzī, *Tahdhīb*, 11:154. For the position of his school, see al-Qaffāl, *Ḥilyat*, 2:104 and *Mughnī I*, 2:149.

TABLE 3.1. *A Summary of the Juristic Treatment of the Basmala*

	Basmala as a Verse at the Start of the *Fātiḥa* and the Other *Sūras*?	*Basmala* Recited at the Start of Prayer?	Nature of the *Basmala* Recitation
Ḥanafīs	No	Yes	Silent
Mālikīs	No	No	Not applicable
Shāfiʿīs	Yes	Yes	Audible – Audible prayers Silent – Silent prayers
Ḥanbalīs	No (independent verse)	Yes	Silent
Imāmīs	Yes	Yes	Audible
Zaydīs	Yes	Yes	Majority: Audible – Audible prayers Silent – Silent prayers Minority: Audible

audibly in audible prayer cycles and silently in silent prayer cycles. The Imāmīs consider the *basmala* a special verse that merits the distinction of audible recitation. The Zaydīs are split on the issue, with the majority adopting a view similar to the Shāfiʿīs but a significant minority advocating a stance that aligns with the Imāmīs.

COMPARING THE KŪFAN TRADITIONS

By the time the systematic legal works discussed in this chapter were composed (mostly after the 3rd/9th century), the early geographical law schools had been superseded by universal schools associated with a juristic master (e.g., Abū Ḥanīfa, Jaʿfar al-Ṣādiq). These new law schools incorporated elements of their geographical predecessors. Thus, the Mālikī school is generally associated with Medina, whereas the origins of the Ḥanafī school are usually traced to Kūfa. Differences between the emerging law schools turned to a great degree on their view of traditions. In the case of the Sunnī law schools, there were notable disagreements between jurists like Mālik and al-Shāfiʿī on the utility and reliability of these accounts in the formation of law.[131] A more fundamental gap existed between the Shīʿī and Sunnī schools regarding the authority of particular historical figures. The Sunnīs generally favor traditions that invoked

131 For al-Shāfiʿī, see al-Shāfiʿī, *al-Umm*, chapter 14 and Schacht, *Origins*. For Mālik, see Dutton, *Origins*.

the Prophet, the Companions and the Successors. The Imāmīs, by contrast, rely on the opinions of their Imāms, while the Zaydīs reference the views of a wide array of ʿAlids. Traditions even play a supportive role in works ascribed to the Zaydī Imām al-Hādī whose motivation was as much polemical as it was legal. The systematic compilation of Prophetic (and non-Prophetic) traditions paralleled the development of the universal law schools but preserved a snapshot of an earlier time. As discussed in Chapter 2, such accounts were circulating in the early 2nd/8th century when the first outlines of sectarian communities were emerging. The second part of this chapter subjects these texts to a systematic structural analysis in an attempt to reconstruct the broad contours of nascent sectarian communities in 2nd/8th century Kūfa.

The Kūfan Traditions – An Overview

The analysis that follows centers on 102 Kūfan traditions[132] that discuss the recitation of the *basmala* in the daily prayer. These are taken from a larger sampling of 233 traditions compiled in a broad survey of the primary Sunnī, Imāmī, and Zaydī *ḥadīth* collections.[133] The process by which these texts were identified as Kūfan is described in detail in Chapter 2. To summarize, particular weight was given to the geographical associations of transmitters from the 2nd/8th century, the period commonly associated with the systematic (and accurate) collection of traditions. Each sectarian community contributed an equal number of traditions (34) to the final total although this constituted only 26 percent (34/131) of the entirety of Sunnī traditions as opposed to 83 percent (34/41) of Imāmī and 71 percent (34/48) of Zaydī traditions.

A survey of the Kūfan traditions (see Table 3.2) suggests a citywide consensus on the need to recite the *basmala* together with a disagreement as to whether the recitation should be audible or silent. A clear majority of Imāmī and Zaydī accounts explicitly endorse the audible *basmala* (i.e., 76 percent – Imāmī and 94 percent – Zaydī) or describe the verse as an integral part of the Qur'ānic text at the start of various *sūra*s (i.e., 6 percent – Imāmī and 6 percent – Zaydī). This data provides strong

[132] Table 3.2 assigns each Kūfan tradition a number based on the death date of authority figures. In such a scheme, a low number (e.g., 001) represents a tradition that cites an early authority (e.g., the Prophet). The Kūfan traditions are not numbered sequentially because they were drawn from a larger overall pool of 233 traditions. For the original sources of each individual numbered text, see www.najamhaider.com/originsoftheshia.

[133] For the canonical and noncanonical sources utilized in this study, see Chapter 2.

TABLE 3.2. *The Kūfan Traditions (Basmala)*

	Audible *Basmala*		Silent *Basmala*		No *Basmala*	Ambiguous[a]
Sunnī	006	105	038	135	095	070
	024	129	068	136		088
	025	130	074	137		106
	026	131	075	149		122
	069	154	076	153		132
	071	155	093	156		138
	085		134			151
Zaydī	020	110				216
	021	111				221
	027	119				
	028	133				
	031	141				
	072	152				
	079	169				
	080	166				
	081	170				
	083	171				
	084	172				
	086	173				
	100	202				
	101	204				
	103	211				
	104	219				
Imāmī	019	193			175	158
	128	194			181	176
	157	196			195	177
	162	197				212
	174	198				215
	178	199				
	179	200				
	180	206				
	182	222				
	183	224				
	189	225				
	191	226				
	192	227				

[a] This category includes (1) traditions that assert that the *basmala* is part of the *Fātiḥa*, thereby supporting both the audible and silent views and (2) traditions that simply state that the *basmala* is "not omitted" without commenting on the manner of its recitation. For complete references corresponding to each numbered tradition, see www.najamhaider.com/originsoftheshia.

evidence that the early Imāmī and Zaydī communities in Kūfa recited the *basmala* audibly in all the daily prayers and considered it the first verse of the *Fātiḥa*. A portion of the Sunnī Kūfan traditions (18 percent) uphold the Qur'ānic standing of the *basmala* but this is not an unambiguous endorsement of audible recitation given the split between texts that favor audible (38 percent) and silent (38 percent) recitation. Overall, the Sunnī traditions suggest that the *basmala* may be recited (1) silently in all prayers (the eventual Ḥanafī view), (2) audibly in all prayers (the eventual Imāmī and majority Zaydī view), or (3) audibly in audible prayer cycles and silently in silent prayer cycles (the eventual Shāfi'ī view and minority Zaydī view).[134]

Authorities

Although all Muslims acknowledge the Prophet's unique religious authority, sects differ significantly regarding his Companions and Successors.[135] In this section, we examine the degree to which different groups invoke the authority of the same historical figures with the understanding that such intersections demonstrate sectarian overlap. If, by contrast, sects rely on distinctive and unique sets of authority figures, this is interpreted as proof for the existence of demarcated communal boundaries. As a reminder, we are primarily interested in evaluating the classical narratives for the emergence of Imāmī and Zaydī identity.

Table 3.3 lists the primary authorities mentioned in the traditions of each sectarian group. The number in the parenthesis before each name represents the total number of traditions that invoke that figure. Those texts that cite the Prophet or the first four caliphs are counted twice, once in accordance with the primary authority (that is, themselves) and a second time with respect to the first transmitters. This is done because Prophetic and caliphal traditions contain significant contradictions which disappear when analysis is extended to first transmitters.[136] Additionally,

[134] Recall that the Mālikī position – not found in Kūfan Sunnī traditions – held that the *basmala* was intended as a marker dividing one *sūra* from the next. Consequently, it was not to be recited within the daily prayer at the start of the *Fātiḥa*.

[135] This issue is discussed in greater detail in Chapter 2.

[136] These traditions are generally characterized by a narrow base of transmitters and significant internal contradictions. The Prophet, Abū Bakr, 'Umar, 'Uthmān, and 'Alī are politically charged figures, who carry a disproportionate authority in legal debates. This makes any attempts at discerning a singular "correct" orthopraxy on their opinions difficult, if not impossible. By citing first transmitters, I attempt to mitigate the impact of the contradictory positions ascribed to these singular early authorities so that

TABLE 3.3. *Authorities Cited (Basmala)*

	Sunnī	Zaydī	Imāmī
Unique	(1) Abū Bakr (d. 13/635)	(2) 'Abd Allāh b. 'Umar (d. 73/692)	**None**
	(2) Abū Hurayra (d. 58/678)	(1) 'Abd Allāh b. al-Zubayr (d. 73/692)	
	(3) Shaqīq b. Salama (d. 82/701)	(1) Mujāhid b. Jabr (d. c 100 or 104/718 or 722)	
	(5) Ibrāhīm al-Nakha'ī (d. 96/714)	(1) Ṭawūs b. Kaysān (d. 106/724)	
	(1) Ḥasan al-Baṣrī (d. 110/728)	(1) 'Aṭā' b. Abī Rabāḥ (d. 115/733)	
	(1) Ṭalḥa b. Muṣarrif b. 'Amr /'Ubayd (d. 113/731)	(1) Zayd b. 'Alī b. al-Ḥusayn (d. 122/740)	
	(4) Ḥammād b. Abī Sulaymān (d. 119/737)	(3) 'Abd Allāh b. Ḥasan b. al-Ḥasan (d. 145/763)	
		(2) Muḥammad b. 'Abd Allāh b. al-Ḥasan (d. 145/763)	
		(1) 'Abd Allāh b. Mūsā b. 'Abd Allāh (d. 247/861)	
		(1) Aḥmad b. 'Īsā b. 'Abd Allāh (d. before 220/835)	
Shared	¥ (5) Muḥammad (d. 11/632)	¥ (6) Muḥammad (d. 11/632)	¥ (6) Muḥammad (d. 11/632)
	¥ (1) Muḥammad al-Bāqir (d. 117/735)	¥ (3) Muḥammad al-Bāqir (d. 117/735)	¥ (4) Muḥammad al-Bāqir (d. 117/735)
	ZS (5) 'Umar b. al-Khaṭṭāb (d. 23/644)	**ZS** (1) 'Umar b. al-Khaṭṭāb (d.23/644)	
	ZS (1) 'Ammār b. Yāsir b. 'Āmir (d. 37/657)	**ZS** (1) 'Ammār b. Yāsir b. 'Āmir (d. 37/657)	
	ZS (5) 'Alī b. Abī Ṭālib (d. 40/661)	**ZS** (9) 'Alī b. Abī Ṭālib (d. 40/661)	
	ZS (7) 'Abd Allāh b. 'Abbās (d. 68/688)	**ZS** (4) 'Abd Allāh b. 'Abbās (d. 68/688)	
	ZS (5) Sa'īd b. Jubayr (d. 95/713)	**ZS** (4) Sa'īd b. Jubayr (d. 95/713)	
	ZS (3) Ḥakam b. 'Utayba (d. 113/731)	**ZS** (2) Ḥakam b. 'Utayba (d. 113/731)	
	ZS (3) 'Amr b. 'Abd Allāh b. 'Alī (d. 127/745)	**ZS** (1) 'Amr b. 'Abd Allāh b. 'Alī/'Ubayd (d. 127/745)	
		ZI (2) 'Alī al-Sajjād (d. 94/712)	**ZI** (1) 'Alī al-Sajjād (d. 94/712)
		ZI (1) Ja'far al-Ṣādiq (d. 148/765)	**ZI** (28) Ja'far al-Ṣādiq (d. 148/765)

Note: Intersections between all three groups are denoted by the symbol "**¥**." Intersections between the Zaydīs and Imāmīs are denoted by the symbol "**ZI**." Intersections between Sunnīs and Zaydīs are denoted by "**ZS**." The raw data can be accessed via www.najamhaider.com/originsoftheshia

in some of these traditions, the opinions of early transmitters are preserved alongside their recollections of the Prophet or Abū Bakr. As a result of this multiplicity of authorities in a single text, the total number of accounts ascribed to each sectarian group does not necessarily add up to thirty-four.

Three important conclusions can be drawn from the data in Table 3.3. First, there is no substantive overlap between the Imāmīs and the Sunnīs. Imāmī traditions rely heavily on the opinions of their contemporary 2nd/8th century Imāms (al-Sajjād, al-Bāqir and al-Ṣādiq), whereas Sunnī accounts draw on a wide range of non-ʿAlids, including important early Companions (Abū Bakr, ʿUmar b. al-Khaṭṭāb) and prominent jurists (Saʿīd b. Jubayr, Shaqīq b. Salama – d. 82/701, Ibrāhīm al-Nakhaʿī). Although al-Bāqir appears in Sunnī traditions, he is depicted as an advocate of the silent *basmala*, in direct opposition to Imāmī practice.[137] It is likely that this isolated Sunnī tradition was used by Kūfan supporters of the silent *basmala* against their largely (though not exclusively) Shīʿī opponents. It is also significant that this particular text is not found in any of the Imāmī collections even though there are cases where deviant traditions (by Imāmī standards) are preserved (and explained away) by Imāmī jurists.[138] Overall, there is a near-total lack of overlap between the Imāmīs and the Sunnīs in the area of authorities.

Second, Table 3.3 indicates a small but significant intersection between the Imāmīs and the Zaydīs. In contrast to the Imāmīs who exclusively revere a specific line of ʿAlids, Zaydī traditions are characterized by a general veneration of ʿAlids. The effects of this difference are evident in a numerical comparison of each sect's traditions. The Kūfan Imāmīs cite either al-Bāqir or al-Ṣādiq in 82 percent (28/34) of their accounts. The Zaydīs, by contrast, include these two Imāms among a litany of other ʿAlids, none of which are mentioned in more than three traditions. In five cases, the opinion of an ʿAlid authority is only preserved in a single Zaydī tradition.

a tradition in which Anas b. Mālik states that the Prophet recited audibly is treated as a reflection of Anas' view, as well as, that of the Prophet. This is not to say that these traditions are not authentic; it is entirely possible that a number of them reach back to the time of the Prophet and the early caliphates. In this study, however, I am more concerned with the 2nd/8th-century Muslim world and Kūfa in particular. The "original" practice of the Prophet and the caliphs is not nearly as important as the views preserved in city-based law schools which drew primarily on the authority of Companions and Successors.

137 *MIAS*, 1:361 – 4147.

138 For examples, see *ṬT*, 2:68 – 15 and 2:288 – 12; *ṬI*, 1:358 – 6; *WS*, 6:62 – 7352.

Third (and most significantly), there is a strong overlap between Sunnī and Zaydī traditions prior to 127/745 and an equally strong divergence after 127/745. A startling 50 percent (7/14) of Zaydī authorities who lived before 127/745 are mentioned in Sunnī traditions.[139] This number, however, underestimates the scope of the intersection since five (of the seven) remaining Zaydī authorities are frequently referenced in Sunnī traditions from *outside* Kūfa. 'Aṭā b. Abī Rabāḥ, Ṭawūs b. Kaysān (d. 106 or 110/724 or 728), and Mujāhid b. Jabr (d. 100 or 104/718 or 722) are standard Sunnī authorities in Meccan accounts, while 'Abd Allāh b. 'Umar and 'Abd Allāh b. al-Zubayr (d. 73/692) are found in Sunnī traditions from Baṣra and Medina.[140] The end result is remarkable. Nearly every figure cited by the Zaydī traditions from the period preceding 127/745 is regularly found in Sunnī *ḥadīth* collections. This consists of both Companions ('Umar b. al-Khaṭṭāb, 'Ammār b. Yāsir – d. 37/657, 'Alī b. Abī Ṭālib, 'Abd Allāh b. 'Abbās) and prominent jurists (Ḥakam b. 'Utayba[141] – d. 113/731, Sa'īd b. Jubayr, 'Amr b. 'Abd Allāh b. 'Alī[142] – d. 127/745). The link falls apart after 127/745 as the Zaydīs begin relying exclusively on Kūfan and Medinan 'Alids. This change, however, does not bring the Zaydīs any closer to the Imāmīs because five of the six post-127/745 'Alids mentioned in Zaydī traditions do not appear in Imāmī *basmala* traditions at all.[143]

139 This does not include the Prophet and 'Umar b. al-Khaṭṭāb.

140 For 'Aṭā' b. Abī Rabāḥ, see *MAR*, 2:59 – 2618. For Ṭawūs b. Kaysān, see *MIAS*, 1:361 – 4153; *MAR*, 2:59 – 2615. For Mujāhid b. Jabr, see *MAR*, 2:60 – 2621; *MIAS*, 1:361 – 4153. For 'Abd Allāh b. al-Zubayr, see the Baṣran traditions in *MIAS*, 1:361 – 4154 and 1:362–4156; *SKB*, 2:71 – 2406 and 2407. For 'Abd Allāh b. 'Umar, see the Medinan and Baṣran traditions in *MIAS*, 1:362 – 4155; *MAR*, 2:58 – 2610; *SKB*, 2:70 – 2402 and 2:71 – 2404.

141 Madelung describes Ḥakam b. 'Utayba as one of the Kūfan chiefs of the Batriyya in the time of al-Bāqir (*EI*[2] supplement, s.v. Batriyya (Madelung)).

142 The Kūfan jurist 'Amr b. 'Abd Allāh b. 'Alī is a figure of disputed sectarian affiliation. The Imāmī *rijāl* literature considers him a companion of al-Ṣādiq with no suggestion of Sunnī tendencies (al-Tustarī, *Qāmūs*, 8:111). The Sunnī *rijāl* literature changes his grandfather's name to 'Ubayd (the Imāmī version is also listed as a possibility) and acclaims his reliability as a transmitter (al-Mizzī, *Tahdhīb*, 22:102). The Zaydīs also claim him as one of their own (al-Ṣan'ānī, *Ra'b*, 3:1689). In 'Amr b. 'Abd Allāh, we have a Kūfan on the boundary between two communities (Sunnī and Shī'ī) in a period characterized by the growth of sectarianism. Figures of this type are discussed in Chapter 7.

143 In addition to Zayd b. 'Alī, these include the 'Alid rebel Muḥammad al-Nafs al-Zakiyya and his father 'Abd Allāh b. al-Ḥasan b. al-Ḥasan b. 'Alī b. Abī Ṭālib (d. 145/763), along with 'Abd Allāh b. Mūsā b. 'Abd Allāh b. al-Ḥasan (d. 247/861) and Aḥmad b. 'Īsā b. 'Abd Allāh b. al-Ḥasan (d. early 3rd/9th century). For 'Abd Allāh b. Mūsā, see *DIQ*, Index 259; al-Tustarī, *Rijāl*, 6:630; al-Ṣan'ānī, *Ra'b*, 3:1689. For Aḥmad b. 'Īsā b. 'Abd Allāh, see al-Ṣan'ānī, *Ra'b*, 3:1708.

Overall, the data attests to Imāmī independence. Imāmī traditions do not exhibit any substantive overlap with Sunnī traditions and only intersect with those of the Zaydīs on a limited number of historically important ʿAlids. By contrast, the results point to a problem in the classical narrative of the origins of Zaydism. While it is clear that some type of change occurred within Zaydism in the mid 2nd/8th century, there is little evidence for the merging of Batrīs and Jārūdīs. Early Zaydī traditions exhibit *exclusively* Batrī characteristics through their citation of the legal opinions of Companions and non-ʿAlid jurists. The situation appears to change in the mid 2nd/8th century with a decidedly Jārūdī shift towards a distinct set of ʿAlid legal authorities.

Chains and Transmitters

Our second comparison focuses on transmitters, both in isolation and as part of extended chains of transmission (shared links). The central concern in this section is determining the extent to which different sects relied on the same pool of individuals for the transmission of legal information.[144] Instances of shared links are especially significant as they suggest that two sectarian groups agreed not only regarding a specific transmitter's veracity but his/her intellectual affiliations as well.[145] As in the previous section, we are foremost interested in signs of the crystallization of Imāmī and Zaydī identity.

Tables 3.4a and 3.4b detail the transmitters and links shared between the Sunnī, Zaydī, and Imāmī traditions. The first (Table 3.4a) lists individual transmitters cited in isolation in chains of transmission by more than one sectarian community. As mentioned in Chapter 2, a large number of common transmitters would suggest a degree of overlap while a complete absence would intimate separation. The second (Table 3.4b) focuses on strings of shared transmitters that imply an even greater degree of overlap between two communities. Divergences in these shared links also allow us to infer the point when groups may have begun to develop independent identities.

According to Tables 3.4a and 3.4b, Imāmī traditions are unique with respect to both their transmitters and their *isnād*s. The intersection between the Imāmīs and the Sunnīs is limited to the Kūfan Jābir b. Yazīd

[144] In the following analysis, the sectarian allegiances of specific transmitters are not as important as the degree to which sects rely on identical *isnād*s and common transmitters. Saʿīd b. Jubayr's appearance in the Sunnī and Zaydī traditions, for example, is far more significant than his status as a 'Sunnī' or 'Zaydī' because it suggests a link between the two communities.

[145] For a detailed discussion of the premises and method employed in this section, see Chapter 2.

TABLE 3.4a. *Single Transmitters (Basmala)*

	Transmitters in Isolation	Traditions
Sunnī/Zaydī	ʿĀṣim b. Bahdala (d. 127/745)*	2 Sunnī (095, 122) 2 Zaydī (101, 103)
	ʿAmr b. ʿAbd Allāh b. ʿAlī (ʿUbayd) (d. 127/745)	1 Sunnī (074) 3 Zaydī (080, 081, 169)
	Saʿīd b. Marzubān (d. 140/758)	1 Sunnī (074) 3 Zaydī (080, 081, 169)
	Sharīk b. ʿAbd Allāh (d. 177/793)	1 Sunnī (074) 2 Zaydī (101, 103)
	Muʿtamar b. Sulaymān b. Ṭarkhān (d. 187/804)*	3 Sunnī (006, 025, 026) 2 Zaydī (110, 141)
	Yūnus b. Bukayr b. Wāṣil (d. 199/814)	1 Sunnī (024) 1 Zaydī (219)
Zaydī/Imāmī	Muḥammad al-Bāqir (d. 117/735)	4 Zaydī (020, 021, 031, 216) 1 Imāmī (222)
	Jaʿfar al-Ṣādiq (d. 148/765)	2 Zaydī (020, 021, 031, 216) 3 Imāmī (019, 206, 226)
	ʿAmr b. Shimr (d. 157/774)	1 Zaydī (027) 1 Imāmī (226)
Sunnī/Imāmī	Jābir b. Yazīd al-Juʿfī (d. 128/746)	1 Sunnī (156) 1 Imāmī (224)

* See also Shared Links in Table 3.4b. For complete references corresponding to each numbered tradition, see www.najamhaider.com/originsoftheshia

al-Juʿfī (d. 128/746), a distinguished (and prolific) Kūfan traditionist scholar who eventually became a disciple of al-Bāqir and al-Ṣādiq and adopted "extremist" beliefs.[146] Given the absence of even a single additional shared transmitter and the complete lack of shared links, the data suggests a clear separation between Sunnī and Imāmī traditions.

The intersection between the Imāmīs and the Zaydīs is more substantial and consists of three single links: al-Bāqir, al-Ṣādiq, and ʿAmr b. Shimr (d. 157/774). Both the Zaydīs and the Imāmīs rely on al-Bāqir and al-Ṣādiq as transmitters[147] in traditions that preserve the opinions of

[146] See *EI*² supplement, s.v. Jābir al-Juʿfī (Madelung); and, especially, Modarressi, *Tradition*, 86–103.

[147] Here, I am not including traditions in which each sect uses the two ʿAlids as legal authorities, as that issue was discussed in the previous section. It should be noted, however, that al-Bāqir and al-Ṣādiq are primarily employed by the Imāmīs as authority figures as opposed to transmitters.

TABLE 3.4b. *Shared Links (Basmala)*

	Shared Links	Traditions
<u>Sunnī/Zaydī</u>		
#1	ʿUmar b. Dharr b. ʿAbd Allāh (d. 153/770) | Dharr b. ʿAbd Allāh b. Zurārā (d. early 2nd/8th c) | Saʿīd b. ʿAbd al-Raḥmān b. Abzā (d. late 1st/7th c) | ʿAbd al-Raḥmān b. Abzā (d. mid to late 1st/7th c) | ʿUmar b. al-Khaṭṭāb (d. 23/644)	1 Sunnī (069) 1 Zaydī (072)
#2	ʿUmar b. Dharr b. ʿAbd Allāh (d. 153/770) | Dharr b. ʿAbd Allāh b. Zurārā (d. early 2nd/8th c) | Saʿīd b. ʿAbd al-Raḥmān b. Abzā (d. late 1st/7th c)	1 Sunnī (071) The same Zaydī (072) as in Table 3.4a
#3	Asbāṭ b. Naṣr (d. 180/796) | Ismāʿīl b. ʿAbd al-Raḥmān b. Abī Karīma (d. 127/745) | ʿAbd al-Khayr b. Yazīd (late 1st/7th c) | ʿAlī b. Abī Ṭālib (d. 40/661)	1 Sunnī (088) 1 Zaydī (221)

#4	‘Āṣim b. Bahdala (d. 127/745) | Sa‘īd b. Jubayr (d. 95/713) | ‘Abd Allāh b. ‘Abbās (d. 68/688)	1 Sunnī (105) 2 Zaydī (101, 103)
#5	Sa‘īd b. Jubayr (d. 95/713) | ‘Abd Allāh b. ‘Abbās (d. 68/688)	The same Sunnī (105) as in Table 3.4a 1 Zaydī (104)
#6	‘Āṣim b. Bahdala (d. 127/745) | Sa‘īd b. Jubayr (d. 95/713)	2 Sunnī (130, 131) The same 2 Zaydī (101, 103) as in Table 3.4a
#7	Mu‘tamar b. Sulaymān b. Ṭarkhān (d. 187/804) | Layth b. Abī Sulaym (Ayman) (d. 133–43/751–61)	1 Sunnī (151) 1 Zaydī (141)
#8	Hushaym b. Bashīr (d. 181/797) | Sa‘īd b. Marzubān (d. 140/758)	1 Sunnī (093) 1 Zaydī (100)
Zaydī/Imāmī	**None**	**None**
Sunnī/Imāmī	**None**	**None**

Note: For complete references corresponding to each numbered tradition, see www.najamhaider.com/originsoftheshia

Muḥammad and 'Alī through broken chains of transmission. Although this highlights a common Imāmī and Zaydī veneration of 'Alids, its value in establishing an overlap between the two groups is minimal. The lone remaining link is the Kūfan 'Amr b. Shimr al-Ju'fī, a moderate Shī'a associated with the aforementioned Jābir al-Ju'fī. The case of 'Amr (like that of Jābir) exposes the ease with which some individuals could cross early communal boundaries.[148] It does not, however, provide definitive (or even probable) proof of an intersection between the Zaydīs and the Imāmīs, especially given the lack of a single shared link.

The Zaydī and Sunnī texts exhibit a significant overlap through (1) eight shared links[149] spread across 26 percent (9/34) of the Sunnī and 24 percent (8/34) of the Zaydī accounts and (2) six common transmitters extending through the end of the 2nd/8th century. The shared links are long, often stretching from the Prophet or a Companion into the middle of the 2nd/8th century. Shared link #1, for example, transmits an opinion from 'Umar through 'Abd al-Raḥmān b. Abzā, Sa'īd b. 'Abd al-Raḥmān b. Abzā and Dharr b. 'Abd Allāh b. Zurārā (d. early 2nd/8th century) before splitting up in the mid 2nd/8th century after 'Umar b. Dharr b. 'Abd Allāh (d. 153/770). No shared links extend beyond 187/804 and a majority (5/8) terminate prior to 153/770. The common transmitters yield similar results, with half pre-dating 140/758 and the last (Yūnus b. Bukayr) ending in 247/861. Overall, the data provides strong evidence for a substantial long-term overlap between the Sunnīs and the Zaydīs that survived into the mid 2nd/8th century.

The picture that emerges from the comparison of transmitters and chains aligns with that of the previous section. The data supports the existence of a clearly demarcated Imāmī communal identity in the early 2nd/8th century. The Imāmī traditions generally rely on the opinions of their Imāms related by a distinctive pool of transmitters. The results also indicate that the early portions of Zaydī texts are predominantly Batrī in tenor, as reflected in their overlap with traditions circulating in a proto-Sunnī milieu. In the middle of 2nd/8th century, the Zaydī traditions change in a fundamental manner, decreasing their reliance on transmitters (and chains of transmission) routinely found in proto-Sunnī Kūfan collections in favor of distinctive transmitters generally identified as Zaydī. It is only at this point – in the mid to late 2nd/8th century – that we begin to observe a noticeable Jārūdī presence in Zaydī *isnāds*.

148 Modarressi, *Tradition*, 204–5.

149 This number includes shared links that are subsets of larger chains. In other words, link #2 is counted as an independent link even though it is a subset of a larger chain (link #1). This is done because the sublink also occurs in a different set of traditions.

Narrative Style

Whereas the first two comparisons dealt with individual authorities and *isnāds*/transmitters, our final comparison focuses on narrative type. In other words, what styles do traditions employ in presenting information? Are distinct literary forms particular to a given sect? And if sects share styles, what does this tell us about their potential intersections? Do they overlap in a consistent and continuous manner, or do they diverge after a certain point? Table 3.5 organizes the 102 Kūfan traditions on the basis of six of the eight narrative styles discussed in Chapter 2.

In Table 3.5, the Imāmīs are distinguished by their extensive use of the question-and-answer and exegetic narrative types, and the absence of exemplary statements. While only 15 percent of Sunnī and 3 percent of Zaydī traditions are in the form of questions, 35 percent of the Imāmī accounts depict disciples asking an Imām to confirm or reject the audible *basmala*. Imāmī traditions are also unique in their use of exegesis (18 percent), regularly referencing Q17:46 as a proof text for the validity of the audible *basmala*. As a whole, Imāmī narrative structure suggests little overlap with the Sunnīs and only a limited intersection with the Zaydīs.

Both the Zaydīs and Imāmīs make use of eyewitness reports, which constitute 35 percent of Imāmī and 47 percent of Zaydī traditions. The authorities who appear in these traditions, however, are invariably ʿAlids with Imāmī traditions preserving eyewitness accounts of al-Ṣādiq's prayer and Zaydī traditions focusing on a variety of ʿAlids such as Zayd b. ʿAlī and Muḥammad al-Nafs al-Zakiyya. In fact, every Zaydī tradition which mentions an authority that died after 127/745 is in the eyewitness form, and all but one of these figures is an ʿAlid. Rather than supporting the possibility of an *early* interaction between the two groups, these results suggest the prevalence of a common narrative style for the preservation of ʿAlid opinions, which the Zaydīs only adopted in the mid to late 2nd/8th century.

Finally, Table 3.5 reveals a strong overlap between Sunnī (41 percent) and Zaydī (44 percent) accounts through their common use of the exemplary narrative style. In the Sunnī case, such accounts are unexceptional and cite a wide range of authorities scattered throughout the 1st/7th and 2nd/8th century. Zaydī exemplary accounts, by contrast, exhibit two distinctive features. First, they only mention those authorities the Zaydīs share with the Sunnīs; not a single prominent ʿAlid (other than ʿAlī) is mentioned in an exemplary tradition. Second, every figure preserved by the Zaydīs in the exemplary form died prior to the mid 2nd/8th century.

TABLE 3.5. *Narrative Style (Basmala)*

	Sunnī		Zaydī		Imāmī	
Question/Answer	088	154	221*		157	181
	149	155			162	192
	153				175	195
					176	200*
					177	212*
					178	225*
Eyewitness Accounts	068	122	027	169	174	193
	070	129	028	170	179	194
	071	151	072	171	180	196
	085		080	172	182	197
			086	173	183	199
			119	202	189	227
			133	204		
			166	211		
Direct Quotes	105	136	021	216	128	215
	106	137			198	224*
	134	138				
	135	156				
Exemplary Statements	006	075	020	103	191	206
	024	076	031	104		
	025	093	079	110		
	026	095	081	111		
	038	130	083	141		
	069	131	084	152		
	074	132	100	219		
			101			
Written Correspondence	None		None		158	
Sign/List Traditions	None		None		200*	224*
Exegesis	None		221		019	222
					200*	225*
					212*	226
Overall	Q/A – 15% Eyewitness – 21% Direct – 24% Exemplary – 41% Written – 0% Lists/Signs – 0% Exegesis – 0%		Q/A – 3% Eyewitness – 47% Direct – 6% Exemplary – 44% Written – 0% Lists/Signs – 0% Exegesis – 3%		Q/A – 35% Eyewitness – 35% Direct – 12% Exemplary – 6% Written – 3% Lists/Signs – 6% Exegesis – 18%	

* Denotes traditions that fall into more than one category. This also explains why the percentages do not always add up to 100, especially in the case of the Imāmīs. For complete references corresponding to each numbered tradition, see www.najamhaider.com/originsoftheshia

As mentioned above, Zaydī traditions that quote 'Alids from the middle of the 2nd/8th century (e.g., 'Abd Allāh b. Mūsā b. 'Abd Allāh b. al-Ḥasan – d. 247/861) employ a narrative style (i.e., eyewitness reports) characteristic of Imāmī accounts. Once again, the middle 2nd/8th century seems to signal a transformation in Zaydī traditions from a narrative style in line with Sunnī traditions (i.e., exemplary statements) to one more congruent with contemporaneous Shī'ī (and particularly Imāmī) preferences.

Overall, the narrative style comparisons agree with the results from the two previous sections. The Imāmīs are distinguished from the Sunnīs and the Zaydīs in two important ways: (1) they restrict themselves to the opinions of a single 'Alid line of descent through (2) question-and-answer and exegetic styles rarely found in the Sunnī or Zaydī *basmala* traditions. The intersection between Sunnī and Zaydī narrative types is strongest for authorities from the 1st/7th century and falls off almost completely in the early 2nd/8th century. Traditions of this type exhibit a Batrī influence in that they align with generic proto-Sunnī Kūfan styles and accept the veracity of non-'Alid Sunnī authorities. In the course of the 2nd/8th century, however, the Zaydīs adopt a different narrative technique for relating the views of strictly 'Alid authorities. These latter texts are best characterized as Jārūdī.

CONCLUSION

The case study presented in this chapter is the first of three designed to test the narratives for the emergence of sectarian identity. The chapter began with a broad survey of the *basmala* issue, highlighting the different approaches (and conclusions) articulated by different law schools. The raw materials for each school's position consisted of ritual law traditions gathered together in large comprehensive collections. The second part of the chapter centered on these traditions, operating on the premise (detailed in Chapter 2) that they were accurately recorded (or in circulation) as early as the 2nd/8th century. In the first step of the analysis, 102 Kūfan traditions were separated from a larger corpus of 233 texts on the basis of the geographical associations of their 2nd/8th century transmitters. In the second, Kūfan traditions preserved by each of the sectarian communities were compared on the basis of their authorities, chains of transmission, and narrative style.

Before proceeding to the second case study in Chapter 4, it may be useful to examine the implications of our results for the classical sectarian narratives. Recall that the heresiographical and historical sources depict the Imāmī community as an independent entity in the early 2nd/8th century.

They also claim that Zaydism emerged in the aftermath of the 122/740 revolt of Zayd b. ʿAlī through the merging of Batrī and Jārūdī Shīʿism. The former aligned in many respects with the proto-Sunnīs whereas the latter bore a resemblance to the Imāmīs. In time, the tensions between these factions erupted into a power struggle that ultimately resulted in Jārūdī dominance. Recall also that the potential skepticism surrounding these narratives stemmed from the noncontemporaneous nature of their sources.

Our tentative findings offer mixed support to the sectarian narratives. They seem to corroborate the presence of an independent Imāmī communal identity in the early 2nd/8th century. Imāmī traditions are characterized by the use of unique authority figures transmitted through independent *isnād*s in distinctive narrative styles.[150] By contrast, they appear to contradict some fundamental aspects of the narrative of early Zaydism. First and foremost, the data does not support the view that early Zaydism was an aggregate of Batrism and Jārūdism. Rather, it suggests that early Zaydīs were predominantly (if not overwhelmingly) Batrī, and Jārūdīs only emerged gradually over the course of the 2nd/8th century. Second, there is no indication of an internal struggle between Batrī and Jārūdī Zaydīs. In particular, if Zaydism only became Jārūdī in the 3rd/9th century,[151] we would expect to find a persistence of Batrī influence through the 2nd/8th century literature. Instead, there is a clear decline in Batrī traditions after the mid-2nd/8th century at the expense of Jārūdī traditions, which restrict legal authority to prominent ʿAlids whose opinions are transmitted through distinctive *isnād*s and narrative styles. If this process was the result of a Zaydī civil war, we would expect the victors (the Jārūdīs) to eliminate (or at least try to eliminate) the traces of their defeated Batrī opponents embodied in traditions preserving the opinions of ʿUmar b. al-Khaṭṭāb and other non-ʿAlid jurists. But these Batrī accounts survive and, in many cases, dominate the collections of prominent Jārūdīs such as Aḥmad b. ʿĪsā. It remains to be seen whether these results are repeated in the final two case studies.

150 The evidence from the comparison of narrative style was less decisive but it serves to reinforce the thesis of a separation between the Imāmīs and the Sunnīs. The mild overlap between Imāmī and Zaydī narrative style was insignificant in relation to the large differences in other areas of comparison and restricted to the end of the 2nd/8th century when the Zaydīs had moved closer to the Imāmīs on a number of issues.

151 This is implied in the classical narrative that depicts a struggle between the initial Batrī and Jārūdī constituents of Zaydism resulting in a 3rd/9th-century Jārūdī victory. For more on this narrative, see Chapter 1.

4

Curses and Invocations

The Qunūt in the Ritual Prayer

At a number of points in the course of his life, the sources depict the Prophet as both offering prayers for individuals/tribes by name and cursing them for perceived betrayals or transgressions. In many cases, these invocations/curses were integrated into the daily prayer at a point between the Qur'ānic recitation and the *sajda* (prostration) in a gesture referred to as the *qunūt*.[1] This much is known and accepted by each of the Islamic law schools under consideration. The problem arises in determining whether the Prophet's actions were meant as an example for future generations or whether they were restricted to a particular historical moment. As with the *basmala*, the issue is tied to the very integrity of the prayer that serves as a cornerstone of Muslim ritual life.

This chapter centers on the *qunūt*, which is defined as either an invocation to God (often on behalf of a group of people) or a curse against an enemy recited in the course of the ritual prayer. Specifically, it focuses on the performance of the *qunūt* in the five mandatory daily prayers and the *witr* prayer (performed between *'ishā'* and *fajr*).[2] Two notable absences in this discussion are the Friday prayer, and the group/congregational prayer, both of which are governed by idiosyncratic legal rules.[3] The logic behind the inclusion of *witr*, but not of the other supererogatory prayers,

[1] For a very basic overview of the *qunūt*, see *EI*², s.v. Qunūt (A. J. Wensinck). For an account of the *qunūt*'s origins (also discussed below), see Kister, "Expedition," 337–57.

[2] There is a significant debate concerning the length and the appropriate time for *witr* but a detailed discussion of these issues is peripheral to this study.

[3] Each of these prayers has generated an enormous mass of legal literature that cannot practically be covered in the current work given basic space constraints.

lies in the controversy surrounding its status[4] and its absolute centrality in juristic discussions of the *qunūt*.

As in the previous chapter, this chapter is divided into two sections. The first provides a legal survey of the views of six prominent Sunnī and Shī'ī law schools regarding the *qunūt*. The second applies the methodology detailed in Chapter 2 to the Kūfan *qunūt* traditions. The chapter ends by appraising the degree to which the results of the analysis align with the sectarian narratives outlined in Chapter 1.

THE JURISTIC CONTEXT

The legal debate over the *qunūt* involves two primary and three secondary issues. The primary questions concern (1) the identity of prayers for which the *qunūt* is mandatory and (2) its wording and content. Identifying the prayers is complicated by opinions that limit the *qunūt* to a specific time of the year (i.e., the second half of Ramaḍān). The juristic discourse surrounding these two issues is Qur'ānic in nature, concentrating on the legal implications of Q3:128[5] and the permissibility of inserting non-Qur'ānic elements (invocations and curses) into the obligatory prayers. The secondary questions focus on (3) practical details such as the location of the *qunūt* in the prayer (before vs. after the *rak'a*[6]), (4) the raising of the hands during the *qunūt*, and (5) the prefacing of the *qunūt* with a *takbīr* (recitation of the phrase "God is the Greatest"). Arguments about these matters draw almost entirely on competing Prophetic traditions and juristic opinions. Whereas each legal school (with the exception of the Zaydīs) came to an internal consensus regarding the primary issues, secondary issues remained problematic and unresolved well into the postformative period.

As in Chapter 3, the section below discusses the works of one or two representative jurists from each of the selected law schools. This is

4 There was a view that considered *witr* a mandatory sixth prayer. This is suggested in the exegesis of Q2:238 (for text, see footnote 67 in this chapter) by a number of scholars including the Ḥanafī al-Jaṣṣāṣ (*Aḥkām*, 1:443) and the Mālikī al-Qurṭubī (*al-Jāmi'*, 3:213). The Ḥanafīs still view the *witr* prayer as *wājib*.

5 Q3:128 – "You have no concern in the affair whether He relent toward them or punish them; for they are evil-doers."

6 The *rak'a* is the point in prayer after the recitation when the worshipper bends down with his/her hands placed on the knees. There is a general consensus that he/she must then return to a standing position and pause before proceeding to the *sajda* (prostration). The issue at stake here is whether the *qunūt* is inserted after the recitation or before the *sajda* when the worshipper is in an upright position.

intended to convey the general tenor of their legal discourse; it is not meant to be exhaustive in scope. There were often significant differences among jurists of the same school both in the form and substance of their arguments.

The Ḥanafīs

The Ḥanafīs categorically reject the *qunūt* for all the obligatory prayers but consider it a required element of the *witr* prayer. This opinion is based on a broad interpretation of Q3:128 in which God reprimands the Prophet for his cursing of individuals by name. Secondary issues are addressed through traditions (on the authority of the Prophet and the Companions) and the opinions of prominent jurists. The broad outlines of the school's position were first articulated by Muḥammad al-Shaybānī and then expounded upon by Aḥmad b. Muḥammad al-Ṭaḥāwī (d. 321/933).

In his *Kitāb al-āthār*, al-Shaybānī provides the basic framework for subsequent Ḥanafī discussions of the *qunūt*.[7] He affirms the obligatory status of the *witr qunūt*[8] throughout the year and places it after the recitation and before the *rak'a*.[9] The raising of the hands is categorically rejected and the worshipper is instructed to preface the *qunūt* with a *takbīr*.[10] This is crucial as a means of differentiating the Qur'ānic recitation (considered *farḍ*) from the *qunūt* (considered *wājib*).[11] Although al-Shaybānī acknowledges the Prophet's use of the *fajr qunūt* in cursing the Banū Sulaym and the Banū 'Āmir after the treacherous 4/626 ambush of a delegation of Muslim missionaries at a location identified as Bi'r Ma'ūna,[12] he argues that the practice was abrogated by the revelation

[7] *KAS I*, 1:569–602.

[8] My use of term "*witr qunūt*" and similar phrases is not technical, and the syntax is not Arabic. The term is shorthand for "*qunūt* in the *witr* prayer," which can become a cumbersome literary construct in the course of a long discussion.

[9] *KAS I*, 1:578 and 585. For the traditions, see *KAS I*, 1:569 – 211 and 1:579 – 212.

[10] *KAS I*, 1:578 and 585. For the tradition, see *KAS I*, 1:579 – 212.

[11] The Ḥanafīs differentiate between *farḍ* and *wājib* on the basis of certainty. Whereas *farḍ* implies certain proof on the basis of clear textual evidence, *wājib* connotes less certainty and the lack of unambiguous textual support. The legal weight of the terms is equal in that, in both cases, the act is deemed obligatory.

[12] *KAS I*, 1:593. This episode appears repeatedly in legal discussion regarding the *qunūt*. Upon learning of the killings, the Prophet is said to have either cursed both tribes collectively or individuals from within each tribe for thirty to forty days before receiving a divine injunction against the practice. Traditions that cite this incident will subsequently be referred to as "Bi'r Ma'ūna traditions." For more on the incident itself, see al-Ṭabarī, *Tārīkh*, 2:219–23.

of Q3:128 (see later in the chapter for more details).[13] The *qunūt* was (illegally) reinstated during the first civil war between ʿAlī in Kūfa and Muʿāwiya in Syria.[14] This final statement suggests that the *fajr qunūt* was still practiced in Kūfa in the mid-2nd/8th century and had to be explained in historical terms. It should also be noted that al-Shaybānī ascribes all of these opinions to Abū Ḥanīfa, the eponymous founder of the Ḥanafī legal school.

In *Sharḥ maʿānī al-āthār*, al-Ṭaḥāwī utilizes a wide range of textual evidence to reinforce most of al-Shaybānī's conclusions.[15] His basic approach consists of listing individual traditions (seventy-six in all) pertaining to the *qunūt* and systematically dismissing those which disagree with the Ḥanafī stance. The discussion begins with thirty traditions that claim that the Prophet cursed his enemies in the *qunūt* during the *fajr*, *maghrib*, and *ʿishāʾ* prayers.[16] Although he affirms the soundness of these accounts, al-Ṭaḥāwī argues that they predate the revelation of Q3:128, which prohibited cursing and (by extension) the *qunūt* in all obligatory prayers.[17] Even though the exact historical context of the verse's revelation is contested, there is a general consensus across all the Sunnī legal schools that it descended after the Prophet cursed or resolved to curse a group of his opponents.[18] The verse was a clear injunction against the

[13] This is attested to in a number of traditions. See *KAS I*, 1:590 – 214 (on the authority of ʿAbd Allāh b. ʿUmar), 1:595 – 216 (on the authority of ʿUmar), 1:589 – 213 (on the authority of ʿAbd Allāh b. Masʿūd), and 1:593 – 215 (on the authority of the Prophet and Abū Bakr). It is also significant that al-Shaybānī's version of Mālik's *Muwaṭṭaʾ* includes a tradition that condemns the *fajr qunūt* and which is described as the view of Abū Ḥanīfa (Mālik b. Anas, *Muwaṭṭaʾ* (1967), 1:91).

[14] See *KAS I*, 1:595 – 216, where the view that the *fajr qunūt* was an innovation from the civil war is identified as the "doctrine of Abū Ḥanīfa." See also *KAS I*, 1:590.

[15] al-Ṭaḥāwī, *Sharḥ*, 1:241–54. The issue is also discussed with considerable less detail in al-Ṭaḥāwī, *Mukhtaṣar*, 28.

[16] This is an obvious reference to the massacre at Biʾr Maʿūna. It would be immensely tedious with little benefit to cite a source reference for each of the seventy-six traditions. Instead, I will attempt to summarize their content (without citation) and focus on the broader features of al-Ṭaḥāwī's criticism.

[17] al-Ṭaḥāwī, *Sharḥ*, 1:245.

[18] The dominant opinion among Muslim exegetes links the revelation of the verse to the Battle of Uḥud (4/627), which marked the first military defeat for the young Muslim community. In the course of the fighting, the Muslim army failed to follow orders and retreated in disarray after the Prophet received a head wound. The commentators disagree as to whether the Prophet's anger was directed against those who had fled the battlefield or his Meccan Qurashī enemies. There is also a difference of opinion as to whether he actually carried out the cursing that prompted the revelation of the verse, or whether he intended to curse and was preempted by the revelation of the verse. For specific discussions, see al-Ṭabarī, *Tafsīr*, 2:384–5; al-Samarqandī, *Tafsīr*, 1:297; al-Qurṭubī, *al-Jāmiʿ*, 4:199–201; and al-Ṭabrisī, *Majmaʿ* (1958), 2:462–4.

practice but its legal scope was ambiguous. Did it abrogate one historically specific act of cursing, or did it apply to the performance of the *qunūt* as a whole?[19] The Ḥanafīs clearly side with the latter interpretation and make it the central pillar in their rejection of the *fajr qunūt*.

Al-Ṭaḥāwī employs a similar style of argumentation in confronting apparent textual contradictions regarding the *qunūt*'s placement in the prayer. He starts by listing a series of traditions and juristic opinions that advocate the *qunūt* both before and after the *rak'a*.[20] At this point, he reiterates his previous conclusion that the *qunūt* was abrogated by Q3:128 for obligatory prayers but remained valid for the *witr* prayer.[21] Most of those traditions/opinions that endorse the *qunūt* after the *rak'a* are then associated with the obligatory prayers (abrogated), whereas those that support the *qunūt* before the *rak'a* are linked with the *witr* prayer (still valid).[22] Texts that do not fit this dichotomy are characterized as either (1) personal opinions (e.g., that of Anas b. Mālik)[23] or (2) the result of misinterpretations of Q3:128 (e.g., that of Abū Hurayra).[24] The section ends with sixteen traditions that depict 'Umar, 'Alī, and 'Abd Allāh b. 'Abbās performing the *qunūt* to curse their enemies during military conflicts alongside a series of countertraditions that reject the *qunūt* (for obligatory prayers) in both wartime and peacetime. Al-Ṭaḥāwī explains this contradiction by noting that the Companions in question employed the measure in a special unidentified supererogatory prayer as opposed to an obligatory one.[25]

The Ḥanafī stance on the *qunūt* is grounded in a broad interpretation of Q3:128[26] and a specific set of Prophetic and Companion traditions.

[19] This question lies at the heart of Mālikī and Shāfi'ī discourse, which takes great pains to limit the scope of Q3:128 to the act of cursing as opposed to the *qunūt* as a whole.

[20] al-Ṭaḥāwī, *Sharḥ*, 1:246–7.

[21] Al-Ṭaḥāwī's proof for the validity of the *witr qunūt* consists (in its entirety) of a statement near the end of the discussion where he says, "we hold the *witr qunūt* as valid at all times and, in particular, for the second half of Ramadan in accordance with most jurists" (*Ibid.*, 1:254).

[22] *Ibid.*, 1:248.

[23] *Ibid.*, 1:248. He acknowledges cases where this strategy breaks down but these are considered exceptional.

[24] *Ibid.*, 1:248–9.

[25] *Ibid.*, 1:251–4.

[26] Despite the importance of Q3:128 in Ḥanafī legal arguments surrounding the *qunūt*, Ḥanafī exegetical works are surprisingly silent on the issue. Al-Samarqandī concentrates on the permissibility of cursing without establishing any link to the performance of the *qunūt* (al-Samarqandī, *Tafsīr*, 1:297). Specifically, he claims that the cursing prohibition was limited to a very specific historical situation as God knew that many of those who fought the Prophet would eventually repent and become Muslims. Al-Zamakhsharī is

Ḥanafī jurists universally uphold the *qunūt* as an integral part of the *witr* prayer performed before the *rak'a* and prefaced by a *takbīr* in order to differentiate it from the Qur'ānic recitation.[27] Whereas both al-Shaybānī and al-Ṭaḥāwī condemn the raising of the hands during *qunūt*, a number of Ḥanafī jurists are more ambivalent on the issue.[28] Integrating curses into the *qunūt* recitation[29] is discouraged but very little attention is devoted to identifying appropriate invocations. Instead, most Ḥanafī efforts are directed toward refuting the *fajr qunūt* based on Q3:128.[30]

The Mālikīs

The Mālikī treatment of the *qunūt* is shaped by an overarching ambiguity rooted in the views of Mālik b. Anas. With respect to the obligatory prayers, Mālik narrates two contradictory opinions preserved in different versions of the *Muwaṭṭa'*. The first contends that 'Abd Allāh b. 'Umar "did not perform the *qunūt* in any of his prayers."[31] The second depicts al-Zubayr b. al-'Awwām as utilizing the *qunūt* during the last cycle of the *fajr* prayer.[32] This latter tradition also explicitly rejects the *qunūt* in the *witr* prayer, while other independent accounts seem to suggest that Mālik upheld the *witr qunūt* for the second half of Ramaḍān.

The lack of clarity regarding Mālik's opinion permeates most subsequent Mālikī legal discussions of the issue as jurists struggle to ascertain

equally silent in the *Kashshāf*, focusing instead on the nature and scope of God's authority in the matter of punishment and forgiveness (al-Zamakhsharī, *al-Kashshāf*, 1:413).

27 See al-Qudūrī, *Mukhtaṣar*, 29; al-Marghīnānī, *al-Hidāya*, 1:153–8; Ibn al-Humām, *Fatḥ*, 1:423–38.

28 Al-Qudūrī's stance on the raising of the hands is vague. Whereas al-Ṭaḥāwī states clearly that the hands are raised for the *takbīr* and then "lowered" (*arsilhumā*), al-Qudūrī removes this second phrase, indicating perhaps his preference for the raising of the hands (*Mukhtaṣar*, 29). An unambiguous endorsement for raising the hands is forwarded by Ibn al-Humām who ascribes the practice to Abū Yūsuf (*Fatḥ*, 1:430).

29 The term "*qunūt* recitation" refers to the words uttered during the *qunūt* which may include curses, invocations, or Qur'ānic phrases.

30 This argument provides the framework for Mālikī and (especially) Shāfi'ī attempts at restricting the scope of Q3:128 to the practice of cursing alone. Given this dynamic, it is not surprising that Mālikī and Shāfi'ī legal criticism is directed almost exclusively against the Ḥanafīs.

31 This tradition is preserved in the four primary transmissions of the *Muwaṭṭa'*. These include the texts of Yaḥyā b. Yaḥyā al-Laythī [*Muwaṭṭa'*, (1996), 1:226]; Suwayd b. Sa'īd [*Muwaṭṭa'*, (1994), 123]; 'Abd Allāh b. Maslama al-Qa'nabī [*Muwaṭṭa'* (1999), 205]; and Muḥammad b. al-Ḥasan al-Shaybānī [*Muwaṭṭa'*, (1967), 91].

32 Of the four versions consulted in this study, this tradition is only found in the texts of Suwayd b. Sa'īd, *Muwaṭṭa'* (1994), 123 and 'Abd Allāh b. Maslama al-Qa'nabī, *Muwaṭṭa'* (1999), 205.

the authoritative position of the founder of the school. Saḥnūn does not acknowledge these discrepancies and simply states that the *fajr qunūt* is valid.[33] Muḥammad al-ʿUtbī (d. 255/869), by contrast, directly confronts the contradictions, concluding that Mālik (1) permitted the *fajr qunūt* without considering it mandatory[34] and (2) categorically rejected the *witr qunūt* for the entire month of Ramaḍān.[35] Ibn Abī Zayd associates Mālik with an opinion in favor of the *fajr qunūt* and addresses the *witr* prayer through an argument grounded in the living tradition of Medina.[36] Specifically, he concedes that Medinans in Mālik's time did not perform the *witr qunūt*, but upholds the practice for the second half of Ramaḍān based on Medinan *ʿamal*[37] (during ʿUmar's caliphate) and a tradition on the authority of ʿAlī.[38]

Ibn ʿAbd al-Barr's *al-Istidhkār* offers a typical Mālikī approach to the *qunūt* covering all the major primary and secondary issues.[39] The relevant section begins by utilizing Medinan living tradition to affirm both the *witr qunūt* and its potential use for the cursing of enemies.[40] Ibn ʿAbd al-Barr notes that when the Medinans would perform the *witr qunūt* during Ramaḍān, the Imām would shift to a silent recitation thereby signaling the congregation to curse the nonbelievers.[41] This was in emulation of the Prophet's actions after the massacre at Biʾr Maʿūna.[42] Despite ascribing this practice to all the Companions and Successors in Medina, Ibn ʿAbd al-Barr only backs it with a solitary Prophetic tradition.[43] He concludes the section by restricting the *witr qunūt* to the second half of Ramaḍān based on the example of prominent Companions and the evident (*ẓāhir*) practice (*ʿamal*) of Medina at that time.[44] Although the *fajr qunūt* is not discussed at length, Ibn ʿAbd al-Barr quotes a number of supporting traditions[45] supplemented by a long list of assenting juristic

33 Saḥnūn, *Mudawwana*, 1:226–9. Saḥnūn does not discuss the *witr qunūt*.
34 Muḥammad al-Utbī al-Qurṭubī's *ʿUtbiyya* is preserved in Ibn Rushd al-Jadd's commentary entitled *al-Bayān wa'l-taḥṣīl*, 17:292 and 2:185.
35 Ibn Rushd al-Jadd, *al-Bayān*, 17:292.
36 Ibn Abī Zayd, *al-Nawādir*, 1:191–2.
37 For *ʿamal*, see footnotes 19 and 33 in Chapter 3.
38 Ibn Abī Zayd, *al-Nawādir*, 1:192 and 1:490.
39 Ibn ʿAbd al-Barr, *al-Istidhkār*, 2:337–40. For a similar (albeit less comprehensive) Mālikī discussion of the issue, see Ibn Rushd al-Ḥafīd, *Bidāyat*, 1:301–3.
40 Ibn ʿAbd al-Barr, *al-Istidhkār*, 2:337.
41 *Ibid.*, 2:337.
42 For this episode, see footnote 12 in this chapter.
43 *Ibid.*, 2:339.
44 *Ibid.*, 2:339.
45 Relying particularly on *Ibid.*, 2:339 – 1.

opinions. The placement of the *qunūt* (before or after the *rakʿa*) is left to the discretion of the worshipper.

Ibn ʿAbd al-Barr then turns to the apparent contradiction in the views ascribed to Mālik. As noted earlier, the *Muwaṭṭaʾ* preserves a tradition (on the authority of ʿAbd Allāh b. ʿUmar) that rejects the *qunūt* and another tradition (on the authority of al-Zubayr) that accepts it for *fajr*. With respect to the first, Ibn ʿAbd al-Barr cites an account in which ʿAbd Allāh b. ʿUmar affirms the *qunūt*. This discredits both traditions by exposing a contradiction in Ibn ʿUmar's opinions.[46] Turning to the second, he argues that Mālik completely abandoned the *witr qunūt* near the end of his life and placed a renewed emphasis on the *fajr qunūt*.[47] This is not surprising given the lukewarm nature of Mālik's initial endorsement of the *witr qunūt* and his refusal to sanction the cursing of nonbelievers.[48] The practical implication of this shift was the circulation of two different opinions, preserved by Mālik's Medinan and Egyptian students and representing different periods in his life. The Medinans (like Ibn ʿAbd al-Barr) upheld the *witr qunūt* for the second half of Ramaḍān in accordance with Mālik's original ruling, while the Egyptians rejected it in line with his later position. Ibn ʿAbd al-Barr prefers the early (Medinan) stance over the late (Egyptian) one.

Although most Mālikī jurists do not mention Q3:128 in their general discussions of the *qunūt*, they address it in their defense of the validity of the *fajr qunūt*.[49] Specifically, they counter the Ḥanafī claim that the verse abrogated the *qunūt* in all obligatory prayers by limiting its scope to the issue of cursing. In his *Jāmiʿ li-aḥkām al-Qurʾān*, for example, al-Qurṭubī interprets Q3:128 as (1) an explicit proclamation of God's authority and (2) an implicit repudiation of cursing within the prayer.[50] A similar strategy is employed by Abū Ḥayyān al-Andalūsī (d. 745/1344) in his *Baḥr al-muḥiṭ*.[51]

The Mālikī position on the *qunūt* is primarily a product of (1) efforts at reconciling contradictions in views ascribed to Mālik b. Anas and (2)

46 *Ibid.*, 2:339.
47 *Ibid.*, 2:339.
48 *Ibid.*, 2:339. For Mālik and the issue of cursing, see *SKB*, 2:298.
49 This is exemplified by the fact that not a single Mālikī exegetical work links the incident at Biʾr Maʿūna to the revelation of Q3:128. The Mālikīs universally prefer the view that the verse was revealed in the aftermath of the Battle of Uḥud. See footnote 18 in this chapter.
50 al-Qurṭubī, *al-Jāmiʿ*, 4:200.
51 Abū Ḥayyān, *al-Baḥr*, 3:56. The verse is not discussed by Ibn al-ʿArabī in his *Aḥkām al-Qurʾān*.

the *'amal* of Medina. Even though all Mālikīs espouse the *fajr qunūt*, there is a clear division between Egyptian Mālikīs who reject the *witr qunūt* and Medinan Mālikīs who limit it to the second half of Ramaḍān. This rift may derive from a change of heart by Mālik b. Anas in the latter part of his life. As for the *qunūt* recitation, Mālikī jurists prefer (but do not require) invocations that petition God for forgiveness and aid (in this world and the next) over cursing. There is no school consensus on placement, despite an acknowledgment that the *qunūt* was originally performed before the *rak'a*. The *takbīr* and the raising of hands are not discussed at length in most Mālikī works.

The Shāfi'īs

Similarly to the Mālikīs, Shāfi'ī jurists expend much of their efforts toward defending the *qunūt* against those who claim its abrogation. But whereas the Mālikīs are comfortable with simply asserting the primacy of Medinan living tradition, the Shāfi'īs structure their arguments around textual proofs. This requires navigating through large amounts of contradictory evidence that encompasses both Prophetic traditions and the opinions of prominent early jurists.

The basic contours of the Shāfi'ī approach are articulated by Muḥammad b. Idrīs al-Shāfi'ī in his *Kitāb al-umm*.[52] He starts by asserting that the *qunūt* should only be recited in the *fajr* prayer.[53] In times when the community is afflicted with a difficulty (*tanzilū nāzilatun*), however, prayer leaders have the option of performing the *qunūt* in every prayer. This is a special circumstance and should not be viewed as a general dispensation.[54] Although al-Shāfi'ī permits the *witr qunūt*, he does so without recourse to any textual proofs or logical arguments, suggesting a degree of ambivalence or uncertainty. On secondary issues, he highlights his differences with the Kūfans (i.e., the Ḥanafīs).[55] Specifically, he quotes a tradition (on the authority of 'Alī) which places the *qunūt* after the *rak'a* and states that the *takbīr* should follow the *qunūt*.[56] The discussion concludes by recommending invocations (as opposed to curses) in both the *fajr* and the *witr qunūt* (during the second half of Ramaḍān).

[52] al-Shāfi'ī, *al-Umm*, 1:260–2, 1:351.
[53] *Ibid.*, 1:351.
[54] *Ibid.*, 1:351.
[55] *Ibid.*, 1:261.
[56] *Ibid.*, 1:261. See also *AA*, 1:291 – 426.

Subsequent Shāfi'ī jurists expounded on these positions by providing additional textual proofs, reconciling contradictory evidence, and explicitly attacking the arguments of their opponents (i.e., the Ḥanafīs). A typical example of a later Shāfi'ī approach is found in 'Alī b. Muḥammad al-Māwardī's *al-Ḥāwī al-kabīr*.[57] The section begins by contrasting al-Shāfi'ī's support for the *fajr qunūt* and the *witr qunūt* (during the second half of Ramaḍān) with the Ḥanafī claim that it should only be performed in the *witr* prayer (year-round).[58] According to al-Māwardī, the Ḥanafīs rely on opinions ascribed to 'Abd Allāh b. 'Abbās and 'Abd Allāh b. 'Umar in combination with variants of the Bi'r Ma'ūna traditions.[59] He also mentions a Ḥanafī argument (not found in the texts above) that rejects the *fajr qunūt* through an analogy with the other obligatory prayers, none of which include the *qunūt*.

Al-Māwardī then offers a series of textual and logical proofs that both support the Shāfi'ī position and refute that of the Ḥanafīs. He quotes a tradition[60] narrated by Abū Hurayra in which the Prophet performs a *fajr qunūt* after the *rak'a*. This is followed by a second tradition,[61] which recounts the incident at Bi'r Ma'ūna,[62] acknowledging the transformative effect of the revelation of Q3:128, but limiting its scope to the issue of cursing in the non-*fajr* obligatory prayers.[63] He cites a third tradition that supports this interpretation by observing that the Prophet continued to perform the *fajr qunūt* until his death.[64] These accounts are supplemented by a logical argument that disputes the analogy between *fajr* and the other mandatory prayers, emphasizing its uniqueness as the only daytime prayer with audible recitation and its distinctive "call to prayer."[65] He

[57] al-Māwardī, *al-Ḥāwī*, 2:150–5. For similar Shāfi'ī approaches to the *qunūt*, see al-Shīrāzī, *al-Muhadhdhab*, 1:271–80; al-Baghawī, *Sharḥ*, 2:275–84; al-Rāfi'ī, *al-'Azīz*, 1:515–20 and 2:126–9; and al-Nawawī, *Majmū'*, 3:474–521.

[58] al-Māwardī, *al-Ḥāwī*, 2:250–1.

[59] al-Māwardī, *al-Ḥāwī*, 2:151. In the case of 'Abd Allāh b. 'Abbās, he cites the *isnād* of a tradition from *SAD*, 2:68 – 1445 attached to the text found in *SKB*, 2:285 – 3098 and 2:301 – 3153. For traditions similar to the one he ascribes to 'Abd Allāh b. 'Umar, see *MIAS*, 2:208 – 9 and 15, 2:209 – 17 and 18, and 2:210 – 38; *MAR*, 3:27 – 4966, 3:28 4968–8; and *SKB*, 2:302–3157.

[60] See *SKB*, 2:281 – 3086; *SN III*, 1:201 – 4.

[61] See *SM*, 1:470 – 308.

[62] For this episode, see footnote 12 in this chapter.

[63] al-Māwardī, *al-Ḥāwī*, 2:152.

[64] *Ibid.*, 2:152. For the traditions, see *SKB*, 2:287 – 3104 and 3105.

[65] *Ibid.*, 2:152. The *fajr adhān* (for the Sunnīs) is distinguished by the *tathwīb* (literally recitation of the phrase, "Prayer is better than sleep (*ṣalāt(u) khayr(un) min al-nawm*)") which is recited twice; once right before dawn and again at the proper time.

also notes that every mandatory daytime prayer (e.g., the Friday prayer) is characterized by a special invocation; the *qunūt* is the equivalent of the *khuṭba* (sermon) of the Friday prayer.[66] The discussion then shifts to a closer examination of those Companions depicted as opponents of the *fajr qunūt*. Al-Māwardī exposes a contradiction in the views of ʿAbd Allāh b. ʿAbbās by citing his interpretation of Q2:238,[67] which explicitly endorses the *fajr qunūt*.[68] ʿAbd Allāh b. ʿUmar poses more of a problem because a large number of traditions emphasize his opposition to the *fajr qunūt*. Al-Māwardī dismisses this opposition through a tradition in which Saʿīd b. al-Musayyab explains that, in his old age, Ibn ʿUmar forgot he had performed the *fajr qunūt* with his father.[69] With respect to the *witr qunūt*, al-Māwardī employs a strategy wherein he highlights the strength of Shāfiʿī textual proofs as compared with the weakness of those utilized by the Ḥanafīs.[70]

The text concludes with an examination of secondary issues. Al-Māwardī devotes significant effort to specifying the manner (silent) and wording (invocations over cursing) of the *qunūt*.[71] Aside from these basic requirements, the worshipper is accorded considerable latitude in choosing his/her own formula, which may include Qur'ānic passages as long as they resemble invocations.[72] For the less ambitious worshipper, al-Māwardī recommends two invocations that either ask for God's guidance in this life or beseech His forgiveness.[73] Turning to placement,

[66] *Ibid.*, 2:152.

[67] Q2:238 – "Attend strictly (*ḥāfiẓū*) to your prayers, and to the midmost prayer (*al-ṣalāt al-wusṭā*), and stand up with devotion (*qānitīn*) to Allāh." This translation reflects the general Sunnī interpretation that does *not* draw a link between the word *qānitīn* and the act of *qunūt*. In this case, al-Māwardī is citing the minority view (for the Sunnīs) in which ʿAbd Allāh b. ʿAbbās interprets the verse as referring to the *qunūt*. A majority of Sunnī exegetes tied the verse to the issue of conversation within the prayer as opposed to the Imāmīs who used it as proof for their general validity of the *qunūt*. For a detailed treatment of the Sunnī approach, see footnote 117 in this chapter.

[68] al-Māwardī, *al-Ḥāwī*, 2:152. He is alluding to traditions recorded in *MIAS*, 2:212 – 416 and 2:215 – 149, and *SKB*, 2:291 – 3118.

[69] *Ibid.*, 2:152.

[70] *Ibid.*, 2:290–3.

[71] *Ibid.*, 2:153.

[72] *Ibid.*, 2:153.

[73] *Ibid.*, 2:152. Specifically, he recommends (1) an invocation (mentioned by al-Dārimī, *Sunan* (2000), 2:992 – 1632–3 and *SN II*, 1:248 – 1) narrated by al-Ḥasan b. ʿAlī on the authority of the Prophet and (2) the "two *sūra*s of Ubayy" (mentioned in *MAR*, 3:30 – 4948 and *MIAS*, 2:213 – 147). The Iraqs considered the latter Qur'ānic based on their inclusion in the codex of Ubayy b. Kaʿb as two independent *sūra*s with the names, *al-Khalʿ* and *al-Ḥafd*. For more on Ubayy's codex, see Jeffery, *Materials*, 180–1. Al-Māwardī

al-Māwardī quotes a Prophetic tradition that unambiguously locates the *qunūt* after the *rak'a*.[74] Although he accepts the veracity of a Ḥanafī account in which 'Uthmān b. 'Affān performs the *qunūt* before the *rak'a*, he reduces its legal importance for two reasons: (1) it was only utilized to allow latecomers to join the congregational prayers,[75] and (2) it was an act of 'Uthmān's personal discretion (*ra'y*) with no textual support. It is notable that al-Mawārdī does not address the issue of raising the hands. This is owing, perhaps, to a general lack of consensus among Shāfi'ī jurists.

The Shāfi'īs align with the Mālikīs in upholding the *fajr qunūt* (year-round) and the *witr qunūt* (during the last half of Ramaḍān) after the *rak'a* in the final prayer cycle. Whereas the Mālikīs base their arguments primarily on the living tradition of Medina, the Shāfi'īs rely on textual evidence. In general, they cite a variant of the Bi'r Ma'ūna tradition that rejects cursing together with another that affirms the Prophet's adherence to the *fajr qunūt* throughout his life.[76] Their argument in favor of the *witr qunūt* is primarily grounded in the opinions of early Companions (especially 'Umar). Finally, the Shāfi'īs reject prefacing the *qunūt* with a *takbīr* and leave recitation (invocation vs. cursing) to the discretion of individual worshippers. They are internally divided on the necessity of the raising of hands.[77]

The Ḥanbalīs

Ḥanbalī discussions of the *qunūt* are characterized by brevity and a limited scope. The school is particularly concerned with the question of whether the *witr qunūt* is restricted to the second half of Ramaḍān or valid throughout the year. With the notable exceptions of Aḥmad ibn Ḥanbal and Ibn Qudāma, most Ḥanbalī jurists do not mention the *fajr qunūt* and (often) offer only a cursory examination of secondary issues.

expresses a preference for combining (1) and (2) into a single invocation, citing traditions taken from Ibn Māja (*SIM*, 1:373 – 1179) and al-Nasā'ī (*SN II*, 1:248 – 3).

74 *Ibid.*, 2:154. For the tradition, see *SM*, 1:470 – 308.

75 *Ibid.*, 2:154. A latecomer may join a group prayer at any point prior to and including the *rak'a*. Should one arrive after the *rak'a*, he/she must wait till the start of the next cycle.

76 Both Shāfi'ī and Mālikī commentators also limit the abrogatory scope of Q3:128 to the act of cursing as opposed to the *qunūt* as a whole. For the Shāfi'ī view, see Fakhr al-Dīn al-Rāzī, *Tafsīr*, 8:231–4 and Ibn Kathīr, *Tafsīr* (2000), 2:178–82.

77 Compare, for example, al-Shīrāzī, *al-Muhadhdhab*, 1:271–80 and al-Baghawī, *Sharḥ*, 2:275–84 with al-Rāfi'ī, *al-'Azīz*, 1:515–20 and 2:126–9.

As mentioned in the previous chapter, the earliest sources for Ḥanbalī law are the collections of responsa ascribed to Ibn Ḥanbal. Three exchanges from these works are directly pertinent to the issue of the *qunūt*. The first upholds the *witr qunūt* (implicitly) and *fajr qunūt* (explicitly)[78] throughout the year and permits the use of curses (alongside invocations) within its recitation.[79] In the second, 'Umar is depicted as performing the *qunūt* (in an unspecified prayer) after the *rak'a* and cursing nonbelievers.[80] The third affirms the *fajr qunūt* on the condition that it include invocations and curses.[81] On the basis of these responses, it appears that Ibn Ḥanbal (1) supported the *fajr qunūt* (year-round) and the *witr qunūt* (during the second half of Ramaḍān), (2) placed it after the *rak'a*, and (3) advocated (and, in some cases, required) cursing. We might expect these views to shape subsequent Ḥanbalī discourse but (as will become clear below) they were often neutralized (if not ignored) by later jurists.

As is the case with many issues, the most comprehensive Ḥanbalī discussion of the *qunūt* is found in Ibn Qudāma's *Mughnī*.[82] The relevant section opens with an unconditional affirmation of the *witr qunūt*.[83] Although Ibn Qudāma concedes that Ibn Ḥanbal originally restricted it to the second half of Ramaḍān (above), he argues that his opinion changed over time. Specifically, he quotes a passage in which Ibn Ḥanbal discovers traditions that convince him to accept the *qunūt* as a recommended part of the *witr* prayer throughout the year.[84] The section ends with a barrage of textual evidence that relates the concurring opinions of many prominent Companions and jurists.[85]

[78] There is some ambiguity here regarding the identity of these prayers. Some later jurists interpreted the response as addressing whether the *witr qunūt* was valid for the entire year or just for the second half of Ramaḍān. Although this is a possible (and very literal) reading of the text, Ibn Ḥanbal's transmission (see footnote 81 in this chapter) of a tradition that explicitly mentions the *fajr* (*ghadā*) prayer suggests that he was, in fact, referring to two different prayers.

[79] Ibn Ḥanbal, *Masā'il*, (1999), 1:71–2 and 1:101. The tradition in question is a variant of a popular strain cited by *MIAS*, 2:215 – 150 and *SKB*, 2:281 – 3086 and 2:294 – 3127.

[80] Ibn Ḥanbal, *Masā'il* (1999), 1:223.

[81] Ibn Ḥanbal, *Masā'il* (1988), 3:211.

[82] *Mughnī I*, 2:580–8.

[83] *Ibid.*, 2:580.

[84] *Ibid.*, 2:581. Ibn Qudāma makes particular reference to *SIM*, 1:374 – 1182 (narrated on the authority of Ubayy b. Ka'b and affirming the *witr qunūt* before the *rak'a*) and *SIM*, 1:373 – 1179 and *SN II*, 1:248 – 3 (both narrated on the authority of 'Alī). Ibn Ḥanbal dismisses a contrary opinion ascribed to Ubayy (similar to *SAD*, 2:65 – 1429) as a case of personal judgment (*rā'y*).

[85] *Mughnī I*, 2:580–1. These include Muḥammad b. Sīrīn, Sa'īd b. Yasār, al-Zuhrī, Yaḥyā b. Thābit, al-Shāfi'ī and Mālik.

Ibn Qudāma then turns to disputes between the Ḥanbalīs and the other Sunnī law schools. The most important of these concerns the *fajr qunūt*, which the (Egyptian) Mālikīs and the Shāfiʿīs uphold on the basis of two traditions that draw on the authority of the Prophet[86] and ʿUmar.[87] He interprets these texts in light of a third account (attributed to Ibrāhīm al-Nakhaʿī), which relates ʿAlī's attempts at incorporating the *qunūt* into communal prayer during the first civil war.[88] The Kūfans resisted (presumably because they felt it had been abrogated) until ʿAlī explained that the practice was permissible in times of crisis.[89] Ibn Qudāma then utilizes this same reasoning to counter Mālikī and Shāfiʿī claims in favor of the *fajr qunūt*. Specifically, he argues that the *qunūt* may only be performed in the *fajr* prayers during times of exceptional difficulty such as wide-scale civil strife. It is invalid at all other times – a view that finds support in a preponderance of the textual evidence[90] and a wide cross-section of juristic opinions.[91]

The remainder of Ibn Qudāma's analysis deals with secondary issues. He confirms the placement of the *qunūt* after the *rakʿa*[92] and suggests (as opposed to requiring) invocations found in a wide cross-section of Sunnī juristic works.[93] The fact that he does not mention cursing indicates a tacit acceptance of the practice, which (it should be recalled) was also

[86] See *SKB* 2:287 – 3104 and 3105.

[87] The tradition is a variant of *SKB*, 2:289 – 3111 and 3112.

[88] *Mughnī I*, 2:586. The tradition is a variant of *KAS I*, 1:595 – 216.

[89] *Ibid.*, 2:586.

[90] *Ibid.*, 2:586. He explicitly cites *SM*, 1:469 – 304 and alludes to *SAD*, 2:68 – 1442 (relating the opinion of Abū Hurayra) and *SKB*, 2:302 – 3155 (relating the opinion of ʿAbd Allāh b. Masʿūd). He also quotes *ST*, 1:118 – 402 and 1:120 – 403 in which Ṭāriq b. Ashyam b. Masʿūd tells his son the *qunūt* is an innovation. Ibn Qudāma considers this last tradition the strongest textual evidence against the *qunūt*.

[91] *Ibid.*, 2:585–6. He explicitly cites Sufyān al-Thawrī and Abū Ḥanīfa as well as a number of legal authorities and Companions, including ʿAbd Allāh b. ʿUmar and ʿAbd Allāh b. Masʿūd.

[92] *Ibid.*, 2:582. The Ḥanbalī view that the *witr qunūt* is placed after the *rakʿa* is supported by allusions to traditions related by Abū Hurayra (e.g., *SKB*, 2:281 – 3086; *SM*, 1:467 – 294; *SN II*, 1:202 – 6, etc ...) and Anas b. Mālik (e.g., *SN II*, 1:200 – 1; *SKB*, 2:293 – 3124 and 2:296 – 3137; al-Dārimī, *Sunan* (2000). 2:995–6 – 1640, etc ...). Ibn Qudāma only offers complete *isnād*s for three traditions (i.e., *SKB*, 2:281 – 3085 and 3086 and 2:294 – 3126).

[93] *Ibid.*, 2:583. The recommended invocation for the *witr qunūt* is ascribed to both al-Ḥasan b. ʿAlī (see al-Dārimī, *Sunan* (2000), 2:992 – 1632; *SN II*, 1:248 – 1) and ʿAlī (*AA*, 1:290–1 – 423). A second acceptable invocation is attributed to ʿUmar (the account is a variant of two traditions from *MIAS*, 2:213 and one from *SKB*, 2:298 – 3143). For more on the second invocation associated with the codex of Ubayy b. Kaʿb, see footnote 73 in this chapter.

endorsed by Ibn Ḥanbal. Finally, Ibn Qudāma notes that the hands should be raised during the *qunūt*, citing the general etiquette of worship.[94] He observes that all the Companions raised their hands when they recited invocations both within and outside the context of the ritual prayer.[95]

Overall, the Ḥanbalīs align with the Ḥanafīs in limiting the *qunūt* to the *witr* prayer and with the Shāfiʿīs and Mālikīs in placing it after the *rakʿa*. As for the *qunūt* recitation, the Ḥanbalīs favor the use of invocations while also permitting the cursing of non-believers. They clearly support the raising of the hands but hold no clear position on the introductory *takbīr*. In terms of method, Ḥanbalī jurists (as represented by Ibn Qudāma) draw extensively on textual evidence with contradictory traditions either (1) dismissed as possessing weak chains of transmission or (2) characterized as either contingent (special cases) or early (abrogated).[96]

The Imāmīs

The Imāmīs require the *qunūt* in all obligatory prayers based primarily on (1) traditions that relate the opinions of the Imāms and (2) distinctive interpretations of certain Qur'ānic verses. Many Imāmī jurists assume the validity of the *qunūt* and concentrate instead on ancillary issues such as the raising of the hands or the manner of recitation (audible vs. silent).[97] The most comprehensive discussions of the *qunūt*, therefore, are found in (1) comparative works intended to legitimize the school's position vis-à-vis the Sunnī law schools (i.e., Ibn al-Muṭahhar) or (2) exegetical works

[94] *Ibid.*, 2:584–5.

[95] *Ibid.*, 2:585.

[96] Note that most Ḥanbalī works are not as exhaustive as the *Mughnī*. Both al-Khiraqī (*Mukhtaṣar*, 30) and Abū Yaʿlā (*al-Jāmiʿ*, 50) simply state their opinions without providing any additional evidence or commentary.

[97] The *qunūt* is discussed in a cross section of Imāmī legal works. Al-Shalmaghānī offers a succinct analysis – typical of *fiqh* manuals – which focuses exclusively on (a) the mandatory nature of the *qunūt* and (b) its recitation (*Fiqh*, 107, 110–11, and 119). Ibn Bābawayh provides significantly more details, quoting numerous Imāmī traditions and supporting the mandatory nature of the *qunūt* for all prayers through interpretations of Q2:238 ascribed to al-Bāqir and al-Ṣādiq (*Faqīh*, 1:315–9 and 1:485 with a much briefer discussion in *Muqniʿ* [115 and 133]). He also suggests recitations for the *qunūt* that include calls for forgiveness, the cursing of enemies, and prolific glorifications of God. For similar treatments, see al-Sharīf al-Murtaḍā, *al-Intiṣār*, 1:46–7 and *Masāʾil al-nāṣiriyyāt*, 230–2. The latter follows Ibn al-Muṭahhar in its inclusion of comparisons with the Sunnī law schools. Al-Ḥalabī's *al-Kāfī* is distinguished by the claim that *qunūt* is recommended rather than mandatory and by his endorsement of raising the hands, an issue not generally discussed in earlier Imāmī legal works (*al-Kāfī*, 120–3). See also, al-Ṭūsī, *al-Nihāya*, 1:297–300 and 354–7; al-Ṭūsī, *Khilāf*, 1:379–80; and Ibn Idrīs, *al-Sarāʾir*, 1:128–9.

that articulate arguments only implicitly referenced in legal manuals or large compendiums of Imāmī law (e.g., al-Ṭabrisī).

Though late, Ḥasan b. Yūsuf (Ibn al-Muṭahhar) al-'Allāma al-Ḥillī's (d. 726/1325) comparative *fiqh* work entitled *Tadhkirat al-fuqahā'* presents a thorough and detailed analysis of the *qunūt*.[98] It begins by verifying the practice for all prayers (obligatory and supererogatory) on the basis of the consensus of the school, the text of Q2:238,[99] and a combination of Imāmī[100] and Sunnī[101] traditions.[102] Additional proof is furnished by Q40:60[103] in which God instructs his slaves to direct invocations toward Him and the argument that, since invocations are the best type of worship, they cannot (and should not) be eliminated from the daily prayer.[104] Ibn al-Muṭahhar restricts the scope of traditions that characterize the *qunūt* as a temporary measure[105] to the issue of cursing, an argument he also ascribes to al-Shāfi'ī.[106] Finally, he notes that those traditions routinely cited by Shāfi'ī jurists to support the *fajr qunūt* are equally applicable to the *qunūt* for the non-*fajr* prayers.[107]

In the second section of the *Tadhkira*, Ibn al-Muṭahhar turns to the placement of the *qunūt*, the content of its recitation, and the raising of the hands. In all three cases, he highlights similarities between Imāmī positions and those of the Sunnī law schools. In other words, he shows that, whereas the Imāmī stance may be unique as a whole, each individual element finds support in the Sunnī sources. The Ḥanafīs (and some Mālikīs), for example, agree with the Imāmīs that the *qunūt* should be performed before the *rak'a*,[108] whereas the Shāfi'īs articulate similar preferences for

[98] Ibn al-Muṭahhar, *Tadhkira*, 3:254–265. The *qunūt* is not discussed in al-Muḥaqqiq al-Ḥillī's *Sharā'i'*.

[99] For the Sunnī perspective on this verse, see footnote 117 in this chapter.

[100] *ṬI*, 1:388 – 495 and 1:390 – 501 (on the authority of al-Bāqir).

[101] *SKB*, 2:283 – 3092 (on the authority of the Prophet); *MAR*, 3:32 – 4990 (on the authority of 'Alī).

[102] Ibn al-Muṭahhar, *Tadhkira*, 254–6.

[103] Q40:60 reads, "And your Lord has said: Pray unto Me and I will hear your prayer. Surely those who scorn My service, they will enter hell, disgraced."

[104] Ibn al-Muṭahhar, *Tadhkira*, 3:256.

[105] This view is attributed to numerous authorities, including 'Abd Allāh b. 'Abbās and 'Abd Allāh b. Mas'ūd. He quotes a tradition (*SKB*, 2:303 – 3160) in which Umm Salama states that the Prophet prohibited the *fajr qunūt*. He also alludes to Prophetic traditions narrated by 'Abd Allāh b. Mas'ūd (*SKB*, 2:302 – 3155; *MIAS*, 2:209 – 27) and Anas b. Mālik (too numerous to list but including *SB*, 1:254 – 3; *SM*, 1:469 – 304; *SAD*, 2:68 – 1445; and *MIAS*, 2:209–21).

[106] Ibn al-Muṭahhar, *Tadhkira*, 3:256–7.

[107] *Ibid.*, 3:257. He specifically makes use of two traditions (*SKB*, 2:287 – 3104 and 3105) which are also central to al-Shāfi'ī's analysis (see earlier discussion in this chapter).

[108] *Ibid.*, 3:258.

the *qunūt* recitation.[109] On the issue of raising the hands, the Imāmī view is shared by both the Ḥanafīs and the Shāfiʿīs.[110] Ibn al-Muṭahhar demonstrates the magnitude of this overlap by offering evidence drawn from both Imāmī[111] and Sunnī[112] collections.

The third and final part of Ibn al-Muṭahhar's discussion focuses on contentious issues within Imāmī juristic circles, namely (1) the *qunūt*'s legal status (mandatory or recommended), (2) the manner of its recitation (audible vs. silent), and (3) the insertion of an introductory *takbīr*. In each of these cases, Ibn al-Muṭahhar relates traditions that either support his preferred view or contradict those of his opponents. Specifically, he denies the mandatory nature of the *qunūt* through selective interpretations of three Imāmī traditions[113] and then upholds audible recitation[114]

109 *Ibid.*, 3:260.

110 *Ibid.*, 3:262. As previously noted, a difference of opinion regarding this issue persisted among Ḥanafī and Shāfiʿī jurists.

111 *Ibid.*, 3:259. Imāmī traditions on placement include *ṬI*, 1:388 – 495 and *KK*, 3:340 – 7. For invocations, a worshipper may recite one of his own choosing (a freedom granted by al-Ṣādiq in *WS*, 6:275–7950) as long as it exceeds five *tasbīḥ*s or roughly ten words (on the basis of *KK*, 3:340 – 11). Alternately, he may choose an invocation ascribed to one of the Imāms.

112 With respect to placement, Ibn al-Muṭahhar quotes *MAR*, 3:37 – 5006 (narrated by ʿAbd Allāh b. Masʿūd); traditions similar to *SAD*, 2:64 – 1427 and *SIM*, 1:374 – 1182 (narrated by Ubayy b. Kaʿb); and *SM*, 1:469 – 301 (narrated by Anas b. Mālik). In terms of recitation, he favors the invocation ascribed to al-Ḥasan b. ʿAlī (see al-Dārimī, *Sunan* (2000), 2:992 – 1632–3; *SN II*, 1:248 – 1) along with the shortened form of an invocation mentioned by Ibn Abī Shayba (*MIAS*, 2:214 – 6) and al-Bayhaqī (*SKB*, 2:299 – 3144) on the authority ʿUmar. The latter is considered acceptable, but it is clearly inferior to invocations traced back to the Imāms. For the raising of the hands, Ibn al-Muṭahhar quotes a variant of *SKB*, 2:299 – 3145.

113 A longer and more thorough analysis of this issue can be found in Ibn al-Muṭahhar's *Mukhtalaf al-shīʿa* (2:189–90), a work primarily concerned with legal debates within Imāmī juristic circles. The discussion here centers on the *qunūt*'s status as a mandatory or recommended part of prayer. The latter is the dominant view among Imāmī jurists. The two primary proponents of the mandatory position are Ibn Abī ʿAqīl and Ibn Bābawayh, both of whom contend that the omission of the *qunūt* leads to the invalidation of the prayer. Ibn al-Muṭahhar's refutation of this opinion rests on an Imāmī *ḥadīth* (*ṬI*, 1:390–502) wherein al-Ṣādiq accepts the *qunūt* either before or after the *rakʿa*. This tradition is deemed sound yet it contradicts the consensus view of the Imāmīs that the *qunūt* is recited after the *rakʿa*. Ibn al-Muṭahhar notes that traditions appearing to negate acts of worship are actually negating only their mandatory status. Furthermore, he cites a tradition (identical in content to both *ṬI*, 1:391–505 and *WS*, 6:269 – 7931) in which al-Riḍā relates from al-Bāqir that the worshipper can choose whether to perform the *qunūt* or not. In cases of *taqiyya*, al-Riḍā acknowledges that he himself does not perform the *qunūt*. If the *qunūt* was considered mandatory, this act on the part of an Imām would be unthinkable (*Mukhtalaf*, 2:190).

114 Ibn al-Muṭahhar, *Tadhkira*, 3:261.

and the introductory *takbīr*[115] based on the opinions of multiple authority figures including 'Alī, al-Bāqir, al-Ṣādiq, and 'Abd Allāh b. Mughīra (d. after 184/800).

The purpose of Ibn al-Muṭahhar's *Tadhkira* is to carve out a space for the Imāmīs in a legal landscape dominated by the Sunnī schools of law. This requires a detailed and careful defense of the *qunūt* for each of the daily prayers. It also impacts the type of arguments Ibn al-Muṭahhar employs because his audience consists primarily of jurists from rival law schools. Imāmī works that lack this comparative dimension emphasize a completely different set of proofs resting on unique interpretations of Q2:238 and Q3:128. Detailed versions of these arguments (alluded to in juristic works) are predominantly found in the school's exegetical literature.

Muslim commentators divide the most prominent and important of these verses (Q2:238) into two distinct parts: (1) "Hold fast to your prayers and the *ṣalāt al-wusṭā*" and (2) "stand up for God in the act of *qunūt* (*qūmū li-llāhi qānitīn*)."[116] Sunnī exegetical works focus almost entirely on the first segment, proposing multiple possible meanings for *ṣalāt al-wusṭā* and settling (in most cases) on either the *'aṣr* or *fajr* prayer.[117] Given their support for the *fajr qunūt*, we might expect Shāfi'ī

115 *Ibid.*, 3:264. For traditions, see *TI*, 1:386 – 488 (on the authority of al-Ṣādiq) and 1:387 – 490 (on the authority of 'Alī).

116 For examples of early Imāmī exegetical works, see al-Qummī(?), *Tafsīr*, 1:79 and al-'Ayyāshī, *Tafsīr* (2000), 1:235–6.

117 Mālikī exegetical works are generally concerned with determining the identity of the mysterious *ṣalāt al-wusṭā*. In *al-Jāmi'*, al-Qurṭubī proposes ten different interpretations-before identifying the *fajr prayer* as the most likely candidate because of its inclusion of the *qunūt* (al-Qurṭubī, *al-Jāmi'*, 3:209–12). In doing so, al-Qurṭubī interprets the word *qānitīn* to refer to "individuals who recite invocations," drawing on an opinion from 'Abd Allāh b. 'Abbās (a variant of texts from *MIAS*, 2:212 – 3 and 2:215 – 3; *SKB*, 2:291 – 3118) and further supported by two Prophetic traditions (a variant of a text from *SM*, 1:466 – 294 and 1:468 – 299; *SKB*, 2:294 – 3127) (al-Qurṭubī, *al-Jāmi'*, 3:212–4). Abū Ḥayyān argues that the phrase *al-ṣalāt al-wusṭā'* most likely refers to the *'aṣr* prayer (Abu Ḥayyān, *Baḥr*, 2:249–50). This opinion is the majority view among the Mālikīs. Shāfi'ī exegetical works rarely mention the *qunūt* in their commentaries on Q2:238. Although both Fakhr al-Dīn al-Rāzī and Ibn Kathīr acknowledge the potential link between the *fajr* prayer and *al-ṣalāt al-wusṭā* through the *qunūt*, this interpretation is dismissed as unsound and problematic (al-Rāzī, *Tafsīr*, 6:160; Ibn Kathīr, *Tafsīr* (2000), 2:392). Al-Rāzī concludes that *fajr* is most likely the *al-ṣalāt al-wusṭā* because of (1) its location between night and day and between the daytime and nighttime prayers combined with (2) five Qur'ānic verses which emphasize its importance (al-Rāzī, *Tafsı ̄r*, 6:158–60). Ibn Kathīr, by contrast, identifies *'aṣr* as the most likely candidate (Ibn Kathīr, *Tafsīr* (2000), 2:394). Both exegetes connect the second part of the verse containing the word *qānitīn* to the prohibition of conversation in the congregational prayer

or Mālikī jurists to emphasize the connection between *ṣalāt al-wusṭā* in the first half of the verse and the term "*qānitīn*" in the second. In actuality, however, there are few (if any) references to Q2:238 in Sunnī discussions of the issue.

The Imāmīs, by contrast, view Q2:238 as explicit proof for the general validity of the *qunūt*. A typical Imāmī interpretation of the verse is offered by al-Faḍl b. al-Ḥasan al-Ṭabrisī in his *Majmaʿ al-bayān*.[118] The text begins in a manner reminiscent of Sunnī exegetical works by laying out a variety of possible explanations for the *ṣalāt al-wusṭā*. Instead of selecting one of these, however, al-Ṭabrisī concedes the impossibility of determining the exact identity of the prayer and draws parallels with the uncertainty associated with the "night of power" (*laylat al-qadr*) in Ramaḍān.[119] He then turns to the second segment of the verse and interprets the word *qānitīn* to mean supplicants who recite an "invocation in the prayer while standing."[120] The result is a general affirmation of the *qunūt* for all prayers including *ṣalāt al-wusṭā*, a term taken to refer to one of the five daily prayers or any number of supererogatory prayers.

A second verse of particular import in Imāmī discussions of the *qunūt* is Q3:128. While there is a general consensus among Muslim exegetes regarding the historical context of its revelation, there are significant differences regarding its legal implications.[121] The verse is broadly associated with the Prophet's cursing of enemies during the Battle of Uḥud or in the aftermath of the massacre at Biʾr Maʿūna. Sunnī scholars are concerned with defining the scope of Q3:128. Did it abrogate the act of cursing or was it a general injunction against the *qunūt* in prayer? The Imāmīs, by contrast, restrict its scope to one incident of cursing at one historical moment. Al-Ṭabrisī's analysis of Q3:128 emphasizes God's unitary power to punish and forgive as the Prophet is instructed to persevere with his job of warning nonbelievers and guiding them to truth.[122] Although it is possible to see this as a prohibition against cursing, al-Ṭabrisī portrays

(al-Rāzī, *Tafsīr*, 6:163 and Ibn Kathīr, *Tafsīr* (2000), 2:405–6). For a succinct summary of the range of opinion, see al-Ṭabarī, *Tafsīr*, 2:69–75. See also footnote 67 in this chapter.

[118] al-Ṭabrisī, *Majmaʿ* (1958), 2:163–5.

[119] *Ibid.*, 2:165.

[120] *Ibid.*, 2:165.

[121] al-ʿAyyāshī is unique his attempts to connect Q3:128 to the Prophet's desire to designate ʿAlī as his successor at a time when the community was growing increasingly jealous of his special status and disproportionate honors (al-ʿAyyāshī, *Tafsīr* [1961–2], 1:197).

[122] al-Ṭabrisī, *Majmaʿ* (1958), 2:462–5.

it more as a historical curiosity than a legal injunction. Similarly, in *Nahj al-bayān*, Muḥammad b. al-Ḥasan al-Shaybānī limits the verse's impact to the aftermath of the massacre at Bi'r Ma'ūna with no indication of a wider legal applicability.[123]

Overall, the Imāmīs (through *ikhtilāf* works) uphold the *qunūt* in all obligatory and supererogatory prayers on the basis of (1) traditions citing the opinions of their Imāms and (2) an extension of the Shāfi'ī arguments in favor of the *fajr qunūt*. For systematic discussions of the *qunūt*, however, it is necessary to examine the exegetical literature that forwards distinctive interpretations of Q2:238 and Q3:128. There is a general school consensus on most issues (i.e., the placement of the *qunūt* before the *rak'a* and prefacing it with a *takbīr*), but differences persist on the raising of the hands and the validity of cursing.[124]

The Zaydīs

Although the Zaydīs affirm the validity of the *fajr* and *witr qunūt*, they disagree sharply on most other issues including (but not limited to) its placement and recitation. These differences were first articulated by a group of prominent 3rd/9th-century Kūfan jurists who supported their views through competing sets of textual evidence. Over time, the Hādawī school triumphed over rival opinions and came to represent a majority of Zaydīs. The discussion that follows (1) examines the dominant Hādawī stance (as first detailed by al-Hādī in the 3rd/9th century) and (2) surveys a range of divergent opinions (as catalogued by al-'Alawī in the 5th/11th century).[125]

The earliest systematic Zaydī analysis of the *qunūt* is ascribed to al-Hādī and preserved in his *Kitāb al-aḥkām* and *Kitāb al-muntakhab*.[126] Both works describe the *qunūt* as a recommended part of the *fajr* and *witr*

[123] al-Shaybānī, *Nahj*, 3:67–8.

[124] One might be tempted to forge a connection between the Imāmī approval of *qunūt* in all prayers and the school's adherence to *barā'a* (disassociation from enemies of 'Alī) which may take the form of cursing in the context of prayer. The dispute in Imāmī juristic circles over the validity of cursing during the *qunūt* argues against this interpretation. Moreover, Baṣran traditions from Sunnī collections support the *qunūt* in all prayers suggesting that this position was present among the proto-Sunnīs in Iraq even if it only survived among the Imāmīs. For the Baṣran evidence, see Haider, *Birth*, 179–90.

[125] Throughout this section, the Nāṣirī position is elaborated in the footnotes for purposes of comparison when necessary.

[126] For similar (though less detailed) articulations of the Hādawī view, see al-Mu'ayyad bi-Allāh Aḥmad b.al-Ḥusayn, *al-Tajrīd*, 65; al-Nāṭiq bi'l-Ḥaqq, *al-Taḥrīr*, 1:89; and Ibn al-Murtaḍā, *Azhār*, 1:40.

prayers, place it after the *rak'a*, and reject the introductory *takbīr*.[127] The *takbīr* does not invalidate the prayer (or impugn a worshipper), but al-Hādī still discourages it in the strongest terms based on the established practice of the family of the Prophet.[128] He also does not require the raising of the hands in the course of the *qunūt* recitation.[129] With one exception (i.e., the use of the *witr qunūt* year-round), al-Hādī's stance aligns with that of the Shāfi'īs, and he consciously positions himself in opposition to the Ḥanafīs whose opinions he often conflates with the Sunnīs as a whole.[130]

A disproportionate amount of space in both the *Aḥkām* and the *Muntakhab* is devoted to identifying permissible texts for the *qunūt* recitation. Al-Hādī requires these to be Qur'ānic and expresses a particular preference for invocations from the latter half of *surat al-baqara* including Q2:136,[131] Q2:286[132] and Q2:201.[133] He must contend, however, with numerous Sunnī and Imāmī traditions that prefer non-Qur'ānic invocations. The most famous of these is ascribed to al-Ḥasan b. 'Alī b. Abī Ṭālib and recommended by a broad cross section of scholars from a number of law schools.[134] Even though al-Hādī acknowledges the validity (and merit) of this invocation, he offers two explanations for its exclusion from the *qunūt* recitation. The first is historical, as he notes that the revelation of Q2:238 abrogated conversation in the prayer.[135]

127 al-Hādī, *al-Aḥkām*, 2:107–9; al-Kūfī, *al-Muntakhab*, 1:58–60.

128 al-Hādī, *al-Aḥkām*, 2:108; al-Kūfī, *al-Muntakhab*, 1:58.

129 al-Kūfī, *al-Muntakhab*, 1:59.

130 See, for example, his discussion of Sunnīs who limit the *qunūt* to *witr* or place it before the *rak'a* (al-Kūfī, *al-Muntakhab*, 1:58). That he makes such a conflation is not surprising considering the influence of the Ḥanafī school in Kūfa.

131 Q2:136 – "Say: We believe in Allāh and that which is revealed unto us and that which was revealed unto Abraham, and Ishmael, and Isaac, and Jacob, and the tribes, and that which Moses and Jesus received, and that which the prophets received from their Lord. We make no distinction between any of them, and unto Him we have surrendered."

132 Q2:286 – "Allāh burdens not a soul beyond its capacity. For it (is only) that which it has earned, and against it (only) that which it deserves. Our Lord! Condemn us not if we forget, or miss the mark! Our Lord! Lay not on us such a burden as thou did lay on those before us! Our Lord! Impose not on us that which we have not the strength to bear! Pardon us, absolve us and have mercy on us, Thou, our Protector, and give us victory over the disbelieving folk."

133 al-Hādī, *al-Aḥkām*, 2:108 and al-Kūfī, *al-Muntakhab*, 1:59. Q2:201 – "And there are some amongst them who say: Our Lord! Give unto us in the world that which is good and in the Hereafter that which is good, and guard us from the doom of Fire."

134 al-Hādī, *al-Aḥkām*, 2:109. There are slight differences in the text of this invocation as preserved in the *Aḥkām* (*SKB*, 2:296 – 3138) and the *Muntakhab* (*SN II*, 1:248 – 1).

135 al-Hādī, *al-Aḥkām*, 2:109; al-Kūfī, *al-Muntakhab*, 1:59. This interpretation is favored by most Sunnī exegetes including al-Zamakhsharī who enjoyed considerable status within Zaydī circles for his Mu'tazilī beliefs (al-Zamakhsharī, *al-Kashshāf*, 1:287–8).

He then characterizes all non-Qur'ānic invocations (including that of al-Ḥasan) as variations of conversational speech, thereby deeming them inappropriate for the *qunūt*.[136] The second is locational in that such invocations should be recited exclusively at the end of the prayer. Al-Hādī concludes that traditions in favor of non-Qur'ānic invocations either (1) date from a period before Q2:238 or (2) support their recitation at the conclusion of the ritual prayer. In the *Muntakhab*, he makes a slight concession, allowing al-Ḥasan's non-Qur'ānic invocation (but no others) in the recitation of the *witr qunūt* due to the prayer's supererogatory status.[137]

Al-Hādī's views did not go unchallenged by his Zaydī contemporaries. This fact is strikingly evident in the depiction of Kūfan Zaydism preserved in Muḥammad b. 'Alī al-'Alawī's *al-Jāmi' al-kāfī*.[138] Al-'Alawī begins by claiming a general consensus among the Family of the Prophet in favor of the *fajr qunūt* and a strong majority opinion in favor of the *witr qunūt*.[139] There is a great deal more divisiveness regarding the other prayers with Muḥammad b. Manṣūr (d. 290/903) and Ḥasan b. Yaḥyā (d. 260/874) endorsing the *qunūt* in all audible prayers[140] (*fajr*, *maghrib*, *'ishā'*, and *jum'a*) and the Hādawīs (associated with al-Qāsim b. Ibrāhīm al-Rassī – d. 246/860) and Aḥmad b. 'Īsā rejecting it.[141]

A similar rift is apparent regarding secondary issues. Whereas the Hādawīs locate the *qunūt* after the *rak'a*, a majority of the major Kūfan jurists (Aḥmad b. 'Īsā, Ḥasan b. Yaḥyā,[142] and Muḥammad b. Manṣūr) place it before the *rak'a*.[143] Aḥmad b. 'Īsā, in particular, attacks the Hādawīs for relying on Baṣran traditions rather than the example of 'Alī who lived in Kūfa and was known to perform the *qunūt* before the *rak'a*.[144]

136 al-Hādī, *al-Aḥkām*, 2:109; al-Kūfī, *al-Muntakhab*, 1:59.

137 al-Kūfī, *al-Muntakhab*, 1:59.

138 al-'Alawī, *al-Jāmi'*, 2:68–72; See also Sharaf al-Dīn, *Shifā'*, 1:292–4; and Ibn Miftāḥ, *Sharḥ*, 2:268–71. For a description of the *Jāmi'*, see Chapter 2.

139 *Ibid.*, 2:69. A single opposing opinion is ascribed to al-Kāẓim via *AA*, 1:283 – 407 but dismissed as an instance of *taqiyya*.

140 *Ibid.*, 2:70. This view is supported by two traditions on the authority of al-Bāqir (*AA*, 1:288 – 415 and 416). It bears a striking resemblance to that of al-Shalmaghānī (*Fiqh*, 110) and is ascribed by al-Sharīf al-Murtaḍā to the Nāṣirī Zaydīs (*Masā'il al-nāṣiriyyāt*, 230–2). It may have represented an early Kūfan position that, although discarded early on by both the Sunnī and Imāmī Shī'ī law schools, remained the dominant Nāṣirī view through at least the 5th/11th century.

141 *Ibid.*, 2:70.

142 *Ibid.*, 2:69. Ḥasan b. Yaḥyā's view is complicated by his support for the *qunūt* before the *rak'a* in *fajr* and after the *rak'a* in *witr*.

143 *Ibid.*, 2:69.

144 *Ibid.*, 2:69.

Muḥammad b. Manṣūr additionally contests the Hādawī rejection of the *takbīr* prior to the *qunūt* and the raising of the hands. He agrees (in principle) that the *takbīr* should not precede the *qunūt* but permits the practice on the basis of a tradition on the authority of 'Alī.[145] A stronger disagreement is evident in the raising of the hands where Muḥammad b. Manṣūr distinguishes between obligatory (no raising of the hands) and supererogatory (raising of the hands) prayers.[146]

As in the legal works of al-Hādī, a large section of al-'Alawī's discussion is concerned with the issue of recitation. Each of the four major Kūfan authorities is linked to a particular set of preferred invocations. Al-Qāsim b. Ibrāhīm, as the mouthpiece of the Hādawī school, strongly advocates Qur'ānic invocations such as Q2:201.[147] Unlike al-Hādī's uncompromising stance on the recitation in the obligatory prayers (above), however, al-Qāsim permits invocations that only resemble the Qur'ān.[148] Aḥmad b. 'Īsā, by contrast, endorses two invocations on the authority of the Prophet and 'Umar with no mention of the Qur'ān.[149] He claims that the worshipper is free to choose a method of addressing God and may pray for specific people by name. This practice is ascribed to 'Alī in the context of *witr* and is extended to *fajr* through the principle that "whatever is permitted in the supererogatory is permitted in the mandatory."[150] Ḥasan b. Yaḥyā and Muḥammad b. Manṣūr favor the use of Qur'ānic passages but also permit non-Qur'ānic invocations.[151] In a significant departure from both the Hādawīs and Aḥmad b. 'Īsā, they also allow the cursing of individuals in emulation of the Prophet's cursing after the Bi'r Ma'ūna massacre and the Battle of Uḥud.[152] Ḥasan b. Yaḥyā explicitly denies that cursing was abrogated in Q3:128 by noting that 'Alī and 'Abd Allāh b. 'Abbās cursed Mu'āwiya during the first civil war.[153] They would not have done so had

145 *Ibid.*, 2:69.

146 *Ibid.*, 2:69.

147 *Ibid.*, 2:71. As an example, he quotes *AA*, 1:290 – 423, which relates the invocation of al-Ḥasan b. 'Alī.

148 *Ibid.*, 2:71.

149 *Ibid.*, 2:71. For the Prophetic invocation, see *AA*, 1:290 – 423. For the invocation on the authority of 'Umar, see *MIAS*, 2:213 – 2.

150 *Ibid.*, 2:71.

151 *Ibid.*, 2:71–2. Ḥasan b. Yaḥyā recommends Q2:136 (for text, see footnote 131 in this chapter) and Q2:201 (for text, see footnote 133 in this chapter) along with the invocation in *AA*, 1:290 – 423. Muḥammad b. Manṣūr recommends Q2:136 and the invocation found in *MIAS*, 2:213 – 2.

152 *Ibid.*, 2:71–2. Ḥasan b. Yaḥyā mentions the massacre at Bi'r Ma'ūna, whereas Muḥammad b. Manṣūr alludes to the Battle of Uḥud.

153 *Ibid.*, 2:71.

the Qur'ān outlawed cursing absolutely, suggesting that the verse only applied to a specific incident in the life of the Prophet.

The majority view among Zaydī jurists is that of the Hādawīs who limit the *qunūt* to the *fajr* prayer (in line with the Shāfi'īs) and perform the *witr* prayer throughout the year (in line with the Ḥanafīs). On secondary issues, they place the *qunūt* after the *rak'a* and reject both its introduction with a *takbīr* and the raising of the hands. The Hādawīs are distinctive in their emphasis on (and in some cases requirement of) the use of Qur'ānic invocations in the *qunūt* recitation. Challenges to Hādawī dominance were immediate and long-lasting, as exemplified by Muḥammad b. Manṣūr, a 3rd/9th-century Kūfan Zaydī jurist, who extended the *qunūt* to all the audible prayers, placed it before the *rak'a*, prefaced it with a *takbīr*, allowed the raising of hands, and permitted the cursing of individuals. In other words, his view was almost diametrically opposed to that of the Hādawīs, aligning most closely with the Imāmīs.

The Legal Landscape

Table 4.1 provides a summary of each school's legal position on the *qunūt*.[154] The Ḥanafīs restrict the *qunūt* to the *witr* prayer before the *rak'a* and affirm its general validity. They also endorse an introductory *takbīr* and prefer a recitation that consists of invocations rather than curses. Although the school initially seems to have rejected the raising of the hands, later jurists came to accept the practice. The Ḥanafīs were opposed by (Medinan) Mālikīs and Shāfi'īs who affirm the *qunūt* in *fajr* and uphold it in *witr* for the second half of Ramaḍān. Whereas the Ḥanafīs forward a wide interpretation of Q3:128, allowing for the omission of the *qunūt* in all the mandatory prayers, the Mālikīs and the Shāfi'īs restrict the scope of the verse to the issue of cursing. The Mālikīs cite Medinan *'amal* to support their stance whereas the Shāfi'īs navigate

[154] I was unable to find corresponding discussions on the *qunūt* in the daily prayer for the Ẓāhirīs, the Ismā'īlīs, and the Ibāḍīs. According to the *ikhtilāf* literature, Sufyān al-Thawrī favored the *witr qunūt* and rejected the *fajr qunūt*. It should be noted, however, that 75% (18/24) of the traditions he transmits affirm the *fajr qunūt*. He also narrates three traditions which uphold the *maghrib qunūt*. While the *ikhtilāf* works do not discuss his opinion on the placement of the *qunūt*, almost all of his transmitted traditions locate it before the *rak'a*. Overall, Sufyān al-Thawrī's position is broadly in agreement with the *ahl al-ra'y* but it also helps explain the surprising presence of Sunnī Kūfan accounts that support the *maghrib qunūt*. See also, Qaffāl, *Ḥilyat*, 2:134 and *Mughnī I*, 2:580.

TABLE 4.1. *A Summary of the Juristic Treatment of the Qunūt*

	Prayers	Placement	Recitation	*Takbīr*	Hands
Ḥanafīs	*Witr*	Before	Invocations	Yes	No/Yes
Mālikīs	*Fajr* *Witr* (2nd half of Ramaḍān)	Before (preferred) After (permitted)	Invocations	No	No/Yes
Shāfiʿīs	*Fajr* *Witr* (2nd half of Ramaḍān)	After	Invocations	No	No/Yes
Ḥanbalīs	*Witr*	After	Invocations/ Curses	N/A	Yes
Imāmīs	All	Before	Invocations/ Curses	Yes	Yes
Hādawī Zaydīs* (majority)	*Fajr, Witr*	After	Invocations	No	No
Nāṣirī Zaydīs* (minority)	*Fajr, Maghrib, 'Ishā'*	Before	Invocations/ Curses	N/A	N/A

* For the differences between these groups, see footnotes 65 and 66 in Chapter 2.

through the often contradictory textual evidence. Both schools limit the *qunūt* recitation to invocations and reject the insertion of an introductory *takbīr*. The Ḥanbalīs rely solely on traditions, following the Ḥanafīs in their affirmation of the year-round *witr qunūt* but differing on its placement in the prayer. Their position is distinctive among the Sunnīs in that they permit cursing in the *qunūt* recitation. As for the Shīʿī legal schools, the Imāmīs align partly with the Ḥanafīs. They place the *qunūt* before the *rakʿa*, preface it with a *takbīr*, and (after an early disagreement) endorse the raising of the hands. They differ from the Ḥanafīs in extending the *qunūt* to all the prayers and permitting cursing. On the whole, the Imāmīs base their position on a distinct (in its acceptance) interpretation of Q2:238 and provide traditions drawn from both Imāmī and the Sunnī collections. Finally, the Zaydīs are characterized by a fragmented set of views that persist well into the postformative period. The dominant (Hādawī) opinion accords with the Shāfiʿīs and Mālikīs in upholding the *fajr* and *witr qunūt* after the *rakʿa*. At the same time, however, it does not restrict the *witr qunūt* to the second half of Ramaḍān. The primary distinguishing feature of Zaydī legal discourse is its emphasis on Qur'ānic recitation in the *qunūt*.

COMPARING THE KŪFAN TRADITIONS

Many of the traditions utilized by Muslim jurists in their discussions of the *qunūt* predate the formation of the formal law schools and preserve echoes of regional differences in ritual practice. As noted in Chapter 2, these texts were circulating in 2nd/8th-century Kūfa contemporaneous with (according to the heresiographical sources) the emergence of Imāmī and Zaydī sectarian identities. In the second part of this chapter, we evaluate the reliability of the origin narratives for these sectarian groups through a structural analysis of the Kūfan *qunūt* traditions.

The Kūfan Traditions – An Overview

The following section focuses on one issue related to the *qunūt*, namely the identity of those daily prayers for which it is deemed permissible.[155] This narrowing in scope is necessitated by the vast complexity and enormous breadth of the *qunūt* traditions. A comprehensive examination of all *qunūt* texts pertaining to each primary and secondary issue could fill an entire book in its own right. Furthermore, it is possible to meet the goals of this study (i.e., to identify sectarian overlaps) by focusing on a single primary issue (albeit a controversial one in the Kūfan context) as opposed to the myriad of more subtle differences.

Our analysis centers on 242 Kūfan traditions[156] sifted from a larger pool of 469 pertinent texts preserved in the primary (canonical and noncanonical) Sunnī, Imāmī, and Zaydī collections. The procedure for labeling accounts Kūfan is discussed in Chapter 2 and rests on the geographical affiliations of transmitters from the 2nd/8th century. The most striking feature of this data is the discrepancy between the textual contributions of the three sectarian communities. Specifically, a vast majority of the Kūfan *qunūt* accounts are drawn from Sunnī (56 percent or 135 traditions) sources with considerably smaller allotments taken from Imāmī

[155] The discussion here does not include the *witr* prayer, which the Ḥanafīs considered obligatory (*wājib*) but which the other law schools did not regard as mandatory (*farḍ*). It is limited to the five prayers that all the Islamic law schools agree are incumbent on every Muslim. These are the dawn prayer (*fajr*), the noon prayer (*ẓuhr*), the afternoon prayer (*'aṣr*), the sunset prayer (*maghrib*), and the evening prayer (*'ishā'*).

[156] As in Chapter 3, Table 4.2 assigns each Kūfan tradition a number based on the death date of authority figures. In such a scheme, a low number (e.g., 001) represents a tradition that cites an early authority (e.g., the Prophet). The Kūfan traditions are not numbered sequentially because they were drawn from a larger overall pool of 469 traditions. For the original sources of these texts, see www.najamhaider.com/originsoftheshia

(30 percent or 73 traditions)[157] or Zaydī (14 percent or 34 traditions)[158] collections.[159] This numerical disparity will be directly addressed in the structural analyses that follows.

Table 4.2 reflects a particular Sunnī interest in the status of the *qunūt* in the dawn (*fajr*) prayer (62 percent of all Sunnī accounts) with a significant divide between those traditions that endorse its inclusion (36 percent) and those that oppose it (27 percent). There is virtually no support for the *qunūt* in the afternoon prayers (i.e., *ẓuhr* and *ʿaṣr*) and only minimal references to its performance in the sunset (*maghrib*) (9 percent) and evening (*ʿishāʾ*) (2 percent) prayers. The Zaydī Kūfan traditions are unanimous in their approval of the *qunūt* in the *fajr* (53 percent) prayer and offer considerable support for its use in the *maghrib* (21 percent) prayer. Similarly to the Sunnī accounts, they seem to reject the practice in both the *ẓuhr* and *ʿaṣr* prayers. By contrast, the Imāmī texts affirm the *qunūt* for every prayer including (uniquely) the afternoon (27 percent) prayers. Many of these are not simply general endorsements of the *qunūt* but rather very specific statements that mention each of the five prayers by name.

Overall, our findings suggest a primary Kūfan concern with the *witr* and the *fajr* prayers. In the case of *witr*, the *qunūt* was unequivocally sanctioned by all the legal schools. The *fajr qunūt* was more problematic as Sunnī traditions were polarized between those that supported it (e.g., the Shāfiʿīs and Mālikīs) and those that opposed it (e.g., the Ḥanafīs). The Sunnī and Zaydī traditions also intimate the existence of a third group (later embodied by the Nāṣirī Caspian Zaydīs) that permitted the *qunūt* in the *maghrib* and *ʿishāʾ* prayer. The Imāmī Kūfan traditions are singular in extending the *qunūt* to all five daily prayers.

Authorities

As in the previous chapter, the first comparison focuses on authority figures mentioned in the traditions preserved by each sectarian community.

[157] This constitutes 71% of the entirety of 104 Imāmī traditions.

[158] This constitutes 85% of the entirety of 40 Zaydī traditions.

[159] This is in stark contrast to the equal numbers of *basmala* traditions provided by each sectarian group in Chapter 3. Such a disparity must be factored in a consideration of the general applicability of our conclusions; however, its impact should not be overstated. If the patterns evident in the previous analysis hold, then we still have two corroborating sets of data. Also note that given the large differences in the number/scale of traditions preserved by each sectarian community, a disparity is to be expected in almost all cases. The *basmala* was thus an exceptional case as opposed to the general rule.

TABLE 4.2. *The Kūfan Traditions (Qunūt)*

	Sunnī					Zaydī		Imāmī			
	Pro			Anti		All Pro		All Pro*			
Fajr	026	193	265	012	218	018	256	234	406	387	413
	034	208	266	146	219	030	257	235	360	388	414
	038	209	267	149	221	036	280	259	367	389	418
	037	212	268	151	253	039	320	349	369	393	419
	041	214	279	178	273	125	345	350	370	400	420
	042	237	288	181	276	230	346	353	377	402	432
	044	238	289	182	277	232	352	358	382	405	
	070	239	295	183	278	233	409	359	386	407	
	082	243	305	184	287	251	445				
	164	245	308	185	291						
	171	246	309	186	292						
	172	247	310	196	293						
	173	248	316	197	294						
	179	249	317	206	300						
	180	252	348	211	319						
	192	262	375	215	323						
				216	326						
				217	331						
Ẓuhr	044			146		124		259	359	377	402
								349	360	384	405
								350	367	388	413
								353	369	393	414
								358	370	400	418
ʿAṣr	044			146				259	359	377	402
								349	360	384	405
								350	367	388	413
								353	369	393	414
								358	370	400	418
Maghrib	037	044		146		036	320	226	359	382	402
	038	236				039	346	259	360	387	405
	040	241				240	352	349	367	388	407
	041	242				251		350	369	392	413
	042	245						353	370	393	414
	043	348						358	377	400	418
ʿIshāʾ	044			146		346		259	360	387	405
	348					352		349	367	388	407
								350	369	393	413
								353	370	400	414
								358	377	402	418
								359	382		

	Sunnī					Zaydī		Imāmī			
	Pro			Anti		All Pro		All Pro*			
Witr	009	245		146		018	244	131	376	400	411
	010	325				030	345	349	379	405	416
	011	327				230	409	350	385	407	417
	014	328				232		358	390	408	432
	022a	329						366	398	410	
	024	330									
	024a	220									
	025										
Unspecified	022	201	302	013	138	081	264	046	351	381	399
	023	231	303	015	162	123	304	132	355	382	403
	029	250	306	016	166	145	307	133	357	391	404
	158	269	324	073a	169	227	332	148	361	394	412
	159	270	424	121	255	254	362	343	363	395	415
	163	271	422	135	322	260	447	344	368	396	421
	168	272				263		347	378	397	448
											383*

* denotes the only Imāmī tradition that rejects the *qunūt*. For complete references corresponding to each numbered tradition, see www.najamhaider.com/originsoftheshia

In Table 4.3, the number in the parenthesis (prior to each name) represents the total number of accounts that invoke a given authority, and texts that cite the Prophet or the first four caliphs are counted twice.[160] Recall that we are particularly interested in evidence for the emergence of distinct Imāmī and Zaydī sectarian identities. To this end, a large number of authorities shared between groups intimates a degree of overlap, whereas reliance on distinctive authorities suggests independence.

The data in Table 4.3 suggests three primary conclusions. First, there is no significant overlap between the Imāmī and Sunnī traditions. The two sects share four authorities: the Prophet, ʿAlī, ʿAbd Allāh b. Maʿqil (d. 80/699), and al-Bāqir. The Prophet's importance is reduced by the fact that he is cited by all sects for obvious reasons. Although ʿAlī is more controversial, his status is upheld by each of the sects considered in this study as (1) a seminal patriarchal figure for Imāmīs and Zaydīs and (2) the fourth

[160] The first time with respect to their primary authority (e.g., Abū Bakr) and the second time with respect to their first transmitters. As discussed in Chapter 3, this is done because Prophetic and caliphal traditions contain significant contradictions that disappear when analysis is extended to first transmitters. Note that in some traditions, the opinions of early transmitters are preserved alongside their recollections of authorities such as the Prophet or Abū Bakr.

TABLE 4.3. *Authorities Cited (Qunūt)*

	Sunnī	Zaydī	Imāmī
Unique	(5) Ubayy b. Ka'b b. Qays (d. 20/641?) (3) Ṭāriq b. Ashyam (d. 20–50/641–70?) (11) 'Abd Allāh b. Mas'ūd (32/652) (2) Abū Mūsā al-Ash'arī (49/669) (2) Abd al-Raḥmān b. Abzā (d. late 1st/early 8th c) (1) 'Abd Allāh b. Mughaffal (d. 60/680) (2) Rabī' b. Khuthaym (d. 60–7/680–5) (1) 'Abd Allāh b. Sakhbara (d. 60–7/680–5) (2) 'Alqama b. Qays b. 'Abd Allāh (d. 63/682) (1) 'Aṭā' b. Yasār (d. 65/685) (3) 'Abd Allāh b. 'Umar (d. 73/692) (1) Muḥammad b. 'Alī b. Abī Ṭālib (d. 73/692) (3) 'Ubayd b. 'Umayr b. Qatāda (d. 73/692) (6) Aswad b. Yazīd b. Qays (d. 75/694) (2) 'Amr b. Maymūn (d. 75/694) (2) Ṭāriq b. Shihāb b. 'Abd al-Shams (d. 83/702) (1) Māhān (Abū Sālim al-Ḥanafī) (d. 83/702) (1) 'Abd al-Raḥmān b. 'Abd (d. 86/705) (1) 'Awf b. Mālik b. Naḍla (d. 90/708) (6) 'Abd Allāh b. Ḥabīb (d. 105/723?) (2) 'Abd al-Raḥmān b. Malla (d. 95–100/713–8) (2) Zayd b. Wahb (d. 96/714) (1) 'Abd al-Raḥmān b. al-Aswad (d. 100/718) (2) 'Āmir b. Sharāḥīl (d. 107/725) (1) 'Āmir b. Wāthila b. 'Abd Allāh (d. 110/728) (1) 'Amr b. 'Abd Allāh b. 'Ubayd (d. 127/745) (1) Muḥammad b. 'Abd al-Raḥmān (d. 148/765) (1) Sufyān al-Thawrī (d. 161/778)	(1) 'Umar b. 'Alī b. Abī Ṭālib (d. 67/687) (1) 'Arfaja b. 'Abd Allāh (d. 70/689) (1) 'Urwa b. al-Zubayr b. al-'Awwām (d. 83/702) (1) Sa'd (Mughīth) b. 'Amr (d. 85/704) (1) Sa'īd b. al-Musayyab (d. 94/713) (1) Mujāhid b. Jabr (d. 100 or 104/718 or 122) (1) Zayd b. 'Alī (d. 122/740) (1) Ibrāhīm b. Muḥammad (d. 162/779) (1) Qāsim b. Ibrāhīm al-Rassī (d. 246/860) (2) Aḥmad b. 'Īsā b. Zayd (d. 248/862)	(1) 'Abd al-Raḥmān b. Samura (d. 51/671) (1) Ṣabbāḥ b. Yaḥyā (d. mid 2nd/8th c) (1) 'Alī al-Riḍā (d. 203/819) (1) 'Alī al-Hādī (d. 254/868)

Shared	¥ (32) Muḥammad (d. 11/632)	¥ (9) Muḥammad (d. 11/632)	¥ (5) Muḥammad (d. 11/632)
	¥ (21) ʿAlī b. Abī Ṭālib (d. 40/661)	¥ (14) ʿAlī b. Abī Ṭālib (d. 40/661)	¥ (5) ʿAlī b. Abī Ṭālib (d. 40/661)
	¥ (2) Muḥammad al-Bāqir (d. 117/735)	¥ (11) Muḥammad al-Bāqir (d. 117/735)	¥ (18) Muḥammad al-Bāqir (d. 117/735)
	ZS (5) Abū Bakr (d. 13/635)	**ZS** (1) Abū Bakr (d. 13/635)	
	ZS (31) ʿUmar b. al-Khaṭṭāb (d. 23/644)	**ZS** (1) ʿUmar b. al-Khaṭṭāb (d.23/644)	
	ZS (3) ʿUthmān b. ʿAffān (35/655)	**ZS** (1) ʿUthmān b. ʿAffān (35/655)	
	ZS (8) al-Ḥasan b. ʿAlī b. Abī Ṭālib (d. 49/669)	**ZS** (1) al-Ḥasan b. ʿAlī b. Abī Ṭālib (d. 49/669)	
	ZS (14) Barāʾ b. ʿĀzib b. al-Ḥārith (d. 50/670)	**ZS** (2) Barāʾ b. ʿĀzib b. al-Ḥārith (d. 50/670)	
	ZS (1) Ḥārith b. ʿAbd Allāh b. Jābir (d. 65/685)	**ZS** (2) Ḥārith b. ʿAbd Allāh b. Jābir (d. 65/685)	
	ZS (7) ʿAbd Allāh b. ʿAbbās (d. 68/688)	**ZS** (2) ʿAbd Allāh b. ʿAbbās (d. 68/688)	
	ZS (3) ʿAbd al-Raḥmān b. Maʿqil (d. 80/699?)	**ZS** (1) ʿAbd al-Raḥmān b. Maʿqil (d. 80/699?)	
	ZS (4) Ibn Abī Layla (d. 83/702)	**ZS** (2) Ibn Abī Layla (d. 83/702)	
	ZS (5) Saʿīd b. Jubayr (d. 95/713)	**ZS** (1) Saʿīd b. Jubayr (d. 95/713)	
	ZS (12) Ibrāhīm al-Nakhaʿī (d. 96/714)	**ZS** (1) Ibrāhīm al-Nakhaʿī (d. 96/714)	
	IS (3) ʿAbd Allāh b. Maʿqil b.(d. 80/699)		**IS** (1) ʿAbd Allāh b. Maʿqil (d. 80/699)
		ZI (1) Jaʿfar al-Ṣādiq (d. 148/765)	**ZI** (51) Jaʿfar al-Ṣādiq (d. 148/765)

Note: Intersections between all three are denoted by the symbol "¥". Intersections between the Zaydīs and Imāmīs are denoted by the symbol "**ZI.**" Intersections between Sunnīs and Zaydīs are denoted by "**ZS.**" Intersections between Sunnīs and Imāmīs are denoted by "**IS.**" The raw data can accessed via www.najamhaider.com/originsoftheshia

of the "rightly-guided" caliphs for the Sunnīs. 'Abd Allāh b. Ma'qil's significance is tied directly to 'Alī whose opinion he transmits in a limited number (4) of traditions. He is never mentioned as a legal authority in his own right. The significance of al-Bāqir as a common authority is reduced by the extreme numerical disparity between the two groups. He is cited in only 1 percent (2/135) of Sunnī traditions as compared to 25 percent (18/73) of Imāmī traditions. In conclusion, the intersection between the Imāmīs and Sunnīs, although slightly greater in the case of the *qunūt* than that of the *basmala*, remains largely trivial.

Second, there is a substantial overlap between the Sunnī and Zaydī traditions through the 1st/7th century. In addition to the Prophet and the first four caliphs, the two groups share eight common authorities: al-Ḥasan b. 'Alī, Barā' b. 'Āzib (d. 50/670), Ḥārith b. 'Abd Allāh b. Jābir (d. 65/685), 'Abd Allāh b. 'Abbās, 'Abd al-Raḥmān b. Ma'qil, Ibn Abī Layla (d. 83/702), Sa'īd b. Jubayr, and Ibrāhīm al-Nakha'ī. The final three figures (i.e., Ibn Abī Layla, Sa'īd b. Jubayr, and Ibrāhīm al-Nakha'ī) are of notable importance because of their routine appearance in postformative Sunnī legal works both as prominent transmitters and as jurists in their own right. Their presence in the early Zaydī traditions, therefore, suggests a significant intersection between the early Zaydīs and their proto-Sunnī counterparts. Further corroboration is found in Zaydī references to 'Urwa b. al-Zubayr (d. 83/702), Sa'īd b. al-Musayyab (d. 93–4/712–3), and Mujāhid b. Jabr. Although these men are not found in Kūfan Sunnī *qunūt* traditions, they are central figures in Sunnī jurisprudence and rarely (if ever) mentioned by the Imāmīs.

Third, the relationship between the Sunnīs and Zaydīs disintegrates at the start of the 2nd/8th century. As in the case of the *basmala*, the two groups have no significant overlaps after 100/718, with the singular exception of al-Bāqir.[161] At this point, the Zaydīs begin relying almost exclusively on Medinan and Kūfan 'Alids. While this includes figures revered by the Imāmīs (e.g., al-Bāqir and al-Ṣādiq), their use in Zaydī traditions is fundamentally different. Specifically, they are listed alongside a myriad of equally authoritative and distinctly Zaydī 'Alids such as Zayd b. 'Alī, Ibrahīm b. Muḥammad (d. 162/779), al-Qāsim b. Ibrāhīm, and Aḥmad b. 'Īsā.

[161] The numerical disparity in the use of al-Bāqir between the Zaydīs and Sunnīs is even greater than that between the Imāmīs and Sunnīs. Al-Bāqir is mentioned in 32% (11/34) of Zaydī traditions as compared with 1% (2/135) Sunnī traditions.

As a whole, the data clearly attests to Imāmī independence. Imāmī traditions do not exhibit any substantive overlap with the Sunnī traditions and only intersect with the Zaydīs on a limited number of historically important 'Alids. By contrast, the data falls short of supporting the classical narrative of Zaydism. Zaydī traditions prior to the 2nd/8th century predominantly preserve the opinions of Batrī authority figures (i.e., Companions, non-'Alid jurists) with little evidence of a Jārūdī (i.e., 'Alid) presence. The situation changes rather dramatically in the early to mid-2nd/8th century, with the disappearance of non-'Alid figures and a growing reliance on a pool of distinctive 'Alid authorities.

Chains and Transmitters

The second comparison of Kūfan traditions is concerned with single common transmitters and shared links. As in Chapter 3, we are interested in the degree to which different sects trusted the same individuals for the transmission of traditions. Shared links are even more significant as they suggest an agreement regarding an individual's scholarly and communal affiliations. Isolated common transmitters are listed in Table 4.4a; shared links are detailed in Table 4.4b.

We can draw two conclusions from Tables 4.4a and 4.4b. First, Imāmī traditions exhibit no substantive overlap with those of other sectarian groups. They only share two single transmitters with the Zaydīs, which, in the absence of shared links, are of marginal overall importance to this study. It may be that some transmitters shifted their allegiances/loyalties in the course of their lives, but this reveals more about these individuals than it does about the convergence between communities.[162] The Sunnī-Imāmī overlap is more pronounced, with three common transmitters and two shared links. One of the three isolated figures (i.e., Sulaymān b. Mihrān al-A'mash) is also common to the Zaydīs, suggesting (once again) that some figures straddled the boundaries of competing sectarian identities[163] The other single transmitters (i.e., Ḥabīb b. Qays – d. 119 or 122/737 or 740, and Jābir b. Yazīd b. Ḥārith – d. 128 or 132/746 or 750)

[162] For more on this category of transmitters, see Chapter 6.

[163] Another possibility is that they were members of one sectarian group but judged trustworthy enough to be cited by others. We would expect some indication of this in the biographical dictionaries. In the case of al-A'mash, however, the Sunnī *rijāl* literature does not categorically dismiss him as Shī'ī and the Imāmī *rijāl* literature does not characterize him as Sunnī. For more on al-A'mash, see Chapter 6.

TABLE 4.4a. *Single Transmitters (Qunūt)*

	Transmitters in Isolation	Traditions
Sunnī/Zaydī	Ibrāhīm b. Yazīd al-Nakhaʿī (d. 96/714)*	6 Sunnī (181, 184, 196, 206, 291, 293, 303) 1 Zaydī (251)
	Mujāhid b. Jabr (d. 100 or 104/718 or 722)	1 Sunnī (277) 1 Zaydī (332)
	ʿAmr b. Murra (d. 116 or 118/734 or 736)*	1 Sunnī (319) 2 Zaydī (036, 039)
	Zubayd (Zubaya) b. Ḥārith (d. 122/740)*	3 Sunnī (009, 010, 011) 2 Zaydī (320, 332)
	ʿAmr b. ʿAbd Allāh b. ʿAlī (ʿUbayd) (d. 127/745)*	12 Sunnī (022, 022a, 023, 024, 024a, 025, 029, 215, 216, 217, 255, 375) 2 Zaydī (230, 232)
	Mughīra b. Miqsam (d. 132/750)*	1 Sunnī (303) 1 Zaydī (251)
	Sulaymān b. Mihrān al-Aʿmash (d. 148/765)*	6 Sunnī (151, 183, 206, 293, 294, 331) 1 Zaydī (240)
	Sharīk b. ʿAbd Allāh (d. 177/793)*	6 Sunnī (013, 022a, 238, 242, 348, 422) 4 Zaydī (081, 244, 280, 352)
	Muḥammad b. Fuḍayl b. Ghazwān (d. 194–5/809–10)	3 Sunnī (214, 269, 270) 1 Zaydī (320)
	Muḥammad b. ʿAlāʾ b. Kurayb (247–8/861–2)	1 Sunnī (073a) 2 Zaydī (232, 409)
Zaydī/Imāmī	Saʿīd b. Musayyib b. Ḥazm (d. 93–4/712–3)	1 Zaydī (145) 1 Imāmī (046)
	Sulaymān b. Mihrān al-Aʿmash (d. 148/765)	1 Zaydī (240) 1 Imāmī (388)
Sunnī/Imāmī	Ḥabīb b. Qays (Ibn Abī Thābit) (d. 119 or 122/737 or 740)*	2 Sunnī (238, 239) 4 Imāmī (234)
	Jābir b. Yazīd b. Ḥārith (d. 128 or 132/746 or 750)	1 Sunnī (151) 2 Imāmī (046)
	Sulaymān b. Mihrān al-Aʿmash (d. 148/765)	7 Sunnī (151, 183, 206, 241, 293, 294, 331) 1 Imāmī (388)

* See also Shared Links in Table 4.4b. For complete references corresponding to each numbered tradition, see www.najamhaider.com/originsoftheshia

TABLE 4.4b. *Shared Links (Qunūt)*

	Shared Links	Traditions
<u>Sunnī/Zaydī</u> #1	Muḥammad (d. 10/632) | Ḥasan b. ʿAlī b. Abī Ṭālib (d. 49/669)	8 Sunnī (022, 022a, 023, 024, 024a, 025, 026, 029) 1 Zaydī (030)
#2	Muḥammad (d. 10/632) | Barāʾ b. ʿĀzib b. al-Ḥārith (d. 50/670) | Ibn Abī Layla (d. 83/702) | ʿAmr b. Murra (d. 116 or 118/734 or 736) | Shuʿba b. Ḥajjāj (160–776)/Sufyān b. Saʿīd (d. 161/778) | ʿAbd al-Raḥmān b. Mahdī b. Hassān (d. 198/813)	1 Sunnī (038) 1 Zaydī (039)
#3	Muḥammad (d. 10/632) | Barāʾ b. ʿĀzib b. al-Ḥārith (d. 50/670) | Ibn Abī Layla (d. 83/702) | ʿAmr b. Murra (d. 116 or 118/734 or 736) | Shuʿba b. Ḥajjāj (160/776)	4 Sunnī (034, 037, 040) 2 Zaydī (036, 039)
#4	ʿAmr b. Murra (d. 116 or 118/734 or 736) | Shuʿba b. Ḥajjāj (160–776)	1 Sunnī (326) The same 2 Zaydī (036, 039) as in Table 4.4a

(*continued*)

TABLE 4.4b *(continued)*

	Shared Links	Traditions
#5	Sufyān b. Sa'īd (d. 161/778) | 'Abd al-Raḥmān b. Mahdī b. Hassān (d. 198/813)	1 Sunnī (265) The same Zaydī (039) as in Table 4.4a
#6	Muḥammad (d. 10/632) | Barā' b. 'Āzib b. al-Hārith (d. 50/670) | Ibn Abī Layla (d. 83/702) | 'Amr b. Murra (d. 116 or 118/734 or 736) | Sufyān b. Sa'īd (d. 161/778)	4 Sunni (037, 040, 041, 042) The same Zaydī (039) as in Table 4.4a
#7	'Alī b. Abī Ṭālib (d. 40/661) | Ḥārith b. 'Abd Allāh b. Jābir (d. 65/685) | 'Amr b. 'Abd Allāh b. 'Alī ('Ubayd) (d. 127/745)	1 Sunnī (231) 2 Zaydī (230, 232)
#8	'Alī b. Abī Ṭālib (d. 40/661) | 'Arfaja b. 'Abd Allāh (d. 70/689?) | Maymūn b. Mihrān (d. 110/728) | Sharīk b. 'Abd Allāh (d. 177/793)	1 Sunnī (219) 1 Zaydī (263)

#9	‘Arfaja b. ‘Abd Allāh (d. 70/689?) | Maymūn b. Mihrān (d. 110/728)	1 Sunnī (218) The same Zaydī (263) as in Table 4.4a
#10	‘Alī b. Abī Ṭālib (d. 40/661) | ‘Abd al-Raḥmān b. Ma‘qil (d. 80/699?) | Anonymous | Sulaymān b. Mihrān al-A‘mash (d. 148/765)	1 Sunnī (241) 1 Zaydī (240)
#11	‘Alī b. Abī Ṭālib (d. 40/661) | ‘Abd al-Raḥmān b. Ma‘qil (d. 80/699?)	2 Sunnī (242, 243) The same Zaydī (240) as in Table 4.4a
#12	‘Alī b. Abī Ṭālib (d. 40/661) | Ibrāhīm al-Nakha‘ī (d. 96/714)	1 Sunnī (250) 1 Zaydī (251)
#13	‘Alī b. Abī Ṭālib (d. 40/661) | Muḥammad al-Bāqir (117/ 735)	1 Sunnī (255) 1 Zaydī (256)
#14	Ibn Abī Layla (d. 083/702) | Zubayd (Zubaya) b. Ḥārith (d. 122/740) | Sufyān b. Sa‘īd (d. 161/778)	1 Sunnī (305) 1 Zaydī (304)

(continued)

TABLE 4.4b *(continued)*

	Shared Links	Traditions
#15	Zubayd (Zubaya) b. Ḥārith (d. 122/740) | Sufyān b. Sa'īd (d. 161/778)	1 Sunnī (011) The same Zaydī (304) as in Table 4.4a
#16	Ibn Abī Layla (d. 083/702) | Zubayd (Zubaya) b. Ḥārith (d. 122/740) | Sharīk b. 'Abd Allāh (d. 177/793)	1 Sunnī (306) 1 Zaydī (307)
#17	Ibrāhīm al-Nakha'ī (d. 96/714) | Mughīra b. Miqsam (d. 132/750)	3 Sunnī (273, 329, 330) 1 Zaydī (251)
<u>Zaydī/Imāmī</u>	**None**	**None**
<u>Sunnī/Imāmī</u> #1	'Alī b. Abī Ṭālib (d. 40/661) | 'Abd Allāh b. Ma'qil (d. 80/699?)	3 Sunnī (236, 237, 262) 1 Imāmī (235)
#2	'Abd al-Raḥmān b. Aswad b. Yazīd (d. 98 or 100/716 or 718) | 'Amr b. Khālid (Abū Khālid) (d. 120/738)	1 Sunnī (252) 1 Imāmī (234)

For complete references corresponding to each numbered tradition, see www.najamhaider.com/originsoftheshia

together with the two shared links suggest a degree of ambiguity on the border between the two communities. It should be kept in mind, however, that the intersection in shared links is limited to just 3% of Imāmī (2/73) and Sunnī (4/135) accounts.

Second, there is a noticeable overlap between the Sunnīs and Zaydīs which consists of seventeen shared links[164] spread across 23 percent (31/136) of the Sunnī and 38 percent (13/34) of the Zaydī traditions along with eleven individual transmitters extending into the early 3rd/9th century. As opposed to the Imāmī/Sunnī case, Zaydī/Sunnī shared links are long, often stretching from the Prophet or an early Companion into the middle of the 2nd/8th century. Shared link #3, for example, narrates a Prophetic opinion through five consecutive transmitters before splitting after Shu'ba b. al-Ḥajjāj who died in 160/776. It is significant that no shared links persist after 198/813 and 88 percent (15/17) terminate before 160/776. As for isolated transmitters, 70 percent (7/10) occur before 148/766, with the last represented by Muḥammad b. al-'Alā' b. Kurayb who died in 247/861. Overall, the intersection between Sunnīs and Zaydīs is both substantial and long-term, surviving well into the middle of the 2nd/8th century.

These results (as in previous cases) support the notion that an independent Imāmī legal identity had materialized by the early 2nd/8th century. There is a small overlap with the Sunnīs, but this is limited to a handful of common transmitters and two shared links that end by 119/737. By contrast, there is a striking disjuncture between the Imāmīs and the Zaydīs. With respect to the classical narrative of early Zaydism, the expected Batrī (proto-Sunnī) elements are present in the Zaydī traditions but the Jārūdī (Imāmī) influences are notably absent. A significant proportion of the Zaydī *ḥadīth* corpus is virtually indistinguishable from that of the Sunnīs through the 1st/7th century. This intersection deteriorates in the mid-2nd/8th century and is restricted by the early 3rd/9th century to the common use of a few isolated transmitters. There is little in the early Zaydī accounts that can be characterized as distinctly Jārūdī with even 'Alī's opinions transmitted through chains shared with the Sunnīs. If the classical narrative is correct, where is the Jārūdī contribution?

[164] This number includes shared links which are subsets of larger chains. In other words, link #4 is counted as an independent link even though it is a subset of a larger chain (link #3). This is done because the sublink also occurs in a different set of traditions.

Narrative Style

The final comparison centers on the narrative style utilized by each sectarian group to preserve information. As in previous comparisons, we are concerned with (1) the extent to which sectarian groups overlap and (2) the point at which intersections disappear suggesting the emergence of an independent communal identity.

Before turning to Table 4.5, we should acknowledge that the large disparity between the contributions of the three sects makes a straight numerical comparison across narrative styles extremely problematic. In the analysis that follows, the potential for distortions or misleading conclusions (due to this disparity) is minimized by focusing on percentages rather than raw numbers. For example, although there are more Sunnī (9) than Zaydī traditions (7) in the 'question-answer' category, the Zaydī use of this style is significant (21 percent of all Zaydī traditions), whereas the Sunnī use (7 percent of the total) is marginal.

The data supports two primary conclusions. First, there is an overlap between the Imāmīs and the Zaydīs, particularly noticeable in accounts citing later authorities. Both the Zaydīs (21 percent) and the Imāmīs (36 percent) rely heavily on the question-and-answer style and minimize the use of eyewitness accounts (9 percent for Zaydī, 5 percent for Imāmī). The most common narrative technique for both communities is the direct quotation (35 percent for Zaydī, 48 percent for Imāmī) from an authority figure. There is no clear correlation between the death dates of Imāmī authorities and the literary forms that preserve their opinions. In other words, the Imāmīs consistently transmit the views of authorities beginning with the Prophet and ending with al-Ṣādiq in the question-and-answer style. In the case of the Zaydīs, however, every authority figure from the 2nd/8th century falls into one of the two narrative types (question/answer or direct quote), which the Zaydīs share with the Imāmīs. These narrative techniques are much less common in Zaydī traditions that cite earlier authorities.

Second, there is a clear intersection in narrative structure between Sunnī and *early* Zaydī traditions. Exemplary statements comprise a majority of the Sunnī accounts (54 percent) and a plurality of the Zaydī (35 percent) accounts. Whereas the Sunnīs utilize this style for a wide range of figures, the Zaydīs restrict its use to the Prophet, the first four caliphs, and the proto-Sunnī jurist Saʿīd b. Jubayr (tradition 320). In other words, the Zaydīs preserve the opinions of early authorities (1st/7th century) in a narrative form they share with the Sunnīs (exemplary statements),

TABLE 4.5. *Narrative Style (Qunūt)*

	Sunnī				Zaydī		Imāmī			
Question/Answer	255	302	348		227	362	131	376	397	413
	292	305	375		254	445	347	378	399	417
	293	322	422		264	447	351	383	403	418
					345		357	384	404	419
							367	387	406	421
							369	392	412	432
							370	395		
Eyewitness Accounts	012	173	186	272	125	280	234	386		
	138	178	193	278	263		377	389		
	162	179	201	288						
	163	180	219	289						
	164	181	238	300						
	166	182	243	319						
	171	183	271	323						
	172	184								
Direct Quotes	022	026	295	326	018	304	132	358	420	400
	022a	073a	306	327	030	307	133	359	385	402
	023	250	309	329	081	332	259	360	388	405
	024	262	324	330	230	346	343	361	390	407
	024a	276	325	424	232	352	344	363	391	408
	025	291			260	409	349	366	393	411
							350	379	394	414
							353	381	396	415
							355	382	398	
Exemplary Statements	009	135	215	253	036	240	148	235		
	010	146	216	265	039	244	226			
	011	149	217	266	123	251				
	013	151	218	267	124	256				
	014	158	220	268	145	257				
	015	159	221	269	233	320				
	016	168	231	270						
	029	169	236	273						
	034	185	237	277						
	037	192	239	279						
	038	196	241	287						
	040	197	242	294						
	041	206	245	308						
	042	208	246	310						
	043	209	247	316						
	044	211	248	317						
	070	212	249	328						
	082	214	252	331						
	121									

(*continued*)

TABLE 4.5 *(continued)*

	Sunnī	Zaydī	Imāmī
Written Correspondence	None	None	448
Exegesis	None	None	046 410 368 416
Overall	Q/A –7 % Eyewitness – 22% Direct – 16% Exemplary – 54% Written – 0% Exegesis – 0%	Q/A – 21% Eyewitness – 9% Direct – 35% Exemplary – 35% Written – 0% Exegesis – 0%	Q/A – 36% Eyewitness – 5% Direct – 48% Exemplary – 4% Written – 1% Exegesis – 5%

Note: For complete references corresponding to each numbered tradition, see www.najamhaider.com/originsoftheshia

while transmitting the opinions of later authorities (i.e., al-Bāqir, Qāsim b. Ibrāhīm, and Aḥmad b. ʿĪsā) in forms prevalent among the Imāmīs.

Overall we find strong support for the assertion of an independent Imāmī communal identity in early 2nd/8th century Kūfa and little evidence corroborating the classical narrative of early Zaydism. The Imāmīs clearly diverge from the Sunnīs in their preferred narrative type but exhibit an overlap with the Zaydīs with respect to ʿAlid authorities from the 2nd/8th century. This might intimate a substantive intersection between the Zaydīs and Imāmīs, but in the absence of any other evidence, it is more likely a stylistic choice common to the depiction of Kūfan ʿAlids. The data also suggests a strong Zaydī reliance on proto-Sunnī Kūfan forms in the 1st/7th and early 2nd/8th century followed by a move toward more Imāmī styles, rather than the (expected) initial mix of Batrī (Kūfan proto-Sunnī) and Jārūdī (roughly Imāmī) elements. As was the case in the two previous comparisons, the Zaydī accounts appear grounded in Kūfan proto-Sunnism until a point, in the mid-2nd/8th century, when they acquire a character similar to – but independent from – that of the Imāmīs.

CONCLUSION

This chapter presents the second of three case studies intended to test the sectarian narratives detailed in Chapter 1 through the utilization of a comparative methodology developed in Chapter 2. Specifically, it centers on the inclusion and performance of the *qunūt* in the daily prayers. The chapter began with a broad legal survey of six major Islamic law schools intended to familiarize the reader with this complicated yet important element of ritual law. It then proceeded to a three-part comparative analysis of 242 Kūfan traditions dealing with the *qunūt* that focused on authority figures, chains of transmission, and narrative styles.

Before proceeding to the third case study, let us evaluate our findings to this point. Recall again that we are primarily concerned with ascertaining evidence for (1) an independent Imāmī identity in the early 2nd/8th century and (2) the birth of Zaydism through the fusion of Batrī and Jārūdī Zaydīs around 122/740. Both case studies provide evidence for an distinct Imāmī communal identity in the early 2nd/8th century through the school's preservation of the opinions of unique authority figures in distinctive *isnād*s and narrative styles. They also point to significant potential discrepancies in the classical narrative of the origins of Zaydism. Rather than an original blend of Batrī and Jārūdī materials that inclines toward the latter in the course of the late 2nd/8th and 3rd/9th century, the data indicates that Zaydism changed at some point in the mid-2nd/8th century. The earliest Zaydī traditions (dating from the early 2nd/8th century) quote proto-Sunnī Kūfan authorities in proto-Sunnī lines of transmission, whereas later accounts (from the mid- to late 2nd/8th century) exclusively cite ʿAlid authorities in distinctive narrative forms. The legal foundation of Zaydism appears almost entirely Batrī (Kūfan proto-Sunnī), with no hint of Jārūdī influence until the mid-2nd/8th century when – although their traditions are preserved – the Batrīs begin to disappear. This suggests a gradual evolution of the movement rather than a merging of two currents. We now turn to the final case study which concerns a famous dietary controversy in the early Muslim world, namely the permissibility of alcoholic drinks.

5

Drinking Matters

The Islamic Debate over Prohibition

Our first two case studies were concerned primarily with ritual practice. The *basmala* and the *qunūt* are actions a supplicant must perform in a particular manner at a specified point in the daily prayer. In addition to mere physical actions, however, Muslims must pray in a lucid, unaltered mental state. The importance of this condition is emphasized in Q4:43 where God orders believers to "not approach prayer when you are drunken, until you know that which you utter."[1] At first glance, the verse seems rather strange given that one of the characteristic features of a pious Muslim in the contemporary world is abstinence from alcohol. Indeed, it would be difficult – if not impossible – to find a single practicing Muslim who would assert the religious permissibility of alcoholic beverages. Medieval legal tracts, however, reveal a raging early controversy over the issue of intoxicants that persisted into the 6th/12th century and was anchored in the writings of a group of early Kūfan Ḥanafī jurists.

Following the model of Chapters 3 and 4, this chapter is divided into two parts. The first provides an overview of prohibition in Islam beginning with an inventory of premodern alcoholic drinks and proceeding to a survey of the six selected law schools. The second applies the methodological approach outlined in Chapter 2 to Kūfan traditions that address the legality of alcohol. The conclusion discusses the extent to which the

[1] Q4:43 – "You who believe! Do not approach prayer when you are drunk, until you know that which you utter, nor when you are sexually polluted except when journeying upon the road until you have bathed. And if you be ill, or on a journey, or one of you comes from the privy, or you have touched women, and cannot find water, then go to high clean soil and rub your faces and your hands (with it). Lo! Allāh is Pardoning, Forgiving."

results align with the sectarian narratives of Chapter 1 and compares the findings to those of the previous two case studies.

THE JURISTIC CONTEXT

The central question in legal discussions of alcohol concerns whether the word *khamr* in Q5:90–1[2] refers exclusively to wine made from uncooked grape juice or whether it can it be broadly applied to intoxicants of all varieties. Although proponents of both views cite supporting traditions, the matter is complicated by slight differences in wording that alter the meaning of proof texts in profound ways. Ancillary issues cover a wide breadth, ranging from the production of vinegar and the legality of certain drinking/storage vessels to the punishment for the consumption of illicit drinks. The positions jurists take on these matters are shaped, to a large extent, by their favoring of either "general" or "narrow" prohibition.[3] For example, if beer is considered a type of *khamr*, it is automatically subject to certain legal restrictions (based on Q5:90–1) including a total ban on its use in cooked foods or in commercial transactions of any kind. A thorough treatment of these matters would require an epic tome far beyond the scope of this modest study. Bearing this in mind, the present chapter will restrict itself to the debate over the legality of alcoholic drinks (the specific question of prohibition). As in previous case studies, the legal survey that follows is not meant to be exhaustive. Rather it is intended to convey a sense of the types of arguments offered by each law school through the examination of a set of representative juristic works.

Visiting a Premodern Kūfan Pub: Definitions and Explanations

Before proceeding to the legal literature, it may be helpful to define the terms used for certain drinks and comment on the standard production

[2] Q5: 90 – "You who believe! *Khamr* and games of chance and idols and divining arrows are only an infamy of Satan's handiwork. Leave it aside so that you may succeed." Q5:91 – "Satan seeks only to cast enmity and hatred amongst you by means of *khamr* and games of chance, and to prevent you from remembrance of Allāh and from prayer. Will you not desist?"

[3] In this chapter, the term "general prohibition" refers to the view that all intoxicants are prohibited in any quantity, as opposed to "narrow prohibition," which restricts the ban to (1) intoxicants drawn from grapes/date or (2) alcohol consumed to the point of intoxication. Proponents of the latter opinion often propose definitions for "intoxication."

methods of the premodern Islamic world.[4] For reasons that will become clear in the course of the chapter, jurists were especially concerned with beverages derived from grapes and dates. The first of these was *khamr*, which was narrowly interpreted as wine derived from raw grape juice. In the early period, there was no legal consensus as to whether the term applied to other intoxicating drinks – a fact that prompted significant disagreements between the Ḥanafīs and the Mālikīs/Shāfiʿīs. *Naqīʿ* (infusion), the second drink with an important role in juristic discussions, was produced by soaking dried fruits (most often dried dates and raisins) until the water acquired the flavor or sweetness of the fruit in question. The third and most problematic of the grape/date drinks was *nabīdh*, described in most traditions[5] as a version of *naqīʿ* in which the fruit was left at the bottom of a glass or vessel rather than being removed after the transfer of flavor. There were other traditions, however, that expanded the sources of *nabīdh* from dried fruit to include fresh fruits (e.g., grapes)[6] and even cooked juice.[7] Jurists also discussed a vast number of intoxicating substances prepared from nongrape/date sources, including barley/millet (*mizr*,[8] *jiʿa*,[9] *fuqqāʿ*[10]), honey (*bitʿ*[11]), wheat/millet (*ghubayrāʾ*[12]), quinces (*mayba*[13]), and even milk (*rūba*[14]).[15]

4 For a discussion of the issues in question, see Hattox, *Coffee*, 50–2 and *EI*², s.v. Khamr (A. J. Wensinck). Bear in mind that the meaning of names given to specific drinks varied by region. The best example is *nabīdh*, which refers to radically different beverages depending on period and location. In the discussion that follows, I have tried to make sense of the chaos by organizing drinks in accordance with their most common usage in the legal sources. Although there are cases in which my use of a name does not align with that of a specific jurist, I feel it is important to maintain a terminological consistency so that, at the very least, the reader can be certain of the identity of the drink in question.

5 See Mālik b. Anas, *Muwaṭṭaʾ* (1951), 2:844 – 8; *SN III*, 5:69 – 5057 and 5:125 – 5229; *SB*, 1102 – 5602; *SIM*, 4:77 – 3397; *SKB*, 8:520 – 17420, 8:521 – 17421, and 8:527 – 17436.

6 See *KK*, 6:392 – 3; *MIAS*, 5:75 – 23837 and 5:76 – 23840.

7 See *KAS II*, 184 – 837.

8 See *SM*, 3:1586 – 71 and 3:1587 – 72; *SAD*, 3:328 – 3684; *MAR*, 9:133 – 17312 and 17313.

9 See *MIAS*, 5:69 – 23765; *SKB*, 8:508 – 17370.

10 The reference to the source of the drink is mentioned in al-Sharīf al-Murtaḍā, *al-Intiṣār*, 1:199 and al-Ṭūsī's *Khilāf*, 5:489–90. See also al-Qalahjī, *Muʿjam*, 317, which defines *fuqqāʿ* as a drink made from barley that has acquired a froth.

11 See *SAD*, 3:328 – 3682; *SN III*, 5:77 – 5083; *SB*, 1100 – 5586.

12 See *SKB*, 8:508 – 17368; *SAD*, 3:328 – 3685; *MAR*, 9:139 – 17337.

13 See *KK*, 6:427 – 3.

14 See *MIAS*, 5:89 – 23982.

15 Mixtures were categorized separately due to their known tendency to ferment more quickly than pure juices. This is made explicit in a number of places, including Ibn Idrīs, *Sarāʾir*, 3:129.

As for production methods, the legal literature was particularly concerned with the cooking of juices. This resulted from a realization that fermentation began at the bottom of a drink where pulp and bits of fruit gathered in a composite known as "the dregs" (*ʿakar*, *durdī*). Once the bottom layer made its way to the top, the drink lost its sweetness and was said to have "intensified." Cooking accelerated the natural process by prematurely pushing the problematic bottom layer to the top. Jurists dealt with this complication by promoting production standards aimed at guarding against the possibility of fermentation. Specifically, they focused on (1) whether a drink had begun to boil and (2) what percentage of its volume had been lost in the cooking process. The ensuing classification of drinks included *bādhiq*,[16] which was produced by briefly cooking grape juice at low heat (so as to not cause boiling), and *ṭilāʾ*,[17] which resulted from cooking grape juice[18] until it had been reduced to one-third of its original volume. On a more general level, all drinks – regardless of source – reduced to one-third of their original volume were called *muthallath*,[19] whereas those reduced to half were labeled *munaṣṣaf*.[20]

This section is intended as a guide for helping the reader navigate through the maze of names mentioned in the juristic literature rather than as a systematic study of premodern drinks. A comprehensive survey of the topic would require a comparison of drinks from a multitude of regions and cultures that confused even the earliest Muslim legal authorities. This is evident in a number of often comical traditions where questioners are asked by authority figures (including the Prophet) to explain the process by which an unfamiliar drink is prepared before ruling on its permissibility.[21] The discussion that follows will assume familiarity with the terminology of drinks and preparations detailed in this section.

The Ḥanafīs

The Ḥanafī treatment of intoxicants is distinguished by an insistence that the Qurʾānic injunction against *khamr* found in Q5:90–1 is limited in

[16] See *MAR*, 9:136 – 17326; *SKB*, 8:511 – 17379.

[17] See *WS*, 25:286–31922; *EI*², s.v. Khamr (A. J. Wensinck).

[18] The date equivalent of this drink is called *sakar*.

[19] See *EI*², s.v. Khamr (A. J. Wensinck); al-Sarakhsī, *al-Mabsūṭ*, 24:15.

[20] al-Sarakhsī, *Mabsūṭ*, 24:15; al-Marghīnānī, *al-Hidāya*, 4:1530.

[21] One tradition (*WS*, 25:352–3 – 32170), for example, mentions a Yemenī beverage called *ḥathā* whose origin remains obscure, whereas another tradition (*SKB*, 8:506 – 17361) depicts the Prophet asking a visiting delegation to describe the manner in which they produce drinks that he subsequently identifies as *bitʿ* and *mizr*.

scope to fermented uncooked grape juice. Even though Ḥanafī jurists acknowledge that *khamr* is illegal in all quantities, they refuse to extend this absolute/strict prohibition to other intoxicants. This stance is aggressively opposed by rival law schools (i.e., the Mālikīs and the Shāfiʿīs), which advocate general prohibition based on analogical reasoning and a number of well-known traditions. The Ḥanafīs defend their position with arguments grounded in etymology and strict logic as well as a series of countertraditions. By the end of the 6th/13th century (and probably much earlier), however, the dominant Ḥanafī view shifts dramatically with the school's embrace of general prohibition.

The earliest formulation of the Ḥanafī position is ascribed to Abū Ḥanīfa who restricts prohibition to wine made from uncooked grape juice while allowing all other drinks unless consumed to the point of intoxication.[22] Muḥammad al-Shaybānī goes slightly further by extending the definition of *khamr* to cover alcoholic drinks made from cooked grape juice (e.g., *muthallath* and *munaṣṣaf*).[23] The most detailed and systematic explanation of the early Ḥanafī stance, however, is found in the juristic works of Aḥmad b. Muḥammad al-Ṭaḥāwī. In the *Mukhtaṣar*, al-Ṭaḥāwī identifies four primary areas of disagreement among the Ḥanafīs, including (1) the evidence for fermentation in grape-based drinks, (2) the impact of cooking on grape-based drinks, (3) the status of water-based intoxicants, and (4) the definition of intoxication.[24]

The first issue centers on whether natural bubbling is sufficient evidence of fermentation (the view of Abū Yūsuf – d. 192/808), or whether frothing is also necessary (the view of Abū Ḥanīfa and al-Shaybānī). The second controversy concerns whether cooking grape juice transforms it into a new substance that can then be fermented to produce a legal drink. The third dispute focuses on water-based drinks. All Ḥanafī jurists (to this point) agree that such drinks are legal if derived from sources other than grapes (e.g., grain, honey); but what about drinks made by fermenting water infused with the flavor of grapes or dates?[25] Al-Ṭaḥāwī notes that Abū Ḥanīfa and Abū Yūsuf recommend avoiding these substances altogether. He then ascribes an even stricter view to al-Shaybānī, claiming that he made reprehensible (*makrūh*) "the consumption of [any drink]

22 *KAS II*, 1:182–5.

23 *Ibid.*, 1:183. See also *KAS II*, 1:184 – 836–838

24 al-Ṭaḥāwī, *Mukhtaṣar*, 1:277–81.

25 Because dates (as a dried fruit) can only be used to make water-based drinks, the issue of intoxicating drinks connected to dates refers exclusively to *naqīʿ* or *nabīdh*.

which intoxicates in large quantities."[26] Finally, although the Ḥanafīs allow the consumption of some intoxicating drinks, they strictly punish those who drink to the point of intoxication.[27] This leads to the fourth contentious issue among Ḥanafī jurists, namely the definition of intoxication. Abū Ḥanīfa and al-Shaybānī forward a definition in which an individual is deemed intoxicated when he cannot differentiate the ground from the sky and a man from a woman, whereas Abū Yūsuf opts for a simple slurring of speech.[28]

In *Sharḥ maʿānī al-āthār*, al-Ṭaḥāwī confronts the mass of textual evidence utilized in legal polemics against the Ḥanafīs with interpretations that carve out a space for the school's views.[29] He begins by defining *khamr* through a tradition (subsequently referred to as "the two plants tradition") in which the Prophet states, "*khamr* is derived from two plants: the date-palm and the grapevine."[30] In an obvious attempt to limit the scope of *khamr* to grapes – and in clear opposition to its plain sense – al-Ṭaḥāwī offers a grammatical gloss of this account based on a series of Qur'ānic verses with the same linguistic structure. For example, he cites Q6:130[31] in which God speaks of messengers sent from "*jinn* and humankind" and observes that God only sent messengers from among humans, indicating that – despite the inclusion of both groups – the verse was intended to refer specifically to humanity. He applies the same logic to the "two plants" tradition, arguing that it is perfectly reasonable to hold that – despite mentioning both the grapevine and the date-palm – the Prophet only intended to link the former to *khamr*.[32]

26 al-Ṭaḥāwī, *Mukhtaṣar*, 1:278. Note that this goes far beyond (and even contradicts) the view articulated by al-Shaybānī in his *Kitāb al-āthār*. Even though al-Ṭaḥāwī includes a quote in which al-Shaybānī says "I am not forbidding such a drink," it is still a puzzling characterization and foreshadows the manner in which subsequent Ḥanafī jurists appropriate al-Shaybānī as a mouthpiece for general prohibition.

27 Note that the Ḥanafīs did not allow the consumption of intoxicants for the express purpose of getting drunk. They maintained that legal intoxicants could only be consumed with food and could not be used exclusively for leisure or entertainment.

28 al-Ṭaḥāwī, *Mukhtaṣar*, 1:278. The latter definition was upheld by a majority of Ḥanafīs. Full punishment was applied for the consumption of even the smallest amount of *khamr*. The standards mentioned here were only applicable to water-based intoxicants like *nabīdh* and *naqīʿ*.

29 al-Ṭaḥāwī, *Sharḥ*, 4:211–22.

30 See *SM*, 3:1573 – 13; *SN III*, 5:72 – 5064; *MAR*, 9:145 – 17365; *SAD*, 3:327 – 3678.

31 Q6:130 – "O' assembly of jinn and humankind! Did there not come to you messengers from among you who recounted my signs and warned you of the meeting of this your Day? They will say, 'We testify against ourselves.' It was the life of this world that deceived them. And they will testify against themselves that they were disbelievers."

32 al-Ṭaḥāwī, *Sharḥ*, 4:212. The confusion regarding the permissibility of date-based intoxicants stems from the tension between the "two plants" tradition and Q16:67 ("And of

In addition to this grammatical argument, al-Ṭaḥāwī consistently highlights ambiguities in the textual evidence used against the Ḥanafīs. In the "two plants" tradition, for example, he observes that it is impossible to prove the superiority of either the inclusive (*khamr* is derived from both plants) or the exclusive (*khamr* is only derived from the grapevine) interpretation.[33] The result is a general affirmation of both. He employs a similar logic when faced with traditions that extend the definition of *khamr* to intoxicants produced from a myriad of nongrape sources[34] such as barley, wheat, and honey (subsequently referred to as the "multiple sources tradition"), or to others that declare that "all intoxicants (*muskir*) are prohibited" (subsequently referred to as the "all intoxicants tradition").[35] These accounts are invariably followed by a series of countertraditions that depict the Prophet[36] and important Companions (1) drinking small quantities of intoxicants,[37] (2) differentiating between *khamr* and other intoxicants,[38] and (3) forbidding intoxication rather than intoxicants.[39] Al-Ṭaḥāwī observes that the only way to resolve these contradictions is to interpret the word "*muskir*" as "the final cup that directly leads to intoxication" rather than simply "an intoxicant."[40] At the very least, this argument strives to demonstrate the legal viability of narrow prohibition based on the copious (but often contradictory) source material.[41]

the fruits of the date-palm, and grapes from which you derive strong drink and good nourishment. Therein is a sign for people who have sense"). The former strongly suggests that date-based intoxicants are *khamr*, whereas the latter has God characterizing date *sakar* (clearly an intoxicant) as "good nourishment." Within the Ḥanafī school, date-based intoxicants were gradually prohibited (without being designated *khamr*), whereas other schools simply declared, from the outset, that Q16:67 had been abrogated by Q5:90–1.

33 *Ibid.*, 4:212.

34 See *SN III*, 5:73 – 5068; *SAD*, 3:324 – 3669; *SB*, 1099 – 5581 and 1100 – 5588; *SKB*, 8:501 – 17346.

35 There are countless variations of this simple formula. See *WS*, 25:334 – 32054; *SKB*, 8:506 – 17362; *MIAS*, 5:66 – 23741; *SIM*, 4:74 – 3389; and *SM*, 3:1587 – 73.

36 See *SKB*, 8:529 – 17446; *MIAS*, 5:78 – 23867; and 5:81 – 23889. Variants are found in *SN III*, 5:114 – 5193 and *MIAS*, 5:79 – 23868.

37 'Umar is cited more often than any other Companion in this regard. He drinks intoxicants after diluting them with water (*MIAS*, 5:79 – 23877; *SAD*, 3:324 – 3669), as well as intensified *nabīdh* (*SKB*, 8:519 – 17416). Anas is also said to have indulged in intensified *nabīdh* (*MIAS*, 5:91 – 23998).

38 See al-Ṭaḥāwī, *Sharḥ*, 4:214.

39 *Ibid.*, 4:220.

40 *Ibid.*, 4:219. This would resolve the most important of the contradictions, as the tradition stating that "all intoxicants are prohibited" would now mean that all final cups that directly intoxicate are forbidden. The Ḥanafī traditions that depict 'Umar (and the Prophet) drinking diluted intoxicants and punishing drunkenness would then make more sense, because prohibition would be limited to cases of intoxication.

41 *Ibid.*, 4:212, 214.

Al-Ṭaḥāwī concludes by affirming the basic parameters of the Ḥanafī position. He asserts a juristic consensus linking fermented grape juice to *khamr* and confirms a strong Ḥanafī aversion toward alcoholic *naqīʿ* and *nabīdh*, albeit restricting punishment (in these cases) to instances of public intoxication.[42] While al-Ṭaḥāwī does not place any credence in the cooking of juices, he concedes that the dominant Ḥanafī view (ascribed to Abū Ḥanīfa, Abū Yūsuf, and al-Shaybānī) assigns a special status to drinks reduced to one-third their original volume in the cooking process.[43]

Subsequent centuries witnessed a gradual movement of the Ḥanafī position toward general prohibition that was legitimized primarily through a transformation in the portrayal of al-Shaybānī. In his *Kitāb al-mabsūṭ*, Muḥammad b. Aḥmad al-Sarakhsī's (d. 483/1090–1) constructs careful etymological arguments and analogies that favor narrow prohibition.[44] A slight shift, however, is perceivable in his declaration that all alcoholic date/grape drinks are unlawful, including *naqīʿ* and *nabīdh*.[45] Al-Sarakhsī justifies the change based on three competing opinions that he ascribes to al-Shaybānī, including one in favor of the complete prohibition of this category of drinks.[46] This contrasts with al-Ṭaḥāwī's claim that al-Shaybānī discouraged these drinks but did not prohibit them. A century later, al-Marghīnānī (d. 593/1196–7) goes even further by condemning the consumption of (1) all grape/date-based intoxicants regardless of their base (water or juice) or their preparation (cooking reduction to half the volume), as well as (2) intoxicants produced from any other substance (grain, honey, etc).[47] Remarkably, these restrictive views are once again traced to al-Shaybānī who, according to al-Marghīnānī and in clear opposition to his own writings, believed that "all intoxicants" were prohibited.[48]

Even in the work of al-Marghīnānī, however, the Ḥanafīs resisted extending the definition of *khamr* beyond wine fermented from uncooked

42 *Ibid.*, 4:215.

43 *Ibid.*, 4:222.

44 Al-Sarakhsī's extensive and detailed examination of *khamr* includes (1) a historical chronology of the Qur'ānic verses pertinent to prohibition; (2) an array of unique arguments centered on logic, rhetoric, and etymology; (3) and discussions about the nature of food and drink (al-Sarakhsī, *al-Mabsūṭ*, 24:2–39). See also al-Qudūrī, *Mukhtaṣar*, 204.

45 Contrast this with Abū Ḥanīfa, who considered such drinks permissible, and al-Ṭaḥāwī, who deemed them reprehensible (*makrūh*).

46 al-Sarakhsī, *al-Mabsūṭ*, 24:15.

47 al-Marghīnānī, *al-Hidāya*, 4:1527–32.

48 *Ibid.*, 4:1531.

grape juice[49] and continued to argue for the permissibility of some intoxicating drinks.[50] Still, the building blocks for a Ḥanafī embrace of general prohibition were now in place, rooted in a new set of opinions ascribed to Muḥammad al-Shaybānī. Despite the gradual evolution in the school's position, its ability to hold out against the combined opinion of every other major Sunnī and Shīʿī law school for more than five hundred years is remarkable.[51]

The Mālikīs

Mālikī jurists endorse general prohibition through the application of analogical reasoning to Q5:90–1. Specifically, they identify *khamr*'s ability to cause enmity among Muslims and hinder remembrance of God as the operative cause (*ʿilla*) of the Qur'ānic prohibition and reinforce this view with etymological and textual evidence. As opposed to the Ḥanafīs, who construct a typology of drinks based on source and preparation, the Mālikīs categorize drinks as either legal (not intoxicating) or illegal (intoxicating). The resulting juristic discourse contrasts sharply with the Ḥanafīs in both style and substance.

A representative example of Mālikī discussions of intoxicants is provided by Ibn Abī Zayd in his *Kitāb al-nawādir wa'l-ziyādāt*.[52] After relating the basic sequence of Qur'ānic verses relevant to the subject

49 In practical terms, this meant that an individual could only be punished for drinking non-grape substances to the point of intoxication. By contrast, consuming even a single drop of *khamr* carried a Qur'ānic punishment.

50 Drawing on the belief that *khamr* compels an individual to drink in excess, al-Marghīnānī observes that *muthallath* is coarse, offers little pleasure, and is more akin to food than drink, thereby making it permissible despite its intoxicating power (al-Marghīnānī, *al-Hidāya*, 4:1533).

51 al-Walwālijīya (d. 540/1145) (*al-Fatāwā*, 5:502–6) adopts the same basic argument as al-Marghīnānī, allowing for the consumption of alcoholic *muthallath* and depicting al-Shaybānī as being opposed to all intoxicants. Al-Kāsānī (d. 587/1191) (*Badā'iʿ*, 6:2944–6) also follows al-Marghīnānī in permitting *muthallath* (as long as it is not consumed to the point of intoxication) and interpreting "*muskir*" as "the final cup that directly causes intoxication." Although I have not conducted an exhaustive survey of every Ḥanafī legal work, the first Ḥanafī jurist (I found) advocating for the complete prohibition of intoxicants was al-Maḥbūbī (d. 747/1346) (*Mukhtaṣar*, 2:224–8), who states that "the ruling in our time agrees with Muḥammad's [al-Shaybānī's] doctrine" that all intoxicants are prohibited (*Mukhtaṣar*, 2:226). The jurists likely lagged behind popular Ḥanafī attitudes/practice on this issue. In other words, whereas most (non-Turkish?) Ḥanafīs were probably conforming to a general prohibition much earlier than the 5th/11th century, the jurists likely felt an obligation to defend the views of Abū Ḥanīfa, the eponymous founder of their law school, from the attacks of rivals.

52 Ibn Abī Zayd, *al-Nawādir*, 14:282–95.

(Q2:219,[53] Q4:43, and Q5:90–1), Ibn Abī Zayd identifies intoxication rather than any physical quality (e.g., color, taste, smell) as the *'illa* for the prohibition of *khamr*.[54] He claims that any drink with the capacity to intoxicate is *khamr* and therefore unlawful in all quantities.[55] Unlike the Ḥanafīs, Ibn Abī Zayd does not attach any importance to the cooking of juice or water-based drinks outside of the fact that, once cooking has started, it must continue until the drink has been reduced to one-third of its original volume.[56] The sole factor in determining the legal status of a drink is its intoxicating power. Thus, juice presses are forbidden because they accumulate residue known to ferment quickly,[57] whereas the dregs of most drinks are rejected because fermentation begins at the bottom of a drinking vessel.[58] As for evidence of fermentation, Ibn Abī Zayd rejects tests based on bubbling or fizzing because many nonintoxicating drinks exhibit these characteristics.[59] The only physical evidence for intoxication is the "intensification" of a drink, usually accompanied by a loss of sweetness.[60] Once again, the effect of a substance trumps all other characteristics in determining its legal status.

[53] This is universally regarded as the first verse revealed on the issue of alcohol. Q2:219 – "They question thee about strong drink and games of chance. Say: In both is great sin and some utility for men but the sin of them is greater than their usefulness. And they ask you what they ought to spend. Say: that which is superfluous. Thus Allāh makes plain to you His signs so that you may reflect."

[54] Ibn Abī Zayd, *al-Nawādir*, 14:283.

[55] *Ibid.*, 14:283. Ibn Abī Zayd also contends that the extension of prohibition from grapes to all other substances is strengthened by Q16:67, which implies that a wine/intoxicant (*sakar*) may be derived from dates as well as grapes.

[56] Ibn Abī Zayd, *al-Nawādir*, 14:292. As mentioned in the first section of this chapter, the issue here is the mixing of the bottom layer with the top by virtue of boiling which can initiate or accelerate the rate of fermentation. It was generally believed that when a drink had been reduced by two-thirds of its original volume, it was (theoretically) no longer an intoxicant. Saḥnūn affirms the need to cook to this point but adds that subsequent fermentation would make the drink illegal. The early Ḥanafīs, by contrast, felt that the reduced substance was fundamentally different from uncooked grape juice so that the product of its subsequent fermentation could not be considered *khamr* (Saḥnūn, *al-Mudawwana*, 6:2460–1).

[57] Ibn Abī Zayd, *al-Nawādir*, 14:293.

[58] *Ibid.*, 14:289.

[59] *Ibid.*, 14:294.

[60] *Ibid.*, 14:285. Ibn Abī Zayd supports these opinions with five proof texts: an "all intoxicants" tradition (see *SIM*, 4:74 – 3390 and 4:75 – 3391; *SN III*, 5:78 – 5087), a tradition that states that anything that is prohibited in large quantities must be prohibited in small quantities (see *SKB*, 8:514 – 17394 and 8:515–17395; *ST*, 3:442 – 1865), a modified "multiple sources" tradition on the authority of 'Umar, which explicitly contains an expansive definition of *khamr* (see *MAR*, 9:144 – 17361; *SN III*, 5:73 – 5068; *SB*, 1099 – 5581; *SKB*, 8:501 – 17346), an account in which Abū Mūsā returns from Yemen

In addition to laying out the general contours of the Mālikī position, Ibn Abī Zayd offers a systematic refutation of the Ḥanafīs. He categorizes arguments that favor narrow prohibition into two groups:[61]

1. Arguments that claim that the operative cause of prohibition is not the drinking of intoxicants but rather the state of intoxication. The implication of this view is that only the final cup of an intoxicant – which directly leads to intoxication – is prohibited.[62]
2. Arguments that draw an analogy between intoxicants and either medicine or food. They are permissible (and beneficial) in small amounts but lead to problems when consumed in large quantities.[63]

In response to the first, Ibn Abī Zayd concedes – on the basis of Q5:91 – that the cause for prohibition is intoxication that hinders a person from prayer and remembrance of God while sowing the seeds of enmity between Muslims.[64] He disagrees, however, with the conclusion that Ḥanafīs draw from this statement. Specifically, he offers three reasons for rejecting the view that prohibition is limited to the final cup of a drink that directly produces intoxication. First, he notes that intoxicants by their nature compel individuals to drink greater amounts so that they invariably reach a state of intoxication.[65] Thus, the nature of the substance in question demands total prohibition. Second, he argues that the Ḥanafī prohibition of only "the final cup" is problematic because of its inherent ambiguity. How can the point of intoxication be determined with any degree of accuracy? If smell is used as the standard, then

and asks the Prophet about the permissibility of *bitʿ* only to receive a stern reprimand (a variant of *MIAS*, 5:66 – 23738, *SN III*, 5:80 – 5094; *SM*, 3:1586 – 70; *SKB*, 8:506 – 17362), and an account of the original prohibition narrated by Anas b. Mālik (a variant of *SB*, 1100 – 5583; *SM*, 3:1571 – 5).

[61] In what follows, Ibn Abī Zayd articulates a series of logical critiques. One of the reasons for this may be the large gulf between the traditions invoked by the Ḥanafīs and those quoted by the other law schools, which made textual debate very difficult. Even though both sides offer a *similar* set of proof texts with small variations, even a slight modification in content (*sukr* versus *muskir*) has profound legal consequences. The frustration over these differences is apparent in Ibn Abī Zayd's use of a statement where the Prophet predicts the rise of a group of Muslims who will try to make intoxicants lawful by changing their names. For examples, see *MIAS*, 5:68 – 23759 and 5:70 – 23776; *SIM*, 4:72 – 3384 and 3385; *SKB*, 8:512 – 17382.

[62] Ibn Abī Zayd, *al-Nawādir*, 14:285.

[63] *Ibid.*, 14:284, 286.

[64] *Ibid.*, 14:285.

[65] *Ibid.*, 14:285.

intoxication has to be discarded altogether, because there is no definite connection between smell and an individual being intoxicated. Any possible physical test is – by its very nature – arbitrary with results that will differ from individual to individual.[66] Third, he maintains that the impact of the final cup cannot be judged in a vacuum. Intoxication results from the cumulative effect of a series of cups, with each playing an equal role in the ultimate outcome. If the final cup is unlawful, then every cup must be equally unlawful.[67]

Turning to the second category of Ḥanafī arguments, Ibn Abī Zayd agrees that medicine is permissible in small quantities despite causing harm in large quantities. Attempts at drawing an analogy between medicine and intoxicants, however, are flawed for three reasons. First, whereas medicine is unwillingly taken to preserve life, intoxicants are consumed on a whim, with the express desire to – at the very least – approach a state of inebriation. In addition, the intoxicated individual does not derive any health benefit from his altered state; rather he is more likely to ignore his sickness altogether. This argument takes a noble substance (medicine) and slanders it by association with something impure (alcohol).[68] Second, intoxicants (unlike medicine) compel an individual to drink more by impairing judgment and breaking down internal resistance.[69] Third, the logical extension of the analogy demands that people who take medicine to the point of impairing their mental capacity be subject to the punishment for intoxication. This is not advocated by any known jurist.[70]

The Mālikī school as a whole follows Ibn Abī Zayd in (1) its primary concern with validating a broad inclusive prohibition of all intoxicating substances and (2) its rejection of the significance of methods of production unless they have a direct bearing on the rate of fermentation[71] and thereby threaten to pollute an otherwise legal drink.[72] In concrete terms, Mālikī jurists draw on Q5:90–1 in combination with analogical, etymological, and tradition-based arguments to extend the scope of

[66] *Ibid.*, 14:287.

[67] *Ibid.*, 14:286.

[68] *Ibid.*, 14:284 and 286.

[69] *Ibid.*, 14:286.

[70] *Ibid.*, 14:286.

[71] This concern with rates of fermentation is evident in Ibn Abī Zayd's strict rulings on issues outside the scope of this study, including mixtures (*Ibid.*, 14:288–9), jars (*Ibid.*, 14:290–1), and dregs (*Ibid.*, 14:289, 291).

[72] Similar Mālikī views are articulated by (1) Mālik b. 'Anas in his *Muwaṭṭa'* (1951), 2:845–7, with no substantive differences between competing versions including that of al-Shaybānī and (2) Saḥnūn in *al-Mudawwana*, 6:2459–61.

the word "*khamr*" to any drink with intoxicating power.[73] They identify "the ability to intoxicate" as the *'illa* of Q5:90–1 through which they generalize prohibition to all alcoholic drinks.[74] The sole standard for determining the legal status of a drink is its potential to intoxicate, regardless of source (dates/raisins or grain/honey) or preparation (cooked or uncooked).

The Shāfiʿīs

Shāfiʿī jurists are not as concerned as the Mālikīs with determining the *'illa* of Q5:90–1 because they believe traditions offer a sufficient level of proof for the prohibition of all intoxicants. They also do not offer a detailed typology of drinks because their affirmation of general prohibition renders such a discussion legally irrelevant. The Shāfiʿīs counter Ḥanafī arguments in a manner virtually indistinguishable from the Mālikīs, with the two schools spearheading a Ḥijāzī response to a (largely) Kūfan espousal of narrow prohibition.

In *al-Ḥāwī al-kabīr*, al-Māwardī presents a typical Shāfiʿī discussion of intoxicants in an argumentative style reminiscent of the Mālikīs.[75] He begins by affirming the unlawful status of *khamr* through a detailed exegesis of six verses (Q2:219, Q4:43, Q16:67, Q5:90–1, and Q7:33[76]),[77] which both (1) discusses the historical circumstances of their revelation[78] and (2) relies heavily on juxtaposition.[79] This is

[73] For a slightly different Mālikī discussion of the issue rooted primarily (though not exclusively) in Qur'ānic arguments, see Ibn Rushd al-Jadd, *al-Muqaddamāt*, 1:439–42. For a later Mālikī engagement of the Ḥanafī position, see Ibn Rushd al-Ḥafīd, *Bidāyat*, 2:912–17, 919–21.

[74] As will become more evident in the next section, the Shāfiʿīs reverse this process by using textual evidence to establish general prohibition that they then connect to *khamr* through Q5:90–1.

[75] al-Māwardī, *al-Ḥāwī*, 13:376–410. As mentioned previously, *al-Ḥāwī* is a commentary on al-Muzanī's *Mukhtaṣar*, which, in the case of intoxicants, draws on al-Shāfiʿī's *al-Umm* and concludes that "every drink which intoxicates in large quantities is also unlawful in small quantities" (al-Muzanī, *Mukhtaṣar* in al-Shāfiʿī, *Mukhtaṣar*, 9:280).

[76] Q2:219 is juxtaposed with Q7:33. This is done by using the fact that Q2:219 associates *khamr* with a great sin (*ithm*) together with Q7:33 ("Say: My Lord forbids only indecencies, such of them as are apparent and such as are within, and sin and wrongful oppression, and that you associate with Allāh that for which no warrant has been revealed, and that you tell concerning Allāh that which you know not.") where sin (*ithm*) is explicitly forbidden. See also, Ibn Rushd al-Jadd, *al-Muqaddamāt*, 440.

[77] al-Māwardī, *al-Ḥāwī*, 13:376–85.

[78] *Ibid.*, 13:377–8.

[79] These arguments are virtually identical in tenor to those articulated by Ibn Rushd al-Jadd (see footnote 76 in this chapter and *Ibid.*, 13:378). Al-Māwardī also addresses issues

supplemented by an inventory of traditions drawn primarily from al-Shāfiʿī's *Kitāb al-umm*.[80] General prohibition is not addressed until al-Māwardī summarizes the legal differences between Iraqī (linked with Kūfa and Baṣra) and Ḥijāzī (linked with Mecca and Medina) jurists. He claims that the former limit the definition of *khamr* to alcoholic drinks derived from uncooked grape juice and allow for the consumption of non-grape/date-based intoxicants.[81] The latter, by contrast, maintain that any drink "which intoxicates in large amounts is unlawful in small amounts."[82]

Al-Māwardī criticizes the Iraqīs for two of their claims: (1) that *khamr* is specific to grapes, and (2) that the word "*muskir*" in traditions narrated from the Prophet refers to "the final cup that directly produces intoxication" rather than intoxicants as such. With respect to the first, he quotes a series of traditions, including one in which the Prophet utters the statement that "all intoxicants are *khamr* and all *khamr* is prohibited"[83] and variants of the "multiple sources" tradition.[84] He vigorously rejects claims that these traditions are fabrications[85] and quotes (yet another)

that have a tangential bearing on this case study, such as Q5:93 ("There shall be no sin [imputed] unto those who believe and do good works for what they may have eaten [in the past]. So be mindful of your duty [to Allāh], and believe, and do good works; and again: be mindful of your duty, and believe; and once again: be mindful of your duty, and do right. Allāh loves those who do good."), which was mistakenly held by one Companion, Qudāma b. Maẓʿūn, to allow early Muslims to drink *khamr*. I am not discussing these verses because they lie outside the scope of this study. None of the legal schools argued over the prohibition of *khamr*. The issue was upheld by such an overwhelming general consensus that any disagreement was considered an act of *kufr* (*Ibid.*, 13:384–5). For more on the story of Qudāma b. Maẓʿūn, see footnotes 97 and 139 in this chapter.

80 *Ibid.*, 13:383–5. For the traditions, see Mālik b. Anas, *Muwaṭṭa'* (1951), 2:845 – 9; *ST*, 3:441 – 1863; and *SN III*, 5:75 – 5075. For al-Shāfiʿīs discussion of intoxicants, see al-Shāfiʿī, *al-Umm*, 6:247–53, which privileges traditions over Qur'ānic evidence in upholding general prohibition.

81 *Ibid.*, 13:387.

82 *Ibid.*, 13:387.

83 *Ibid.*, 13:391. For identical texts, see *SIM*, 4:74 – 3390; *SKB*, 8:509 – 17374; and *SM*, 3:1588 – 75. For the exact chain of transmission, see *SN III*, 5:74 – 5072; and *SM*, 3:1587 – 74.

84 *Ibid.*, 13:395–6. One of these traditions cites the Prophet (see *SN III*, 5:63 – 5036), but most draw on the authority of Companions including ʿUmar (see *SB*, 1099 – 5581; *SKB*, 8:501 – 17346) and ʿAbd Allāh b. ʿAbbās (see *SB*, 1102 – 5598; *SKB*, 8:511 – 17378; *SN III*, 5:80 – 5096).

85 *Ibid.*, 13:391. As an example of such claims, al-Māwardī quotes Yaḥyā b. Maʿīn's statement that the tradition "all intoxicants are *khamr*" was one of three lies attributed to the Prophet. Al-Māwardī notes that Ibn Ḥanbal accepted the veracity of this tradition and highlights its narration through reliable transmitters.

account in which the Prophet anticipates a time when people will try to justify the consumption of *khamr* by changing its name.[86]

Al-Māwardī offers four logical counterarguments against the view that "*muskir*" signifies "the final cup that directly produces intoxication."[87] First, he asserts that *sukr* (intoxication) is a physical characteristic specific to a category of substances as opposed to quantity. Second, he points to the legal ambiguity inherent in gradation. Specifically, if both the first and last sip of that final intoxicating drink are prohibited, then why should there be a difference between the first and final cup? The decision to frame the issue in terms of "cups" is arbitrary. Third, al-Māwardī notes the disparity in tolerance between various people, arguing that every amount of intoxicant has the capacity to intoxicate someone. Finally, he follows Ibn Abī Zayd in observing that intoxication results from a series or drinks rather than a single drink in isolation. Al-Māwardī concludes that narrow prohibition is untenable given the non-Ḥanafī juristic consensus and the overwhelming mass of textual evidence favoring general prohibition.[88]

Although al-Māwardī's refutation of the Ḥanafī position includes logical proofs, his central argument rests on a firm textual foundation. Subsequent Shāfiʿī jurists increasingly emphasized traditions that related the opinions of the Prophet and the Companions as opposed to logical arguments or Qur'ānic exegesis.[89] By the 6th/12th century, there was a

[86] *Ibid.*, 13:392. For the tradition, see *SAD*, 3:329 – 3688.

[87] For the arguments that follow, see *Ibid.*, 13:392–3. In addition, al-Māwardī quotes a series of traditions that ostensibly state that all intoxicants are prohibited in all amounts (see al-Dārimī, *Sunan* (2000), 3:1333 – 2144; *SN III*, 5:81 – 5098).

[88] In fairness to the Ḥanafīs, it should be mentioned that al-Māwardī does not engage their logical arguments. He is aware of these arguments because he summarizes them among the Iraqī proofs for narrow prohibition. Specifically, he ascribes the following three opinions to the Ḥanafīs: (1) While *khamr* is rare in Medina because it must be imported from Syria, *nabīdh* is common. This being the case, we would expect *nabīdh* to be specified by name (in the Qur'ānic text) if it were forbidden. The fact that *khamr* was mentioned indicates a specific prohibition rather than a general one. (2) God routinely prohibits one item from a category while allowing benefit from another. Thus, we can see that cotton is permitted for men whereas silk is not; camel meat is lawful whereas pig meat is not. In the same manner, *nabīdh* is permitted but *khamr* is not. (3) Objects exist on earth that give us a taste of heaven. They are not identical but similar and intended to increase our desire for heaven. God has promised *khamr* in heaven, and the object that approximates it in this world is *nabīdh* (al-Māwardī, *al-Ḥāwī*, 13:391).

[89] In his *Muhadhdhab* (5:454–8), Abū Isḥāq al-Shīrāzī follows the opinion of the school very closely in extending the definition of *khamr* to include all intoxicants. The argument is supported through Q5:90–1 and four traditions that include an "all intoxicants" tradition (see *SIM*, 4:74 – 3390), a "multiple sources" tradition (see *SAD*, 3:326 – 3677)

distinct change in the tone of Shāfiʿī juristic discourse, suggesting that the issue may have lost its previous divisive connotations. In Abd al-Karīm b. Muḥammad al-Rāfiʿī's (d. 623/1226) *al-ʿAzīz*[90] (a commentary on al-Ghazālī's *Wajīz*), for example, Abū Ḥanīfa is identified as the primary proponent of narrow prohibition as opposed to previous works that had ascribed the view to either the Ḥanafī school (in general) or the Iraqīs.[91] Moreover, when al-Rāfiʿī describes the early Ḥanafīs who differentiated drinks on the basis of source (grape/date vs. everything else), preparation (cooked or uncooked, juice or water), and physical characteristics (bubbling or foam), he does so in a detached historical manner.[92] By disrupting juristic consensus, the example of Abū Ḥanīfa also enables al-Rāfiʿī to shield prominent early scholars (predominantly Iraqī Ḥanafīs) who upheld narrow prohibition from accusation of *kufr*.[93] Finally, al-Rāfiʿī does not relate the logical and textual arguments of earlier Shāfiʿīs (e.g., Māwardī) and Mālikīs (e.g., Ibn Abī Zayd), intimating the issue's transformation into a matter of settled law.

Both the Mālikīs and the Shāfiʿīs support general prohibition, but they differ in methodology. The Mālikīs primarily focus on establishing intoxication as the *ʿilla* of Q5:90–1, whereas the Shāfiʿīs cite textual proofs that support an expansive interpretation of prohibition. Instead of the broad application of the principle that "all intoxicants are prohibited" employed by Mālikīs jurists, the Shāfiʿīs are concerned with finding individual texts to justify specific extensions of prohibition. Neither group constructs a typology of drinks or discusses the cooking of juice; once general prohibition is established, these matters are no longer relevant.

The Ḥanbalīs

The Ḥanbalīs are the first of three schools (along with the Imāmīs and Zaydīs) whose legal works do not seem expressly concerned with the Ḥanafīs. They affirm general prohibition largely on the basis of traditions and devote most of their efforts to issues of punishment that lie outside

and two variants of the "large/small" tradition (See al-Dārimī, *Sunan* (2000), 3:1333 – 2144; *SN III*, 5:81 – 5098; and *MIAS*, 5:66 – 2374). A similar discussion is elaborated in al-Baghawī's *Sharḥ*, which utilizes a range of traditions to attack the Ḥanafī position (6:532–44).

[90] al-Rāfiʿī, *al-ʿAzīz*, 11:273–6.

[91] *Ibid.*, 11:275.

[92] *Ibid.*, 11:275.

[93] *Ibid.*, 11:274–5.

the scope of this study. The Ḥanbalīs do not address or even mention any of the logical or etymological arguments characteristic of Ḥanafī, Mālikī, and Shāfiʿī juristic works. Their legal discussions are marked by a literalist reading of the textual evidence, which, on occasion, leads to stipulations that cut against a logical application of the principle that "all intoxicants are prohibited."

Ibn Qudāma's *al-Mughnī* (unsurprisingly) preserves the most comprehensive rendering of the Ḥanbalī position on intoxicants.[94] As opposed to other Ḥanbalī juristic works,[95] Ibn Qudāma surveys the extended legal landscape and offers a detailed and systematic argument for general prohibition. He starts by affirming the unlawfulness of *khamr* based on the Qur'ān (Q5:90–1), the *sunna* of the Prophet,[96] and the unanimous consensus of the community.[97] He then cites a tradition that states that any substance that intoxicates in large quantities is forbidden in small quantities (subsequently referred to as the "large/small tradition"),[98] along with a myriad of opinions from Companions and Ḥijāzī jurists (including Mālik

[94] *Mughnī I*, 12:493–517.

[95] For the earliest Ḥanbalī discussion of intoxicants, see Ibn Ḥanbal's responses in *Masā'il* (1999), 1:157, 325 and *Masā'il al-imām* (Riyadh 2004), 2:379 and 382. Ibn Ḥanbal also authored a *Kitāb al-ashriba*, which consists of 242 traditions dealing with intoxicants but which provides no legal commentary/discussion. See also al-Khiraqī, *Mukhtaṣar*, 196 and Abū Yaʿlā, *al-Jāmiʿ*, 321. Early Ḥanbalī jurists were particularly interested in determining the moment (i.e., three days) at which a drink (with the potential for fermentation) became unlawful.

[96] *Mughnī I*, 12:493. Ibn Qudāma cites two traditions. The first is a popular variant of the "all intoxicants" tradition, which explicitly links intoxicants to *khamr* (*SIM*, 4:74 – 3390; *SKB*, 8:509 – 17374; *SM*, 3:1588 – 75). The second states that God curses *khamr* along with individuals who aid its production in any capacity.

[97] *Ibid.*, 12:494. Ibn Qudāma identifies two challenges to prohibition that were predicated on Q5:93 (for text of verse, see footnote 79 in this chapter). The first involved Qudāma b. Maẓʿūn who argued that Q5:93 constituted permission for Emigrants (like himself) who took part in the battle of Badr to consume any food or drink of their choosing. ʿUmar solicited the general population of Medina for a refutatione of this claim but received no satisfactory answers. He then turned to ʿAbd Allāh b. ʿAbbās, who asserted that Q5:90 abrogated Q5:93, and ʿAlī, who specified a punishment of eighty lashes. In another version of the encounter, ʿUmar admonished Qudāma to be fearful of God and avoid that which He has prohibited. A more detailed variant of this story is preserved in al-Hādī's *Aḥkām* (see footnote 139 in this chapter). The second challenge resulted from Yazīd b. Abī Sufyān's encounter with a group of Syrians who openly drank *khamr* and justified their behavior on the basis of Q5:93. Yazīd wrote to ʿUmar informing him of the situation and sent the group to Medina so as to avoid any potential *fitna*. ʿUmar convened a council to deal with the issue during the course of which ʿAlī declared that these men had made laws without God's permission. If they persisted in their claims that *khamr* was lawful, then they should be killed. If they repented, then they should be punished with eighty lashes for making false attributions to God.

[98] *Ibid.*, 12:495.

and al-Shāfiʿī) that prohibit intoxicants in any quantity. The only opposition to this view is ascribed to Abū Ḥanīfa (as opposed to the Ḥanafīs), who permitted grape *muthallath*, lightly cooked date/raisin *naqīʿ*, and all intoxicants from non-grape/date sources based on a tradition (found in nearly every Ḥanafī discussion) wherein the Prophet distinctly condemns "*khamr* and intoxication from other drinks."[99] In addition to emphasizing this account's dubious transmission history,[100] Ibn Qudāma offers five countertraditions[101] in support of general prohibition on the authority of the Prophet and ʿUmar.[102] He observes that these traditions do not permit a change in a substance's legal status through cooking, as intoxication is independent of a drink's manner of preparation.[103] The section ends with an authorization to punish those who consume intoxicants regardless of whether they consider them legal or not.[104]

Ibn Qudāma then turns to the issue of determining when a drink has acquired the capacity to intoxicate. He notes that most Ḥanbalī jurists set three days as a strict limit regardless of whether a juice drink has begun to bubble. The other law schools, by comparison, allow the consumption of juice beyond three days as long as it does not exhibit clear signs of fermentation through either bubbling (e.g., the Ḥanafīs) or an intensification in taste (e.g., the Mālikīs and Shāfiʿīs).[105] On the basis of previously cited traditions,[106] Ibn Qudāma concludes that the common element for prohibition is fermentation rather than the passage of time. In light of this fact, he interprets accounts in which the Prophet or ʿUmar refrain from consuming drinks after three days as acts of precaution and not as evidence for legal prohibition.[107] Thus three-day-old drinks with

99 See *SN III*, 5:108 – 5174; al-Ṭaḥāwī, *Sharḥ*, 4:214. Ibn Qudāma does not mention any of the logic-based Ḥanafī arguments.

100 *Mughnī I*, 12:496–7. He observes that, in the canonical collections, the tradition only goes back to ʿAbd Allāh b. ʿAbbās as opposed to the Prophet.

101 These include (1) a variant of the "all intoxicants" tradition, which explicitly mentions *khamr* (see *SIM*, 4:74 – 3390; *SKB*, 8:509 – 17374; *SM*, 3:1588 – 75), (2) three groups of traditions that advocate punishment for all quantities of intoxicants (see *ST*, 3:442 – 1865 and 3:443 – 1866; *SIM*, 4:76 – 3393; *MIAS*, 5:66 – 23741; *SAD*, 3:329 – 3687), and (3) a variant of the "multiple sources" tradition (see *SAD*, 3:324 – 3669; *SKB*, 8:501 – 17346).

102 *Mughnī I*, 12:496–7.

103 *Ibid.*, 12:514.

104 *Ibid.*, 12:497–8.

105 *Ibid.*, 12:512–3.

106 For these traditions, see footnote 101 in this chapter.

107 *Ibid.*, 12:512–3. He cites a tradition where the Prophet makes *nabīdh* and drinks it for three days (see *SAD*, 3:335–3713; *SN III*, 5:125 – 5229), a tradition in which the Prophet allows nonbubbling juice for three days (a variant of *MIAS*, 5:77 – 23857 which is *not* Prophetic), and a tradition in which ʿAbd Allāh b. ʿUmar specifies three days as the point at which the *shayṭān* of a substance manifests itself (see *MAR*,

the potential for fermentation (e.g., *nabīdh* or *naqī'*) but lacking clear physical signs of intoxicating capacity are deemed permissible.[108]

The Ḥanbalīs are not important players in the debate over intoxicants. Although they side with the Mālikīs and Shāfi'īs in affirming general prohibition, they limit their proof to Q5:90–1 and a small number of authoritative traditions. Ḥanbalī criticisms of the early Ḥanafīs are limited to the listing of a set of texts that are characterized as decisive, with little additional commentary.

The Imāmīs

Similarly to the Ḥanbalīs, the Imāmīs affirm general prohibition but exhibit little concern for debates between the Ḥanafīs and the Mālikīs/Shāfi'īs. The school's position – based primarily on textual proof (Qur'ān and traditions) as opposed to analogical reasoning or etymology – differentiates between *khamr* and other intoxicants but subjects both to the same legal constraints.[109] A majority of Imāmī jurists accept this position and focus instead on ancillary issues such as the production of vinegar, medicinal/cosmetic use, and cases of extreme thirst/hunger.

The first Imāmī jurist to offer a systematic analysis of intoxicants is Muḥammad b. al-Ḥasan al-Ṭūsī.[110] In *al-Nihāya*,[111] he upholds the

9:131 – 17302; *MIAS*, 5:78 – 23863). He actually projects this view backward, asserting that Ibn Ḥanbal (in contradiction to his responses) considered three-day-old juice *makrūh* due to the *likelihood* that it had fermented.

108 On the whole, Ibn Qudāma urges caution in dealing with intoxicants but he does not hold to previous Ḥanbalī rulings (e.g., the three day time limit, a ban on all mixtures) that ignore intoxicating capacity. With respect to mixtures (outside the scope of this study), for example, Ibn Qudāma explains that the Ḥanbalī prohibition is based on the tendency of mixed juices to speed up the fermentation process. Against the dominant school opinion, he asserts that mixtures are permissible until they acquire the capacity to intoxicate (*Mughnī I*, 12:515–17). In the case of thirst and hunger, he breaks with Abū Ya'lā and allows the consumption of intoxicants if they are diluted with water (given that pure alcohol does not alleviate thirst). He supports this view through an account in which the Companion 'Abd Allāh b. Ḥudhayfa is imprisoned by the Byzantines and offered only roast pork and diluted alcohol. He is compelled to eat the pork and drink the alcohol for fear of death, but does not accrue any sin in the process (*Mughnī I*, 12:499–500).

109 This is apparent as early as al-Kulaynī's *al-Kāfī*, where sixty of ninety-one traditions ban intoxicants without linking them in anyway to *khamr*. The overwhelming majority of these accounts focus on cooked juice, *nabīdh*, or *ṭilā'* (*KK*, 6:392).

110 The topic is covered in similar terms (but with much less detail) by al-Shalmaghānī, *Fiqh*, 1:280; Ibn Bābawayh, *Muqni'*, 450–5 and *Faqīh*, 4:55–60; Ibn Idrīs, *Sarā'ir*, 3:128–35; and al-Muḥaqqiq al-Ḥillī, *Sharā'i'*, 3:204–8, 4:172–6. A more limited discussion that focuses on a specific drink (*fuqqa'*) is found in al-Sharīf al-Murtaḍā, *al-Intiṣār*, 1:197–200.

111 al-Ṭūsī, *al-Nihāya*, 3:108–14.

general prohibition of all alcoholic drinks in any quantity but maintains a clear separation between *khamr* and other intoxicants.[112] Rather than characterizing *fuqqāʿ* (or *nabīdh*) as *khamr*, he states that "the legal ruling (*ḥukm*) for *fuqqāʿ* is [identical] to the legal ruling for *khamr*."[113] The importance of this distinction lies in the school's general belief that *khamr* was prohibited by God whereas other intoxicants were made unlawful by the Prophet with God's permission. In determining the permissibility of specific drinks, al-Ṭūsī stresses the importance of natural bubbling/fizzing (a strong indicator of intoxicating power).[114] He notes that fire-induced bubbling (e.g., boiling) accelerates fermentation by pushing the bottom layers to the top and must continue until two-thirds of a drink's original volume has evaporated, the taste sweetens, and the pot becomes stained.[115] Al-Ṭūsī also identifies a number of substances that remain permissible even if they emit the odor of alcohol. These include drinks derived from mulberries (*tūt*), pomegranates (*rummān*), quinces (*safarjal*), honey (*sakanjabīn*),[116] and rose water (*julāb*), which – according to al-Ṭūsī – do not "intoxicate in large amounts."[117] On the whole, *al-Nihāya* suggests a broad consensus among the Imāmīs on general prohibition. The school's primary internal rifts center on ritual purity (e.g., can an individual pray with *khamr* on his clothing?),[118] punishment (e.g., is the death penalty applicable after the third or fourth violation?),[119] and necessity (e.g., is *khamr* permissible in cases of extreme thirst/hunger?), all of which lie outside the scope of this study.[120]

In *al-Mabsūṭ fī fiqh al-imāmiyya*,[121] al-Ṭūsī offers additional proofs for the Imāmī view while also addressing oppositional assertions/interpretations – primarily Ḥanafī – that he finds particularly problematic. He begins with the claim that *khamr* is outlawed on the basis of the Qur'ān, the *sunna* of the Prophet and the Imāms, and consensus.[122] This is followed by ten Qur'ānic arguments in favor of this opinion – drawing on Q2:219, Q7:33, and Q5:90–1 – none of which rest on

[112] *Ibid.*, 3:108.
[113] *Ibid.*, 3:109.
[114] *Ibid.*, 3:109.
[115] *Ibid.*, 3:109.
[116] Apparently this is a mixture of honey, water, vinegar, and spice, made into syrup and often used as an expectorant.
[117] *Ibid.*, 3:114.
[118] *Ibid.*, 3:111.
[119] *Ibid.*, 3:119.
[120] *Ibid.*, 3:111.
[121] al-Ṭūsī, *al-Mabsūṭ*, 8:57–70.
[122] *Ibid.*, 8:57.

analogy or juxtaposition.[123] Al-Ṭūṣī then cites three traditions[124] that link prohibition (but not the word *khamr*) to all alcoholic drinks.[125] In terms of consensus, he concedes the initial objection of Qudāma b. Maẓ'ūn, a prominent early Companion, but emphasizes that he eventually realized the error of his ways and accepted the unlawfulness of *khamr*.[126] As for the historical causes of prohibition, al-Ṭūsī mentions recurring outbreaks of violence, 'Umar's beseeching of God to clarify the matter, and other stories that are "agreed upon by the consensus of the community."[127]

Turning to non-grape-based intoxicants, al-Ṭūsī declares that all alcoholic drinks are governed by the same legal injunctions as *khamr*.[128] Rather than leave the issue here, however, he proceeds to explain Imāmī reasoning in greater detail, observing that:

> If it is established that every intoxicant is prohibited, then it is not – according to us – on the basis of an operative cause but rather on the basis of proof texts (*naṣṣ*) since we consider analogical reasoning invalid.[129]

The Sunnīs, he continues, are divided between one group (particularly Mālikīs but also Shāfi'īs) that outlaws alcohol by applying analogical reasoning to Q5:90–1 and another group (Ḥanafīs) that rejects this particular analogy but applies the same method to another text – the "two plants" tradition – to prohibit date drinks.[130] This debate is pointless given the fact that general prohibition can easily be demonstrated through a literal reading of Qur'ānic verses and a small sampling of traditions.[131]

[123] *Ibid.*, 8:57–8.

[124] The first is a version of the "all intoxicants" tradition (*SKB*, 8:509 – 17371 with close Imāmī variants *KK*, 6:409 – 9; *WS*, 25:339–40 – 32069). The second speaks of the consequences for drinking on the acceptance of an individual's prayer (a variant of *MIAS*, 5:78 – 23859, which stops at al-Bāqir instead of extending back to the Prophet). The third advocates the cursing of those who drink *khamr* or aid in its dissemination in any capacity.

[125] al-Ṭūsī, *al-Mabsūṭ*, 8:58.

[126] *Ibid.*, 8:58–9. The complete story of Qudāma b. Maẓ'ūn is cited by both Ibn Qudāma (see footnote 97 in this chapter) and al-Hādī (see footnote 139 in this chapter).

[127] *Ibid.*, 8:58. This is one of the reasons why this chapter does not cover exegetical works. Even though the legal schools disagree over the historical circumstances surrounding the revelation of important prohibition verses (e.g., Q5:90–1, Q2:219), there is no difference of opinion regarding the necessary unlawfulness of *khamr*. Thus, the juristic debate dealing with intoxicants focuses on logical arguments and legal traditions as opposed to the interpretation of specific Qur'ānic verses.

[128] *Ibid.*, 8:59.

[129] *Ibid.*, 8:59.

[130] *Ibid.*, 8:59.

[131] *Ibid.*, 8:59.

The first outlaws *khamr* and the second prohibits a broader category of intoxicants that includes alcoholic drinks made from grain, honey, or any nongrape substance.[132]

In the following centuries, Imāmī jurists largely accepted the distinction between *khamr* and other intoxicants articulated by al-Ṭūṣī. The situation appears to have changed fundamentally by the time of Ibn al-Muṭahhar, however, who conflate these categories by expanding the definition of *khamr* to cover all alcoholic drinks.[133] This shift is most apparent in the section of his *Muntahā al-maṭlab*, which deals with the contaminating effects of alcoholic drinks other than *khamr*.[134] After affirming the impurity of all intoxicants and paraphrasing ʿUmar's opinion that *nabīdh* was ritually unclean, Ibn Muṭahhar cites four Imāmī traditions that support his opinion.[135] The second and fourth of these shed particular light on the difference between Ibn al-Muṭahhar's conception of prohibition and that of previous Imāmī jurists. In the second, the Prophet declares that "all intoxicants are prohibited and all intoxicants are *khamr*,"[136] whereas the fourth quotes al-Kāẓim as saying "God did not prohibit *khamr* for its name, but rather prohibited it for its consequences."[137] Taken together, these accounts blur the distinction between *khamr* and other intoxicants at the core of earlier Imāmī discussions of alcohol.

The Imāmī stance on intoxicants agrees with a majority of the Sunnī (i.e., Mālikī, Shāfiʿī, Ḥanbalī) law schools in prohibiting all intoxicants and linking their legal status to that of *khamr*. The Imāmīs are distinguished by their rejection of analogical reasoning and exclusive reliance on the Qur'ān and other textual evidence. Specifically, the prohibition of *khamr* is a consequence of Q5:90–1, whereas other intoxicants are outlawed by Prophetic and Imāmī traditions.

The Zaydīs

Much like the Ḥanbalīs and the Imāmīs, the Zaydīs support general prohibition without participating in the dispute between the Ḥanafīs and the Mālikīs/Shāfiʿīs. This is made apparent by the lack of detailed discussions of

132 For al-Ṭūṣī's views on the debate among Sunnī jurists and an attempt to place the Imāmī position in the context of the broader legal landscape, see al-Ṭūsī, *Khilāf*, 5:473–98.

133 He was not, however, the first Imāmī jurist to broach the issue from this perspective. See, for example, the brief discussion of intoxicants in al-Ḥalabī, *al-Kāfī*, 279.

134 Ibn al-Muṭahhar, *Muntahā*, 3:213–9.

135 *Ibid.*, 3:218–9.

136 *Ibid.*, 3:219. For the tradition, see *KK*, 6:408 – 3.

137 *Ibid.*, 3:219. For the tradition, see *KK*, 6:412 – 1 and 2.

general versus narrow prohibition in their legal works. Instead, a majority of Zaydī texts focus on marginal issues such as the permissibility of using alcohol in medicine or the criteria for classifying new drinks as intoxicants.

The basic parameters of the Zaydī approach to intoxicants (in general) are articulated by al-Hādī in his *Kitāb al-aḥkām* and *Kitāb al-muntakhab*.[138] He starts by affirming the prohibition of *khamr* on the basis of Q5:90 and the overwhelming[139] weight of juristic consensus.[140] This is followed by an etymological argument (similar to that of Mālikī jurists) that associates any drink that obscures the intellect (*li-mukhāmaratihā li-l-ʿaql*)[141] with *khamr* regardless of its source or preparation.[142] This conclusion finds further support in Q5:91, which attributes the prohibition of *khamr* to its ability (1) to cause enmity and hatred and (2) to hinder Muslims from the remembrance of God and prayer.[143] The section concludes with a series of supportive traditions that relate the opinions of distinctly Shīʿī (and particularly Zaydī) authority figures including the Prophet,[144] ʿAlī,[145] and al-Qāsim b. Ibrāhīm.[146] Overall, al-Hādī's stance

138 al-Hādī, *al-Aḥkām*, 1:263–6, 408–10; al-Kūfī, *al-Muntakhab*, 1:120–1.

139 At this point, al-Hādī cites the most complete version of the Qudāma b. Maẓʿūn story that I have found in any juristic work. According to al-Hādī, Abū Hurayra imposed the punishment for drinking *khamr* on Qudāma b. Maẓʿūn in Baḥrayn after which Qudāma came to ʿUmar and lodged a complaint. ʿUmar summoned Abū Hurayra to Medina along with the witnesses to the crime. Qudāma did not contest the testimony and instead argued that he was exempt from the prohibition of *khamr* on the basis of Q5:93, which allowed "those who believe and do good" to eat and drink without any conditions. ʿUmar had no response to this argument so he summoned ʿAlī, who explained that Q5:93 had been revealed in response to inquiries from Muslims *after* the enforcement of prohibition. Specifically, they were concerned about the status of deceased relatives who had consumed *khamr* and died before the descent of Q5:90–1. Q5:93 was intended to reassure Muslims that their relatives would not be punished for drinking *khamr* and had no bearing on the validity of Q5:90. For the entire episode, see al-Hādī, *al-Aḥkām*, 1:265–6.

140 *Ibid.*, 1:263.

141 *Ibid.*, 1:264. He also cites examples of names derived from fundamental aspects of an object's nature, including *insān* (from *nisyān*) and *jinn* (from *istijān*).

142 al-Hādī, *Aḥkām*, 1:264; al-Kūfī, *al-Muntakhab*, 120. In the *Muntakhab*, al-Hādī states that *khamr* "is from grapes, raisins, dates, millet, barley, wheat and the entirety of substances ... [The word originates] in the obscuring of the intellect."

143 al-Hādī, *al-Aḥkām*, 1:264.

144 *Ibid.*, 1:409, 410. He cites two variants of the "all intoxicants" tradition on the authority of the Prophet (see *AA*, 3:1565 – 2608ff).

145 *Ibid.*, 1:409, 410. He cites four traditions on the authority of ʿAlī. The first affirms punishment for drinking intoxicants (*AA*, 3:1569 – 2615). The second is a variant of the "all intoxicants" tradition (*AA*, 3:1569 – 2616). The third and fourth are variants of the "large/small" tradition, affirming punishment for the consumption of any amount of intoxicant (*AA*, 3:1569 – 2617 and 1618).

146 Two opinions are attributed to al-Qāṣim b. Ibrāhīm al-Rassī. In the first, he describes all intoxicants as *khamr*. In the second, he refuses to differentiate between substances on

is grounded in Qur'ānic exegesis combined with a mixture of rational and textual proofs.[147]

Sharaf al-Dīn Ḥusayn b. Muḥammad presents a dramatically different argument in *Shifā' al-uwām*, confirming general prohibition but in a manner reminiscent of Māliki or Shāfi'ī legal works.[148] He first asserts the unlawfulness of *khamr* through (1) three interpretations[149] of Q5:90–1 juxtaposed with Q7:157 and Q26:60 and (2) an interpretation[150] of Q2:219 juxtaposed with Q7:33.[151] These Qur'ānic proofs are reinforced by seven[152] variants of the "all intoxicants" tradition and two[153] variants of the "large/small" tradition, which draw on the authority of the Prophet. It is particularly striking that all but one[154] of these accounts are taken from Sunnī rather than Zaydī collections and that the pertinent section includes no references to any 'Alid jurists or Imāms.

In the second part of his analysis, Sharaf al-Dīn turns to the definition of *khamr*. In a manner reminiscent of al-Hādī, he argues that the term refers to any drink that obscures and corrupts the intellect/reason

the basis of their origins or preparation and argues that a drink that intoxicates in any quantity is prohibited (al-Hādī, *al-Aḥkām*, 1:409, 410).

147 Al-Hādī's formulation of general prohibition informs the minimalist *fiqh* works of al-Mu'ayyad bi-Allāh Aḥmad b. Ḥusayn (*al-Tajrīd*, 347) and al-Nāṭiq bi'l-Ḥaqq (*al-Taḥrīr*, 2:500).

148 Sharaf al-Dīn, *Shifā'*, 1:178–82, 1:332–6.

149 *Ibid.*, 1:178–9. The first interpretation focuses on the link between *khamr* and *rijs* (foul impurity) in Q5:90, which is juxtaposed with Q7:157 ("Those who follow the messenger, the Prophet who can neither read nor write, whom they will find described in the Torah and the Gospel [which are] with them. He will enjoin on them that which is right and forbid them that which is wrong. He will make lawful for them all good things and prohibit for them only the foul; and he will relieve them of their burden and the fetters that they used to wear. Then those who believe in him, and honor him, and help him, and follow the light which is sent down with him: they are the successful.") to affirm prohibition. The second draws on the characterization of *khamr* as "Satan's work," which is juxtaposed with Q36:60 ("Did I not enjoin on you, O ye Children of Adam, that you should not worship Satan; for that he was to you an enemy avowed?"). Serving Satan is prohibited, and so are any actions that serve his ends, such as drinking *khamr*. The third and final interpretation focuses on the use of the phrase "avoid it" (*ijtanibūh*), which is interpreted as a clear divine command.

150 *Ibid.*, 1:179–80. For the juxtaposition, see footnote 76 in this chapter. He also quotes a famous poetic couplet (often mentioned in Sunnī texts) that equates drinking *khamr* with sin.

151 All of these arguments are also found in al-Ṭūsī, *Mabsūṭ*, 8:57–8.

152 Sharaf al-Dīn, *Shifā'*, 1:178. For the traditions, see *SAD*, 3:329 – 3686 and *MIAS*, 5:67 – 23746; *SN III*, 5:77 – 5083; *SAD*, 3:327 – 3680, 3:328 – 3682 and 3684; *ST*, 3:441 – 1864; a variant text in *SN III*, 5:75 – 5083; *SIM*, 4:73 – 3388.

153 *Ibid.*, 1:178. For the traditions, see *AA*, 3:1562 – 2599.

154 *Ibid.*, 3:178.

by means of its intoxicating powers.[155] He then cites a tradition[156] that unambiguously declares that "all intoxicants are *khamr*" alongside two[157] variants of the "multiple sources" tradition, which expand the definition of *khamr* beyond simply grapes and dates. Whereas the etymological aspect of this argument may be linked to al-Hādī, the textual support is (once again) drawn from Sunnī sources.

The natural question to ask at this point is why does Sharaf al-Dīn quote Sunnī as opposed to Zaydī arguments and traditions? To answer this question, it is necessary to expand the scope of our analysis. In his discussion of punishment for the consumption of intoxicants, for example, Sharaf al-Dīn relies exclusively on traditions preserved in Zaydī collections.[158] He outlines differences of opinion among Zaydī Imāms and explicitly searches for the consensus view of the Family of the Prophet.[159] Even the historical anecdotes he narrates are distinctly Zaydī and bear little resemblance to those found in Sunnī or Imāmī legal tracts.[160] Sharaf al-Dīn apparently felt comfortable citing Sunnī evidence for general prohibition because of the overwhelming consensus on the issue; even the Ḥanafīs had changed their minds by the late 7th/14th century. In the case of punishment, by contrast, there remained significant disputes both among the Zaydī jurists themselves and between different law schools. It is in these divisive areas that Sharaf al-Dīn's work assumes a notably Zaydī character.

Zaydī juristic discourse surrounding intoxicants is characterized by a broad affirmation of general prohibition. Early jurists (e.g., al-Hādī) advance arguments centered on Q5:90–1 along with etymological claims that associate *khamr* with the ability to "obscure and corrupt the intellect." The school's position remains steadfast throughout the centuries, but there is a subtle shift in method of argumentation, exemplified by a growth in the importance of analogical reasoning. Later Zaydī jurists identify the operative cause for Q5:90–1 as intoxication in line with the Mālikīs and (to a lesser extent) the Shāfiʿīs. The overall consensus of the school, however, renders the issue largely irrelevant as jurists concentrate on areas of internal dispute such as the use of intoxicants in medicines/cosmetics or commercial transactions.[161]

155 *Ibid.*, 1:180.
156 *Ibid.*, 1:180. For the tradition, see *AA*, 3:1561 – 2597; *SIM*, 4:74 – 3390.
157 *Ibid.*, 1:180. For the traditions, see *AA*, 3:1562 – 2598; *SKB*, 8:502 – 17347.
158 *Ibid.*, 1:332–6.
159 *Ibid.*, 1:333.
160 *Ibid.*, 1:333–5.
161 See, for example, Ibn al-Murtaḍā, *al-Baḥr*, 2:348–52, 6:191–6 and Ibn Miftāḥ, *Sharḥ*, 9:204–6, 10:113–9. Both focus on the rehabilitation of early Ḥanafīs, who were

The Legal Landscape

Table 5.1 provides a summary of the views and legal arguments utilized by different law schools in their treatment of intoxicants.[162] The early Ḥanafīs are distinguished by their belief in a narrow prohibition limited to drinks produced from grapes and dates. Other alcoholic drinks are deemed permissible as long as they are not consumed to the point of intoxication. With this in mind, early Ḥanafī jurists consider the final cup that pushes a person over the edge of sobriety as particularly problematic. Punishment is limited to cases where an individual drinks *khamr* (in any quantity) or water-based grape/date intoxicants (*naqī‘*, *nabīdh*) to the point of inebriation. There is no penalty for drinking intoxicants such as beer (*mizr*) or mead (*bit‘*). The strongest opposition to the early Ḥanafī position comes from the Mālikīs and the Shāfi‘īs, who favor general prohibition of all intoxicants. The Mālikī stance is grounded in an analogical analysis of Q5:90–1 that links *khamr* to every kind of alcoholic drink, whereas the Shāfi‘ī view draws on a

vulnerable to the accusation of *kufr* for their conspicuous permitting of non-date/grape intoxicants.

[162] Three legal schools not covered in this chapter – the Ẓāhirīs, the Ismā‘īlīs, and the Ibāḍīs – also uphold general prohibition. While the Ẓāhirīs agree with the Ḥanafīs in narrowly interpreting Q5:90, they draw on a wide range of traditions (primarily those mentioned in Shāfi‘ī legal texts) to extend prohibition to all intoxicants. In other words, they craft an argument similar to that of the Imāmīs, which differentiates between a Qur'ānic prohibition of *khamr* and a tradition-based prohibition of other alcoholic drinks. For a detailed treatment of the Ẓāhirī stance, see Ibn Ḥazm, *al-Muḥallā*, 6:176. The Ismā‘īlī position, as represented by Qāḍī Nu‘mān, emphasizes the unlawfulness of all intoxicants, links fermentation to bubbling and fizzing, and permits fresh grape/date drinks. Support for this view is rooted primarily in traditions on the authority of al-Ṣādiq (Qāḍī Nu‘mān, *Da‘ā'im*, 125–7, 129–32). The Ibāḍī literature is frustratingly silent on the issue, but general prohibition appears to have been the norm. In *al-Jāmi‘ al-ṣaḥīḥ* (246–48), Rabī‘ b. Ḥabīb cites many of the same traditions used by opponents of the Ḥanafīs, including an account in which the Prophet predicts the emergence of a group that would call *khamr* by another name, an "all intoxicants" tradition in which the Prophet emphasizes that all intoxicants are *khamr*, and a narrative relating the circumstances of the initial ban of intoxicants in Medina. The issue is discussed with more detailed textual evidence but similar ends in Bishr b. Ghānim, *al-Mudawwana al-kubrā*, 2:227–40. Whereas al-Shammākhī does not mention the issue at all, Yaḥyā b. Sa‘īd permits the destruction of jars containing *nabīdh*, strongly suggesting its prohibition. He does not, however, offer a systematic analysis of the issue. See Yaḥyā b. Sa‘īd, *Kitāb al-īḍāḥ*, 4:78 (for the allusion to intoxicants) and 4:258 (for the section on drinking). Finally, the Kūfan school of Sufyān al-Thawrī also seems to support general prohibition. Ibn Qudāma explicitly singles out Abū Ḥanīfa and his companions as advocating narrow prohibition and implicitly (by exclusion) places Sufyān al-Thawrī in the opposing camp (*Mughnī I*, 12:495).

TABLE 5.1. *A Summary of the Juristic Treatment of Prohibition*

	Prohibition Type	Prohibited Drinks	Methodology (In Order of Importance)
Ḥanafīs	Narrow	1. Alcoholic uncooked grape juice (*khamr*) 2. Undercooked alcoholic grape/date juice (less than 2/3 evaporation) 3. Uncooked raisin/date *naqīʿ* or *nabīdh* 4. The final cup of an alcoholic drink (other than *khamr*) that directly produces intoxication	1. Strict interpretation of *khamr* in Q5:90–1 as alcoholic uncooked grape juice based on etymology and rational proofs. 2. The "two plants" tradition to extend prohibition to dates. 3. Traditions that allow weak intoxicants and punish intoxication.
Mālikīs	General	1. All Intoxicants	1. Broad interpretation of *khamr* in Q5:90–1 through analogical reasoning. 2. Etymology. 3. Traditions that classify all alcoholic drinks as *khamr*.
Shāfiʿīs	General	1. All Intoxicants	1. Traditions that classify all alcoholic drinks as *khamr*. 2. Broad interpretation of *khamr* in Q5:90–1 through analogical reasoning.
Ḥanbalīs	General	1. All Intoxicants	1. Broad interpretation of Q5:90–1 and Q2:219. 2. Traditions that classify all alcoholic drinks as *khamr*.
Imāmīs	General	1. All Intoxicants	1. Strict interpretation of Q5:90–1 and Q2:219 prohibiting wine produced from uncooked grape juice. 2. Traditions that prohibit other alcoholic drinks.
Zaydīs	General	1. All Intoxicants	1. Broad interpretation of *khamr* in Q5:90–1 and Q2:219 on the basis of (1) etymology and (2) analogical reasoning. 2. Traditions that classify all alcoholic drinks as *khamr*.

series of traditions that unambiguously support a broad definition of *khamr*. This is not to say that the Mālikīs ignore traditions or that the Shāfiʿīs ignore analogy. They simply emphasize different aspects of the same evidence.

The three remaining law schools do not participate in this debate with any degree of regularity. Ḥanbalī jurists affirm general prohibition through Qur'ānic proofs and traditions but – rather than taking an active role in the dispute – concentrate on issues that arise from a literal reading of the evidence. Specifically, early Ḥanbalī legal tracts focus on whether juice may be consumed after three days even if it is clearly not alcoholic. Given that they reject analogical reasoning as a source of law, early Imāmī jurists actually agree with the Ḥanafīs in limiting the definition of *khamr* to fermented uncooked grape juice. Other alcoholic drinks are prohibited on the basis of traditions as opposed to rationalist arguments. The Zaydīs combine etymological arguments with traditions and analogical reasoning to forward a broad interpretation of Q5:90–1 in favor of general prohibition.

COMPARING THE KŪFAN TRADITIONS

Juristic discussions of intoxicants from each of the major law schools routinely invoke traditions either to restrict or expand the definition of *khamr*. As shown in Chapter 2, these accounts can be tied to particular cities in the 2nd/8th-century Muslim world where they likely preserved echoes of local ritual practice. Similarly to Chapters 3 and 4, the second part of this chapter subjects Kūfan traditions that address the issue of alcohol to a comparative analysis in an attempt to test the veracity of sectarian narratives drawn primarily from the heresiographical sources.

The Kūfan Traditions – An Overview

As in previous chapters, we begin with a broad overview of the legal landscape of Kūfa, in this case focusing on permissible and prohibited drinks. Table 5.2 utilizes 363 Kūfan traditions[163] taken from a larger corpus of 695 pertinent accounts preserved in the primary (canonical and

[163] As in Chapters 3 and 4, Table 5.2 assigns each Kūfan tradition a number based on the death date of authority figures. In such a scheme, a low number (e.g., 001) represents a tradition that cites an early authority (e.g., the Prophet). The Kūfan traditions are not numbered sequentially because they were drawn from a larger overall pool of 469 traditions. For the original sources of these texts, see www.najamhaider.com/originsoftheshia

TABLE 5.2. *The Kūfan Traditions (Prohibition)*

	Sunnī										Zaydī	Imāmī			
	Prohibited							Permitted			Prohibited	Prohibited			
Unspecified Source	004	030	141	229	354	417	502	019a	208	506	096	260	291	568	619
	005	031	142	246	355	422	504	021a	302	507	097	261	292	569	621
	006	038	144	249	391	423	511	034	329	520	102	262	293	591	630
	017	039	145	250	393	424	516	035	392	543	202	274	299	592	632
	018	095	146	318	396	426	521				269	275	371	594	635
	020	129	147	319	399	428	525				270	277	375	603	637
	021	132	148	320	402	429	531				336	280	378	604	638
	022	133	163	322	403	442	536				360	282	556	609	639
	023	134	172	323	404	443	537				361	283	557	614	645
	024	135	186	324	405	455	539				362	285	558	615	647
	025	136	187	338	405a	456	542				368	286	564	616	677
	026	137	188	347	408	499	548				526	289	567	617	
	027	138	191	348	410	500	555				540				
	028	139	207	353	415	501	571				582				
	029	140									583				

Grape/Date (uncooked)	036	154	174	183	305	350	438	173	328	452	152	159	288	492	607
	037	155	177	184	307	382	491	254	330	454	308	263	294	559	608
	044	156	178	185	315	418	498	306a	331	464	463	265	295	562	610
	093	157	180	192	317	425	503	309	344	514	580	267	296	563	611
	110	158	181	209	321	427	505	310	351	522	643	268	297	590	618
	111	168	181a	210	325	431	651	312	356	560		271	370	595	620
	179	169	182	304	334			316	451	566		278	372	596	644
												281	374	597	646
												284	376	600	685
												287	379	606	
Grape/Date (cooked)	387	457						301	388	494		565	599	628	640
	414	482						306	397	508		570	602	629	641
								314	398	509		593	612	631	642
								363	412	510		598			
								364	419	513					
								366	445	517					
								367	447	518					
								369	448	519					
								381	449	523					
								383	462	524					**636***
								384	469	535					
								385	481	553					

(*continued*)

TABLE 5.2 *(continued)*

	Sunnī		Zaydī	Imāmī
	Prohibited	Permitted	Prohibited	Prohibited
Grain	008 012 155 157 214 321 350	021b	152	159 633 667 678
	009 013 156 158 317 325 431		308	284 634 668 679
	010 154			296 657 669 680
				492 665 670 684
				613 666
Honey	154 156 158 321 350	021b	152	284 492
	155 157 317 325 431		308	296 618
Milk		561		
Overall	Prohibited 69% (158/229) Permitted 31% (71/229)		Prohibited 100% (20/20)	Prohibited* 100% (114/114)

Note: Underlining denotes traditions found in multiple categories because they deal with more than one substance. The traditions are organized around five categories of drinks: uncooked grapes/dates (*naqīʿ*, *nabīdh*), cooked grapes/dates (*ṭılāʾ*), grain alcohol (*mizr*, *jiʿa*, *fuqqāʿ*, *ghubayrāʾ*), honey (*bitʿ*), and milk. Where traditions cite either *muskir* (an intoxicant) or *khamr*, they are placed in the category entitled "unspecified source," because the material sources of these drinks cannot be ascertained with any degree of certainty. * – There is a singular Imāmī tradition (636) that permits juice drinks after they have been boiled to one-third of their original volume. There is no indication (as in the Sunnī case) that these were subsequently fermented or possessed the power to intoxicate. For complete references corresponding to each numbered tradition, see www.najamhaider.com/originsoftheshia

noncanonical) Sunnī, Imāmī, and Zaydī collections. Before turning to the analysis, it is important (as in Chapter 4) to acknowledge the numerical discrepancy between the Kūfan contributions of each sect. The Sunnīs dominate Kūfan intoxicant traditions and provide 63 percent (229/363) of the total, followed by the Imāmīs who contribute a not-insignificant 31 percent (114/363). The Zaydīs supply only 6 percent (20/363) of the Kūfan accounts, raising potentially serious concerns about the integrity of our results. If the present case study was the sole basis for the arguments advanced in this study, then such criticism would undoubtedly be valid. The comparisons that follow, however, come on the heels of two other cases that yielded parallel results. Specifically, they both (1) supported the presence of an independent Imāmī identity in the early 2nd/8th century and (2) cast doubt on the origin narrative of Zaydism. The utility of this third case study lies in its potential to reinforce these conclusions. Phrased differently, we are particularly interested in demonstrating that the intoxicant case study does not directly *contradict* the first two comparisons. With such an objective in mind, numerical equivalence is not nearly as critical as it was in previous chapters.

Recall that one of central issues of debate among the Sunnī schools of law concerned the definition of *khamr*, a substance whose prohibition was accepted by all Muslims. The early Ḥanafīs severely restricted the scope of the term and allowed for the consumption of alcoholic drinks as long as an individual did not become intoxicated. The other Sunnī law schools extended the definition to include all intoxicants. In drafting Table 5.2, it was necessary to make a number of decisions about the intentions of a given text. In some cases, there was no ambiguity as a tradition might state that "all intoxicants are prohibited" or identify a permitted drink made from grain or honey. With others, however, permissibility was predicated on a passage of time (e.g., prohibited after three days) or preparation (e.g., cooking until the loss of one-third or two-thirds of volume). For Table 5.2, temporal conditions are generally interpreted as supporting prohibition as they imply that, prior to the elapse of a specified time, a drink does not become intoxicating. Preparation conditions, by contrast, imply that altering a substance (usually grape juice) is sufficient to make a drink legal even if it subsequently acquires the power to intoxicate. These traditions are considered as permitting intoxicants.

Table 5.2 reflects a broad consensus for general prohibition among Zaydī and Imāmī traditions in line with the formal legal position of each school. The Sunnī accounts, by contrast, are markedly divided among those that reject intoxicants regardless of source (69 percent) and those that make allowances for certain drinks based on preparation or source

(31 percent). Although it is true that most opposing traditions are clustered around grape-based drinks, and there is an apparent agreement on the prohibition of grain and honey drinks, this conclusion is misleading. The Ḥanafīs felt that the burden of proof for the prohibition of these (nongrape) beverages was on their opponents, who wanted to expand the scope of the definition of *khamr*. Thus, most traditions regarding grain/honey drinks were circulated and preserved by non-Ḥanafīs who categorically condemned their consumption. The relatively small number (as well as the uniformity) of such accounts indicates that legal debates among Sunnīs in 2nd/8th-century Kūfa centered overwhelmingly on the status of the grape.

The final point to note about Table 5.2 concerns the striking overlap in the distribution of Sunnī and Imāmī accounts. A nearly identical percentage of each corpus addresses drinks made from unspecified sources (49 percent of Sunnī vs. 41 percent of Imāmī), grapes (48 percent of Sunnī vs. 46 percent of Imāmī), grain (8 percent of Sunnī vs. 16 percent of Imāmī), and honey (4 percent of both). This similarity embodies a common Kūfan sentiment in opposition to the early Ḥanafīs and strongly indicates that the traditions of both sects emerged from a common legal milieu. As such, the comparative analysis that follows is of particular significance. In the previous case studies, there were clear ritual differences between the Imāmīs and the Sunnīs, which – it could be argued – may have contributed to the apparent uniqueness of the former's traditions. In other words, the Imāmīs were the only sect to advocate the audible recitation of the *basmala* at the start of prayer and the performance of the *qunūt* in all of the daily prayers. Perhaps later Imāmī jurists jettisoned contradictory texts that disagreed with the school's official position, thereby skewing the data to suggest a false independence. In the case of prohibition, however, the Imāmī traditions align with a majority of Sunnī traditions and even reproduce their topical distribution. Here, it is a Sunnī law school (the early Ḥanafīs) that stands in clear and distinct opposition to all other groups. Given this fact, a recurrence of the same patterns in authorities, transmitters, and narrative style would substantially reinforce the results of previous chapters that supported the presence of a distinct Imāmī identity in early 2nd/8th-century Kūfa.

Authorities

As with Chapters 3 and 4, we first turn to a comparison of the authorities cited in the traditions of each sect. This information is conveyed

TABLE 5.3. *Authorities Cited (Prohibition)*

	Sunnī	Zaydī	Imāmī
Unique	(2) ʿĀmir b. ʿAbd Allāh b. Jarrāḥ (d. 18/639) (2) Ubayy b. Kaʿb b. Qays (d. 20/641?) (2) Khālid b. Walīd b. al-Mughīra (d. 22/643) (6) ʿAbd Allāh b. Masʿūd (32/652) (1) Abū Dharr al-Ghifārī (d. 32/652) (2) ʿUwaymir b. Ashqar (d. 40/660?) (2) ʿUqba b. Thaʿlaba b. ʿAmr (d. 42/662) (2) ʿUbāda b. al-Ṣāmit b. Qays (d. 45/665) (18) Abū Mūsā al-Ashʿarī (49/669) (1) Al-Ḥasan b. ʿAlī b. Abī Ṭālib (d. 49/669) (1) Abd al-Raḥmān b. Abzā (d. late 1st/early 8th c) (1) Barāʾ b. ʿĀzib b. al-Ḥārith (d. 50/670) (2) ʿUtba b. Farqad b. Yarbūʿ (d. 53/673) (2) Jarīr b. ʿAbd Allāh b. Jābir/Mālik (d. 56/676) (2) Abū Hurayra (d. 58/678) (1) Umm Salama Hind bt. Abī Umayya (d. 59/679) (2) Ṭalq b. ʿAlī b. Mundhir b. Qays (d. 60/680) (1) ʿAbd Allāh b. Sakhbara (d. 60–7/680–5) (1) Umm Salama Asmāʾ bt. Yazīd (d. 62/681) (1) Masrūq b. al-Ajdaʿ (d. 62/681) (13) Burayda b. Ḥuṣayb b. ʿAbd Allāh (d. 63/682) (1) ʿAbd Allāh b. ʿAmr b. al-ʿĀṣ (d. 65/685) (1) Hammām b. Ḥārith (d. 65/685) (1) Marwān b. al-Ḥakam (d. 65/685) (2) Al-Muṭṭalib b. Ḥārith b. Subayra (d. 67/687) (33) ʿAbd Allāh b. ʿAbbās (d. 68/688) (1) Suwayd b. Muqarrin b. ʿĀʾidh (d. 68/688)	(1) Sāʾib b. Yazīd b. Saʿīd (d. 91/709) (1) Aṣbagh b. Nubāta (d. 100/718?) (3) Zayd b. ʿAlī (d. 122/740) (1) Muḥammad b. al-Munkadir (d. 130/748) (1) ʿAbd Allāh b. Ḥasan b. Ḥasan b. ʿAlī (d. 145/763)	(1) Sulaymān b. Khālid (d. 117–48/735–66?) (1) ʿAmr b. Jumayʿ (d. 148–84/766–800?) (1) Yaḥyā b. (Abī) Qāsim (Isḥāq) (d. 150/767) (1) Mūsā al-Kāẓim (d. 184/800) (10) ʿAlī al-Riḍā (d. 203/819) (2) Muḥammad al-Jawād (d. 220/835)

(continued)

TABLE 5.3 *(continued)*

Sunnī	Zaydī	Imāmī
(1) Ḥayyān b. Ḥuṣayn (d. 70/689)		
(1) Muḥammad b. ʿAlī b. Abī Ṭālib (d. 73/692)		
(4) ʿAmr b. Maymūn (d. 75/694)		
(1) ʿAbd al-Raḥmān b. Bishr (d. 77/696?)		
(1) ʿAbd al-Raḥmān b. Ghanm (d. 78/697)		
(1) Shurayḥ b. Hāniʾ b. Yazīd (d. 78/697)		
(1) Wahb b. ʿAbd Allāh (Abū Juḥayfa) (d. 79/698)		
(1) Shaqīq b. Salama (d. 82/701)		
(1) Huzayl (?) b. Shuraḥbīl (d. 82/701)		
(1) Ibn Abī Layla (d. 83/702)		
(1) Māhān (Abū Sālim al-Ḥanafī) (d. 83/702)		
(2) Masʿūd b. Mālik (d. 85/704)		
(1) ʿAbd Allāh b. Ḥabīb (d. 92/710)		
(2) Saʿīd b. al-Musayyab (d. 94/713)		
(8) Saʿīd b. Jubayr (d. 95/714)		
(18) Ibrāhīm al-Nakhaʿī (d. 96/714)		
(2) Shurayḥ b. Ḥārith b. Qays (d. 97/715)		
(2) ʿAbd Allāh b. Muḥayrīz (d. 99/717?)		
(1) ʿUmar b. ʿAbd al-ʿAzīz b. Marwān (d. 101/720)		
(1) Ḥārith (ʿĀmir) b. ʿAbd Allāh (d. 103/722)		
(2) ʿIkrima (d. 105/723–4)		
(1) Bakr b. ʿAbd Allāh b. ʿAmr (d. 106/724)		
(1) Harim (Abū Zurʿa) b. ʿAmr (d. 106/724)		
(3) Ḥasan al-Baṣrī (d. 110/728)		
(1) Ṭalḥa b. Muṣarrif b. ʿAmr b. Kaʿb (d. 112/730)		
(1) Mughīra b. Miqsam (d. 132/750)		
(2) Sufyān al-Thawrī (d. 161/778)		

Shared	¥ (91) Muḥammad (d. 11/632)	¥ (7) Muḥammad (d. 11/632)	¥ (31) Muḥammad (d. 11/632)
	¥ (11) ʿAlī b. Abī Ṭālib (d. 40/661)	¥ (4) ʿAlī b. Abī Ṭālib (d. 40/661)	¥ (8) ʿAlī b. Abī Ṭālib (d. 40/661)
	¥ (5) Nuʿmān b. Bashīr b. Saʿd (d. 64/683)	¥ (1) Nuʿmān b. Bashīr b. Saʿd (d. 64/683)	¥ (1) Nuʿmān b. Bashīr b. Saʿd (d. 64/683)
	ZS (27) ʿUmar b. al-Khaṭṭāb (d. 23/644)	**ZS** (2) ʿUmar b. al-Khaṭṭāb (d.23/644)	
	ZS (2) Abū Burda Hānī' b. Niyār (d. 41/661)	**ZS** (1) Abū Burda Hānī' b. Niyār (d. 41/661)	
	ZS (5) ʿĀ'isha bint Abī Bakr (d. 58/678)	**ZS** (3) ʿĀ'isha bint Abī Bakr (d. 58/678)	
	ZS (30) ʿAbd Allāh b. ʿUmar (d. 73/692)	**ZS** (1) ʿAbd Allāh b. ʿUmar (d. 73/692)	
	ZS (1) Anas b. Mālik (d. 91/709)	**ZS** (1) Anas b. Mālik (d. 91/709)	
	ZS (1) Mujāhid b. Jabr (d. 100–4/718–22)	**ZS** (1) Mujāhid b. Jabr (d. 100–4/718–22)	
	ZS (7) ʿĀmir b. Sharāḥīl (d. 107/725)	**ZS** (1) ʿĀmir b. Sharāḥīl (d. 107/725)	
	ZS (1) Ṭawūs b. Kaysān (d. 110/728)	**ZS** (1) Ṭawūs b. Kaysān (d. 110/728)	
	ZS (2) ʿAṭā' b. Abī Rabāḥ (d. 115/733)	**ZS** (1) ʿAṭā' b. Abī Rabāḥ (d. 115/733)	
		ZI (1) Jaʿfar al-Ṣādiq (d. 148/765)	**ZI** (73) Jaʿfar al-Ṣādiq (d. 148/765)
	IS (2) ʿAlī al-Sajjād (d. 95/714)		**IS** (1) ʿAlī al-Sajjād (d. 95/714)
	IS (4) Muḥammad al-Bāqir (d. 117/735)		**IS** (22) Muḥammad al-Bāqir (d. 117/735)

Note: Intersections between all three groups are denoted by the symbol "¥." Intersections between the Zaydīs and Imāmīs are denoted by the symbol "**ZI**." Intersections between Sunnīs and Zaydīs are denoted by "**ZS**." Intersections between Sunnīs and Imāmīs are denoted by "**IS**.". The raw data can accessed via www.najamhaider.com/originsoftheshia

in Table 5.3, which adopts the same conventions utilized in previous case studies: (1) the number of accounts that invoke a given authority are indicated prior to each name in parenthesis, and (2) texts that cite the Prophet or the first four caliphs are counted twice.[164] We are primarily interested in evidence that either supports or contradicts the classical narratives for the birth of Imāmī and Zaydī sectarian identity. As explained in Chapter 2, shared authorities indicate overlap and a blurring of boundaries between groups whereas distinctive authorities intimate independence.

The table suggests four conclusions that reinforce our earlier findings. First, there is no significant overlap between the Imāmīs and the Sunnīs. They have five authorities in common: Muḥammad, 'Alī, Nu'mān b. Bashīr (d. 64/683), al-Sajjād, and al-Bāqir. The importance of the first two (Muḥammad and 'Alī) is minimal because they command near-universal respect as the Messenger of God and either the first Imāmī Imām or the fourth of the "rightly guided" caliphs. As for the last two figures, al-Sajjād is mentioned in less that 1 percent of the Sunnī (2/229) and Imāmī (1/114) traditions, reducing his significance as a bridge between the two sectarian communities. Al-Bāqir appears in four Sunnī and twenty-two Imāmī accounts, which corresponds to only 2 percent of all Sunnī traditions as compared with 17 percent of the Imāmī total. The single remaining shared authority is Nu'mān b. Bashīr, hailed by the Sunnīs as an early Companion of the Prophet and lauded by the Imāmīs for his opposition to (and death at the hands of) the Umayyads.[165] As a whole, however, there are only one or two commonalities from a pool of sixty-eight Sunnī and twelve Imāmī authorities.

Second, there is no substantive overlap between the Imāmīs and the Zaydīs in the 1st/7th and early 2nd/8th century. The two groups share four figures: Muḥammad, 'Alī, Nu'mān b. Bashīr, and al-Ṣādiq. The significance of the first two is (once again) minimized because of their importance for nearly all Muslims. Nu'mān b. Bashīr may represent a true intersection between the Imāmīs and the Zaydīs but the fact that he is also cited by Sunnī traditions suggests a universality that reduces his

[164] The first time with respect to their primary authority (e.g., Abū Bakr) and the second time with respect to their first transmitters. As discussed in Chapter 3, this is done because Prophetic and caliphal traditions contain significant contradictions, which disappear when analysis is extended to first transmitters. Note that in some traditions, the opinions of early transmitters are preserved alongside their recollections of authorities such as the Prophet or Abū Bakr.

[165] al-Mizzī, *Tahdhīb*, 29:411.

overall value. There is a striking disparity in the use of the final shared authority (al-Ṣādiq) by each community, Specifically, he serves as the primary authority for 64 percent of all Imāmī accounts whereas he is only mentioned in a single Zaydī text. This likely reflects the late Zaydī view that legal authority/knowledge was equally diffused among all ʻAlids as opposed to representing a genuine early overlap between the two sectarian groups.

Third, early Zaydī authorities are (again) drawn exclusively from within the bounds of Kūfan proto-Sunnism. The Zaydī and Sunnī traditions share ten authority figures, six of whom (i.e., Umar al-Khaṭṭāb, Abū Burda – d. 41/661, ʻĀʼisha, Nuʻmān b. Bashīr, ʻAbd Allāh b. ʻUmar) are early Companions mentioned in a wide range of proto-Sunnī Kūfan accounts. A few make it into Imāmī traditions (see Nuʻmān b. Bashīr), but most are condemned by the Imāmīs for their opposition or hostility to the claims of the Prophet's family. The remaining four (i.e., Mujāhid b. Jabr, ʻĀmir b. Sharāḥīl – d. 107/725, Ṭāwūs b. Kaysān, and ʻAṭāʼ b. Abī Rabāḥ) are influential jurists of the late 1st/7th and early 2nd/8th century, who routinely appear in Sunnī *ḥadīth* collections and other legal works. With the sole exception of ʻĀmir b. Sharāḥīl, these individuals are rarely (if ever) mentioned by the Imāmīs.

Fourth, the connection between the Zaydīs and the Sunnīs breaks down in the early to mid-2nd/8th century as the Zaydīs begin relying on the legal opinions of Medinan and Kūfan ʻAlids. The Zaydīs do not share a single common authority with the Sunnīs after the year 115/733 (the death of ʻAṭāʼ b. Abī Rabāḥ). This change, however, does not bring the Zaydīs any closer to the Imāmīs. Whereas the Imāmīs exclusively quote a specific set of legal authorities (i.e., al-Bāqir, al-Ṣādiq, etc.), the Zaydīs subsume these figures under the general heading of the "Family of the Prophet" wherein every member has an equal standing. In other words, they place al-Ṣādiq's opinion on par with that of other post-115/733 ʻAlids such as Zayd b. ʻAlī, Muḥammad b. al-Munkadir b. ʻAbd Allāh (d. 130/748), and ʻAbd Allāh b. Ḥasan b. Ḥasan b. ʻAlī (d. 145/763).

Overall, the data supports the early existence of an Imāmī identity. The authorities cited in their accounts do not (significantly) overlap with those of the Sunnī, and only intersect with those of the Zaydīs in the case of one historically important ʻAlid. The data also falls short of supporting the classical narrative of early Zaydism, as we do not find a combination of Batrī (Companions, jurists, and non-ʻAlids) and Jārūdī (ʻAlid or Imāmī) authorities represented in the Zaydī traditions. Instead, early Zaydī texts exclusively cite Companions and jurists hailed by proto-Sunnī

Kūfans. The dynamic changes in the course of the 2nd/8th century, with a shift toward ʿAlid authority figures. Rather than a movement forged from the merging of Batrīs and Jārūdīs, Zaydism seems to transform rather dramatically from a Batrī to a Jārūdī orientation over the course of the 2nd/8th century.

CHAINS AND TRANSMITTERS

The second set of comparisons focuses on shared transmitters, both in isolation and as part of larger shared links. Here, we are specifically interested in the degree to which sects relied on similar sets of individuals to transmit information. Shared links hold a particular significance as they suggest a consensus on an individual's scholarly and (by extension) communal associations. Tables 5.4a and 5.4b highlight both types of links.

Two conclusions may be drawn from these tables. First, as in the case of the *basmala* and (to a lesser extent) the *qunūt*, the Imāmī traditions exhibit a striking independence. The Imāmīs share only two common Kūfan transmitters (i.e., Sarī b. Ismāʿīl – d. 107/725?, Saʿd b. Ṭarīf – d. after 148/766) with the Zaydīs and only one (i.e., Sulaymān al-Aʿmash) with the Sunnīs; all three sects rely on the narrations of ʿĀmir b. Sharāḥīl. Four shared transmitters might seem significant, but it is important to note that they are not distributed throughout the Imāmī traditions. Specifically, the use of these transmitters is limited to just 4 (i.e., 159, 568, 569, 615) of 114 total Imāmī traditions. Their importance is further reduced by the fact that the Imāmīs share only a single shared link (i.e., Muḥammad – Nuʿmān b. Bashīr) with the other sectarian groups through a single tradition (i.e., 159). Put simply, the Imāmīs utilize the four shared figures in a singular manner, transmitting to and from a larger pool of individuals distinct from that of both the Zaydīs and the Sunnīs. If we further consider that all four of these men were depicted in ambiguous and contradictory ways in Imāmī and Sunnī biographical works, the end result is an affirmation of the independence of the Imāmī traditions. At most, the data suggests that some Kūfans, lacking solid sectarian loyalties, were free to navigate between communities whose boundaries remained somewhat fluid.

Second, the tables suggest a clear connection between the Sunnīs and the Zaydīs through eight shared links and eight common transmitters that persist well into the 2nd/8th century. Half of the shared links

TABLE 5.4a. *Single Transmitters (Prohibition)*

	Transmitters in Isolation	Traditions
Sunnī/Zaydī	ʿAmr b. ʿAbd Allāh b. ʿAlī (ʿUbayd) (d. 127/745)*	12 Sunnī (010, 013, 019a, 020, 021, 021a, 021b, 177, 249, 328, 331, 348) 1 Zaydī (308)
	Layth b. Abī Sulaym (Ayman) (d. 133 or 143/751 or 761)*	3 Sunnī (410, 426, 427) 1 Zaydī (097)
	Sallām b. Sulaym (d. 179/795)*	6 Sunnī (034, 035, 417, 502) 1 Zaydī (308)
	ʿĀʾidh b. Ḥabīb b. Mallāḥ (d. 190/807)	5 Sunnī (214, 325, 338, 366, 425) 4 Zaydī (102, 202, 270, 540)
	ʿAbd Allāh b. Idrīs b. Yazīd b. ʿAbd al-Raḥmān (d. 192/808)*	3 Sunnī (338, 366, 425) 3 Zaydī (102, 202, 270)
	Muḥammad b. Fuḍayl b. Ghazwān (d. 194–5/809–10)	13 Sunnī (023, 137, 138, 139, 367, 383, 412, 419, 447, 454, 464, 494, 531) 4 Zaydī (096, 152, 463, 526)
Zaydī/Imāmī	Sarī b. Ismāʿīl (d. 107/725?)	1 Zaydī (152) 1 Imāmī (159)
	ʿĀmir b. Sharāḥīl (d. 106 or 107/724 or 725)	1 Zaydī (152) 1 Imāmī (159)
	Saʿd b. Ṭarīf (d. mid to late 2nd/8th c)	2 Zaydī (368) 1 Imāmī (568, 569)
Sunnī/Imāmī	ʿĀmir b. Sharāḥīl (d. 106 or 107/724 or 725)	5 Sunnī (154, 155, 156, 157, 158) 1 Imāmī (159)
	Sulaymān b. Mihrān al-Aʿmash (d. 148/765)	20 Sunnī (178, 179, 180, 181, 306a, 312, 356, 385, 398, 412, 414, 419, 428, 429, 445, 517, 518, 519, 523, 524) 1 Imāmī (615)

* See also Shared Links in Table 5.4b. For complete references corresponding to each numbered tradition, see www.najamhaider.com/originsoftheshia

TABLE 5.4b. *Shared Links (Prohibition)*

	Shared Links	Traditions
Sunnī/Zaydī #1	Muḥammad (d. 11/632) | ʿĀʾisha bint Abī Bakr (d. 58/678)	1 Sunnī (093) 1 Zaydī (102)
#2	Muḥammad (d. 11/632) | ʿAbd Allāh b. ʿUmar (d. 73/692)	5 Sunnī (207, 208, 209, 210, 214, 229) Zaydī (202)
#3	Muḥammad (d. 11/632) | Nuʿmān b. Bashīr b. Saʿd b. Thaʿlaba (d. 64/683) | ʿĀmir b. Sharāḥīl (d. 106 or 107/724 or 725)	5 Sunnī (154, 155, 156, 157, 158) 1 Zaydī (152)
#4	Mujāhid (d. 104/722), Ṭawūs (d. 110/728), ʿAṭāʾ (d. 115/733) | Layth b. Abī Sulaym (Ayman) (d. 133 or 143/751 or 761)	1 Sunnī (410) 1 Zaydī (526)
#5	ʿĀmir b. Sharāḥīl (d. 106 or 107/724 or 725) | Yaḥyā b. Saʿīd b. Ḥayyān (d. 145/765)	8 Sunnī (318, 319, 320, 321, 322, 323, 324, 350) 1 Zaydī (540)
#6	ʿAmr b. ʿAbd Allāh b. ʿAlī (ʿUbayd) (127/745) | Sallām b. Sulaym (d. 179/795)	4 Sunnī (012, 329, 330, 347) The same Zaydī (308) as in Table 5.4a

#7	‘Āmir b. Sharāḥil (d. 106 or 107/724 or 725) | Yaḥyā b. Sa‘īd b. Ḥayyān (d. 145/765) | ‘Abd Allāh b. Idrīs b. Yazīd b. ‘Abd al-Raḥmān (d. 192/808)	2 Sunnī (214, 325) 1 Zaydī (540)
#8	Muḥammad (d. 11/632) | ‘Ā’isha bint Abī Bakr (d. 58/678) | Qāsim b. Muḥammad b. Abī Bakr (d. 108/726) | ‘Amr b. Sālim (d. 120/728?) | Layth b. Abī Sulaym (Ayman) (d. 133 or 143/751 or 761) | ‘Abd al-Raḥmān b. Muḥammad b. Ziyād (d. 195/812)	1 Sunnī (095) 2 Zaydī (096, 097)
<u>Zaydī/Imāmī</u> #1	Muḥammad (d. 11/632) | Nu‘mān b. Bashīr b. Sa‘d b. Tha‘laba (d. 64/683)	1 Imāmī (159) 1 Zaydī (152)
<u>Sunnī/Imāmī</u> #1	Muḥammad (d. 11/632) | Nu‘mān b. Bashīr b. Sa‘d b. Tha‘laba (d. 64/683)	5 Sunnī (154, 155, 156, 157, 158) 1 Imāmī (159)

Note: For complete references corresponding to each numbered tradition, see www.najamhaider.com/originsoftheshia

originate with the Prophet, whereas the other half center on figures that lived in the late 1st/7th and early 2nd/8th century, including the ubiquitous ʿĀmir b. Sharāḥīl and the Meccan juristic trio of Mujāhid b. Jabr, Ṭawūs b. Kaysān, and Aṭāʾ b. Abī Rabāḥ. In the first four shared links, the intersection is limited to the 1st/7th and early to mid-2nd/8th century, terminating (in the longest of these chains) with Layth b. Abī Sulaym (d. 133/751). The other shared links extend well into the 2nd/8th century, with the last culminating in ʿAbd al-Raḥmān b. Muḥammad b. Ziyād (d. 195/812).

The eight common transmitters provide further support for an overlap between the Sunnīs and the Zaydīs. These include four figures who died in the early 2nd/8th century (i.e., Abū Burda, ʿĀʾisha, ʿAmr b. ʿAbd Allāh, and Layth b. Abī Sulaym) and four who died in the latter part of the 2nd/8th century (i.e., Sallām b. Sulaym – d. 179/795, ʿĀʾidh b. Ḥabīb b. Mallāḥ – d. 190/807, ʿAbd Allāh b. Idrīs b. Yazīd – d. 192/808, and Muḥammad b. Fuḍayl b. Ghazwān – d. 194–5/809–10). In total, shared links and common transmitters between the Sunnīs and Zaydīs span seventeen individuals spread over 50 percent (10/20) of all Zaydī and 27 percent (61/229) of all Sunnī traditions. These numbers offer strong evidence for an intersection between the two communities stretching well into the second half of the 2nd/8th century. It should be noted, however, that these links are limited to those Zaydī traditions that cite the opinions of either the Prophet or jurists held in high regard by Kūfan traditionists; not a single Zaydī account preserving the opinion of an ʿAlid from the 2nd/8th century includes a transmitter common to either the Sunnīs or the Imāmīs.

The results of this second layer of comparisons (as in the previous two case studies) support two propositions: (1) the Imāmīs functioned as an independent legal entity in the early 2nd/8th century; and (2) there is minimal support for the origin narrative of early Zaydism. With regards to the first, the Imāmī traditions show no significant commonalities with the Sunnīs, consisting of only two common transmitters and one shared link that terminates in 64/683. There is an equally insignificant overlap between the Imāmīs and the Zaydīs embodied by the same shared link and only three common transmitters. As for the second, although the early Zaydī traditions include the expected Batrī (proto-Sunnī) elements, they do not preserve a single link that can be characterized as Jārūdī (Imāmī). Even ʿAlī's opinions are related through chains shared with Sunnī traditions.

Narrative Style

As in previous chapters, we conclude with a comparison of the primary narrative forms employed by each group. In examining Table 5.5, recall that we are looking for overlaps and differences as indicators for the development of independent sectarian identity.

We have already mentioned the numerical disparity between the contributions from the three sectarian groups, but let us recall that – as in the second case study – we overcome this obstacle by examining the *distribution* of narrative forms. Percentages of a community's traditions that employ a particular style are more significant than the actual number of such accounts.

The information in Table 5.5 (once more) reinforces assertions of the presence of a distinct Imāmī communal identity in the early 2nd/8th century. The most common method of preserving information in the Imāmī traditions is the question-and-answer form (36 percent), in contrast to the Sunnī and Zaydī reliance on direct quotes (Sunnī – 37 percent, Zaydī – 75 percent) and exemplary statements (Sunnī – 21 percent, Zaydī – 10 percent). Moreover, the Imāmī accounts utilize written correspondence (7 percent) and exegesis (9 percent), which are rarely found in Sunnī and Zaydī traditions. Finally, the Imāmīs are unique in their use of traditions that link alcohol/prohibition to Biblical figures (3 percent).

Interpreting the Zaydī texts is more difficult because of their small numbers. Even with a limited sampling, however, it is clear that the few Zaydī traditions that convey the opinions of mid- to late-2nd/8th-century 'Alid authorities (e.g., traditions 582 and 643) diverge from the direct-quote style (dominant among Sunnī traditions) and align with the question-and-answer form (characteristic of Imāmī traditions). In the absence of additional evidence, however, it is likely that the similarities between the Imāmīs and the Zaydīs result from a shared stylistic convention common to the preservation of 'Alid legal opinions in Kūfa. When quoting non-'Alids from the 1st/7th and early 2nd/8th century, the Zaydī closely resemble the Sunnīs in their (1) reliance on direct quotes, (2) minimizing of exegetical accounts, and (3) dismissal of written correspondence and Biblical proofs. Whereas the results of this section regarding the Zaydīs are somewhat tenuous and ambiguous, the broader comparative context must be kept in mind. If this singular comparison was our only basis for determining the relationship between the Zaydīs and other sectarian communities, it would be

TABLE 5.5. *Narrative Style (Prohibition)*

	Sunnī					Zaydī		Imāmī			
Question/ Answer	019a	028	305	425	482	582	643	265	559	607	631
	020	030	338	426	502			267	563	608	633*
	021b	031	355	427	503			271	590	609	634*
	022	044	382	429	516			278	591	610	636
	023	132	412	442	543			281	592	614	642
	024	133	414	443	548			285	593	617	645
	025	172	415	454	561			288	595	618	646
	026	192	423	481	651			294	596	620	666
	027	304						297	602	621	667
								556	603	628	678
								558			
Eyewitness Accounts	036	191	309	334	422	None		295	564	633*	635
	037	207	312	344	447			562	606	634*	685
	168	208	316	351	448						
	169	209	319	363	451						
	172	210	321	366	452						
	173	246	322	367	464						
	174	301	323	385	491						
	186	302	324	387	506*						
	187	306a	325	391	555						
	188	307	330	419							

Direct Quotes	004	111	154	347	405a	508	096		159	371	598	632
	005	135	155	348	410	509	097		277	378	599	637
	006	136	156	350	418	511	102		282	492	600	638
	017	137	157	353	428	513	152		284	557	604	639
	018	138	158	354	431	514	202		289	567	612	640
	021	139	163	356	456	521	269		291	568	613	641
	021a	140	214	392	457	535	270		292	569	615	644
	029	141	229	393	498	536	308		296	594	616	647
	034	142	249	396	499	537	336		299	597	630	670
	035	144	250	399	500	539	362					
	038	145	298	402	501	542	368					
	039	146	317	403	504	553	526					
	095	147	329	404	505	560	540					
	110	148	331	405	506c	571	580					
							583					
Exemplary Statements	008	179	310	397	517		360	361	268	287	372	379
	009	180	315	398	518				274	371	374	611
	010	181	328	424	519				275			
	012	181a	364	445	520							
	013	182	369	449	522							
	093	183	381	462	523							
	129	184	383	469	524							
	134	185	384	494	531							
	177	254	388	510	566							
	178	306										

(*continued*)

TABLE 5.5 *(continued)*

	Sunnī	Zaydī	Imāmī
Written Correspondence	314	None	375 665 669 680 376 668 679 684 657
Exegesis	318 408 438 525 320 417 455	463	260 263 286 619 261 280 293 677 262 283
Biblical Stories	None	None	565 570 629
Overall	Q/A – 18% Eyewitness – 21% Direct – 37% Exemplary – 21% Written – <1% Exegesis – 3% Biblical – 0%	Q/A –10 % Eyewitness –0 % Direct – 75% Exemplary – 10% Written – 0% Exegesis – 5% Biblical – 0%	Q/A –36% Eyewitness – 7% Direct – 32% Exemplary – 8% Written – 8% Exegesis – 9% Biblical – 3%

* Denotes traditions that utilize multiple narrative styles. For complete references corresponding to each numbered tradition, see www.najamhaider.com/originsoftheshia

virtually impossible to offer any reasonable conclusions. As it stands, however, we have two previous comparisons that depict a similar alignment of early Zaydī and Sunnī accounts. This final case, although not sufficient on its own, reinforces our earlier results by *not* explicitly contradicting them.

Overall, the results of this section generally agree with those of previous sections. On the one hand, we find support for the presence of an independent Imāmī identity in the early 2nd/8th century embodied in distinctive choices for the presentation and preservation of information. On the other hand, we must question the validity of the view that Zaydism crystallized around the merging of a Batrism closely associated with proto-Sunnī Kūfan traditionism and a Jārūdism reflecting a more Imāmī Shīʿī perspective. Rather than a hybrid combination of both tendencies, the early Zaydī traditions seem to align primarily (if not exclusively) with those preserved in Sunnī collections. Where does that leave the narrative of the origins of Zaydism? Where are the Jārūdīs at the start of the movement and where are the Batrīs at the end?

CONCLUSION

As in Chapters 3 and 4, this chapter focuses on the juristic literature and traditions surrounding a controversial legal issue (i.e., the status of alcoholic drinks). Our specific goal was to test the validity of the classical narratives for the emergence of Imāmī and Zaydī Shīʿism outlined in Chapter 1 through an approach developed in Chapter 2. We began with a survey of the legal literature of six Islamic law schools designed to provide context regarding the broader issue of prohibition. This was followed by structural comparisons of the authorities, chains of transmission, and narrative styles of 363 Kūfan traditions drawn from the most important Sunnī, Imāmī, and Zaydī collections.

The results largely affirmed those of Chapters 3 and 4. Specifically, we found that Imāmī traditions exhibit a strong independence in the individuals they accord authority, the transmitters they deem trustworthy, and the narrative forms they utilize to preserve information. This supports the contention that the Imāmīs had developed an independent communal identity by the early 2nd/8th century. In contrast, we found significant reasons for doubting the view that Zaydism crystallized in 122/740 with the merging of Batrism and Jārūdism. Early Zaydī traditions exhibit characteristics that are overwhelmingly Batrī (proto-Sunnī) whereas Jārūdī (Shīʿī) elements only appear near the middle or end of the 2nd/8th century. The implications of these results will be further developed in Chapters 6 through 8. Chapter 6 offers a revisionist history of early Zaydism that better aligns with the results of our case studies, whereas Chapters 7 and 8 examine the mechanisms through which an Imāmī identity emerged in 2nd/8th-century Kūfa.

PART THREE

THE EMERGENCE OF SHĪ'ISM

6

Dating Sectarianism

Early Zaydism and the Politics of Perpetual Revolution

The case studies in Chapters 3 through 5 offer us a substantive basis for evaluating the validity of the sectarian narratives identified in Chapter 1. Recall that the classical view of the origins of Shīʿī identity which is largely drawn from the heresiographical sources (1) assumes the emergence of an Imāmī identity in the early 2nd/8th century and (2) asserts that Zaydism resulted from the union of two strains of Kūfan Shīʿism (Batrism and Jārūdism) around the 122/740 revolt of Zayd b. ʿAlī.

A BROAD ASSESSMENT

The results of all three of our comparisons support the first claim, as the Imāmīs exhibit a notable independence with respect to authorities, transmitters, and narrative forms. In the limited instances where they share a transmitter with one of the other sects (e.g., Ḥabīb b. Qays cited by both the Imāmīs and the Sunnīs), each group utilizes the given transmitter in considerably different chains of transmission.[1] Even in cases where the Imāmīs hold views similar to those of the Sunnīs and Zaydīs (e.g., the general prohibition of *khamr*), they still quote their own authorities through distinct transmitters in unique narrative styles.[2] If an Imāmī

[1] In other words, the students associated with al-Bāqir and al-Ṣādiq by the biographical literature narrate their opinions in very distinctive chains of transmission. A similar pattern (shared authority/independent chain of transmission) obtains with respect to other shared authorities/transmitters (e.g., Sarī b. Ismāʿīl, Saʿd b. Ṭarīf).

[2] There was a minor overlap in narrative style between ʿAlid traditions quoted by the Imāmīs and the Zaydīs, but this was limited to texts from the mid- to late 2nd/8th century. Although this might intimate a common style of ʿAlid citation, it does not support an intersection between the two groups in the early part of the century contemporaneous with the birth of Zaydism.

identity only crystallized in the mid- or late 2nd/8th century, we would expect the group's literature to include a substantial number of early overlaps with other groups. This is not the case.

It may be possible to argue that the Imāmīs did, in fact, emerge in the mid- or even late 2nd/8th century and then purged problematic traditions, creating the impression that they had differentiated from the larger Kūfan population in a much earlier period. This process, however, would either (1) require a broad consensus on early-2nd/8th-century transmitters who could unambiguously be appropriated by the Imāmīs without opposition from other groups or (2) produce a significant category of transmitters claimed by rival communities. In the first case, the process would have to wait a number of generations for communal boundaries to become clear; back-sifting could not really start until the beginning of the 3rd/9th century. In such a situation, we would expect some remnants or traces of the process to survive in either the Imāmī literature or – if the purge was extremely efficient – in the Sunnī literature. There is no substantive evidence for this hypothesis. In the second scenario, we would likely encounter numerous individuals who were claimed by different communities as one of their own. The actual number of such contested transmitters, however, is minimal. The Imāmīs share only 9 transmitters with the Sunnīs[3] and 6 with the Zaydīs[4] out of a grand total of the more than 1,400 transmitters distributed over 1,388 traditions.[5] The simplest and most logical explanation of the data is that the Imāmīs were an insular and distinctive community at the start of the 2nd/8th century.[6]

[3] These include (in chronological order of death date) Nu'mān b. Bashīr (d. 64/683), 'Abd Allāh b. Ma'qil b. Muqarrin (d. 80/699), Sa'īd b. al-Musayyab (d. 94/713), 'Abd al-Raḥmān b. Aswad b. Yazīd (d. 100/718), 'Āmir b. Sharāḥīl (d. 107/725), Jābir b. Yazīd al-Ju'fī (d. 128/746), Ḥabīb b. Qays b. Dīnār (d. 122/740), Ibrāhīm b. 'Abd al-'Alā' (d. 120/738), and Sulaymān b. Mihrān al-A'mash (d. 148/765).

[4] These include (in chronological order of death date) Nu'mān b. Bashīr (d. 64/683), Sarī b. Ismā'īl (d. 107/725?), 'Āmir b. Sharāḥīl (d. 107/725), Sa'd b. Ṭarīf (d. mid 2nd/8th century), 'Amr b. Shimr (d. 157/774), and Sulaymān b. Mihrān al-A'mash (d. 148/765).

[5] There are three transmitters found in the collections of all three sectarian groups – Nu'mān b. Bashīr (d. 64/683), 'Āmir b. Sharāḥīl (d. 107/725), and Sulaymān b. Mihrān al-A'mash (d.148/765). The first was a universally revered early Companion from a time before the demarcation of sectarian boundaries for which we have no extant written texts. The latter two, by contrast, lived during the period associated with early sectarianism. A closer look at their lives (and the representations of their lives) may provide interesting insights into the dynamics of allocating sectarian identity. For a closer examination of al-A'mash, see Chapter 7 in this volume.

[6] Whether the Imāmī community coalesced earlier (e.g., the late 1st/7th century during the lifetime of al-Sajjād) cannot be answered with any degree of certainty. There are only a handful of traditions that cite authorities predating al-Bāqir.

In contrast to Imāmism, the case studies offer far less support for the origin narrative of Zaydism. Had the sect formed through a merger of Batrism and Jārūdism, we would expect early Zaydī texts to embody the discordant tendencies of both communities. The Batrīs, despite their belief in the rightful succession of ʿAlī, were part and parcel of a general Kūfan traditionism that was eventually incorporated into Sunnism and revered the early Companions as transmitters. The Jārūdīs aligned with more sectarian Shīʿī communities (i.e., the Imāmīs) that rejected the probity of Companions who had fought or opposed ʿAlī. As a general rule, Batrī texts should resemble Sunnī traditions while Jārūdī texts should approximate those of the Imāmīs. The origin narrative further maintains that these two segments of Zaydism vied for control of the movement through the 2nd/8th and (especially) 3rd/9th centuries, a struggle in which the Jārūdīs ultimately triumphed. The impact of this internal conflict on the Zaydī traditions should be significant. We might, for example, expect victorious Jārūdīs to eliminate those traditions transmitted by their opponents, thereby skewing the surviving Zaydī accounts toward a Jārūdī orientation.[7] In general, if the classical origin narrative of early Zaydism is correct, our data should reflect one of the following:

1. A pattern in which Zaydī traditions include equal (or relatively equal) distributions of texts that share features with those of the Sunnīs (the Batrī component) and the Imāmīs (the Jārūdī component).
2. A corpus of Zaydī traditions dominated by a Jārūdī tendency as reflected in significant intersections with Imāmī texts and minimal similarities with Sunnī accounts.

Our results, however, are not indicative of either of these hypotheticals. Rather, we find that the earliest layer of Zaydī traditions are overwhelmingly Batrī in that they resemble Sunnī accounts in their use of authorities, transmitters, and style. In fact, there is a near-complete lack of traditions of a Jārūdī mold in the early 2nd/8th century. It is only in the course of the mid- to late 2nd/8th and early 3rd/9th centuries that Jārūdī accounts begin to appear concurrent with a precipitous decline in Batrī traditions.

[7] The primary Zaydī collection used in this study was compiled by Aḥmad b. ʿĪsā, a Jārūdī and a potential ʿAlid candidate for the Imāmate. If there had been an internal struggle for power between the Batrīs and the Jārūdīs in the 2nd/8th century, we would have expected Aḥmad b. ʿĪsā to expunge Batrī texts in an effort to eliminate all vestiges of their influence. The fact that he did not is telling.

This supports neither (1) an initial division between Batrīs and Jārūdīs nor (2) the removal of Batrī traditions by a victorious Jārūdism.[8]

Given the suspect nature of the classical narrative, it may be fruitful to approach the source materials anew with an eye toward constructing a revised chronology for the origins of Zaydism that finds support in the three case studies. The remainder of this chapter offers such a new framework drawing primarily on historical chronicles as opposed to the heresiographies that have shaped much of the secondary literature.

THE CASE FOR EVOLUTION

Let us begin by proposing an alternate narrative for early Zaydism. In contrast to the classic account that depicts an initially bifurcated Zaydī community consisting of Batrīs and Jārūdīs, the data suggests that the early community was largely Batrī. This meant that when Zayd b. ʿAlī revolted in 122/740, his followers (as Batrīs) were only distinguished from the larger proto-Sunnī Kūfan population by virtue of their avid enthusiasm for ʿAlid political claims. Through the course of the 2nd/8th century, the Zaydīs grew more militant and adopted legal doctrines that brought them closer to the Imāmīs. In other words, they became increasingly Jārūdī so that by the mid-3rd/9th century, the sect had shed much of its initial Batrī characteristics. This process finds support in a general lack of Jārūdī elements in early Zaydī traditions and their increase through the middle and late decades of the 2nd/8th century. Put simply, Zaydism gradually evolved from one orientation (Batrī) to another (Jārūdī). The terms "Batrī" and "Jārūdī" were utilized by scholars (mostly heresiographers) to help explain this dramatic change.

The primary benefit of this reformulation lies in its agreement with the results of the three case studies. In the absence of additional evidence, however, this correlation does not constitute definitive proof. Data can be manipulated to tell many different stories, all of which may be equally conjectural. With this in mind, let us turn to the primary sources (mainly historical chronicles) to ascertain the extent to which they align with and support our revised narrative.[9]

[8] See footnote 122 in this chapter.

[9] The following discussion relies largely on well-known historical chronicles. The primary Zaydī historical sources are al-Iṣbahānī's *Maqātil al-ṭālibiyyīn*, al-Nāṭiq bi'l-Ḥaqq's *al-Ifāda*, and Aḥmad b. Ibrāhīm and ʿAlī b. Bilāl, *al-Maṣābīḥ*. The *Maṣābīḥ* was originally authored by Aḥmad b. Ibrāhīm (d. 353/864) and then supplemented by ʿAlī b. Bilāl (fl. 5th/11th century) beginning with (or after) the entry on Yaḥyā b. Zayd b. ʿAlī. In future

Contesting the Revolt of Zayd b. ʿAlī (122/740)

Any discussion of early Zaydism must begin with the revolt of its apparent founder, Zayd b. ʿAlī, in Kūfa in 122/740. This event is generally acknowledged as the catalyst for the formation of the sect and a critical turning point in the broader history of Shīʿism.

We have previously discussed the manner in which heresiographies interpreted this rebellion (see Chapter 1) as a rallying point around which Batrīs and Jārūdīs coalesced to create a new movement. In the present chapter, we are more interested in their portrayal of the historical circumstances surrounding the revolt. The earliest heresiographies rarely comment on specifics and provide little in the way of detailed information. Pseudo-al-Nāshiʾ al-Akbar's (d. 293/906) *Masāʾil al-imāma* is exclusively concerned with the differences between the Jārūdīs and the Batrīs regarding (1) the nature of ʿAlī's designation as successor and (2) the sources for authoritative religious knowledge.[10] Historical context is limited to a single statement – in the course of a discussion on Jārūdism – which notes that "this sect rose up in rebellion with Zayd b. ʿAlī b. al-Ḥusayn and the Shīʿa named them the Zaydiyya."[11] Al-Nawbakhtī's (d. after 309/922) *Firaq al-shīʿa* and al-Qummī's (d. 301/914) *Kitāb al-maqālāt*[12] recount the Zaydī belief that an Imām who "sits in his house in the ease of his bed" is an "idolatrous non-believer on the wrong path as [are] his followers."[13] They then identify two primary Zaydī subdivisions – termed Jārūdīs and "weak" Zaydīs (later equated with Batrīs) – and discuss their distinctive theological doctrines.[14] Both authors apply the term "Zaydī" to those groups who agreed that ʿAlī was the most virtuous of people

citations, *Maṣābīḥ I* will be used to denote the section of the text authored by Aḥmad b. Ibrāhīm and *Maṣābīḥ II* will be used in reference to the continuation of ʿAlī b. Bilāl. These works were accessed by van Arendonk (*Les débuts de l'imāmat zaidite au Yémen*) and Madelung (*Der Imam al-Qāsim*). The former, however, based much of his narrative on al-Ṭabarī's *Tārīkh*, while the latter – in line with the objectives of his study – utilized many texts that were primarily theological in focus. Sunnī historical sources are mentioned in the course of the footnotes for comparative purposes.

10 *MIm*, 42–5.

11 *Ibid.*, 42.

12 Madelung has posited that al-Nawbakhtī's text – the earlier of the two – may preserve large sections of Hishām b. al-Ḥakam's lost *Kitāb al-ikhtilāf al-nās fiʾl-imāma* ("Remarks," 152–63). Modarressi has challenged this claim with two alternate source possibilities: (1) Hishām b. al-Ḥakam's *Kitāb al-mīzān* or (2) an earlier unidentified Sunnī text (Modarressi, *Tradition*, 266).

13 *KM* 71–2; *FS*, 54–5.

14 *KM*, 72; *FS*, 55. In his discussion of the difference between the two groups, Madelung primarily follows al-Nawbakhtī's narrative (*DIQ*, 47–51).

after the Prophet and supported Zayd b. 'Alī's revolt in Kūfa.[15] Finally, Abū al-Ḥasan al-Ash'arī (d. 324/935–6), in his *Maqālāt al-islāmiyyīn*, summarizes the doctrinal differences between six different Zaydī subdivisions without addressing their historical origins.[16]

The later works of al-Shahristānī (d. 549/1154) (*al-Milal wa'l-niḥal*) and Ibn Ṭāhir al-Baghdādī (d. 429/1037) (*al-Farq bayn al-firaq*) include theological descriptions similar to those mentioned in previous heresiographies. Each identifies the Jārūdīs and the Batrīs as the initial constituents of Zaydism and details their doctrinal beliefs in a typical manner.[17] These works, however, are distinguished by their exploration of the events surrounding Zayd's initial revolt and, in particular, a critical encounter that immediately preceded his final battle against the Umayyad army.

Al-Shahristānī's account begins by mentioning Zayd's education at the hands of the famous Mu'tazilī, Wāṣil b. 'Aṭā' (d. 130/748). This tutelage led him to accept (1) the legitimacy of a "less worthy" Imām and (2) the belief that there was no means for allocating blame in the conflict between Alī and his opponents in the first civil war. The mere act of studying under Wāṣil precipitated a falling-out between Zayd and his half-brother al-Bāqir who accused him of "acquiring knowledge from one who allowed for the possibility that his ancestor ['Alī] has committed a mistake in fighting the perfidious, the unjust, and the apostates."[18]

This argument ultimately had fatal consequences for Zayd as he prepared for battle outside Kūfa in 122/740. Both al-Shahristānī and Ibn Ṭāhir al-Baghdādī note an angry exchange between Zayd and a number of his followers prior to the outbreak of hostilities.[19] The relevant passage in al-Shahristānī's *al-Milal* starts abruptly with Zayd addressing potential supporters who had asked for a clarification of his stance on the early Companions. This speech is worth quoting in its entirety:

> 'Alī b. Abī Ṭālib – God be pleased with him – was the best of the Companions but the Caliphate was delegated to Abū Bakr for the soundness of his judgment and the religious basis of his stewardship in quelling the fire of civil strife and easing the hearts of the general masses. The era of wars which raged in the days of Prophethood was recent. The blood of the Qurashī polytheists and others on the sword of the Commander of the Faithful 'Alī had not yet dried, and the rancor in their chests for revenge remained. Hearts would not incline towards him

[15] *KM*, 72; *FS*, 55.
[16] *MIs*, 1:144–5.
[17] See the discussion of the Batrīs and Jārūdīs in Chapter 1.
[18] *MN*, 155–6.
[19] The same story is found in *Débuts*, 30–1.

and necks would not submit to him. It was in the public benefit (*maṣlaḥa*) that the leader in this situation should be someone known for being gentle, malleable, old, an early convert, and close to the Messenger of God, prayers of God and peace upon him. Consider the fact that when he [Abū Bakr] was stricken with the sickness from which he would die and appointed ʿUmar b. al-Khaṭṭāb, the people cried, "You have appointed a coarse harshness over us!" They were not pleased with the Commander of the Faithful ʿUmar b. al-Khaṭṭāb for his strictness, his rigidity, his religious harshness, and his coarse stubbornness against enemies until Abū Bakr silenced them by saying, "If my Lord asks me, I will say, 'I appointed over them one better than me.'" Therefore it is permitted for the less worthy (*mafḍūl*) to be Imām and have recourse to the more worthy (*afḍal*) in the implementation of legal judgments (*aḥkām*).[20]

Al-Shahristānī continues:

When the Shīʿa of Kūfa heard these doctrinal ideas (*maqālāt*) from him and realized that he did not disavow the two shaykhs [Abū Bakr and ʿUmar], they refused him (*rafaḍūhu*) until he died (lit: his fate came upon him). They were named the *rāfiḍa*.[21]

Ibn Ṭāhir al-Baghdādī relates the same encounter, laying out the situation in greater detail but summarizing the contents of Zayd's speech:

Zayd b. ʿAlī took the oath of allegiance as Imām from 1500 Kūfan men who rebelled with him against Hishām b. ʿAbd al-Malik's governor of Iraq, Yūsuf b. ʿUmar al-Thaqafī.

When fighting broke out between him and [Yūsuf b.] ʿUmar al-Thaqafī, they [the Kūfans] said, "We will help you against your enemies after you tell us your opinion regarding Abū Bakr, ʿUmar, and those who oppressed your forefather ʿAlī b. Abī Ṭālib."

Zayd said, "I only have good things to say about them. I never heard my father say anything but good about them. I only rebelled against the Banū Umayya who killed my grandfather al-Ḥusayn, plundered Medina on the day of *al-ḥarra*, and destroyed the House of God with rocks and fire launched by siege-machines."

They [the Kūfans] distanced themselves from him because of that [opinion] and he labeled them, "Those who refused me." From that day on, they were known as the *rāfiḍa*.

Naṣr b. Khuzayma al-ʿAbsī,[22] Muʿāwiya b. Isḥāq b. Yazīd b. Ḥāritha, and approximately 200 men remained with him [Zayd], fighting the army of Yūsuf b. ʿUmar al-Thaqafī until every last one of them was killed including Zayd whose body was exhumed, crucified, and burned.[23]

[20] *MN*, 155.
[21] *Ibid.*, 155.
[22] The text here appears corrupt with the name given as Naḍr b. Khuzayma al-ʿAnsī [sic].
[23] *FBF*, 44–5.

According to both versions, Zayd's refusal to condemn the first two caliphs for usurping 'Alī's rightful political claims precipitated the withdrawal of most of his Kūfan followers and resulted in his death.

As a whole, the heresiographies leave us with two contradictory propositions. On the one hand, they assert that early Zaydism consisted of distinct streams of Jārūdism and Batrism defined on the basis of theology and brought together in the revolt of Zayd b. 'Alī. On the other hand, they recount Zayd's explicit refusal to condemn the early Companions and his education under a non-'Alid religious authority (i.e., Wāṣil b. 'Aṭā'), positions that align with Batrism and fundamentally contradict Jārūdism. Furthermore, they expressly identify a number of Kūfans who (1) withdrew on the verge of battle and (2) were theologically Jārūdī in their demand that Zayd explicitly denounce Abū Bakr and 'Umar. In other words, the narrative preserved by al-Shahristānī and Ibn Ṭāhir al-Baghdādī allocates responsibility for Zayd's death to a group virtually indistinguishable from the Jārūdīs (although they are never named). It is hard to imagine that these "refusers" would have continued to call themselves Zaydīs after abandoning their Imām on the battlefield. Even if they did, they would have hardly held any credibility in the eyes of those Zaydīs who supported Zayd till the bitter end. Only one of the heresiographers, al-Shahristānī, mentions this paradox, observing that Abū al-Jārūd's followers opposed their own Imām on a number of fundamental theological issues.[24] He offers no further commentary on the matter.

If we accept the validity of Zayd's exchange with his followers (and there is no real reason to doubt it), this seems to undermine the claim that Zaydism initially consisted of Batrī and Jārūdī subdivisions.[25] It does, however, support our revised narrative that (1) most (if not all) of Zayd's initial followers were Batrīs,[26] and (2) the Jārūdīs emerged over

[24] *MN*, 158. Van Arendonk also points out the apparent disjuncture in these accounts (*Débuts*, 32–3).

[25] Crone offers a different perspective (drawing on a version of the revolt transmitted through Abū Mikhnaf) by classifying the Jārūdīs as "Rāfiḍī Zaydīs" who were much closer to – if not indistinguishable from – the Imāmīs. They were eventually drawn into Zaydism as a result of their political activism. This still leaves open the puzzling question of how the Jārūdīs could have been accepted within Zaydī circles if they (1) existed as defined group at the time of Zayd's revolt but (2) abandoned the cause at a critical juncture (Crone, *God's Rule*, 100).

[26] If we adopt this approach, then the events could be explained as follows: Zayd b. 'Alī led a group of (moderate) Batrī Shī'a united in their refusal to condemn the early Companions. Initially, he also garnered the support of other (possibly even early Imāmī) Shī'a who left after the battlefield incident. The term "*rāfiḍa*" was applied to this group and persisted as a pejorative condemnation of their last-minute rejection of Zayd. For more on this term

the next few decades as Zaydism underwent a internal transformation. This allows us to avoid the improbable assertion that the Jārūdīs abandoned the founder of their faith to certain death and then proceeded to seize control of his movement.

As opposed to the heresiographical literature, the Zaydī historical sources present a narrative of the revolt that is both internally consistent and strikingly devoid of theological complications. A representative example is Abū al-Faraj al-Iṣbahānī's (d. 356/967) *Maqātil al-ṭalibiyyīn*, a work organized around Ṭālibid struggles to wrest political power from the Umayyads and 'Abbāsids.[27] Al-Iṣbahānī does not mention theological disputes over the status of the first two caliphs and offers no indication of tensions among Zayd's core supporters. The account begins with Zayd b. 'Alī's arrival in Iraq and details his efforts toward building a covert missionary infrastructure designed to secure military and political support. He was especially successful in the traditional Shī'ī stronghold of Kūfa and the outlying provinces of Khurāsān, Jurjān, and Rayy.[28] In the face of growing pressure from Hishām's governor of Iraq (Yūsuf b. 'Umar al-Thaqafī), Zayd was forced to rebel prior to completing his preparations and before he was able to muster his full strength.[29] Once the revolt was public, Yūsuf b. 'Umar al-Thaqafī intimidated Zayd's Kūfan followers by rounding them up in the Friday mosque and threatening to kill anyone who ventured out.[30] They buckled under pressure and refused to respond to Zayd's call to arms, leaving him with an army of only 218 men.[31] Zayd was categorically unsympathetic toward these Kūfans and accused them of treachery.[32] The charge

and its varied usage, see Kohlberg, "*Rāfiḍa*," 677–9, and Jarrar, "Aspects," 213–4. Jarrar's piece is an English adaptation of one part of a larger study of Zaydī dogmatic epistles entitled "Arba'u rasā'il Zaydiyya mubakkira."

[27] Al-Iṣbahānī covers the biography of every prominent Ṭālibid (descendant of Abū Ṭālib) who died in the course of a rebellion or by order of a caliph through the 3rd/9th century. In the period between Zayd b. 'Alī's initial rebellion in 122/740 and the end of the 2nd/8th century, al-Iṣbahānī recounts the biographies of no less than fifty-five 'Alids. Although bearing a symbolic importance, many of these figures exerted only a limited influence on the overall evolution of Zaydism. The remainder of this chapter concentrates on the handful of 'Alids whose lives were especially pivotal in the sect's transformation from a Batrī moderation to a Jārūdī radicalism, drawing on al-Iṣbahānī's text for the basic historical framework and supplementing it with al-Nāṭiq bi'l-Ḥaqq's *al-Ifāda* and Aḥmad b. Ibrāhīm and 'Alī b. Bilāl's *al-Maṣābīḥ*

[28] *Maqātil*, 130–2.

[29] *Ibid.*, 132.

[30] *Ibid.*, 132–3.

[31] *Ibid.*, 134.

[32] *Ibid.*, 134.

was further justified after Zayd's small force stormed into the city, took control of the mosque, and cleared the way for the besieged Kūfans to fulfill their oaths. Even the removal of the immediate threat, however, failed to spur them into action, prompting one of Zayd's companions to exclaim, "Rise up from lowliness to honor and from this world to your religion!"[33] The end came swiftly as the Umayyad forces systematically struck down many of Zayd's closest supporters (e.g., Naṣr b. Khuzayma and Muʿāwiya b. Isḥāq al-Anṣārī) and finally killed him with a poisoned arrow to the head.[34]

Some Zaydī historical sources identify additional causes for Zayd's loss of support. In *al-Maṣābīḥ*, a work covering the lives of Zaydī Imāms through the mid-4th/10th century, Aḥmad b. Ibrāhīm (d. 353/864) records a number of encounters between Zayd and the Kūfans in which the latter attempt to circumvent their oath of allegiance.[35] Their complaints range from the assertion that al-Ṣādiq was the rightful Imām to pleas of financial hardship, prompting Zayd to label them *rawāfiḍ*. The account then describes the round-up of many Kūfans in the Friday mosque and the Umayyad threats that cow them into breaking their oaths. It is significant to note that neither Aḥmad b. Ibrāhīm nor any other Zaydī author mentions the battlefield theological exchange over the status of the first two caliphs.

As a whole, Zaydī historical chronicles frame the rebellion as a strictly political act. Although they mention prominent Batrī traditionists (e.g., Salama b. Kuhayl – d. 122/740 and Hārūn b. Saʿd al-ʿIjlī – d. 145/763)[36] and important early Jārūdīs (e.g., Fuḍayl b. al-Zubayr[37] and Abū al-Jārūd[38]) among Zayd's partisans, they offer conspicuously little information regarding their theological views. The sole factor uniting Zayd's supporters appears to be a shared belief in ʿAlid political claims against the Umayyads. Of particular interest in this regard is al-Iṣbahānī's depiction of Abū al-Jārūd as a prototypical young Kūfan who preferred Zayd b. ʿAlī's call to arms over the political pacifism of other prominent

33 *Ibid.*, 135.
34 *Ibid.*, 137.
35 *Maṣābīḥ I*, 390–2. A similar version of the revolt is preserved by two non-Zaydī Shīʿī scholars: al-Yaʿqūbī (*Tārīkh*, 2:325–6) includes a summary of important events but suggests that Zayd was never given the chance to network with his Kūfan supporters. Al-Masʿūdī covers the rebellion but does not offer an explanation for its failure in either the *Murūj* (3:206–7) or *Kitāb al-tanbīh wa al-ishrāf* (323).
36 *Ifāda*, 63.
37 Ibn al-Murtaḍā, *Ṭabaqāt*, 2:204.
38 *Maqātil*, 133.

'Alids (i.e., al-Bāqir and – in particular – al-Ṣādiq).[39] Even in the case of the eponymous founder of Jārūdism, however, al-Iṣbahānī offers no hint of his adherence to what would eventually become 'Jārūdī' theological doctrines.[40]

The Sunnī historical chronicles preserve a hybrid account combining the theological encounter detailed in the heresiographies with the political chronology of the Zaydī sources.[41] The theological controversy is placed well before the actual rebellion and explained as a ploy devised by certain elements of Zayd's supporters to renege on their oaths. This was not a critical blow to Zayd's hopes, which ultimately failed (as in the Zaydī sources) because of the cowardice of the Kūfans barricaded in the central mosque. Once again, the Jārūdīs are notably absent in the rebellion. The only group ascribed seemingly Jārūdī beliefs abandons Zayd well before the start of hostilities, whereas the bulk of his supporters seem perfectly comfortable with his adherence to an unambiguous Batrism.

It is significant to note that all three sets of sources discussed in this section support our revised narrative for the origins of Zaydism rather than its classical analogue.[42] Both the heresiographies and the Sunnī sources place Zayd (and his followers) firmly within the boundaries of Batrī Zaydism; any Jārūdīs would have abandoned the cause after his refusal to condemn Abū Bakr and 'Umar. The Zaydī chronicles are devoid of any theological discussions and intimate unanimity among his followers. This does not necessarily mean that there were no theological factions within Zaydism, but it is difficult to find any evidence for the existence of a discernible and relevant Jārūdī component. We are left with the impression of a Zaydism dominated by a perspective best characterized as Batrī.

[39] Modarressi, *Tradition*, 121.

[40] For an analysis of some of the purported theological views of Abū al-Jārūd that differ from the Batrīs, see Jarrar, "*Tafsīr*," 37–9.

[41] See al-Ṭabarī, *Tārīkh*, 5:497–503; Ibn al-Jawzī, *al-Muntaẓam*, 7:210–1; al-Nuwayrī, *Nihāyat*, 24:401. These accounts integrate the heresiographical narrative into the historical narrative. Al-Balādhurī does not include the theological exchange between Zayd and his followers, but the issue is discussed indirectly (*Ansāb*, 2:520–41 and especially 528–9). It is worth noting that al-Balādhurī employs the term "Zaydī" (in one instance) to refer to those of Zayd's followers who agreed with him regarding Abū Bakr and 'Umar (*Ansāb*, 2:529). This is likely an anachronistic label rather than evidence for the existence of a distinct Zaydī community.

[42] Al-Iṣbahānī's account seems the most persuasive, offering reasons for Zayd's failure that extend beyond a battlefield theological debate. The Umayyad army had a reputation for invincibility in the 2nd/8th-century Muslim world, which could intimidate supporters of potential rebels. It seems far more likely that Zayd b. 'Alī's abandonment resulted from a frightened populace than from a public finally deciding to ask Zayd his opinion of Abū Bakr on the eve of battle.

The Consolidation of Batrī Zaydism (122–45/740–63)

After Zayd's death, his eldest son Yaḥyā attempted (unsuccessfully) to rally the remnants of his forces, drawing on the remorse of those who had abandoned the cause.[43] He fled to Khurāsān where he solicited the military support of a number of local leaders sympathetic to ʿAlid political aspirations.[44] The region, however, had been thoroughly infiltrated by the Hāshimī movement led by Bukayr b. Māhān (d. after 127/744–5) and Abū Muslim (d. after 136/753–4) that would eventually bring the ʿAbbāsids to power.[45] After a series of run-ins with both Hāshimī and government agents, Yaḥyā reached Balkh where he found shelter with al-Ḥarīsh b. ʿAmr b. Dāwūd al-Shaybānī (d. mid-2nd/8th century),[46] a prominent local with Shīʿī sympathies.

When Yaḥyā persisted in his efforts at organizing an armed rebellion, the Umayyads redoubled their pursuit. The governor of the province, Naṣr b. Sayyār (d. 131/748), had al-Ḥarīsh arrested and tortured to the brink of death, prompting his son, Quraysh, to reveal Yaḥyā's location.[47] When news of the ʿAlid's capture reached the Umayyad caliph, Walīd II b. Yazīd, in 125/743, he granted Yaḥyā a conditional pardon and ordered Naṣr to monitor his movements in Khurāsān.[48] Yaḥyā managed to slip away (again) and raised a small military force of no more than seventy Khurāsānī supporters near the eastern frontier. He rebelled late in 125/743 and was quickly defeated and killed by a small provincial army.[49] Van Arendonk observes that Yaḥyā's death left "a deep impression among those in Khurāsān,"[50] but its impact in Kūfa appears to have been marginal at best. There are no indications of widespread Kūfan or

[43] For similar accounts of Yaḥyā's movements, see al-Balādhurī, *Ansāb*, 2:542–7; al-Yaʿqūbī, *Tārīkh*, 2:262–3; al-Ṭabarī, *Tārīkh*, 5:536–8; and *Débuts*, 33–4. A shortened version is preserved in Masʿūdī, *Murūj*, 3:212–3.

[44] *Maqātil*, 145–50.

[45] *EI*², s.v. Yaḥyā b. Zayd (Madelung).

[46] This is the correct name as mentioned by al-Ṭabarī, *Tārīkh*, 5:536 as opposed to al-Iṣbahānī who identifies him as al-Ḥarīsh b. ʿAbd al-Raḥmān.

[47] *Maqātil*, 146–47.

[48] *Ibid.*, 248.

[49] *Ibid.*, 149–50.

[50] Van Arendonk examines the manner in which the ʿAbbāsids manipulated Yaḥyā's death to mobilize support in Khurāsān (*Débuts*, 41–2). Al-Masʿūdī claims that all male children born in 125/743 were named either Yaḥyā or Zayd (*Murūj*, 3:213). See also *EI*², s.v. Yaḥyā b. Zayd (Madelung).

Zaydī support for the young 'Alid. Al-Iṣbahānī notes that he was only able to garner ten supporters in all of Iraq.[51]

A more serious 'Alid revolt was organized by two of Yaḥyā's distant cousins, al-Nafs al-Zakiyya Muḥammad b. 'Abd Allāh and his brother, Ibrāhīm, in 145/763. The sources claim that al-Nafs al-Zakiyya was groomed for the caliphate from an early age so that many 'Alids referred to him by the title "al-Mahdī."[52] After Yaḥyā b. Zayd's death and Walīd II's murder in 125/744, 'Abd Allāh b. al-Ḥasan called a council of the family of the Prophet for the express purpose of securing a consensus in favor of his son's candidacy for the caliphate.[53] Most of those present – with the exception of al-Ṣādiq and his followers[54] – pledged their allegiance to al-Nafs al-Zakiyya, who began building a missionary network that stretched as far east as India. After the 'Abbāsid revolution, al-Nafs al-Zakiyya and Ibrāhīm went underground and continued their preparations for rebellion. Al-Manṣūr's drive to find the brothers bordered on the maniacal, as he imprisoned and murdered numerous prominent 'Alids including their father, 'Abd Allāh.[55] In 145/763, under considerable pressure from al-Manṣūr and against the advice of his brother, al-Nafs al-Zakiyya emerged from hiding, declared himself the legitimate Imām, and took control of Medina.[56] Ibrāhīm simultaneously rebelled in Baṣra and quickly gained control of the city with the aid of a sympathetic governor and broad military support from the garrison towns.[57] Al-Manṣūr was ecstatic at the unorganized and ill-advised rebellion. In a matter of months, he was able to crush al-Nafs al-Zakiyya's forces in Medina and turn his attention to the more formidable military challenge posed by Ibrāhīm in Baṣra.[58] By the end of the year, the brothers

[51] *Maqātil*, 146.

[52] For use of this title, see *Maqātil*, 206–7, 210–17 and *Débuts*, 46, 50. For an alternate view that casts al-Nafs al-Zakiyya as a well-intentioned but doomed martyr in the mold of al-Ḥusayn b. 'Alī, see *Maqātil*, 217–27.

[53] *Maqātil*, 184–7; *Maṣābīḥ II*, 427–8; *Débuts*, 46–8

[54] For the Ḥusaynid opposition voiced by Ja'far al-Ṣādiq, see *Maqātil*, 186–7.

[55] See *Maqātil*, 178–83 where he offers a long list of 'Alids imprisoned by al-Manṣūr. Beginning on page 184, he recounts the direct causes of 'Abd Allāh's imprisonment, emphasizing his efforts at securing support for his two sons. See also, al-Ya'qūbī, *Tārīkh*, 2:307–8 and *Débuts*, 49–50.

[56] *Maqātil*, 230.

[57] For specifics of the brothers' movements, see *Débuts*, 49.

[58] For a detailed narrative of the rebellion, see *Maqātil*, 229–44; al-Balādhurī, *Ansāb*, 2:417–26 and 437–48; al-Ya'qūbī, *Tārīkh*, 2:315–19; al-Ṭabarī, *Tārīkh*, 6:183–95,

were dead and 'Abbāsid power had been consolidated in both the Ḥijāz and Iraq.

In their accounts of Ibrāhīm's revolt,[59] the historical sources offer strong indications of a distinctive Zaydī identity,[60] explicitly referring to a segment of his supporters – led by Hārūn b. Sa'd al-'Ijlī[61] – as "Zaydīs."[62] These men were noted for their religious tenacity[63] and their propensity to question (and confront) Ibrāhīm on a wide range of practical and religious matters.[64] Al-Iṣbahānī preserves a series of such encounters that center on the allocation of funds,[65] the proper method for performing the funeral prayer,[66] and battlefield tactics.[67] They eventually pressured Ibrāhīm to name their favorite candidate, 'Īsā b. Zayd, as his political and religious successor.[68] Tensions were also apparent in Ibrāhīm's ambiguous attitude toward their leader, Hārūn b. Sa'd, whom he refused to meet in the early stages of the rebellion.[69] A dispute even erupted over the use

199–230, and 250–63; and *Débuts*, 50–60. A shorter account of the conflict is preserved in Ibn Sa'd, *al-Ṭabaqāt al-kubra'*, 4:438–42.

[59] After al-Nafs al-Zakiyya's defeat, the Zaydīs considered Ibrāhīm the legitimate Imām. See al-Ya'qūbī, *Tārīkh*, 2:318.

[60] The earliest testimony for a distinct group of Zaydīs in the Sunnī historical chronicles occurs in al-Ṭabarī's *Tārīkh* with respect to the 127/744 rebellion of 'Abd Allāh b. Mu'āwiya. See *Tārīkh*, 5:599–604 for the revolt and 5:600 and 603 for explicit mention of the Zaydīs. This contrasts with the Zaydī sources that either ignore this rebellion altogether (e.g., 'Alī b. Bilāl's *al-Maṣābīḥ II* or al-Nāṭiq bi'l-Ḥaqq's *al-Ifāda*) or cast it in a highly negative light without noting any explicit Zaydī involvement (*Maqātil*, 152–9).

[61] Yaḥyā b. al-Ḥusayn emphasizes the traditionist credentials of Hārūn b. Sa'd. He is depicted as a prominent jurist with a reputation for good works and piety who transmitted traditions from Ibrāhīm al-Nakha'ī and 'Āmir b. Sharāḥīl (*Ifāda*, 85). Al-Balādhurī refers to Hārūn b. Sa'd as a Shī'a and quotes some of his verse (*Ansāb*, 2:442–3).

[62] The Zaydīs are a clearly demarcated segment of Ibrāhīm's supporters in *Maqātil*, 289, 296, 299, 308; al-Balādhurī, *Ansāb*, 2:440–41; al-Ya'qūbī, *Tārīkh*, 2:318; al-Ṭabarī, *Tārīkh*, 6:262; and *Débuts*, 57–8.

[63] They are characterized as crude (*kathīf*) and appear to have functioned as an independent military force (*Maqātil*, 308 and al-Ya'qūbī, *Tārīkh*, 2:318). This suggests that they constituted a preexisting community.

[64] In addition to the Zaydīs, the brothers were able to secure the support of Abū Ḥanīfa (*Ifāda*, 84; *Débuts*, 58 and 315; *DIQ*, 74), Mālik b. Anas (*Ifāda*, 77; *Débuts*, 50; *DIQ*, 74) and a number of unaffiliated Shī'a of dubious allegiances, such as Sulaymān b. Mihrān al-A'mash (*Ifāda*, 86–7; *Débuts*, 315–6; *DIQ*, 74). For a broad list of the companions of each of the prominent 'Alid rebels, see *Débuts*, 307–19 (Appendix 1).

[65] *Maqātil*, 288.

[66] *Ibid.*, 288–9.

[67] *Ibid.*, 296–9.

[68] *Ibid.*, 289, 342–3 and 345.

[69] *Ibid.*, 286 and 309; See also al-Ṭabarī, *Tārīkh*, 6:253–4.

of the term "Zaydī." When Ibrāhīm observed them chanting "We are the Zaydīs and the sons of Zaydīs," he exclaimed, "God have mercy on you! Is this word [Zaydī] better than the word Islam? Say we are Muslims and the sons of Muslims!"[70] Despite these tensions, the Zaydīs continued supporting Ibrāhīm to the end and mourned his death in a very vocal public display of grief.[71]

As a whole, these disagreements embodied a striking difference in perspective between the Ḥasanid Imāms and the early Zaydīs who – in the words of Veccia Vaglieri – "formed what was in effect a political party"[72] and were clearly advocates of a proto-Sunnī Kūfan traditionism. If Ibrāhīm performed the funeral prayer in an idiosyncratic style or allocated funds in a manner at odds with their traditions, they would – and did – object vociferously. This made them Batrīs (though the term is not used in the sources) in that they subordinated the religious authority of their 'Alid Imam to the transmitted knowledge of the Companions and early jurists. There are no indications that a sizable contingent of al-Nafs al-Zakiyya or Ibrāhīm's supporters held views that could be characterized as legally (or theologically) Jārūdī. If Abū al-Jārūd was still alive (likely) and took part in the rebellion (unclear), he does not appear to have played a role of even marginal importance in the larger Zaydī movement.

At this point, it may be useful to take a step back and consider the historical situation. The revolt of al-Nafs al-Zakiyya was especially significant because it included one of the earliest references to a distinct group of Zaydīs. These Zaydīs were most likely the same contingent of Kūfans that had supported (or regretted not supporting) Zayd b. 'Alī twenty years earlier. That initial revolt had united them based on a common commitment to the 'Alid political cause. In every other way, however, they continued adhering to a legal methodology and religious orthopraxy consistent with the proto-Sunnī Kūfan legal milieu. The next twenty years provided adequate time for them to construct an independent identity, undoubtedly aided by the missionary networks of al-Nafs al-Zakiyya and other 'Alids. When the brothers finally revolted, these partisans constituted a distinct faction that the historical literature labeled Zaydīs but which the heresiographers (eventually) identified as

[70] *Maṣābīḥ II*, 451; *Débuts*, 58.
[71] *Maṣābīḥ II*, 451.
[72] *EI*[2], s.v. Ibrāhīm b. 'Abd Allāh (L. Veccia Vaglieri).

Batrī Zaydīs. The problem with speaking of Batrī Zaydīs in 145/763 is that the term is redundant as it is likely that being a Zaydī at this time meant being a Batrī.

The Tipping Point (145–68/763–85)

The first signs of a change in Zaydism materialized in the twenty years following al-Nafs al-Zakiyya's death. The 'Abbāsids instituted a massive wave of repressive measures that forced the Zaydīs underground. In this period, the titular head of the movement in Iraq was Zayd's eldest living son, 'Īsā,[73] who spent the last few decades of his life (following Ibrāhīm's defeat in 145/763) under the protection of his Kūfan followers. 'Īsā had commanded the right flank of al-Nafs al-Zakiyya's army in his final stand against al-Manṣūr[74] before fleeing to Baṣra where he became one of Ibrāhīm's closest political and military advisors.[75] As mentioned earlier, he was held in high regard by the Kūfan Zaydīs who regretted their complicity in the violent deaths of both his father (Zayd b. 'Alī) and his brother (Yaḥyā b. 'Zayd).[76] By 156/773, 'Īsā had received the Zaydī oath of allegiance and was in the early stages of planning a rebellion that never came to fruition.[77] Al-Manṣūr and al-Mahdī (rl. 158–69/775–85) pursued him with tenacity, offering large monetary rewards for information and making (probably insincere) offers of amnesty during the Ḥajj seasons.[78] The accounts in the *Maqātil* and the *Maṣābīḥ* differ regarding 'Īsā's movements, with the former observing that he was unable to garner any significant

[73] For his succession to leadership, see *Débuts*, 61; *DIQ*, 52.

[74] *Maqātil*, 344; *Maṣābīḥ II*, 487.

[75] *Maṣābīḥ II*, 487–8.

[76] There are strong indications that the Kūfan Zaydīs preferred 'Īsā b. Zayd to Ibrāhīm b. 'Abd Allāh after observing the latter perform the prayer in an unfamiliar manner. There are even reports that al-Manṣūr promised 'Īsā a large sum of money if he would convince the Zaydīs to abandon Ibrāhīm. Aware of al-Manṣūr's reputation for betrayal, 'Īsā rejected the proposal in the harshest of terms (*Maqātil*, 343–4; *Débuts*, 61).

[77] Aḥmad b. Ibrāhīm reports that Ibrāhīm was succeeded by his son, al-Ḥasan, who failed to live up to expectations (*Maṣābīḥ II*, 488; *Débuts*, 59–60). Al-Iṣbahānī, by contrast, strongly asserts that the Zaydī elements in Ibrāhīm's forces were intent on 'Īsā's succession. He even offers an account in which Ibrāhīm formally designates 'Īsā b. Zayd as his heir apparent (*Maqātil*, 342–3 and, especially, 345).

[78] See *Maṣābīḥ II*, 488 and *Maqātil*, 343–53, with numerous examples of the search for 'Īsā b. Zayd and other prominent 'Alids. Multiple versions of the Ḥajj episode are presented on pages 350–1 of the *Maqātil*.

support[79] and the latter asserting that he was about to rebel when he was poisoned by 'Abbāsid agents.[80]

From 145/763 to his death in 168/785, 'Īsā lived covertly in the household of the famous Batrī al-Ḥasan b. Ṣāliḥ b. Ḥayy (d. 168/785) and met frequently with a number of prominent Zaydīs, including Isrā'īl b. Yūnus (d. 160 or 162/776 or 778) and Ṣabbāḥ al-Za'farānī (d. mid-2nd/8th century).[81] The sources suggest that the community grew impatient with 'Īsā's careful and cautious style, a style likely aggravated by the relentless pressures of governmental pursuit and the memory of the deaths of his father and brother.[82] Al-Iṣbahānī depicts an exchange in which several Zaydīs urged 'Īsā to revolt with the claim that they had the backing of 10,000 men in Iraq and the Ḥijāz. The Imām replied that he would gladly rebel "before the day has dawned" if he could count on even 300 of these supporters "to expend their lives" against the enemies of God.[83] Although the encounter successfully silenced the Zaydīs in the short term, they continued to agitate for a fight.

The repeated and growing calls for a military uprising did not produce any change in the dominant Batrism of the early Zaydīs. This was apparent in a dispute over an episode from the Prophet's *sīra* that broke out between Ḥasan b. Ṣāliḥ and 'Īsā b. Zayd during the Ḥajj.[84] The matter was only settled when the two parties covertly approached the famous traditionist Sufyān al-Thawrī for his opinion.[85] The episode suggests that the Zaydīs continued to adhere to the Batrī view that denied an 'Alid Imām any special status vis-à-vis non-'Alid Muslim scholars.

The strains of living underground under the constant watch of the 'Abbāsid authorities pushed many Zaydīs to the breaking point, and some began clamoring for an accommodation with governmental power. These internal divisions remained hidden during 'Īsā's lifetime but erupted immediately after his death in an argument over the fate of his sons,

79 *Maqātil*, 353.
80 *Maṣābīḥ II*, 388–9.
81 *Maqātil*, 345–51; *Débuts*, 62; *DIQ*, 51. For a historiographical analysis of this period in 'Īsā's life, see Haider, "Contested."
82 *Maqātil*, 345–6.
83 *Ibid.*, 353.
84 Although the text does not explicitly identify the contentious issue, it likely involved the succession to the Prophet with implications for the political legitimacy of non-'Alid rulers.
85 *Ibid.*, 350–1.

Zayd and Aḥmad, between Ṣabbāḥ al-Za'farānī[86] and al-Ḥasan b. Ṣāliḥ.[87] Ṣabbāḥ was blunt in his appraisal of the situation:

> Consider the fact that the pain and struggle we have endured has been without meaning. 'Īsā b. Zayd has died and gone [lit: gone on his way]. We are only persecuted because of ['Abbāsid] fears of him. If it is known that he has died, they [the 'Abbāsids] will feel safe from him and will leave us alone. Let me seek out this man – meaning al-Mahdī – and inform him of his ['Īsā's] death so that he will stop searching for us and we will stop fearing him.[88]

Al-Ḥasan refused to go along with the plan, declaring, "By God, do not bring joy to the enemy of God by informing him of the death of the friend (*walī*) of God and the descendant of the Prophet of God.... His [al-Mahdī] spending a night in fear of him ['Īsā'] is better to me than a year of fighting and worship."[89] The matter resolved itself when al-Ḥasan b. Ṣāliḥ died a few months later and Ṣabbāḥ proceeded to al-Mahdī's court where he announced 'Īsā's death and shamed the caliph into caring for the children of the dead 'Alid.[90]

The Kūfan Zaydīs were faced with two alternatives: renounce the revolutionary struggle in exchange for material security, or continue it under intense governmental pressure. Those Zaydīs (e.g., Ṣabbāḥ al-Za'farānī) who chose to make peace with the 'Abbāsids returned to their Kūfan traditionist roots and assimilated into a community that would eventually coalesce into Sunnism. The choice of continued revolution, by contrast, had consequences that extended beyond the political sphere (see further discussion).[91] Subsequent Zaydī Imāms embraced "Jārūdī" positions,

[86] al-Tustarī very briefly mentions Ṣabbāḥ as a companion of al-Ṣādiq (*Qāmūs*, 5:479). He is not found in al-Mizzī's *Tahdhīb*.

[87] For this exchange, see *Maqātil*, 354–61.

[88] *Ibid.*, 355.

[89] *Ibid.*, 355.

[90] For more on 'Īsā b. Zayd's eldest son, Aḥmad, see footnote 122 in this chapter.

[91] This framework of an accommodationist/revolutionary divide is indebted to Marshall Hodgson's analysis of a "piety-minded" movement that included a wide array of religious groups opposed to the Umayyads. After the 'Abbāsid revolution, many of these groups accommodated the new regime. Specifically, they accepted its political legitimacy but claimed a scholarly monopoly on legal and religious matters. Hodgson contends that the formal break between Proto-Sunnīs and the Shī'a can be traced to this fateful decision. The Zaydīs were faced with the same choice. Those that accommodated were eventually integrated into Sunnism, whereas those that sought revolutionary change were forced to elaborate independent positions, which – in the legal sphere – often resembled those of the Imāmīs. This point becomes more evident over the next few decades in the build-up to the battle at Fakhkh and the dispersal of rebellion to the Muslim East and West (Hodgson, *Venture*, 1:272–9). See also Chapter 1.

which brought them closer to the Imāmīs in law and theology. In fact, after 'Isā's death, the sources rarely mention disputes between Zaydīs and their Imāms on facets of ritual law, and there is a dramatic diminishing of reverence for traditionist figures such as Sufyān al-Thawrī.

The Emergence of Jārūdī Zaydism (169/786)

The next major Zaydī military rebellion erupted in Medina in 169/786 under the leadership of Ṣāḥib Fakhkh al-Ḥusayn b. 'Alī b. al-Ḥasan b. al-Ḥasan b. al-Ḥasan b. 'Alī b. Abī Ṭālib (d. 169/786).[92] During the reign of al-Mahdī, al-Ḥusayn had enjoyed a degree of influence and prestige as the caliph routinely granted him large sums of money and even acceded to his amnesty requests for prominent imprisoned 'Alids.[93] The political landscape changed dramatically in 168/785 with the deaths of both 'Īsā b. Zayd and al-Mahdī. The new caliph, al-Hādī (rl. 169–70/785–6), was much more aggressive in his dealing with the 'Alids, and the Iraqī Zaydīs were spoiling for a fight after a long period of political quiescence. When al-Hādī heard whispers of a possible Kūfan insurrection, he ordered al-Ḥusayn b. 'Alī and other prominent 'Alids residing in Iraq to Medina, where they could be kept under the watchful eye of the newly appointed governor of the Ḥijāz, 'Umar b. 'Abd al-'Azīz b. 'Abd Allāh al-'Umarī (d. after 169/786).[94]

The sources are unanimous in ascribing the subsequent revolt to a series of repressive measures instituted by al-'Umarī. The 'Alids were particularly enraged by the imposition of a daily roll call.[95] If any descendant of the Prophet failed to appear when his name was called, his relatives were held accountable and threatened with physical and fiscal sanctions. A few months into the policy, al-Ḥasan b. Muḥammad b. 'Abd Allāh b. al-Ḥasan b. al-Ḥasan b. 'Alī b. Abī Ṭālib disappeared, prompting a particularly harsh exchange between al-'Umarī and al-Ḥusayn b. 'Alī that culminated in the former threatening the latter with physical violence.[96] The

[92] A parallel but slightly different version of the revolt is found in al-Ya'qūbī, *Tārīkh*, 2:348–9.

[93] *Débuts*, 62–3; *EI*², s.v. al-Ḥusayn b. 'Alī Ṣāḥib Fakhkh (L. Veccia Vaglieri). The Zaydī sources contend that this relationship was a façade for a covert rebellion brewing in Kūfa (*Maṣābīḥ II*, 466–7).

[94] *Maqātil*, 371; *Maṣābīḥ II*, 465 and 468; *Ifāda*, 93–4; *Akhbār*, 132 and, for more on this important source, Jarrar. "Arba'u," 267–8; *Débuts*, 62.

[95] *Ifāda*, 94; *Débuts*, 63.

[96] Veccia Vaglieri's account is based almost entirely on al-Ṭabarī (*Tārīkh*, 6:410–6 and 417–20), depicting the rebels as arrogant and selfish. The impetus for their hostility is

'Alids (and Ṭālibids) in Medina were furious at the governor and convened an emergency meeting where they gave the oath of allegiance to al-Ḥusayn b. 'Alī and decided (in a rather short-sighted manner) to revolt the next day.[97]

The rebellion was dominated by the hot-headed and charismatic Yaḥyā b. 'Abd Allāh b. al-Ḥasan b. al-Ḥasan b. 'Alī b. Abī Ṭālib (d. 189/805) and his brother Idrīs (d. 175/791), who were placed in charge of al-Ḥusayn's military affairs. On the morning of the uprising, before the *fajr* prayer, the brothers led a small force that seized control of the Prophet's mosque.[98] But when al-Ḥusayn b. 'Alī took the pulpit and appealed for support against the 'Abbāsids, he found the Medinans wholly unenthusiastic. In fact, many locals immediately returned to their homes in anticipation of the 'Abbāsid military response.[99] The Zaydī historical sources claim that the decision to rebel in Medina was rash and ill-conceived because a revolt had been meticulously planned for Mecca following the Ḥajj with the pledged support of 30,000 pilgrims.[100] If the 'Alids had just waited a month and declared their intentions in Mecca, they could have posed a serious threat to 'Abbāsid power. In Medina, however, al-Ḥusayn b. 'Alī was isolated with a limited support base (no more than 300 men)[101] drawn primarily from his own family. The only viable option was to flee to Mecca where the bulk of the pilgrims (unaware of the events in Medina) were gathered (allegedly) in eager anticipation of a rebellion. When the 'Abbāsids learned of the uprising, however, they were able to raise a patchwork army and intercepted the 'Alids at Fakhkh (six miles outside of Mecca).[102] Al-Ḥusayn b. 'Alī and more than a hundred of his 'Alid supporters lost

traced back to al-'Umarī's decision to punish al-Ḥasan b. Muḥammad (who later disappeared) for drinking wine. This version of the revolt also notes that the 'Alids who seized the Prophet's mosque left it in a scandalous state of impurity. In the larger chronology, however, Veccia Vaglieri aligns with the Zaydī historical chronicles (Veccia Vaglieri, "al-Ḥusayn b. 'Alī," 3:615–17). For parallel Zaydī accounts, see *Maqātil*, 373–5; *Maṣābīḥ II*, 471; *Ifāda*, 94; *Akhbār*, 133–4; *Débuts*, 63–4.

97 The sources identify al-Kāẓim and al-Ḥasan b. Ja'far b. al-Ḥasan b. al-Ḥasan b. 'Alī b. Abī Ṭālib as the only 'Alids who refused to take the oath or support the rebellion (*Maqātil*, 375–6; *Ifāda*, 94).

98 The brothers play a central role in almost every account of the rebellion with Yaḥyā holding (an apparent) seniority over Idrīs (*Maṣābīḥ II*, 472–5; *Ifāda*, 94–5; *Akhbār*, 140).

99 Aḥmad b. Ibrāhīm, *al-Maṣābīḥ*, 472 and 474–8; *Ifāda*, 95.

100 *Akhbār*, 142 and 146.

101 *Maqātil*, 377; *Ifāda*, 95.

102 *Ifāda*, 95–6; *Débuts*, 64.

their lives in the subsequent battle.[103] Many of the survivors (including Yaḥyā and Idrīs) fled to Mecca where they escaped pursuit by dispersing among the crowds of pilgrims.

Al-Ḥusayn b. 'Alī's revolt offers significant evidence for the emergence of a Jārūdī Zaydism. First, the native Medinan population soundly rejected the 'Alid call to arms and withdrew to their homes[104] to await the end of the conflict.[105] More significantly, there was no indication of the slightest traditionist (or proto-Sunnī) support for the rebellion. This was a striking change from previous 'Alid revolts, which garnered the tacit (if not explicit) support of local scholars including Abū Ḥanīfa, Mālik b. Anas, and Sufyān al-Thawrī.[106] By 169/786, however, most traditionist scholars had adopted an accommodating (as opposed to a revolutionary) stance toward 'Abbāsid power. The withdrawal of this support was critical in the reduction of Batrī influence within Zaydism. Second, there was a marked increase in ritual practices that were clearly Jārūdī in flavor. The very first act of the rebellion was the seizure of the Prophet's mosque and the demand (made vociferously by Yaḥyā and Idrīs b. 'Abd Allāh) that the call to prayer be performed in a distinctly Shī'ī manner, with the inclusion of the phrase, "Hurry to the best of works." When the *mu'adhdhin* hesitated, the brothers drew their swords and threatened his life.[107] This was a clear public declaration that (at least some important) Zaydī 'Alids had embraced ritual law positions that differed significantly from those of proto-Sunnī Kūfan (and by association Batrī) scholars.

After the 'Abbāsid revolution and the failed revolt of al-Nafs al-Zakiyya and Ibrāhīm b. 'Abd Allāh, the Zaydīs endured a period of intense oppression that exacted a heavy toll. Like many other segments of the population, they were forced to choose between accommodating 'Abbāsid power or continuing the revolutionary struggle. Most groups – including the

[103] *Maqātil*, 378–81; *Ifāda*, 96; *Akhbār*, 152–5; *EI*², s.v. al-Ḥusayn b. 'Alī Ṣāḥib Fakhkh (L. Veccia Vaglieri).

[104] *Maṣābīḥ II*, 470–1 and especially 476.

[105] *Ibid.*, 474–5.

[106] Abū Ḥanīfa is reported to have backed the rebellions of Zayd b. Alī and the brothers, al-Nafs al-Zakiyya and Ibrāhīm b. 'Abd Allāh. Mālik b. 'Anas and Sufyān al-Thawrī are also counted among the followers of al-Nafs al-Zakiyya, with the latter showing extreme deference to 'Īsā b. Zayd. See also footnote 64 in this chapter.

[107] *Maṣābīḥ II*, 474; *Ifāda*, 94. Al-Iṣbahānī (*Maqātil*, 375) and Aḥmad b. Sahl al-Rāzī (*Akhbār*, 138) preserve the incident but do not portray the brothers as voicing the demand. These details are not mentioned by al-Ṭabarī despite his depiction of Yaḥyā as one of the leading voices in the revolt. For the call to prayer, see footnote 68 in Chapter 8 of this volume.

various streams of Kūfan traditionism and the *ahl al-ra'y* – chose accommodation. They renounced the legality of armed rebellion while asserting their monopoly over religious matters and ritual law. This change made life very difficult for those Zaydīs identified as Batrī because their loyalties were drawn in contradictory directions. If they disavowed revolution, they could no longer consider themselves Zaydī in any real sense as they would lose the very element that differentiated them from Kūfan proto-Sunnism. If they rejected their links to a Kūfan proto-Sunnism that was moving toward accommodation, then how would they define themselves in terms of law and practice? There were no easy answers to this dilemma. The most obvious solution might have been for the Zaydīs to maintain their proto-Sunnī positions independent of the larger Kūfan community. Most Zaydīs, however, chose a different path, adopting a "Jārūdism" that incorporated many elements of Imāmī ritual practice and legal methodology. The driving forces behind this transformation were the brothers who played such a pivotal role in al-Ḥusayn b. 'Alī's rebellion, namely Yaḥyā and Idrīs b. 'Abd Allāh.

Marginality and the Triumph of Jārūdī Zaydism (170–89/787–805)

The failure of the rebellion at Fakhkh triggered a Zaydī migration to the physical (and intellectual) margins of the Islamic world.[108] This was best embodied by Yaḥyā b. 'Abd Allāh who had lent support to al-Ḥusayn b. 'Alī despite his own apparent seniority among the Ḥasanids. His actions in the course of the revolt reflected his devotion to a religious ideal that can only be characterized as Jārūdī (e.g., the demand for a Shī'ī call to prayer). This was hardly surprising given that Yaḥyā was brought up and educated in the home of al-Ṣādiq in Medina.[109] After the defeat at Fakhkh, Yaḥyā made his way to Daylam, where he led a small military rebellion in 176/792 that ended with his acceptance of an offer of security from al-Rashīd.[110] The sources attribute his failure to the lukewarm

[108] See al-Balādhurī, 2:449–53; al-Ṭabarī, *Tārīkh*, 6:416–7; and *Débuts*, 65.

[109] Madelung attributes Yaḥyā's adoption of practices that may be characterized as Jārūdī to the influence of al-Ṣādiq. Specifically, he states that "[Yaḥyā] followed [al-Ṣādiq] in his ritual practice and transmitted from him. He appears in Imāmī works as a transmitter from Ja'far" (*EI*², s.v. Yaḥyā b. 'Abd Allāh (Madelung); *idem*, *DIQ*, 51).

[110] For a detailed itinerary of his travels, see *Débuts*, 65–6. Ibn Sa'd offers a brief entry on Yaḥyā that notes his participation in the battle at Fakhkh and al-Rashīd's pardon but does not mention the revolt in Daylam (*al-Ṭabaqāt al-kubra'*, 5:442). For similarly bare accounts of Yaḥyā's fate after the rebellion, see al-Balādhurī, *Ansāb*, 2:449 and al-Ya'qūbī, *Tārīkh*, 2:353. The latter condenses events to the extent that it appears

support of his Kūfan followers, in particular the (unnamed) son of the famous Batrī Zaydī, al-Ḥasan b. Ṣāliḥ.[111] The problems between the two parties stemmed from Yaḥyā's adherence to a Jārūdī ritual orthopraxy heavily influenced by Imāmism.[112] He repeatedly (and unsuccessfully) tried to convince the Kūfans to abandon the "wiping" of leather socks in the ablution and the drinking of date wine (an *ahl al-ra'y* practice). The relationship became so strained that Yaḥyā ultimately refused to lead them in group prayer, which understandably provoked a scathing response from the Kūfans.[113]

The Kūfan Zaydīs were still clinging to a proto-Sunnī Batrism, which put them at odds with their new Jārūdī Imām. This disconnect – ten years removed from the death of 'Īsā b. Zayd – strongly intimated the direction Zaydism was heading in the mid- to late 2nd/8th century. The primary engine in the transition was Yaḥyā, who survived for two decades as the focal point for Zaydī hopes in both the Muslim heartlands and the frontiers. His influence increased greatly when he returned to Medina after the caliphal pardon and provided financial support for 'Alid families who had lost relatives in the Battle of Fakhkh.[114] In Yaḥyā, the Zaydīs finally had an Imām-in-waiting with the ability to move freely between Iraq and the Ḥijāz, the influence to secure the release of imprisoned 'Alids, and access to large sums of money. These conditions (set in writing in the document of security) enraged al-Rashīd who searched desperately for a legal means of circumventing his oath.[115] Eventually, in 189/805, he managed to imprison and kill Yaḥyā, but twenty years of the 'Alid's political machinations and proselytizing had

al-Rashīd broke his agreement immediately and threw Yaḥyā in jail for what would amount to thirteen years! Al-Ṭabarī mentions Yaḥyā's rebellion and emphasizes the erratic nature of the relationship between the 'Alid and al-Rashīd (*Tārīkh*, 6:450–7 and 485–7). There is no discussion of Yaḥyā's interactions with his followers or indication of his degree of freedom. In general, al-Ṭabarī's depiction of Yaḥyā centers on his repeated imprisonments and releases interspersed with the bestowing of large sums of money.

111 *Maqātil*, 391–3; Jarrar, "Imāmī," 210; This is one of the last revolts that won proto-Sunnī support, with Aḥmad b. Ibrāhīm and Aḥmad b. Sahl al-Rāzī counting al-Shāfi'ī among Yaḥyā's supporters (*Maṣābīḥ II*, 491; *Akhbār*, 197; *Débuts*, 318; *DIQ*, 74; Jarrar, "Aspects," 205–6). See also footnote 64 in this chapter.

112 Jarrar makes a similar point ("Aspects," 210).

113 For these examples and the Batrī reactions, see *Maqātil*, 392–3; *Maṣābīḥ II*, 494; *Ifāda*, 101. The tensions are also discussed in *EI*², s.v. Yaḥyā b. 'Abd Allāh (Madelung).

114 *Maqātil*, 394–400. For more on the agreement between al-Rashīd and Yaḥyā, see *Débuts*, 68–70.

115 In fact, many biographies of Yaḥyā are devoted almost entirely to al-Rashīd's relentless efforts to revoke the security guarantee (*Maqātil*, 393–400; *Maṣābīḥ II*, 494–500; *Débuts*, 67).

left a permanent mark on Zaydism with a precipitous decline in the influence of Batrism.[116]

The tensions that accompanied this transition from a Batrī to a Jārūdī Zaydism erupted in a dramatic way in North Africa, where Yaḥyā had sent his brother Idrīs.[117] Recall that Idrīs had been at his brother's side when al-Ḥusayn b. 'Alī's supporters seized control of the Prophet's mosque and demanded the Shī'ī call to prayer. Idrīs was also depicted in the sources as one of the main firebrands of the uprising and a military leader in many of the initial battles in Medina.[118] In the Maghrib and Ifrīqiyya, Idrīs began proselytizing among the Berber tribes and building an army that eventually became the foundation for an independent local dynasty.[119] When news of Idrīs' movements reached al-Rashīd, he dispatched an agent who infiltrated the 'Alid's entourage and poisoned him in 175/791. The identity of the assassin remains in doubt, but two possible suspects are mentioned in all the historical sources: a client of al-Mahdī known as al-Shammākh al-Yamāmī and Sulaymān b. Jarīr.[120] Little information survives about the former, but the latter was none other than the eponymous founder of the Sulaymāniyya branch of Zaydism, which agreed in substance with most Batrī (Kūfan Proto-Sunnī) legal and theological positions.[121] The mere possibility of Sulaymān's involvement speaks volumes about the state of Zaydism at

[116] Jarrar's analysis of four epistles ascribed to either Yaḥyā or Idrīs allows for a similar conclusion. He notes that at least two of the texts bear signs of potential authenticity thereby dating the proliferation of Jārūdī ideas to their lifetimes. See Jarrar, "Aspects," 217 and the more expansive conclusions of *idem*, "Arba'u," 288–90.

[117] Other 'Alids alleged to have headed to the Maghrib included another of Idrīs' brothers, Ibrāhīm, and the senior member of the group, Muḥammad b. Ja'far b. Yaḥyā b. 'Abd Allāh b. al-Ḥasan b. 'Alī b. Abī Ṭālib (*Maqātil*, 408; *Akhbār*, 164). For a heavily textual discussion of the murder of Idrīs and its broader implications for Zaydism, see Haider, "Community," 459–76, and the sources mentioned therein. For the text and analysis of an epistle sent by Yaḥyā with Idrīs, which conveyed a distinctive Jārūdī message, see Jarrar, "Aspects," 201–19 and *idem*, "Arba'u," 269–77.

[118] *Maṣābīḥ II*, 474–5; *Akhbār*, 140.

[119] The most thorough account of his movements is found in *Akhbār*, 171–89, with a less detailed version preserved in *Maqātil*, 407.

[120] See *Maqātil*, 407 and *EI*[2], s.v. Idrīs I al-Akbar (D. Eustache). Aḥmad b. Sahl al-Rāzī (*Akhbār*, 171–2) names al-Shammākh without any further commentary, whereas Alī b. Bilāl (*al-Maṣābīḥ II*, 511–12) offers both possibilities before citing an opinion from Aḥmad b. 'Īsā, which exonerates Sulaymān b. Jarīr. The skepticism in 'Alī b. Bilāl's account, however, is palpable. Van Arendonk mentions Sulaymān's possible role in the poisoning without assessing its historicity (*Débuts*, 81; *DIQ*, 62).

[121] al-Iṣbahānī describes him as "one of the leading theologians of the Zaydī Batrīs" (*Maqātil*, 407). For more on the Sulaymāniyya, see Chapter 1.

the time as Jārūdī Imāms were pressuring doctrinal Batrīs to declare their loyalties.[122]

ZAYDISM REINTERPRETED

This chapter began by questioning the view (derived primarily from the heresiographical sources) that Zaydism was created through the merger of two early Shīʿī groups, namely the Batrīs and the Jārūdīs. The results of the three case studies did not support this account of the origins of Zaydism. In its place, we proposed a revised narrative in which early Zaydism was overwhelmingly Batrī and only acquired a Jārūdī character in the course of the 2nd/8th century. This alternative chronology implied that the terms "Batrī" and "Jārūdī" were heresiographical constructs utilized to explain the group's gradual transformation from one orientation to the other. The revision found strong support in the comparative analyses of traditions conducted in Chapters 3 through 5.

In the second part of the chapter, we examined the historical sources for evidence for our reformulated narrative. We found significant indications that the supporters of Zayd b. ʿAlī (and his son Yaḥyā) were primarily Batrī in that they (1) were Kūfan traditionists (a movement associated with proto-Sunnism) and (2) supported the political claims and legality of ʿAlid military uprisings.[123] The lack of a significant Jārūdī presence persisted through the revolt of al-Nafs al-Zakiyya, with even Abū al-Jārūd appearing unconcerned with (or unaware of) Zayd's opinion of the status of the early Companions. The first indications of a change

[122] This Jārūdization of Zaydism finds further support in the life of ʿĪsā b. Zayd's eldest son Aḥmad who, after his father's death, was raised in Baghdād under the watchful eye of al-Mahdī and al-Hādī before being sent to Medina by al-Rashīd (*Maqātil*, 355, 358–61). Aḥmad went underground and managed to evade the authorities for a number of years (*Maqātil*, 496–8). At one point, he was arrested along with his cousin, Qāsim b. ʿAlī b. ʿUmar b. ʿAlī b. al-Ḥusayn, but managed to escape with the help of Zaydīs who laced his guard's food with *banj*, a strong narcotic (*Maqātil*, 492–3). Aḥmad then fled to Iraq where he divided his time between Kūfa and Baṣra, eluding al-Rashīd's forces that – at one point – searched the home of every Medinan known to harbor any pro-Shīʿī sympathies (*Maqātil*, 494). Even though Aḥmad b. ʿĪsā never rose up in rebellion, he was hailed as one of the most promising Zaydī candidates for the Imāmate. He maintained close ties to a number of prominent ʿAlids including the aforementioned Yaḥyā and Idrīs, the sons of ʿAbd Allāh b. al-Ḥasan b. al-Ḥasan (*Maqātil*, 497). Aḥmad b. ʿĪsā is best known for his *Amālī*, the most important Zaydī *ḥadīth* collection and the primary source for the majority of Zaydī traditions cited in this study.

[123] It can even be argued that the revolutionary beliefs of these Batrīs were in accord with a particular strain of traditionism that originally included Mālik b. Anas and Sufyān al-Thawrī.

materialized around al-Manṣūr's consolidation of ʿAbbāsid power, when many prominent ʿAlids and their followers were forced underground and most proto-Sunnī groups adopted an accommodationist stance toward political power. The conjunction of these historical forces left the Zaydīs in a difficult position, caught between a nascent Sunnī traditionism that rejected rebellion and a strident political activism that defined their larger movement. It was Yaḥyā and Idrīs b. ʿAbd Allāh who facilitated the "Jārūdization" of Zaydism through (1) their staunch preservation of its revolutionary character and (2) their introduction of ritual positions and theological tenets drawn from Imāmī Shīʿism.[124]

[124] These conclusions must be qualified by two important observations: (1) It is necessary to approach some of our historical chronicles with a degree of caution as they derive from a branch of literature known as *maqātil*, characterized by the recurrence of a particular set of literary topoi (Gunther, "*Maqātil*," 192–212). It should be noted, however, that I am not using these sources to construct a new historical narrative, but rather to test a narrative derived from independent sources (i.e., ritual law traditions) uninterested in perpetuating a specific *historical narrative*. Utilized in this limited manner, the historical sources offer a valuable tool for assessing the accuracy of a revised version of early Zaydism. (2) The general paucity of Zaydī traditions in Chapters 3 through 5 should temper any broad overarching claims. Even though I am arguing that Zaydism evolved from a Batrī to Jārūdī orientation, this does not mean that the change happened with great suddenness and rapidity or that there were no figures who defied this classification. It is possible that there were individuals who self-identified at Zaydīs in the early 2nd/8th century but held views similar to the "Jārūdīs." This study, however, suggests that they were exceptionally rare.

7

The Problem of the Ambiguous Transmitter

Ritual and the Allocation of Identity

In Chapters 3 through 5, ritual law texts were used to evaluate the hypothesis that Shīʿī sectarian identities first coalesced in Kūfa during the early 2nd/8th century. Chapter 6 presented a revised chronology for early Zaydism that aligned with the results of the three case studies. The final two chapters of this book shift from the question of *when* sectarian groups emerged to the equally important question of *how* they demarcated themselves from broader Kūfan society. Most modern studies emphasize the role of theological doctrines in this process, but such an approach has a number of drawbacks. Firstly, there are no extant theological works (i.e., heresiographies) contemporaneous with the beginnings of Shīʿī identity in the early 2nd/8th century. Secondly, later heresiographical works ascribe sects with coherent and mature doctrines, thereby eliding the gradual and piecemeal process by which theological positions develop. This does not necessarily mean that theological explanations are incorrect. After all, they proved quite reliable in dating the birth of Imāmī identity. It does, however, highlight the need for exploring avenues for the study of early sectarianism grounded in nontheological sources.

This chapter offers one such alternative, focusing on visible differences in ritual practice.[1] Kūfa in the 2nd/8th century was home to a myriad of rival groups that advocated often contradictory positions on basic aspects of ritual law. The most famous of these differences concerned the status of alcoholic beverages derived from substances other than grapes or dates (Chapter 5) with a number of prominent authorities (e.g., Abū

[1] Ritual, in the context of this chapter, refers to the basic acts of worship in Islam (*ibādāt*) including the daily prayer, purity rules, dietary restrictions, dress codes, and so on.

Ḥanīfa and Muḥammad al-Shaybānī) allowing limited consumption.[2] Others involved the structure of the daily prayer such as the recitation of the *basmala* (Chapter 3) and the performance of the *qunūt* (Chapter 4). It is possible that individuals were initially free to choose from a range of practices without being criticized or accused of innovation. At some point, however, adherence to a particular ritual form appears to have acquired a material significance – a change that had profound implications for the development of communal identity.

The central argument of this chapter is that ritual form functioned as a visible marker for sectarian identity in early 2nd/8th-century Kūfa. There may have been rare instances in which a single practice sufficed to establish an individual's standing in a particular community.[3] In most cases, however, the process was complicated and multifaceted, requiring the examination of a set of rituals. The Imāmīs, for example, agreed with most proto-Sunnī groups on the general prohibition of alcohol but were unique in combining this position with the recitation of an audible *basmala* and the insertion of the *qunūt* into the second cycle of each prayer.[4] The sum of these acts constituted the performance of an Imāmī identity and amounted to a public declaration of communal membership. The potency of ritual practice in allocating identity is evident in (1) discussions of transmitter veracity in the premodern biographical literature and (2) judgments regarding the loyalties of figures on the boundaries between communities.

THE EXAMINATION OF MEN

The first three Islamic centuries saw the birth and gradual victory of traditionism embodied by the production of large voluminous *ḥadīth* collections.[5] Over time, regional variations in practice were justified on the basis of accounts ascribed to either early legal authorities or, in some cases, to the Prophet himself. As the importance of traditions increased, considerable effort was devoted to evaluating their veracity, with a particular emphasis on chains of transmission. It was assumed that the reliability of a given text was largely predicated on the quality and reputation of its individual transmitters. The 3rd/9th century witnessed the

[2] *KAS II*, 1:182–6.

[3] The *ahl al-ra'y* (representing the early Ḥanafīs) were singular in asserting the legality of some alcoholic drinks.

[4] Lalani dates the use of these rituals as identity markers to the lifetimes of either al-Bāqir or al-Ṣādiq (*Early Shī'ī Thought*, 122–5).

[5] This process is documented in Lucas, *Constructive*, and Brown, *Canonization*.

proliferation of complicated categorizations of transmitters that could include up to thirty different gradations ranging from trustworthy *(thiqa)* to worthless (*laysa bi-shay'*).[6] These frameworks were the finished products of a process that began generations earlier with scholars scrutinizing figures central to the preservation and transfer of traditions. In most cases, conclusions about an individual's veracity were listed without a detailed explanation of standards. This section is interested in interrogating the processes involved in the evaluation of a transmitter. Specifically, what qualities were most important in determining reliability? Did theological positions or sectarian loyalties matter, or was a general reputation for honesty sufficient?

Even though some scholars identify suspect figures and craft guidelines for the use of their traditions, it is rare to find a detailed discussion of the criteria necessary for assessing general reliability.[7] A notable exception to this rule is the Samarqandī scholar 'Abd Allāh b. 'Abd al-Raḥmān al-Dārimī (d. 255/869) who, in the preface to his *Sunan*, offers important details about the means by which earlier scholars ascertained transmitter veracity. He begins with a series of narrations that emphasize the central role of traditions (*ḥadīth*) in the articulation of proper "religion" (*dīn*).[8] There is a danger that, in the absence of sound textual guidance, an individual may fail to perform rituals correctly or adhere to deviant beliefs, with dire consequences in the afterlife. With the stakes so high, it is incumbent upon the Muslim community to develop a systematic method for testing the men and women who transmit religious knowledge. Al-Dārimī notes that the Baṣran scholar Muḥammad b. Sīrīn (d. 110/728)[9] advocated "examining men" before utilizing their traditions (and opinions) as proof texts in questions of religion.[10] Other sources

[6] Lucas, *Constructive*, 287–326, but especially 291, 298–9, and 303, where he examines the categorizations of three 3rd/9th-century scholars.

[7] Muslim offers one of the earliest discussions of traditionist methodology in the introduction to his *Ṣaḥīḥ* (3–35).

[8] al-Dārimī, *Sunan* (2000), 1:397 – 433 and 1:398–9 – 438. Muslim quotes a similar tradition with two chains of transmission, substituting the term "science (of *rijāl*)" for "*ḥadīth*" (*SM*, 1:14).

[9] A Baṣran traditionist of high reputation famed for his interpretation of dreams. See *EI*², s.v. Ibn Sīrīn (T. Fahd).

[10] al-Dārimī, *Sunan* (2000), 1:397–8 – 438. Variants of this tradition include: one account in *SM*, 1:14; four accounts in Ibn Abī Ḥātim, *Jarḥ*, 2:15–6; two accounts in Ibn 'Abd al-Barr, *al-Tamhīd*, 1:46–7; and one account in Sulaymān b. Khalaf al-Bājī, *al-Ta'dīl*, 1:267. These texts are implicitly referencing Q49:6 ["O you who believe, if an evil-doer comes to you with a report, look carefully (*tabayyanū*) into it, lest you harm a people in ignorance, then be sorry for what you have done"].

ascribe similar views to Muḥammad b. Sīrīn's brother, Anas (d. 120/738) in Baṣra,[11] al-Ḍaḥḥāk b. Muzāḥim (d. 105/724) in Khurāsān,[12] Ibrāhīm al-Nakhaʿī in Kūfa,[13] and Mālik b. Anas in Medina.[14] The regional distribution of these calls for examination strongly suggests that this sentiment was common to traditionist circles across the Muslim world.

Despite their broad agreement on the need for examination, the sources offer little in the way of details. Later works enumerate a wide set of relevant factors that should be considered in the evaluation process, including (1) the power and reliability of a transmitter's memory, (2) the transmitter's willingness to collaborate with government, (3) the transmitter's propensity to eliminate intermediate links from chains of transmission, (4) the itineraries of individual transmitters' travels, and even (5) personal attributes like piety or generosity. Al-Dārimī, by contrast, conceives of the examination in a fundamentally different manner, as exemplified by a series of reports that document the investigative efforts of late 1st/7th and early 2nd/8th-century religious scholars and students. In one such account, Ibrāhīm al-Nakhaʿī recalls that "if they [previous generations] wanted to narrate [traditions] from a man, then they would follow him, examining his prayer, his practice (*sunna*), and his appearance. [Only then] would they transmit from him."[15] Other sources relate variants of this tradition that substitute the word "*sima*" (form) for "*sunna*," emphasizing the particular importance accorded to the form of an individual's prayer.[16] A view virtually identical to that of Ibrāhīm al-Nakhaʿī in Kūfa is ascribed to al-Ḥasan al-Baṣrī (d. 110/728)[17] in Baṣra indicating that this

[11] Ibn Abī Ḥātim, *Jarḥ*, 2:15–6. Anas b. Sīrīn was a prominent Baṣran traditionist. For his life, see al-Mizzī, *Tahdhīb*, 3:346.

[12] Ibn Abī Ḥātim, *Jarḥ*, 2:15. Like Anas and Muḥammad b. Sīrīn, al-Ḍaḥḥāk b. Muzāḥim enjoyed a high standing in traditionist circles. For his life, see al-Mizzī, *Tahdhīb*, 13:291.

[13] Ibn ʿAbd al-Barr, *Tamhīd*, 1:47. Ibrāhīm b. Yazīd b. Qays al-Nakhaʿī was a prominent Kūfan jurist from the late 1st/7th century. For his life, see al-Mizzī, *Tahdhīb*, 2:233 and *EI*², s.v. al-Nakhaʿī (Lecomte).

[14] Ibn ʿAbd al-Barr, *Tamhīd*, 1:47. For his life, see also al-Mizzī, *Tahdhīb*, 27:91 and *EI*², s.v. Mālik b. Anas (Schacht).

[15] al-Dārimī, *Sunan* (2000), 1:397 – 435.

[16] For variants of this tradition, which include the term *sima*, see: Ibn ʿAbd al-Barr, *Tamhīd*, 1:47; Sulaymān b. Khalaf al-Bājī, *al-Taʿdīl*, 1:268; al-Khaṭīb al-Baghdādī in both (1) *al-Kifāya*, 157 and (2) *al-Jāmiʿ*, 1:128. A number of variants are also cited by Ibn Abī Ḥātim (*Jarḥ*, 2:16), including a hybrid that combines the words *sunna* and *sima* in a single formula. A similar text is quoted in the biographical entry on Ibrāhīm al-Nakhaʿī by Abū Nuʿaym (*Ḥilyat*, 2:224). The use of "appearance" in these texts may refer to disputes over the permissibility of praying in certain types of clothing.

[17] al-Mizzī, 6:95; *EI*², s.v. Ḥasan al-Baṣrī (H. Ritter).

attitude (similarly to the previously mentioned call for examination) was widespread among traditionists in important Muslim urban centers.[18]

One of the clearest and most unambiguous affirmations of the centrality of ritual is found in the following tradition, which quotes the Baṣran scholar, Abū al-ʿĀliya Rufayʿ b. Mihrān (d. 90/708):[19]

> We would follow the man from whom we wanted to transmit [traditions] to observe him when he prayed. If he knew how to perform [the prayer] expertly, we would sit down with him and say, "He must be correct in other matters." But if he performed [the prayer] incorrectly, we would move away from him and say, "He is wrong in other matters."[20]

Here, the prayer functions as a decisive shorthand for determining the reliability of a transmitter. This is not surprising given the fact that nearly every step of the prayer is subject to some form of controversy, from the *basmala* and the *qunūt* to the placement of the hands while standing, the raising of the hands when reciting the phrase "God is the greatest" (*takbīr*), and even the selection of Qur'ānic verses for the formal recitation.[21] In Abū al-ʿĀliya's account, the ritual prayer serves as an effective means for quickly identifying an individual's communal loyalties.

Overall, the sources suggest that ritual practice was one of the central standards employed by scholars in the late 1st/7th and early 2nd/8th centuries to establish transmitter probity.[22] Rather than sitting with

18 al-Dārimī, *Sunan* (2000), 1:398 – 436.

19 al-Mizzī, *Tahdhīb*, 9:214.

20 al-Dārimī, *Sunan* (2000), 1:398 – 437.

21 There are a number of similar controversies surrounding the ablution prior to the ritual prayer, which include the proper method for washing the face (see Ṭūsī, *Khilāf*, 1:76–7 and *Mughnī I*, 1:161–6), the washing versus rubbing of the feet (Ṭūsī, *Khilāf*, 1:89–92 and *Mughnī I*, 1:184–9), and the passing the hand over slippers (*masḥ ʿala al-khuffayn*) (Ṭūsī, *Khilāf*, 1:97 and *Mughnī I*, 1:360ff). For the controversy over *masḥ*, see Jarrar, "Ibn Abī Yaḥyā."

22 In addition to its utility in assessing an individual's veracity, ritual law steadily acquired a political significance. The following anecdote from Muḥammad b Yūsuf al-Kindī (d. 349/961) emphasizes the importance of enforcing a specific ritual regimen in the 3rd/9th-century Muslim world:

> During his appointment as chief of the police (*shurṭa*), Azjūr prohibited women from the bath houses, cemeteries, female prisons, and loud weeping [for the dead]. He also prohibited the audible recitation of the *basmala* in prayers at the Friday Mosque (*al-masjid al-Jāmiʿ*). He ordered al-Ḥasan b. al-Rabīʿ, the Imām of the Friday Mosque, to abandon it [i.e., the audible *basmala*]. That was in Rajab of the year 253. The people of Miṣr had continually recited [the *basmala*] audibly in the Friday Mosque since the coming of Islam until its prohibition by Azjūr. The people in the Friday Mosque were forced to complete rows [in the prayers, a task] for which he sent a foreign man with the *kunya* of Abū Dawuh (?). He would push people forward from the back of the mosque

individuals and questioning them on theological issues such as God's justice or the institution of the Imāmate, they could simply follow them into mosques and observe them pray.[23] This would provide the necessary insight to identify a figure's communal identity and thereby ascertain his reliability as a conveyer of religious knowledge. Such accounts confirm that ritual was important, but they do not help in determining the relative value of practice as compared to theology. It may be that ritual was little more than an indicator of theological beliefs and – quite simply – a less confrontational way of gauging loyalties than a full-blown debate over, for example, the status of sinners. To further explore this dimension of the ritual-theology dynamic, let us turn to a category of figures who hovered at the edges of multiple sectarian communities.

THE LOYALTIES OF THE AMBIGUOUS

The issue of communal identity for individuals with relatively clear theological positions and a concurrent ritual practice is rather straightforward.

with a whip and order those [lit: the people] in study circles to orient their faces to the *qibla* before the *iqāma* [the second call announcing the immediate start of prayer] of the prayer.... He [also] ordered that the *tarāwīḥ* prayers [supererogatory prayers performed by Sunnīs exclusively in Ramaḍān] in the month of Ramaḍān be performed in five sets. The people of Miṣr had continually prayed six sets of *tarāwīḥ* until Azjūr made it five in the month of Ramaḍān of the year 253. Azjūr [also] ordered the recitation of the *tathwīb* [the phrase 'prayer is better than sleep'] in the [morning] call to prayer and had the call to prayer performed at the rear of the mosque. (*Wulāt Miṣr*, 238)

By this point, ritual practice in Egypt (the setting for the account) was an important arena for conflict between the Mālikī and the Shāfiʿī schools of law. The measures above appear directed against the Shāfiʿīs, forcefully denying them the latitude to perform (in public) distinctive Shāfiʿī practices such as the audible recitation of the *basmala* in audible prayer cycles. Thanks to Lennart Sundelin for this reference.

[23] This is not to say that theological views were irrelevant, but rather to suggest that in the late 1st/7th and early 2nd/8th centuries, ritual practice was useful shorthand in ascertaining an individual's communal self-identification. This dynamic changed in later centuries, with a decline in anecdotes of scholars being followed to the mosque and a rise in systematic norms for evaluating transmitter veracity. In the comprehensive *rijāl* works that began emerging in the 3rd/9th century, Sunnī traditionists were classified into one of three groups. The first allowed transmission by any figure with a reputation for honesty regardless of his/her theological beliefs so long as these did not include proselytizing or "extremism." The second accepted traditions narrated by individuals with problematic beliefs as long as they did not consider lying permissible. The third required independent verification of any and all traditions related by transmitters who held suspect views or were known "innovators." This framework can be found in (among other works) al-Dhahabī's *Mīzān* (1:29–30), where the author differentiates between "extremist" and "non-extremist" Shīʿa based on their cursing of early Companions. Muslim adopts a similar approach in the introduction to his *Ṣaḥīḥ* (3–35, but especially 4–9 and 12–16). For an annotated translation of Muslim's discussion, see Juynboll, "Introduction," 263–311.

But what about those who performed rituals associated with one group while championing theological views characteristic of a different group? Where would they fit in the social geography of 2nd/8th-century Kūfa, where identities were still in the process of crystallization and boundaries remained highly permeable and fluid? The sources do, in fact, mention a number of such ambiguous figures, and the process by which their loyalties were determined provides considerable insight into the role of ritual practice in the allocation of sectarian identity.

To demonstrate this process, let us examine the case of Sulaymān b. Mihrān al-Aʿmash, an early Kūfan transmitter generally acknowledged by the later sources as an important Sunnī authority. According to most reports, al-Aʿmash was either born in a village near Rayy in the Iranian province of Jibāl or in Kūfa where his family eventually moved and settled.[24] Ibn Saʿd (d. 230/845) and Aḥmad b. ʿAbd Allāh al-ʿIjlī (d. 261/875) date his birth to ʿĀshūrāʾ of 61/680, the same day that al-Ḥusayn and his family were killed at Karbalāʾ.[25] Shortly after his arrival in Kūfa, al-Aʿmash was purchased by an Asadī clansman and given his freedom. He spent the remainder of his life living as a client of the Kāhilī branch of the Asad tribe in their quarter of the city.[26] He earned a reputation as one of the city's most prominent traditionist scholars of his generation and was greatly mourned at his death in either 147/764 or 148/765.[27]

The Sunnī sources depict al-Aʿmash as a dominant intellectual figure with a wide ranging breadth of knowledge. He was particularly renown for his expertise in the Qur'ān, especially his mastery of the variant reading of ʿAbd Allāh b. Masʿūd (d. 32/652), which retained a particular popularity in Kūfa. People would reportedly gather once a year (often in the month of Shaʿbān) to hear him recite the entire Qur'ān and correct transcription mistakes in their own texts.[28] His fame as a Qur'ān scholar even extended beyond the confines of Kūfa as he was considered eleventh among the fourteen most prominent readers (*qurrāʾ*) in the greater Muslim world.[29]

Al-Aʿmash's reputation as a *ḥadīth* transmitter was generally positive, albeit with some notes of caution and concern. Ibn Saʿd praises him as

[24] al-Mizzī, *Tahdhīb*, 12:76.

[25] Ibn Saʿd, *al-Ṭabaqāt al-kubra'*, 6:332 and al-ʿIjlī, *Tārīkh*, 206. The Shīʿī sources place it to two years earlier, in 58/677–8 (al-Tustarī, *Qāmūs*, 5:299).

[26] al-Mizzī, *Tahdhīb*, 12:76.

[27] *Ibid.*, *Tahdhīb*, 12:90.

[28] Ibn Saʿd, *al-Ṭabaqāt al-kubra'*, 6:331.

[29] *EI*[1], s.v. Aʿmash (Kohlberg).

possessing an expertise in *ḥadīth* that even impressed the Medinan jurist Muḥammad b. Muslim al-Zuhrī (d. 124/742), a man notably skeptical of all Iraqī transmitters.[30] Al-'Ijlī recounts that al-A'mash transmitted the most Prophetic traditions among his generational contemporaries.[31] Both al-Dhahabī (d. 748/1347) and al-Mizzī (d. 746/1345) offer similar appraisals of al-A'mash's knowledge of the Qur'ān and the *ḥadīth* but intimate his tendency to (1) change wording[32] and (2) ascribe accounts to individuals who were not necessarily his direct source. In particular, his claims of transmitting traditions from Anas b. Mālik are heavily disputed,[33] as are some of his reports from Mujāhid b. Jabr.[34] Ibn Ḥanbal strongly condemns his traditions as "confused."[35] Overall, however, al-A'mash is portrayed in a positive light,[36] with al-Mizzī relating anecdotes in which he is consulted as an authority in the science of *rijāl* and passes judgment on the veracity of his contemporaries.[37]

In addition to the Qur'ān and traditions, al-A'mash was praised for his legal expertise. Both early[38] and later[39] biographical works characterize him as the premier Kūfan authority in inheritance (*farā'iḍ*) after the death of Ibrāhīm al-Nakha'ī. He is also noted for his knowledge of ritual law, particularly in the realms of purity,[40] prayer,[41] and fasting.[42] In these areas, the sources emphasize his reliance on and narration of traditions as opposed to the issuing of personal legal rulings. Overall, al-A'mash appears to have supported practices that aligned with those of the Kūfan traditionists. Were this not the case, we would expect to find clear indications of his idiosyncrasies in the biographical sources given their propensity to highlight problematic legal positions. They do,

[30] Ibn Sa'd, *al-Ṭabaqāt al-kubra'*, 6:332.
[31] al-'Ijlī, *Thiqāt*, 205.
[32] al-Dhahabī, *al-Jarḥ*, 1:211.
[33] al-Mizzī, *Tahdhīb*, 12:83–4; Ibn Abī Ḥātim, *Jarḥ*, 2:146–7 and particularly al-Dhahabī, *Tārīkh*, 141–60:167.
[34] Ibn Ma'īn, *Kalām*, 43.
[35] al-Dhahabī, *Tārīkh*, 141–60:164. For a similar modern assessment, see Lucas, *Constructive*, 345–6.
[36] al-Dhahabī, *Tārīkh*, 141–60:162 and *Jarḥ*, 1:210; al-Mizzī, *Tahdhīb*,12:89, al-'Ijlī, *Thiqāt*, 204; and Ibn Abī Ḥātim, *Jarḥ*, 2:146–7.
[37] al-Mizzī, *Tahdhīb*, 12:88–89 with similar echoes in Ibn Sa'd, *al-Ṭabaqāt al-kubra'*, 6:331–2.
[38] al-'Ijlī, *Thiqāt*, 8:205.
[39] al-Mizzī, *Tahdhīb*, 12:85; al-Dhahabī, *Tārīkh*, 141–60:162.
[40] *Ibid.*, 141–60:164.
[41] *Ibid.*, 141–60:162 and 166. This is indirectly alluded to by al-Mizzī when he notes a prayer tradition that was falsely ascribed to Anas b. Mālik (*Tahdhīb*, 12:83).
[42] *Ibid.*, 141–60:164.

in fact, repeatedly and consistently condemn al-A'mash's opinion that the pre-fast meal (*suḥūr*) may be eaten *after* the *fajr* prayer. The lack of any other objections, especially with regard to inheritance or ritual, suggests a broad traditionist approval of his legal views.[43] This sentiment is further reflected in an array of positive assessments by al-A'mash's colleagues and students. Al-Mughīra b. Miqsam (d. 132/750), for example, notes that "we frequented al-A'mash regarding inheritance,"[44] whereas Wakī' b. Jarrāḥ (d. 196/811) recalls that al-A'mash never failed to perform a prayer at the proper time.[45] It is also conveyed by later biographers such as al-Dhahabī, who resoundingly praises al-A'mash's understanding of jurisprudence (*fiqh*).[46]

In light of his positive scholarly reputation among traditionists, it is not surprising to find al-A'mash widely hailed as an important member of the early Sunnī community. He is listed as one of a myriad of figures who provided guidance in matters of inheritance and ritual (despite the occasional irregular opinion), while transmitting generally sound traditions (albeit with a few problematic chains of transmission). The reference to inheritance is of particular importance, given the fact that it was (and remains) one of the central points of contention between Sunnī and Shī'ī jurists.[47] That his rulings in law were deemed reliable and his status as a traditionist upheld by his pupils (i.e., Sufyān al-Thawrī, Wakī' b. Jarrāḥ) speaks strongly for his Sunnī credentials.[48]

The discussion to this point has focused on matters of law as opposed to theology, and it is on this basis that Sunnī biographers appear to have approved of (and ultimately appropriated) al-A'mash. There are, however, strong indications in the Sunnī sources of his Shī'ī theological inclinations. The earliest and most commonly cited passage comes from al-'Ijlī who states that al-A'mash "harbored Shī'ism."[49] Specifically, he advocated rebellion against the 'Abbāsids, a view common among the

[43] In other words, the fact that al-A'mash is strongly condemned for his opinion regarding the pre-fast meal suggests that the biographical sources were not shy in highlighting legal views that they considered incorrect. Therefore, their silence with respect to the other fields in which al-A'mash is accorded authority (e.g., inheritance law) implies a broad approval of his rulings.

[44] Al-Mizzī, *Tahdhīb*, 12:85.

[45] *Ibid.*, 12:86.

[46] al-Dhahabī, *Jarḥ* 1:211.

[47] For heirs other than those listed in the Quran, the Shī'a tend to favor matrilineal inheritance whereas the Sunnīs tend to favor patrilineal inheritance.

[48] In his detailed analysis of Sunnī biographical literature, Lucas depicts al-A'mash as a typical Sunnī transmitter from early 2nd/8th-century Kūfa (*Constructive*, 65–6 and 345–7).

[49] al-'Ijlī, *Thiqāt*, 205.

Kūfan Shīʿa and ascribed, most prominently, to the Batrī Zaydī, Ḥasan b. Ṣāliḥ.[50] When al-Nafs al-Zakiyya and Ibrāhīm rebelled in 145/762–3, al-Aʿmash, who was too old to fight himself, endorsed their cause and offered moral support.[51] This approval of insurrection complicated the appraisals of early authorities to a certain extent. In spite of their reservations, however, few went so far as to label him a Shīʿa.[52]

In general, early Sunnī biographers did not seem overly troubled by the disjuncture between al-Aʿmash's legal opinions and his apparent theological inclinations. By contrast, later biographers struggled with this perceived contradiction and strongly de-emphasized his potential Shīʿī associations. Al-Dhahabī, in particular, expresses genuine confusion at the earlier characterizations. In the *Tārīkh*, he quotes al-ʿIjlī's claim regarding al-Aʿmash's Shīʿism but follows it with the statement that "this is what he [al-ʿIjlī] said but it certainly is not correct as he [al-Aʿmash] was a champion (*ṣāḥib*) of the *sunna*."[53] In *Kitāb al-jarḥ*, he notes that "al-Aʿmash was accused of a little Shīʿism but I do not know (for certain)."[54] When al-Mizzī cites al-ʿIjlī's opinion in the *Tahdhīb*, he adds no personal commentary and simply concludes with an affirmation of al-Aʿmash's truthfulness.[55]The reasons for such a conscious dismissal of problematic theological beliefs are difficult to identify with any degree of certainty. Perhaps it was the collective weight of centuries of communal appropriation that produced a general assumption that al-Aʿmash was a Sunnī authority? After all, according to the Sunnī biographical literature, he played a seminal role in the development of traditionism.[56] In the end, it seems that al-Aʿmash's early acceptance as a Sunnī *despite contrary theological views* proved somewhat unsettling for later scholars.

At this point, it is necessary to take a step back and examine the meaning of statements such as "he harbored Shīʿism" (*kāna fīhi tashayyuʿ*). In general, such phrases are interpreted as referring to a nebulous "Shīʿism" that consisted of backing the political claims of ʿAlid rebels and elevating

50 *Ibid.*, 205.
51 *EI*[r], s.v. Aʿmash (Kohlberg).
52 Ibn Qutayba, by contrast, includes al-Aʿmash in a long list of Kūfan Shīʿa (*Maʿārif*, 624). This is not typical of most early Sunnī biographers.
53 al-Dhahabī, *Tārīkh*, 141–60:163.
54 al-Dhahabī, *Jarḥ*, 1:210.
55 al-Mizzī, *Tahdhīb*, 12:87.
56 This point is emphasized repeatedly by Lucas in his analysis of the generations preceding the compilers of the canonical Sunnī collections. See, for example, *Constructive*, 345–7.

ʿAlī and his family above the other Companions. Melchert explicitly associates usage of the term Shīʿa in the Sunnī sources with the Zaydīs[57] and explains it as a preference for ʿAlī over ʿUthmān without a rejection of Abū Bakr and ʿUmar.[58] By contrast, the term "*rāfiḍī*" describes individuals who unequivocally rejected (and even apostatized) Abū Bakr and ʿUmar. Evidence for the importance of these labels in assessing the reliability of transmitters in the 2nd/8th century is minimal. In his study of transmitters in the six Sunnī canonical collections, for example, Melchert identifies sixty from the 2nd/8th-century who were characterized as possessing "*tashayyu*" and another forty-one considered *rāfiḍī*s.[59] The fact that they were unproblematically included in the most authoritative of the Sunnī traditionist works speaks to the secondary import of sectarian theological affiliations in ascertaining transmitter probity for the first two Islamic centuries.[60]

Returning to the case of al-Aʿmash, we might hypothesize that early Sunnī biographers initially considered him a mild Shīʿa (of the Batrī variety) before eventually claiming him as one of their own. After all, his Shīʿism was apparently limited to a subtle endorsement of ʿAlī and an inclination toward rebellion, views that might be overlooked given his stature as a traditionist scholar and his articulation of legal positions that aligned with the broader proto-Sunnī community. In such a scenario, his theology would have been subordinated to his stance on issues like inheritance (and ritual). Before decisively embracing this conclusion, however, we should examine the manner in which he is described in the Imāmī biographical literature.

The Imāmī depiction of al-Aʿmash generally aligns with that of the Sunnīs. It praises him for his theological views while rejecting him both as a transmitter of traditions and a legal authority. Although Kohlberg takes al-Aʿmash's inclusion among the students of al-Ṣādiq as evidence that he was claimed by the Imāmī Shīʿa, this view does not appear to have garnered broad support.[61] The modern Imāmī scholar al-Tustarī, for example, consciously avoids characterizing al-Aʿmash as an Imāmī in his comprehensive compilation of the sect's most important *rijāl*

[57] For more on this point, see later discussion in this chapter.

[58] Melchert, "Sectaries," 291.

[59] Melchert, "Sectaries," 290–2. These figures disappear almost completely at the start of the 3rd/9th century.

[60] Lucas reaches a similar conclusion (*Constructive*, 323).

[61] *EI*ʳ, s.v. Aʿmash (Kohlberg).

works. This is in spite of al-Tustarī's affirmation of al-Aʿmash's connection to al-Ṣādiq[62] and his knowledge of numerous anecdotes that suggest he held views similar to those prevalent among the Kūfan Shīʿa. In one such account, al-Aʿmash stands up to the Umayyad caliph Hishām b. ʿAbd al-Malik and refuses to praise ʿUthmān at the expense of ʿAlī.[63] In another, he is visited on his deathbed by a group of prominent proto-Sunnī scholars, including Ibn Abī Layla (d. 148/765) and Abū Ḥanīfa, who ask him to disavow traditions praising ʿAlī and the family of the Prophet.[64] When al-Aʿmash refuses, they deliver a series of dire warnings, beseeching him to consider the otherworldly consequences of his actions. The scholars depart in frustration when their arguments and protests fail to effect a change and al-Aʿmash grows increasingly hostile and resolute.

It is important to note that the issue that draws the particular ire of these proto-Sunnī jurists is intercession (*shafāʿa*). In the course of their conversation with al-Aʿmash, they cite a few of his narrations, including one that depicts the Prophet and ʿAlī sitting side by side on the Day of Judgment, saving those who loved them and condemning those who opposed them. It would be difficult to find a theological doctrine more unambiguously associated with Imāmī Shīʿism and more resolutely rejected by the wider proto-Sunnī community. The jurists are also disturbed by al-Aʿmash's elevation of ʿAlī above all the other Companions and his espousal of the general superiority of every member of the family of the Prophet. These theological positions are documented by the Zaydī biographical literature as well, suggesting that al-Aʿmash's views were well-known among a broad cross-section of Kūfan society.[65]

This portrait of al-Aʿmash suggests that he held beliefs that extended far beyond a mild Shīʿism consisting of a vague veneration of ʿAlī over ʿUthmān. The Imāmī sources associate him with an endorsement of intercession and seem to ascribe him the belief that legitimate authority rested solely with the descendants of ʿAlī. Even if the Imāmī portrait is a forgery or a back projection of values, it represents the community's overall perceptions of al-Aʿmash. In other words, the Imāmīs did not

[62] al-Tustarī, *Qāmūs*, 5:297. See also, al-Ṭūsī, *Rijāl*, 215.
[63] al-Tustarī, *Qāmūs*, 5:298.
[64] *Ibid.*, *Qāmūs*, 5:297–8.
[65] Ibn al-Murtaḍā, *Ṭabaqāt al-zaydiyya*, 1:374–6.

simply consider al-Aʿmash an adherent of a few Shīʿī political or historical ideas; rather, they associated him with a number of distinctive Shīʿī theological tenets. Yet despite this fact, they never claimed al-Aʿmash as one of their own. It apparently required more than a common theology to be counted as a Shīʿa in 2nd/8th-century Kūfa. Even the late Imāmī biographical literature that often identifies the sectarian allegiances of transmitters (e.g., as Sunnīs, Batrī or Jārūdī Zaydīs, or even smaller Imāmī subsects like Faṭḥīs) does not associate al-Aʿmash with any Shīʿī group. It was clear to both the early Shīʿa and the proto-Sunnī Kūfan traditionists that he fit firmly within the boundaries of the latter. By the 8th/14th century, only the bare outlines of his Shīʿism remained and even those were confusing to a traditionist scholar of the stature of al-Dhahabī.

Al-Aʿmash is not the only example of a 2nd/8th-century Kūfan hovering at the edges of multiple communal identities. Similar patterns hold for an entire category of figures who held (1) theological views that appeared to align with early Shīʿism alongside (2) legal positions that fit within the bounds of Kūfan proto-Sunnism. Such was the case with Sālim b. Abī Ḥafṣa (d. 137/755), who endorsed the practice of wiping leather socks in the performance of the ritual ablution (a Kūfan traditionist opinion) and indulged in an occasional glass of *nabīdh* (as allowed by the Kūfan *ahl al-raʾy*).[66] Sālim enjoyed a high reputation among early Sunnī scholars in matters of ritual law,[67] despite his well-documented transmission of traditions that lowered the rank of Abū Bakr and ʿUmar and his endorsement of the murder of ʿUthmān.[68] Like al-Aʿmash, Sālim's standing was a product of his ritual law positions, which resembled those of the Kūfan proto-Sunnīs, as opposed to his theological views, which inclined toward the Shīʿa. Imāmī biographers agreed with this characterization of Sālim and condemned him for his persistent (and aggressive) questioning of al-Ṣādiq.[69] Biographical entries for al-Ḥakam b. ʿUtayba[70] and al-Ḥasan b. Ṣāliḥ[71]

[66] al-Tustarī, *Qāmūs*, 4:602.

[67] al-Mizzī, *Tahdhīb*, 10:136–8.

[68] al-Dhahabī, *Tārīkh*, 121–40:435.

[69] al-Tustarī, *Qāmūs*, 4:597–5.

[70] al-Ḥakam's Shīʿism is characterized in all the Sunnī biographical sources as subtle and concealed, yet the Imāmī sources consider him a typical Sunnī traditionist scholar. For the Sunnī perspective, see al-Mizzī, *Tahdhīb*, 7:114–20 and al-Dhahabī, *Tārīkh*, 101–20:345–7. For the Imāmī perspective, see al-Tustarī, *Qāmūs*, 3:613.

[71] Although the Sunnī biographical literature emphasizes al-Ḥasan b. Ṣāliḥ's reliability, it concentrates primarily on two controversial opinions: (1) his claim that the Friday

adhere to similar patterns of assessment; both are upheld as proto-Sunnī legal authorities despite their promotion of Shīʿī theological views. Al-Ḥakam is identified as a leader of the traditionist movement whereas al-Ḥasan is counted among the *ahl al-raʾy*. These are but a few individuals in long lists of so-called Shīʿa whose apparent Shīʿism did little to impugn their authority or prevent their eventual appropriation by Sunnī scholars.

A few final thoughts are in order regarding these ambiguous figures. First, bear in mind that this chapter is primarily interested in the calculation involved in allocating identity The case of al-Aʿmash highlights the potential role of ritual in the emergence of discrete sectarian communities. This process is most evident in instances where a transmitter appears to have forwarded disparate positions, namely a Shīʿī theological view in combination with traditionist ritual or law. Second, it follows that many of these early 2nd/8th-century figures at the boundary between the proto-Sunnīs and the Imāmīs were Batrī Zaydīs.[72] This is not overly surprising given the argument (outlined in Chapter 6) that the term "Batrī" essentially denoted traditionists willing to join ʿAlid rebellions. It is likely that such an attitude was ubiquitous among Kūfan traditionists of the 2nd/8th century, although only a few figures were subsequently claimed by the Zaydīs whereas the rest were smoothly incorporated into the ranks of Sunnism. This point resonates with Melchert's observation that the presence of "Batrīs" in the Sunnī biographical literature is severely understated.[73] Overall, it appears that theology, while important, was not decisive in the determination of sectarian identity.[74]

prayer was not mandatory and (2) his endorsement of armed insurrection. Although these views were condemned by later Sunnī scholars, they did not result in al-Ḥasan b. Ṣāliḥ's marginalization. Al-Dhahabī, for example, placed him among the leading jurists of the Kūfan *ahl al-raʾy*. The Imāmī literature stresses that al-Ḥasan b. Ṣāliḥ was not part of the Imāmī community but rather a Batrī Zaydī. For the Sunnī perspective, see al-Mizzī, *Tahdhīb*, 6:177–91, and al-Dhahabī, *Tārīkh*, 161–70:131–6, with the latter strongly affirming al-Ḥasan's juristic authority. For the Imāmī perspective, see al-Tustarī, *Qāmūs*, 3:264–6.

72 For the Batrīs, see *DIQ*, 49–50; *EI*² supplement, s.v. Batriyya (*idem*); Zaydiyya (*idem*). See also Chapter 1 of this book.

73 Melchert, "Sectaries," 291.

74 The conclusions presented in this section remain tentative but point to the need for more work on this category of ambiguous figures. For another study of an ambiguous 2nd/8th-century figure on the margins of multiple sectarian identities, see Maher Jarrar, "Ibn Abī Yaḥyā."

CONCLUSION

Early-2nd/8th-century Kūfa was home to a wide range of ritual practices increasingly associated with demarcated religious communities. In such an environment, the decision to perform the prayer in a particular fashion constituted a public affirmation of communal identity.

In the first part of this chapter, it was shown that ritual practice was one of the fundamental criteria for ascertaining the reliability of *ḥadīth* transmitters. Calls for the examination of these men and women focused on the observation of their ritual form, particularly the daily prayer, which included a series of choices that clearly denoted sectarian loyalties. There is a possibility, however, that ritual merely served as a shorthand for theology. In the case of the Shīʿa, for example, the choice of an Imām was a fundamentally theological decision that carried profound legal implications. Since rules for praying or fasting were determined by the Imām, it is fair to ask whether ritual practice was not just a reflection of theology?

The second part of the chapter explored this question by examining the life of a figure whose theological views did not align with his ritual practice. Al-Aʿmash supported intercession and elevated ʿAlī (and his family) above the other Companions and yet he held to a set of practices (and legal positions) that differed markedly from the early Shīʿa. In the end, it was al-Aʿmash's ritual practice that secured him a place among Sunnī legal authorities. This suggests that, at least in the first few centuries, ritual (1) did not *necessarily* emerge from theology and (2) could at times play a more influential role than theology in the allocation of identity.

The insight these conclusions provide are more nuanced than a simple affirmation or rejection of theology. There is little doubt that theological issues exerted a powerful influence in early Kūfa. The danger lies in adopting a heresiographical framework that overwhelmingly privileges theology as the determining force in the creation of sectarian identity. The actual mechanism for identity formation appears to have been far more complicated. Kūfa in the 2nd/8th century was certainly home to (1) a community of proto-Sunnī traditionists who rejected ʿAlī and the hereditary/activist notions of the early Shīʿa, and (2) a core of Shīʿa who elevated the Prophet's family (or specific members of that family) to a position of unparalleled religious and/or political authority. In the middle, however, were figures who held an eclectic mix of opinions that defied easy classification.[75] Over time, they were appropriated by one group or another in a process heavily informed by political and theological developments.[76] For al-Aʿmash and others located at the center of the spectrum, ritual practice seems to have played a critical role in ultimately determining their respective sectarian identities.

[75] See chapter 1 of Mairaj Syed's forthcoming doctoral dissertation at Princeton University entitled "Coercion in Classical Islamic Legal and Moral Thought."

[76] Recall Chapter 6, which suggests that Zaydism emerged from a proto-Sunnī context before undergoing a radical shift toward a more Shīʿī orientation through the leadership of Yaḥyā b. ʿAbd Allāh.

8

The Mosque and the Procession

Sacred Spaces and the Construction of Community

In Chapter 7, it was shown that ritual practice played a critical role in the construction of sectarian identity. The potency of practice was such that it often trumped adherence to seemingly problematic theological tenets. Traditions depict authorities from the late 1st/7th and early 2nd/8th centuries evaluating figures of uncertain loyalties by following them to mosques and observing them in prayer. These texts suggest that there was no established correlation between specific mosques and ritual practice as Kūfans from a range of sectarian identities might frequent the same venues and perform prayers in their own distinctive ways. This chapter traces the process by which this dynamic began to change through the increasing association of sacred space with ritual. The first section examines the transformation of neighborhood mosques affiliated with tribal groups into sectarian mosques. The second section discusses the integration of these sectarian mosques into a new religious geography comprised of friendly/sacred and hostile/accursed spaces. The final section highlights the merging of ritual and space in a new and powerful public affirmation of sectarian identity, namely pilgrimage (*ziyāra*).

FROM TRIBAL MOSQUE TO SECTARIAN SPACE

To understand the process through which space was gradually appropriated by sectarian groups, it is necessary to begin with an examination of the urban development of Kūfa itself. In his seminal study of the city's transformation from a garrison town to a major Muslim urban center, Hichem Djait highlights small neighborhood mosques founded by tribes and often named after prominent tribal elites.[1] At the turn of the 1st/7th century, most Muslims frequented their local clan mosques except on special occasions (e.g., the Friday prayer) when they would venture to the cathedral mosque in the geographic center of the city.[2]

Djait proposes a tentative spatial reconstruction of Kūfa in which he locates all known mosques in existence between the years 100/718 and 120/738.[3] This map (see Map 2) includes many of the places listed in (later) Shīʿī sources as safe havens or hostile spaces along with tribal mosques mentioned in non-Shīʿī sources. Specifically, Djait places six mosques later renowned for their hostility to the Shīʿa either in the southeast quadrant of the city (the quarters of the Banū Tamīm and the northern quarter of the Banū Asad[4]) or just north of the center (the quarters of the Banū Bajīla and the Banū Thaqīf). By contrast, friendly mosques are found east (the quarters of the Banū Qays and the Banū Ḥamrā') and south (the quarters of the Banū Madhḥij and the Banū ʿAbs and the southern quarter of the Banū Asad) of the center, as well as in one sector in the northwest (the quarters of the Banū ʿAbd al-Qays).

It is likely that many of these early tribal mosques carried a loose sectarian association given the partisan history of some tribes (and clans) in the tumultuous civil wars of the 1st/7th century.[5] For example, the Banū ʿAbd al-Qays had strongly backed ʿAlī in the first civil war and especially in the Battle of the Camel.[6] That their local mosque became a haven for

[1] Djait, *Kūfa*, 297–8. Donner presents a similar portrait of the founding and early development of Kūfa (*Conquests*, 226–36).

[2] *Ibid.*, 297–8.

[3] *Ibid.*, 302–3.

[4] The Asad appear divided in terms of political inclinations between support of and opposition to ʿAlī. Many of the Banū Asad in Kūfa ultimately adopted Shīʿism and contributed significantly to its intellectual development. See *EI*², s.v. Asad, Banū (Kindermann).

[5] It is important to emphasize that this link between tribe and sectarian leanings is not absolute. Hinds has shown that, in fact, most tribes were internally divided between the established pre-Islamic elites (*ashrāf*) and those who owed their status exclusively to their early standing in Islam (*sābiqa*). There were certainly tribes that were inclined toward supporting or opposing ʿAlī, but most elicit no such unanimity. In this regard, Hinds highlights the Bajīla who were among ʿAlī's strongest supporters but whose leadership (e.g., Jarīr b. ʿAbd Allāh al-Bajalī) was (at best) ambiguous, lukewarm, and even hostile. Interestingly, Hinds hypothesizes that most of the pro-Shīʿī elements in Kūfa, lacking tribal standing, would have lived near the outskirts of the city. This is largely confirmed by Map 2 wherein the mosques near the center are considered hostile space in the Imāmī sources with the singular exception of Masjid al-Kūfa. See Hinds, "Alignments," 346–67 and especially 347–8 and 361–8. For a similar analysis of tribal divisions in ʿAlī's Kūfan support and its impact on the Battle of Ṣiffīn, see Madelung, *Succession*, 216–20 and 239–40.

[6] Djait, *Kūfa*, 300–1.

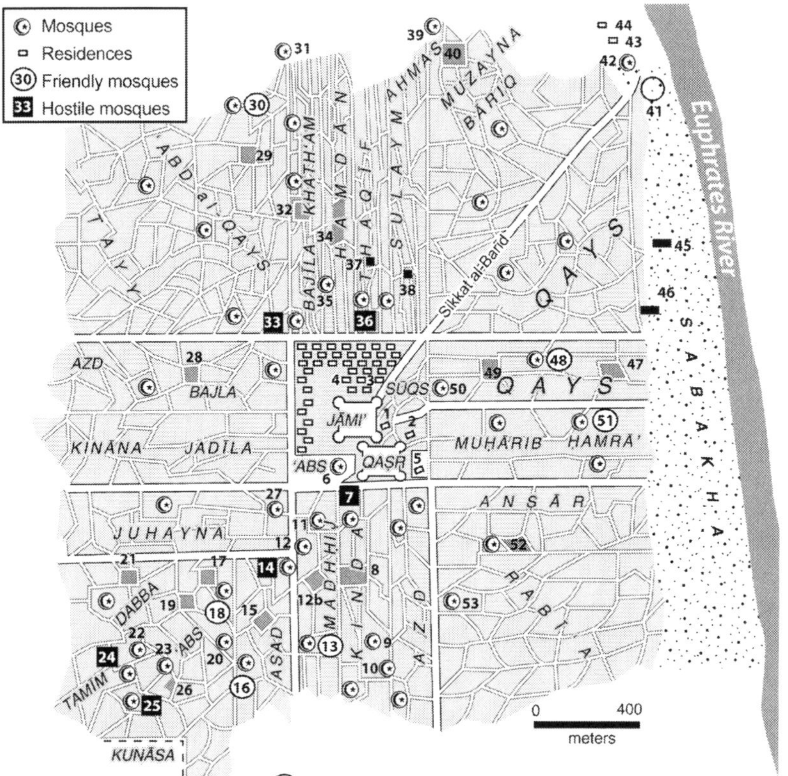

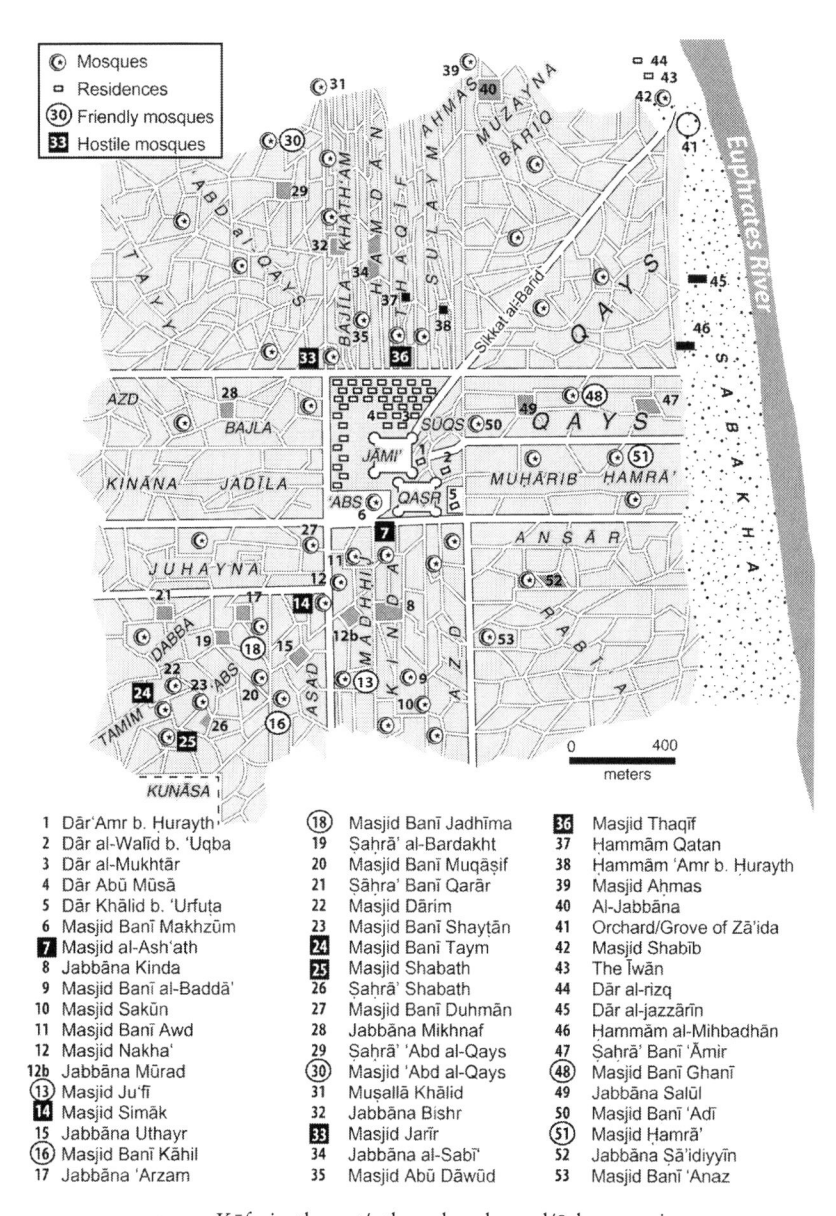

1 Dār'Amr b. Ḥurayth
2 Dār al-Walīd b. 'Uqba
3 Dār al-Mukhtār
4 Dār Abū Mūsā
5 Dār Khālid b. 'Urfuṭa
6 Masjid Banī Makhzūm
7 Masjid al-Ash'ath
8 Jabbāna Kinda
9 Masjid Banī al-Baddā'
10 Masjid Sakūn
11 Masjid Banī Awd
12 Masjid Nakha'
12b Jabbāna Mūrad
13 Masjid Ju'fī
14 Masjid Simāk
15 Jabbāna Uthayr
16 Masjid Banī Kāhil
17 Jabbāna 'Arzam
18 Masjid Banī Jadhīma
19 Ṣaḥrā' al-Bardakht
20 Masjid Banī Muqāṣif
21 Ṣāḥra' Banī Qarār
22 Masjid Dārim
23 Masjid Banī Shayṭān
24 Masjid Banī Taym
25 Masjid Shabath
26 Ṣaḥrā' Shabath
27 Masjid Banī Duhmān
28 Jabbāna Mikhnaf
29 Ṣaḥrā' 'Abd al-Qays
30 Masjid 'Abd al-Qays
31 Muṣallā Khālid
32 Jabbāna Bishr
33 Masjid Jarīr
34 Jabbāna al-Sabī'
35 Masjid Abū Dāwūd
36 Masjid Thaqīf
37 Ḥammām Qatan
38 Ḥammām 'Amr b. Ḥurayth
39 Masjid Aḥmas
40 Al-Jabbāna
41 Orchard/Grove of Zā'ida
42 Masjid Shabīb
43 The Īwān
44 Dār al-rizq
45 Dār al-jazzārīn
46 Ḥammām al-Mihbadhān
47 Ṣaḥrā' Banī 'Āmir
48 Masjid Banī Ghanī
49 Jabbāna Salūl
50 Masjid Banī 'Adī
51 Masjid Ḥamrā'
52 Jabbāna Ṣā'idiyyīn
53 Masjid Banī 'Anaz

MAP 2. Kūfa in the 1st/7th and early 2nd/8th centuries.

his partisans in subsequent centuries is hardly surprising. The same is true of the Banū Madhḥij who were famous for their unwavering support of ʿAlī at Ṣiffīn under the leadership of Mālik al-Ashtar (d. 38/658–9).[7] In an opposing vein, the persistent and intransient hostility of the Banū Thaqīf toward ʿAlī is well documented.[8]

The fact that a tribe backed the political claims of ʿAlī in the 1st/7th century, however, did not necessarily mean that its mosques could be characterized as Shīʿī. To reach this stage, there needed to be a shift from a perspective that privileged tribe to one that emphasized sectarian identity. Such a transformation appears to have taken hold at some point in the mid-2nd/8th century, but the exact timing remains unclear.[9] The situation is complicated by the fact that a preponderance of the material describing the loyalties of mosques is found (almost exclusively) in the Shīʿī literature.[10] In many cases, these texts discuss mosques that do not appear in non-Shīʿī sources or (more often) associate mosques with historical figures as opposed to tribes. The latter are sometimes notoriously difficult to locate in the known geographical landscape of early Kūfa.

The clearest evidence for the correlation between ritual and mosque is found in legal sources that only examine the issue indirectly. In the process of affirming the soundness of a controversial practice, these accounts imply that certain rituals were practiced in specific mosques as early as the mid-2nd/8th century. A typical text of this variety preserves an exchange between the prominent Kūfan jurist Sharīk b. ʿAbd Allāh (d. 177/793)[11] and an unnamed questioner:

In our presence a man asked Sharīk, "What is your opinion regarding a man whose door is located near a mosque where the *qunūt* is not performed while behind that mosque is another mosque where the *qunūt* is performed?" He responded, "He should go to the mosque where the *qunūt* is performed." He then asked, "What is your opinion regarding a man who affirms the *qunūt* but forgets to perform it?" He responded, "He should perform two prostrations of forgetfulness." He continued,

[7] *EI*², s.v. Madhḥij (Smith and Bosworth).
[8] *EI*², s.v. Thaqīf (Lecker).
[9] For a discussion of this transformation, see *EI*², s.v. Masdjid (Pedersen).
[10] Djait, *Kūfa*, 298–301.
[11] The Sunnī sources depict Sharīk as a traditionist Kūfan scholar of considerable standing (al-Mizzī, *Tahdhīb*, 12:462). The Imāmīs agree with this characterization, although they note Sharīk's pro-ʿAlid inclinations and recount a number of his narrations that elevate ʿAlī above the other Companions (al-Tustarī, *Qāmūs*, 8:416–21). For more context regarding the account that follows, see footnote 15 of this chapter.

"What is your opinion regarding a man who rejects the *qunūt* but forgets and performs it?" He laughed and said, "This man forgets and thereby hits the mark!"[12]

As mentioned in Chapter 4, the insertion of the *qunūt* in the daily prayers was a practice present in Kūfa and one that was eventually adopted by the Imāmīs and rejected by the Sunnī law schools.[13] In the given text, Sharīk both endorses the *qunūt* and bestows it a central ritual importance. If forgotten, he requires a worshipper to perform "two prostrations of forgetfulness," a procedure generally reserved for cases where an individual commits a major mistake or omits a required step of the prayer.[14]

On a secondary level, Sharīk's statement suggests that ritual and mosque were increasingly intertwined by the middle of the 2nd/8th century.[15] The Imāmīs were inclined to frequent mosques where the *qunūt* was regularly performed. This was a conscious choice that involved a degree of hardship or, at the very least, annoyance. The Imāmī population was not exclusively concentrated around appropriate mosques and sometimes had to travel inconvenient distances to reach a suitable venue. This was a fact of life for the inhabitants of Kūfa in general. The hypothetical worshipper discussed by Sharīk, for example, is instructed to bypass his neighborhood mosque in favor of another (located at a distance) in which the *qunūt* is integrated into the prayer. There is no indication here that individuals simply attended the mosques associated with their tribe out of habit. Rather, it appears that, by Sharīk's time, ritual practice had begun to eclipse tribal affiliation as the defining feature of many places of worship.

THE DEMARCATION OF SACRED SPACE

The link between sacred spaces and sectarian ritual practice was ultimately institutionalized in the broader Imāmī literature[16] through the

[12] *BM*, 2:46–7 – 1137. See also footnote 15 of this chapter.

[13] Lalani, *Early Shī'ī Thought*, 124–5.

[14] For examples and a discussion of unintentional omission, see *Mughnī II*, 2:214–5.

[15] This anecdote indicates that there remained, during Sharīk's lifetime, segments of the proto-Sunnī population in Kūfa that performed the *qunūt* in some of the daily prayers (i.e., *fajr* and *maghrib*). Bear in mind, however, the conclusion from Chapter 7 that it was a *packet* of rituals, as opposed to a single ritual (e.g., the *qunūt*), which proved decisive in the allocation of sectarian identity. Sharīk was likely directing a proto-Sunnī to a proto-Sunnī mosque. The broader point here regarding the increasing alignment between ritual and mosque remains valid.

[16] Djait is quite critical of the dichotomous framework embedded in the Shī'ī sources and drawn primarily from pilgrimage manuals (discussed later in the chapter). He argues that much of this literature imposes a subsequent historical perspective onto

TABLE 8.1.[17] *The Mosques of Kūfa*

Blessed – Friendly Mosques	Accursed – Hostile Mosques
*Masjid al-Kūfa (the Friday mosque)	*Masjid al-Ashʿath
*Masjid Sahla (aka Masjid ʿAbd al-Qays)	*Masjid Jarīr b. ʿAbd Allāh al-Bajalī
*Masjid Ghanī	*Masjid Simāk b. Makhrama
Masjid Suhayl	*Masjid Shabath b. Ribʿī
*Masjid Juʿfī	*Masjid Taym
*Masjid al-Ḥamrā (aka Masjid Yūnus)	*Masjid Thaqīf
*Masjid Banī Kāhil	Masjid al-Ḥamra (different from Masjid Yūnus)
Masjid Bāhila	Masjid Banī Sayyid
*Masjid Ṣaʿṣaʿa b. Ṣūḥān b. Ḥujr al-ʿAbdī	Masjid Banī ʿAbd Allāh b. Rāzm
Masjid Banī Zafar (identical to Masjid Sahla?)	
Masjid Zayd b. Ṣūhān	
Masjid al-Ḥannāna	
*Masjid Banū Jadhīma b. Mālik	
Masjid Banī ʿAnza (?)	

Note: Mosques identified by Djait in the 1st/7th century are denoted by a *

designation of some mosques (see Table 8.1) as "blessed" and others as "accursed."[18] In time, the Imāmīs developed a religious geography of Kūfa that directed worshippers toward a network of friendly venues and away from regions of particular hostility.

the 1st/7th century, characterizing mosques associated with the Shīʿa as friendly (e.g., the Banū ʿAbd Qays) and those connected with opponents (e.g., ʿAbd Allāh b. Jarīr al-Bajalī) as hostile (*Kūfa*, 300–1). In Djait's view, the Shīʿa coalesced as theologically coherent entities in a later period and then constructed (or revised) their vision of the mosques of Kūfa. Although later Shīʿī scholars might have endowed certain mosques with an increased charismatic reverence or historical importance, it does not follow that such venues necessarily lacked a sectarian dimension at an earlier stage. Given the importance of ritual practice (see Chapter 7) and the circulation of traditions similar to that of Sharīk (see earlier discussion), it is more likely that these mosques were spaces where the early Shīʿa could gather and pray (in a distinctive manner). The fact that this tendency may have been exaggerated in subsequent periods on other (religious and historical) grounds should have no bearing on the potential for an earlier differentiation.

[17] For this table, see al-Ṭūsī, *al-Amālī*, 168–9 – 283 with an important variant in Ibn al-Mashhadī, *al-Mazār*, 117–8. The most comprehensive register of the sectarian inclinations of mosques is found in al-Burāqī, *Tārīkh*, 75–7, with greater detail on 78–91. See also, Djait, *Kūfa*, 296–301, for a general discussion of Kūfan mosques. An abbreviated list of these mosques appears in al-Shaykh al-Mufīd, *Mazār*, 82–3. For details about the location and namesakes of both the "blessed" and "accursed" mosques, see footnotes 1 and 2 in Ibn Bābawayh, *al-Khiṣāl*, 301 and Djait, *Kūfa*, 302–3.

[18] For such a differentiation of mosques, see al-Ṭūsī, *al-Amālī*, 168–9 – 283. A similar tradition is found in al-Kūfī, *al-Ghārāt*, 2:483–5. Although ʿAlī is the most commonly mentioned authority for this account, a number of variants cite either al-Bāqir or al-Ṣādiq. See *KK*, 3:489–90 – 1; Ibn Bābawayh, *al-Khiṣāl*, 300–1 – 75, where the text has Masjid al-Khamrāʾ in place of Masjid al-Ḥamrāʾ; and Ibn al-Mashhadī, *al-Mazār*, 119. The Imāmī typology of blessed/accursed is also discussed by Djait (*Kūfa*, 300–1).

The "blessedness" of mosques was predicated on a combination of historical and religious factors. Masjid Ghanī was founded by "a believer" and was prophesied as being home to the gardens and springs of heaven,[19] whereas al-Bāqir emphasized that "every prophet who God sent" had performed prayers in Masjid Suhayl.[20] Masjid Ju'fī was a gathering place for Bedouin and appears in later traditions as one of the locations in which the hidden Imām would perform his prayers.[21] The significance of Masjid al-Ḥamrā' was tied to its construction over the tomb of the Prophet Yūnus, endowing the land with a special blessing (*baraka*).[22] A fifth mosque, Masjid Banī Kāhil (also known as the Masjid of the Commander of the Faithful), was revered as a location where 'Alī led the *fajr* prayers and performed the *qunūt*.[23] Masjid Zayd b. Ṣūḥān (d. 36/656)[24] was named for a companion of 'Alī and visited by the prophet al-Khiḍr who recited a few special invocations before quickly disappearing.[25] Masjid Bāhila and Masjid Ṣa'ṣa'a b. Ṣūḥān b. Ḥujr al-'Abdī[26] (d. before 60/680) were also honored by the Imāmī community and ascribed unique sets of prayers and invocations.[27] Less is known about

19 Ibn al-Mashhadī, *al-Mazār*, 118–9; al-Burāqī, *Tārīkh*, 75–6; Djait, *Kūfa*, 299–303.

20 *ṬT*, 6:31 – 1, where the mosque is characterized as the "dwelling place of the prophets, successors, and those who do good." See also Ibn al-Mashhadī, *al-Mazār*, 113 and al-Burāqī, *Tārīkh*, 75.

21 For a typical anecdote, see Warrām b. Abī Farrās, *Tanbīh*, 2:303–5. Ibn al-Mashhadī mentions that this mosque was no longer frequented by the Ju'fī tribe in the 6th/12th century (*al-Mazār*, 119). See also al-Burāqī, *Tārīkh*, 75–6; Djait, *Kūfa*, 299–303.

22 al-Ṭūsī, *al-Amālī*, 168–9 – 28; al-Burāqī, *Tārīkh*, 75–7; Djait, *Kūfa*, 299–303. Al-Burāqī explicitly rejects the possibility that the Prophet Yūnus was buried at the site of the mosque and instead ascribes its importance to 'Alī having prayed there.

23 Ibn al-Mashhadī, *al-Mazār*, 120–1; al-Burāqī, *Tārīkh*, 78; Djait, *Kūfa*, 299–302.

24 The brother of Ṣa'ṣa'a (see footnote 26 of this chapter) and a close companion of 'Alī, he was one of the leaders of the Kūfan delegation that traveled to Medina to protest 'Uthmān's economic policies in 35/656. He was killed in the Battle of the Camel in 36/656. See Ibn Sa'd, *al-Ṭabaqāt al-kubra'*, 6:176–8; al-Tustarī, *Qāmūs*, 4:557–8; and Hinds, "Murder," 450–69 and especially 459.

25 al-Burāqī, *Tārīkh*, 87.

26 Abū Ṭalḥa Ṣa'ṣa'a b. Ṣūḥān b. Ḥujr al-'Abdī fought on 'Alī's side at the Battle of the Camel. He was famed as a *khaṭīb* (orator) and narrated a few traditions from 'Alī and 'Abd Allāh b. 'Abbās. He was also part of the Kūfan party that came to Medina in 35/656 to object to 'Uthmān's economic policies. A district in Kūfa was named after him, and he is said to have died during the reign of Mu'āwiya. See Ibn Sa'd, *al-Ṭabaqāt al-kubra'*, 6:244; al-Mizzī, *Tahdhīb*, 13:167. See also, Hinds, "Murder," 459, where he refers to Ṣa'ṣa'a as a member of the *qurrā'*.

27 See Ibn al-Mashhadī, *al-Mazār*, 119 for Masjid Bāhila; see Ibn al-Mashhadī, *al-Mazār*, 142–6; al-Burāqī, *Tārīkh*, 78–80; and Djait, *Kūfa*, 299 for Masjid Ṣa'ṣa'a. Al-Burāqī relates a few anecdotes that suggest that this mosque was frequented by the hidden Twelfth Imām.

Masjid Banī 'Anaza,[28] Masjid Banī Ẓafar,[29] and Masjid Banī Jadhīma b. Mālik,[30] although the latter was loosely connected with (perhaps the clients of?) the Banū Asad. A final Kūfan site of prominence (according to the later sources) was on the desert road to Karbalā', later identified as Masjid al-Ḥannāna.[31] A number of reports note its association with the severed head of al-Ḥusayn, with some alluding to the possibility of its burial at the location.

The most important mosques for the Shī'a were Masjid al-Sahla and Masjid al-Kūfa (also known as the "Big Masjid").[32] Masjid al-Sahla was particularly noteworthy due to its avid sectarian associations. As opposed to Masjid al-Kūfa, which served a broad cross-section of the Kūfan population on important occasions, Masjid al-Sahla was located in the north Kūfan district of the Banū 'Abd al-Qays where it may have initially been established as the neighborhood mosque for the pro-'Alī tribe.[33] Its transformation into a sectarian space was reflected in a wide range of traditions. Masjid al-Sahla was said to possess a green stone bearing the marks of all past prophets.[34] It had been personally visited by Idrīs (Enoch), Ibrāhīm (Abraham), Dāwūd (David),[35] and al-Khiḍr[36] and was constantly

[28] The Banū 'Anaza were an ancient Arab tribe that partially settled in Kūfa and was said to have ties to the Qays (*EI²*, s.v. 'Anaza [Graf]). The tribe fought alongside 'Alī in large numbers (i.e., up to 4,000) during the Battle of Ṣiffīn (Madelung, *Succession*, 246).

[29] The presence of this mosque is affirmed by both al-Burāqī (*Tārīkh*, 75–6) and Djait (*Kūfa*, 300), but neither provides any additional information. The Banū Ẓafar had roots in central Arabia as attested to by their establishment of a tribal mosque in early Medina (*EI²*, s.v. Masdjid [Pedersen]). Masjid Banī Ẓafar in Kūfa was apparently frequented by the Anṣār. Al-Khaṭīb al-Baghdādī recounts an incident in which Thābit b. Qays b. al-Khaṭīm (d. after 40/660) happened upon a large group of disgruntled Anṣār at the mosque in the process of drafting a letter of complaint to Mu'āwiya (al-Khaṭīb al-Baghdādī, *Tārī kh*, 1:526–7). This might suggest a correlation between Masjid Banī Ẓafar and Masjid al-Anṣār, a mosque identified by Djait (*Kūfa*, 298).

[30] al-Burāqī, *Tārīkh*, 90. The Banū Jadhīma b. Mālik b. Naṣr b. Qu'ayn were a part of the Banū Asad and traced their roots to the Najd (Yāqūt, *Mu'jam*, 4:448).

[31] al-Burāqī, *Tārīkh*, 88–90.

[32] Evidence of the importance of Masjid al-Sahla and Masjid al-Kūfa to the early Imāmīs is provided by al-Shaykh al-Mufīd, who places both at the center of a wider religious program for visiting the city (al-Shaykh al-Mufīd, *al-Mazār*, 82–3). The exact identity of Masjid al-Sahla is somewhat disputed, as some sources equate it with Masjid Banī Ẓafar whereas others identify it with Masjid Banī 'Abd al-Qays (Djait, *Kūfa*, 300).

[33] Djait, *Kūfa*, 302–3.

[34] al-Ṭūsī, *al-Amālī*, 168–9 – 283; al-Kūfī, *al-Ghārāt*, 2:483–4; Ibn al-Mashhadī, *al-Mazār*, 134–5.

[35] Ibn al-Mashhadī, *al-Mazār*, 118–9 and 132–6, with special invocations and further historical details on 136–43.

[36] al-Burāqī, *Tārīkh*, 82–3.

circled by worshipping angels.[37] A single two-cycle prayer in Masjid al-Sahla earned a reward exceeding two lesser pilgrimages[38] and (according to al-Sajjād) could add two years to a supplicant's life.[39]

The sources identify Masjid al-Kūfa as the main Shīʿī mosque for the entire city and emphasize its importance through an anecdote about the Prophet's ascent to heaven (*miʿrāj*).[40] In the account, as the Prophet is being carried by Jibrā'īl (Gabriel), he is informed that they are passing above Masjid al-Kūfa where every prophet or servant of God had performed prayers.[41] Muḥammad asks for and is granted the same privilege. The narrator (al-Ṣādiq) observes that "an obligatory prayer within it is equivalent to a thousand prayers [outside it] and a supererogatory prayer in it is equivalent to five hundred prayers [outside it],"[42] with variant accounts increasing the rewards to a greater (*ḥajj*) and lesser (*ʿumra*) pilgrimage, respectively.[43] This mosque was further exalted as being home to people who would be granted intercession on the Day of Judgment,[44] the location of numerous heavenly gardens,[45] and the secret resting place of Nūḥ's (Noah) ark, Mūsā's (Moses) cane, and Sulaymān's (Solomon) signet ring.[46] Such descriptions of Masjid al-Kūfa are a mere sampling of a much larger inventory with entire sections of some works devoted entirely to praising its virtues.[47]

These mosques were part and parcel of a broad network of religious spaces frequented by the nascent Imāmī community. Masjid al-Kūfa was at the core of this sacred geography, but it was also a space visited by a wide cross-section of the population diminishing its utility in identity formation. Given the breadth of Kūfan ritual diversity, one would expect to find groups in the central mosque praying in discordant and different

37 *Ibid.*, 83.
38 *Ibid.*, 83.
39 al-Shaykh al-Mufīd, *al-Mazār*, 26.
40 *KK*, 3:490–1 – 1; *BM*, 1:128 – 149; Ibn al-Mashhadī, *al-Mazār*, 123 and 131. The parallels in the descriptions of Masjid al-Kūfa to that of Masjid al-Aqṣā in Jerusalem (in other accounts of the *miʿrāj*) are striking.
41 Masjid al-Sahla is sometimes described in a similar manner as a venue where every Prophet has offered prayers (al-Burāqī, *Tārīkh*, 82). A vast majority of traditions, however, associate this virtue with Masjid al-Kūfa (Ibn al-Mashhadī, *al-Mazār*, 123).
42 *ṬT*, 6:32–62.
43 *KK*, 3:491–2; *ṬT*, 6:32–4; Ibn al-Mashhadī, *al-Mazār*, 122 and 130.
44 Ibn al-Mashhadī, *al-Mazār*, 125–6. For a thorough compilation of traditions pertaining to Masjid al-Kūfa, see *KK*, 3:494–5 and Ibn al-Mashhadī, *al-Mazār*, 121–31.
45 *BM*, 1:128–149; Ibn al-Mashhadī, *al-Mazār*, 127–8.
46 Ibn al-Mashhadī, *al-Mazār*, 127 and 129.
47 al-Burāqī, *Tārīkh*, 20–31.

ways. The smaller mosques, by contrast, were the prime laboratories for the crystallization of sectarian communal identity. Although many of the traditions explaining their importance were ascribed to either the Prophet or ʿAlī, a comparison of variant accounts suggests that they were originally circulated by the disciples of al-Bāqir and al-Ṣādiq.[48] It was during the lifetimes of these important Imāms (i.e., the late 1st/7th to the mid-2nd/8th century) that such texts gained wide distribution, endowing some spaces with a religious pedigree that significantly elevated their status for the emerging community. It is not surprising that the leaders of these mosques are often portrayed conducting prayers in a distinctively Imāmī manner.[49]

The same traditions that identify "blessed" mosques also document "accursed" mosques (see Table 8.1) that were tainted by their connection to either (1) hostile personalities or (2) unfriendly tribes. The former (all of which have been identified and mapped by Djait – see Map 2) were associated with individuals particularly reviled by the Imāmīs. Al-Ashʿath b. Qays (d. 40/661)[50] fought with ʿAlī in the Battle of Ṣiffīn before pressuring him to (1) accept arbitration and (2) appoint Abū Mūsā al-Ashʿarī as one of the arbiters. The Imāmī sources claim that he turned to Khārijism in his later years.[51] Jarīr b. ʿAbd Allāh b. Jābir al-Bajalī (d. 51–6/671–6)[52] was entrusted by ʿAlī to carry a letter to Muʾāwiya but secretly pledged loyalty to the Umayyads and worked on their behalf.[53] Simāk b. Makhrama b. Ḥumayn al-Asadī (d. mid- to late 1st/7th century)[54] lived in an area

[48] For accounts that cite al-Bāqir and al-Ṣādiq in place of ʿAlī, see Ibn Bābawayh, *al-Khiṣāl*, 300–1 – 75; *TT*, 6:39–26; al-Kūfī, *al-Ghārāt*, 2:483–4.

[49] Modarressi, *Tradition*, 1:204.

[50] Al-Ashʿath b. Qays al-Kindī was a Companion and participated in the *ridda* (apostasy) revolts after the death of the Prophet. He was eventually pardoned and took part in the conquests of Syria. See Ibn Saʿd, *al-Ṭabaqāt al-kabīr*, 6:236–7; *EI*², s.v. al-Ashʿath (Reckendorf); and al-Dhahabī, *Tārīkh*, 11–40:609. By the 6th/12th century, the mosque named after him no longer existed. Some claimed that it originally stood between Masjid al-Kūfa and Masjid al-Sahla but that only a part of its wall had survived, whereas others equated it with the extant Masjid al-Jawāshin (Ibn al-Mashhadī, *al-Mazār*, 120).

[51] For Shīʿī characterizations of his Khārijism, see footnote 1 in Ibn Bābawayh, *al-Khiṣāl*, 301. For the significance of his status as a member of the *ashrāf*, see Hinds, "Alignments," 353, 357, and 361–2. See also, Madelung, *Succession*, 239.

[52] Djait places his mosque just north of the city center in the district of his tribe, the Banū Bajīla (*Kūfa*, 299 and 302–3). Hinds describes Jarīr as a tribal leader whose support for ʿAlī was suspect at best (Hinds, "Alignments," 353 and 361–2). See also, Madelung, *Succession*, 193–5.

[53] Ibn Saʿd, *al-Ṭabaqāt al-kabīr*, 6:288–301 and especially 300–1. See also footnote 1 in Ibn Bābawayh, *al-Khiṣāl*, 301.

[54] Djait places Masjid Simāk in the southwest quarter of Kūfa and, specifically, in the northern half of the Asad tribal district (*Kūfa*, 298, 302–3). In the 6th/12th century, this

of Kūfa known for the pro-ʿUthmān beliefs of its inhabitants (as late as the 4th/10th century), where he built a mosque in which ʿAlī famously refused to offer prayers.[55] A fourth mosque was linked to Shabath b. Ribʿī al-Tamīmī (d. 80/699),[56] an ambiguous figure who supported both ʿUthmān and ʿAlī before joining the Khawārij.[57] He eventually repented of his rejection of ʿAlī and (after the murder of al-Ḥusayn b. ʿAlī) joined Mukhtār, who placed him in charge of the *shurṭa* in Kūfa. Each of these mosques (i.e., Masjid al-ʿAshʿath, Masjid Jarīr, Masjid Simāk, and Masjid Shabath) achieved particular notoriety when, according to al-Bāqir, "they were renovated ... in celebration of the murder of al-Ḥusayn."[58] Given these circumstances, it is highly unlikely that any Imāmī would venture into such locations to perform prayers.

The nascent Imāmī community dubbed five additional mosques as hostile due primarily to their tribal affiliations. According to an early tradition, ʿAlī avoided Masjid Taym[59] because its constituency (consisting largely of the Tamīm) "would not pray with him out of enmity and hatred."[60] A similar dynamic characterized Masjid Thaqīf given the tribe's adversarial relationship with ʿAlī and his partisans.[61] The tribal mosques of the Banū ʿAbd Allāh b. Dārim and the Banū al-Sayyid were identified as hostile spaces without any additional commentary or explanation.[62]

mosque was located near the market of the blacksmiths and had been renamed Masjid al-Ḥawāfir (Ibn al-Mashhadī, *al-Mazār*, 120).

55 al-Iṣbahānī, *al-Aghānī*, 11:4037.

56 Djait positions Masjid Shabath in the tribal district of the Banū Tamīm located in the furthest regions of southwestern Kūfa (*Kūfa*, 298, 302–3). In the 6th/12th century, this mosque stood in the markets at the end of a road called *Darb al-Ḥajjāj* (Ibn al-Mashhadī, *al-Mazār*, 120).

57 Ibn Saʿd, *al-Ṭabaqāt al-kabīr*, 8:335. See also footnote 2 in Ibn Bābawayh, *al-Khiṣāl*, 301. Madelung discusses his place among the early Khawārij in *Succession*, 246–7.

58 Ibn Bābawayh, *al-Khiṣāl*, footnote 1 on 302; *KK*, 3:490–2; Ibn al-Mashhadī, *al-Mazār*, 118–9. The reference here is to the murder of al-Ḥusayn b. ʿAlī b. Abī Ṭālib in 61/680.

59 Djait locates Masjid Taym close to Masjid Shabath in the Tamīmī district far southwest of the city center (*Kūfa*, 299–302).

60 Ibn Bābawayh, *al-Khiṣāl*, 301–2–76. The fact that Abū Bakr was a member of the Banū Taym likely contributed to the clan's animosity. See also, *ṬT*, 6:39–82 and al-Shaykh al-Mufīd, *al-Mazār*, 83–4.

61 Djait places Masjid Thaqīf just north of the city center in the narrow strip associated with the tribe (*Kūfa*, 299 and 300–2). For the mosque's inclusion in lists of "accursed" mosques, see al-Burāqī, *Tārīkh*, 76.

62 al-Burāqī, *Tārīkh*, 76. The text reads "Masjid Banī ʿAbd Allāh b. Razm" but likely refers to the Banū ʿAbd Allāh b. Dārim who occupied a region of Kūfa near the walls, possibly in the eastern districts close to the Euphrates (Yāqūt, *al-Buldān*, 2:611). There is little information regarding the Banū al-Sayyid.

The final "accursed" mosque on the Imāmī lists was the second Masjid al-Ḥamrā',[63] allegedly built on the grave of "one of the pharaohs."[64]

The Imāmī sources depict 2nd/8th-century Kūfa as an amalgamation of safe havens and hostile ground. This division of sacred space is predicated on religious or historical claims that either elevate a mosque's status or render it enemy territory. Though the reality of these unequivocal judgments must be approached with caution,[65] the tendency for a nascent community to endow spaces with a broad charismatic significance is well documented.[66] Thus, although the ascribed virtues of "blessed" mosques may be a later accretion, it is likely that the Shīʿa were frequenting these mosques early on and appropriating them as friendly spaces for the performance of a distinctive ritual prayer.[67] Venturing into Masjid Juʿfī, a worshipper could expect to hear the Shīʿī *adhān*[68] followed by a prayer that included (among other idiosyncrasies) the audible *basmala* and the insertion of a *qunūt* after the recitation in the second cycle.[69]

[63] al-Ṭūsī, *al-Amālī*, 168–9 – 283, with variants in *TT*, 6:39–82; Ibn Bābawayh, *al-Khiṣāl*, 300–1–75; al-Kūfī, *al-Ghārāt*, 3:482–3; and al-Burāqī, *Tārīkh*, 76. The tribal associations of this mosque remain unclear and confused (*Kūfa*, 299 and 300–1).

[64] al-Ṭūsī, *al-Amālī*, 168–9 – 283; Ibn Bābawayh, *al-Khiṣāl*, 300–1 – 75; al-Kūfī, *al-Ghārāt*, 3:482–3; Ibn al-Mashhadī, *al-Mazār*, 118–9; and al-Burāqī, *Tārīkh*, 76. Ibn al-Mashhadī associates this location with the marketplace of the carpenters in 6th/12th-century Kūfa (*al-Mazār*, 120).

[65] See also, footnote 16 in this chapter.

[66] A similar process is explored in a range of theoretical works drawing on Bourdieu's seminal *Distinction*. See, in particular, Kevin Hetherington's *Expressions of Identity*, which focuses on the dynamic process that endows safe spaces with new meaning in the process of identity building. The key point here is that before space acquires charisma, it is already under the control of a given social group.

[67] Although much of this section focuses on the identification of mosques frequented by Imāmīs, there are also accounts that associate specific non-Imāmī Kūfans with particular mosques. For a typical example in which al-Aʿmash is noted as frequenting "Masjid Banī Ḥarām min Banī Saʿd," see Ibn Saʿd, *al-Ṭabaqāt al-kubra'*, 6:331.

[68] There are important differences between the Sunnī and Shīʿī law schools regarding the proper form of the call to prayer (*adhān*). The most prominent concerns the Shīʿī use of the phrase "Hurry to the best of works," a practice attributed to the Prophet, confirmed by ʿAlī, and supported by subsequent Imāms. Within Sunnī juristic circles, there are additional disagreements regarding the use of the *tathwīb* (the phrase "Prayer is better than sleep") before the dawn prayer. For the Imāmī view, see al-Shaykh al-Mufīd, *al-Muqniʿa*, 102; Ibn Bābawayh, *al-Faqīh*, 1:289–90; and *TT*, 2:59–69. For the Sunnī view, see *Mughnī II*, 1:544–7 and 550–2. In the 16th century, the Ṣafawids institutionalized a number of new Imāmī ritual practices, including the insertion of a confirmation of ʿAlī's *wilāya* in the *adhān*. For this issue, see Takim, "*Bidʿa*," 166–77.

[69] For a summary of these differences, see Lalani, *Early Shīʿī Thought*, 119–26. See also Chapters 3 and 4 in this volume.

THE POWER OF PILGRIMAGE

The crystallization of a distinct Imāmī identity was increasingly reflected in a practice that combined ritual and space, specifically pilgrimage to sites of religious importance.[70] The growth in the importance of pilgrimages sparked the proliferation of a new genre of Imāmī literature – the pilgrimage manual – which provided adherents with itineraries and instructions for location-specific prayers and invocations.

An early example of an Imāmī author concerned with pilgrimage was al-Barqī (d. 273/887–8) who emphasized the virtues of the central mosque in Kūfa and the enormous rewards that accrued to those who offered their prayers within.[71] He did not, however, provide a clear itinerary for pilgrims as he was more interested in the sanctity of sites than on the actual details of a visit. Al-Kulaynī, by contrast, devoted extensive space to the subject, quoting traditions that encouraged visits to the shrines of the Imāms with the promise of intercession.[72] He also included accounts that identified important sites in and around Kūfa and specified special invocations for each location.[73]

Beginning as early as the 4th/10th century, Imāmī scholars began producing works that specifically focused on pilgrimage. A typical example of this new genre of religious literature was al-Shaykh al-Mufīd's (d. 413/1022) *Kitāb al-mazār*, which included a careful set of instructions detailing both (1) the order in which places should be visited and (2) the duration of time to be spent at each. Al-Mufīd directed pilgrims returning from a visit to 'Alī's grave to stay at Masjid al-Kūfa for an extended period before proceeding to Masjid al-Sahla, Masjid Ghanī, and Masjid al-Ḥamrā'.[74] In a similar vein, al-Ṭūsī recommended a visit to the Euphrates, quoting al-Ṣādiq's observation that "I do not think anyone

70 For an historical overview of the practice, which can be traced to the pre-Islamic period, see *EI*², s.v. Ziyāra (J. Meri). Leor Halevi examines the prevalence of visiting graves and mourning rituals among the earliest generations of Muslims in *Muhammad's Grave*, ch. 4–5. Although he does not directly address pilgrimage to shrines, his discussion provides insight on how the practice may have developed from roots in popular piety.

71 *BM*, 1:128–149.

72 *KK*, 4:567–2.

73 Al-Kulaynī's section on pilgrimages is very large (4:548–89). For a tradition that cites a specific invocation (to be recited at 'Alī's grave), see *KK*, 4:570–71 – 1. For a tradition that highlights the gradual appropriation of space in a narrative of pilgrimage, see *KK*, 4:571–2 – 1.

74 al-Shaykh al-Mufīd, *al-Mazār*, 83–4. The same work emphasizes the importance of Kūfan mosques by enjoining pilgrims to visit them before proceeding to the grave of 'Alī, especially if they fear that they will not have the opportunity to do so afterward.

experiences the water of the Euphrates without developing a love for us, the family of the Prophet,"[75] before cataloging the merits of the usual set of Kūfan mosques. In his 6th/12th-century pilgrimage manual, the Imāmī Ibn al-Mashhadī (d. 594/1198) identified appropriate prayers for a wide array of Kūfan mosques and arranged them in a hierarchy of importance.[76]

The growing significance of pilgrimage was also reflected in the structure of manuals like those of al-Shaykh al-Mufīd and Ibn al-Mashhadī. These generally began with a discussion of shrines and places of import in the vicinity of Mecca and Medina. In addition to tombs of religious figures or locations associated directly with the Prophet (e.g., his home or a favorite mosque), they included venues of particular significance to the Imāmī community. Special mention, for example, was made of a mosque built near Ghadīr Khumm where it was believed that the Prophet appointed ʿAlī as his successor.[77] Both al-Ṣādiq and al-Kāẓim emphasized this location's centrality to the historical narrative at the heart of Imāmī identity. The former explained that it is "recommended to perform prayers in Masjid Ghadīr Khumm because the Prophet established (*aqāma*) the Commander of the Faithful in it and it is the place where God made the truth manifest,"[78] whereas the latter instructed his followers to "pray in it, for in the prayer is a good benefit, my father [al-Ṣādiq] having commanded it."[79]

In addition to the Ḥijāz, pilgrimage manuals devoted considerable space to Kūfa and its surrounding areas. They offered proper instructions for visiting many of the previously mentioned Kūfan mosques (e.g., Masjid al-Sahla and Masjid al-Kūfa), along with the tombs of ʿAlī (on the outskirts of the city) and al-Ḥusayn (on the battlefield of Karbalāʾ fifty miles away). Every member of the community with the means and opportunity was expected to perform a formal pilgrimage to these shrines as an affirmation of communal identity.

The special importance of ʿAlī's grave was exemplified by regular Kūfan delegations that would travel the short distance in a public procession during the festival commemorating Ghadīr Khumm on the

[75] *ṬT*, 6:39–26.

[76] Ibn al-Mashhadī, *al-Mazār*, 111–80, where the location of each mosque within Kūfa proper is described along with appropriate invocations.

[77] For the importance of this location and the accounts associated with it, see EI^2, s.v. Ghadīr Khumm (L. Veccia Vaglieri) and Dakake, *Charismatic*, 33–48.

[78] *KK*, 4:566–7 – 3; *ṬT*, 6:18–22.

[79] *KK*, 4:566 – 1; *ṬT*, 6:18–21.

10th of Dhū al-Ḥijja. This annual event was a very public declaration of sectarian membership as reflected in the case of Hibat Allāh Aḥmad b. Muḥammad b. al-Kātib (d. early 5th/11th century), popularly known as Ibn Barniyya. The Imāmī biographical sources ascribe him a belief in thirteen Imāms (the twelve in the standard Imāmī genealogy together with Zayd b. 'Alī) and note that he frequented the circles of a prominent Kūfan Zaydī scholar.[80] Rather than condemn Ibn Barniyya for his heterodox views,[81] however, Imāmī scholars claimed him as one of their own, citing his acceptance of Imāms (e.g., al-Sajjād) who were explicitly rejected by the Zaydīs for their political pacifism.[82] This is startling. If Ibn Barniyya held a theological belief (i.e., the acceptance of thirteen Imāms) that fell outside the purview of Imāmī doctrine, how could he be considered a proper Imāmī? Part of the answer is found in al-Najāshī's biographical entry, which states that "this man participated in many pilgrimages. The last pilgrimage where he was present amongst us was in the year 400 on the day of Ghadīr at the tomb of the Commander of the Faithful."[83] This public act constituted a proof of communal identity strong enough to overcome a dramatic departure from Imāmī theology. The case of Ibn Barniyya testifies to the importance of the annual synchronized processions that represented singular occasions where large groups of Imāmīs could assert their loyalties as a collective.[84]

The shrine of al-Ḥusayn in Karbalā' evoked a similar sentiment among the early Imāmīs. Located at a distance that made daily visits from Kūfa difficult, it was nevertheless close enough to serve as a semiregular site for pilgrimage. A number of traditions depict Kūfan Imāmīs in Medina being questioned by either al-Bāqir or al-Ṣādiq about the frequency of their visits to Karbalā'. In a typical example, al-Ṣādiq observes that "our Shī'a [in Kūfa] allow a year or two to pass during which most of them do not visit

80 al-Najāshī, *Rijāl*, 2:408–9; Ibn Dāwūd al-Ḥillī, *Rijāl*, 366. Al-Najāshī identifies his Zaydī teacher as Abū al-Ḥusayn b. Shayba al-'Alawī.

81 One Imāmī authority does condemn him as weak in *ḥadīth* transmission (Ibn Dāwūd al-Ḥillī, *Rijāl*, 366), but others appear to reserve judgment and do not offer a clear opinion regarding his reliability (al-Najāshī, *Rijāl*, 2:408–9).

82 al-Tustarī, *Qāmūs*, 10:499.

83 al-Najāshī, *al-Rijāl*, 2:408.

84 While smaller gathering in mosques for daily prayers or individualized pilgrimages to holy sites carried significance, the processions allowed individuals to be counted as part and parcel of a cohesive community. Similar dynamics are apparent in processions in the modern period in South Asia (among both Muslims and Hindus) and were particularly conspicuous in the millions of pilgrims who gathered in Karbalā' for the first commemoration of 'Āshūrā' after the fall of Saddam Hussein.

al-Ḥusayn b. ʿAlī b. Abī Ṭālib."[85] He notes that they will be surprised in the afterlife by a diminished reward and by being kept at a distance from the Prophet. In another tradition, al-Ṣādiq asks a Kūfan guest (identified as ʿAbd Allāh b. Ṭalḥa al-Nahdī – d. after 148/765) if he has ever visited Karbalāʾ (yes) and then interrogates him as to the regularity of those visits.[86] When al-Ṣādiq learns of the infrequency with which al-Nahdī (along with the larger Kūfan Imāmī community) undertake the short journey, he laments that the act is not intended as a burden, for it garners a reward equal to a greater and lesser pilgrimage. In a third account, al-Bāqir – upon being informed that the travel time between Kūfa and Karbalāʾ is "a little over a day" – observes that if he resided so close to al-Ḥusayn, he would visit often.[87]

In time, pilgrimage became an integral and even necessary component of Imāmī identity. This may (or may not) have been the case as early as the 2nd/8th century, but it was certainly true by the 4th/10th century when traditions explicitly began predicating communal membership on pilgrimage to the tomb of al-Ḥusayn. In the following account, al-Ṣādiq addresses Kūfan Imāmīs who had not undertaken the short trip to Karbalāʾ:

> If one of you performs the *ḥajj* in the course of your lifetime and does not visit al-Ḥusayn b. ʿAlī, then you have departed from one of the claims (*ḥuqūq*) of God and the Messenger of God, because the claim of al-Ḥusayn is a mandatory duty from God Exalted and Mighty and obligatory upon every Muslim.[88]

The Imām's words unambiguously place pilgrimage (to the shrine of al-Ḥusayn) among the core tenets of Imāmī belief and even suggest its superiority to the Ḥajj. In fact, a large portion of some manuals are devoted almost in their entirety to the virtues and benefits of visiting Karbalāʾ, highlighting the act's centrality in the construction of Imāmī identity.[89] In another account, the eleventh Imām Ḥasan al-Askarī (d. 260/874) is asked about the specific characteristics that distinguish an Imāmī from the wider mass of Muslims:

> [T]here are five signs of a believer: fifty-one cycles of prayer, the pilgrimage to al-Ḥusayn's tomb forty days after the anniversary of his death, the wearing of a

85 *ṬT*, 6:45–12.
86 *Ibid.*, 6:21–4.
87 *Ibid.*, 6:46–14.
88 al-Shaykh al-Mufīd, *al-Mazār*, 38.
89 See, for example, Ibn Qulūyah, *Kāmil al-ziyārāt*.

ring on the right hand, the placing of the forehead on the earth in prostration, and the audible recitation of the *basmala*.[90]

Here the Imām includes the ritual among a range of signs that were easily observed and (in most cases) very public in nature. It would be difficult to find a more unambiguous declaration of the functional importance of pilgrimage.

CONCLUSION

The early stages in the development of Kūfa were primarily dominated by tribal forces. The city's spatial layout was organized on a tribal basis and each district neighborhood was home to its own local mosque. Although some of these mosques had a subtle sectarian dimension, this was primarily a consequence of the political loyalties of specific clans as opposed to a conscious religious choice. The situation changed dramatically with the rise of polarized sectarian groups and their gradual appropriation of many of these spaces. This chapter examines the process by which such a change occurred, beginning as early as the 2nd/8th century and extending into the 3rd/9th and 4th/10th centuries.

The first and second sections of this chapter discussed the emerging correlation between sectarian groups and mosques as represented by ritual practice. Mosques that were originally tribal became associated with rituals particular to a given sect (i.e., the Imāmī Shīʿa). A supplicant venturing into these sites would expect the prayer to be performed in a manner that aligned with his communal affiliations.[91] Such a demarcation of sacred space was ultimately embedded in traditions that identified groups of blessed/friendly and accursed/hostile mosques. The exact time frame for the shift from singular sectarian mosques to the networks of friendly spaces listed in pilgrimage manuals is unclear owing, in part, to a scarcity in the source material. It seems likely, however, that the change began in the early 2nd/8th century when the Imāmīs were already adhering to a distinct set of rituals.

[90] al-Shaykh al-Mufid, *al-Mazār*, 60; *TT*, 6:52–37. For more on these signs and their central importance for the Imāmī Shīʿa, see Modarressi, *Sanadīyāt*, 425–6.

[91] This was a marked change from the situation alluded to in the previous chapter wherein mosque attendance was not sufficient to establish the probity of a transmitter. Rather an individual's prayer had to be directly observed before making any judgments regarding reliability.

The third section of this chapter traced the growth of pilgrimage, a ritual predicated on the existence of distinctively Imāmī mosques and shrines. Without the presence of such venues, it would have been virtually impossible to design detailed itineraries for Imāmīs visiting Kūfa. The proliferation of pilgrimage manuals highlighted the practice's seminal importance in articulating Imāmī identity and suggested a clear solidification in the division of sacred space. In such an environment, the very act of marching through the streets of Kūfa side by side with fellow Imāmīs constituted an unambiguous declaration of an individual's sectarian loyalties.

9

Conclusion

Historical studies of early Shīʿism are generally limited by a lack of contemporaneous sources and a reliance on theological works such as heresiographies. Although many scholars have made use of these materials to construct careful and erudite narratives for the origins of sectarianism, it is difficult to dispel doubts that they are simply back-projections intended to validate subsequent political and theological developments. This book is an attempt to make use of recent methodological advances in the dating of early sources (particularly traditions ascribed to the Prophet or other early authorities) to test the reliability of the origin narratives of Imāmī and Zaydī Shīʿism.

Modern studies of early Imāmī Shīʿism emphasize the institution of the Imāmate in a wide variety of interpretive frameworks (from theological to legal) to date the emergence of the sect to the early 2nd/8th century. A particular importance is ascribed to al-Bāqir and al-Ṣādiq who are said to have gathered a circle of disciples in Medina and commanded a large following in Kūfa. The Imāmī community crystallized around a belief in the unquestioned authority of these ʿAlids, although differences over the scope of that authority persisted, with some positing a rationalist position and others venturing into the esoteric. The Imāmī perspective on the Companions aligned with that of the Jārūdī Zaydīs (see further discussion here) and included a total rejection of those who had opposed ʿAlī's claims. These figures were deemed untrustworthy and rarely appeared in the chains of transmission of Imāmī traditions.

Most modern scholars trace the origins of Zaydism to the 122/740 revolt of Zayd b. ʿAlī, which brought together two streams of Kūfan Shīʿism, the Batriyya and the Jārūdiyya. The former were part of a broad traditionist movement that upheld the probity of those early Companions who rejected ʿAlī's political claims. Although strongly supporting ʿAlī's right to rule, the Batrīs felt that the evidence for his appointment was unclear and ambiguous so that opposition was tantamount to a mistake in judgment (*ijtihād*) as opposed to an act of disbelief (*kufr*). The Jārūdīs, by contrast, asserted that the proof for ʿAlī's succession was unequivocal and concluded that most of the Companions had committed apostasy by denying his claims. After Zayd's death, these two groups struggled for control of the Zaydiyya until the Jārūdīs finally triumphed in the 3rd/9th century. The overall picture, then, is one of a radically divided community experiencing severe internal conflict rooted in disagreements over the status of the Prophet's Companions and, by extension, the proper standard for preserving and transmitting knowledge.

The last few decades have produced new opportunities for testing these narratives on the basis of contemporaneous sources. Recent scholarship has demonstrated that traditions were being accurately recorded and transmitted (as opposed to fabricated) in the early 2nd/8th century (and possibly much earlier). Even though much of this research has centered on Sunnī (i.e., the work of Harald Motzki) and Imāmī (i.e., the articles of Etan Kohlberg and Hossein Modarressi) collections, it suggests a broader 2nd/8th-century societal investment in the written compilation of traditions. The question of whether such materials preserve the opinions of the generation of the Prophet and his Companions remains unclear. For the 2nd/8th century, however, they constitute an array of potentially useful and valuable materials. What is needed is the development of new techniques and approaches that can be used to mine these texts for historical information.

This book offers one potential methodological approach that utilizes these traditions to evaluate the veracity of early sectarian narratives. Specifically, it compares the structural characteristics of Kūfan texts drawn from the Sunnī, Imāmī, and Zaydī collections to determine the point at which sectarian groups appear to have developed a sense of being "different." The primary focal points for the analysis are authority figures, transmitters, and narrative style. It is argued that the citation of unique authorities through distinct chains of transmission in particular narrative forms is indicative of the presence of an *independent* sectarian identity. Conversely, shared authorities, transmitters, and styles suggest a degree of overlap between groups. To what extent, then, do these comparisons support the views that (1) Imāmī Shīʿī identity was present in the early 2nd/8th century and (2) Zaydī Shīʿism was initially rent by a conflict between Batrīs and Jārūdīs that culminated in the victory of the latter over the former?

Given the breadth and scope of the *ḥadīth* literature, it is necessary to restrict our analysis to a specific set of manageable issues. In the process of choosing these issues, this study privileges ritual practice over theological doctrines. Such a decision is predicated on the realization that theological traditions have a well-documented tendency to back-project doctrinal developments. Moreover, theological controversies are at the very core of sectarian polemics, increasing their likelihood for being altered to further the agenda of a specific party (or parties). There appears to have been a far greater societal tolerance for diversity in ritual practice among the various sectarian groups and legal schools. This was particularly true in Kūfa, which was characterized by a striking degree of variation that sometimes placed the (proto-Sunnī) traditionists closer to the Imāmī Shī'a than the (proto-Sunnī) *ahl al-ra'y*. It is never possible to completely eliminate the potential for tampering, but an emphasis on ritual law may reduce the risk significantly.

The three case studies discussed in this book are deliberately selected to reflect a range of relationships between the legal communities in Kūfa. The *basmala* was a topic of broad disagreement, with many Kūfan proto-Sunnīs endorsing the same positions as the Imāmīs and the Zaydīs. The *qunūt*, by contrast, placed the Imāmī Shī'a in direct opposition to the Zaydīs and proto-Sunnīs. The dynamic was reversed in the case of prohibition, with a large segment of proto-Sunnīs openly advocating the consumption of nongrape alcoholic drinks. The choice of these issues as opposed to strictly sectarian ones (i.e., the wiping/washing of the feet in the ritual ablution or the placement of the hands in prayer) is intended to ensure that our results are not simply a product of selection bias.

The structural comparisons of traditions across all three case studies reveal support for one sectarian narrative and serious questions about the other. The Imāmī texts consistently demonstrate independence from their Sunnī and Zaydī counterparts with respect to their use of authorities, transmitters/chains of transmission, and narrative style. The striking lack of overlap affirms the view of many modern scholars that an Imāmī sectarian identity originated in the early 2nd/8th century. In this instance, the heresiographical information appears to have been relatively accurate.

The Zaydī traditions, by contrast, do not support the view that Zaydism was the product of the merging of Batrīs and Jārūdīs. While the texts provide evidence for the existence of Batrīs in the early 2nd/8th century (through clear overlaps between Zaydī and Sunnī traditions), there is little indication of any Jārūdī presence. In the course of the next century, however, Jārūdī influences appear to grow (gradually) until they wholly replace those of the Batrīs by the late 2nd/8th and early 3rd/9th century. These results raise significant doubts regarding the veracity of the narrative of early Zaydism drawn from the heresiographical (and secondary) literature.

An examination of the historical sources offers a possible alternate narrative for early Zaydism that better aligns with our results. Specifically, it may be argued that an overwhelming majority of Zaydīs were initially Batrī. This perspective finds support in the case of Zayd b. ʿAlī who consistently articulated views that were (1) Batrī in character (i.e., regarding the status of Abū Bakr and ʿUmar) and (2) actively opposed by groups with a Jārūdī orientation. Such a state persisted through the early and mid-2nd/8th century, with Zaydī Imāms ascribed various Batrī positions including a belief in the authority of non-ʿAlīd legal scholars (i.e., as in the case of ʿĪsā b. Zayd). A noticeable change occurred in the aftermath of the Battle of Fakhkh (169/786), when the movement's leadership was inherited by Yaḥyā b. ʿAbd Allāh who had been raised in the household of al-Ṣādiq and upheld ritual practices and (possibly) theological doctrines today associated with Jārūdī Zaydism. In the subsequent two decades, Yaḥyā overcame the strident opposition of his (predominantly Batrī) Kūfan followers and reoriented Zaydism in a Jārūdī direction.

This revised narrative closely fits the data from the case studies. It suggests that rather than a merging of Batrī and Jārūdī Shīʿism and a subsequent civil war, Zaydism evolved from one theological position to another through the efforts of a few strong, long-lived leaders. The heresiographical narrative may have simply been an attempt at explaining this transformation. Rarely do heresiographies depict a natural evolution in a sect; rather, they speak of groups differentiating into smaller and smaller subunits as a result of the personal disagreements of their leaders. Zaydism, by contrast, retained a singular name and identity while adopting a new set of central theological (and ritual law) positions. Perhaps the heresiographers attributed these changes to the presence of both tendencies in 122/740? In such a scenario, there would have been no actual evolution but only the resolution of internal tensions between two component factions. These observations about the heresiographical literature remain largely conjectural, but it is worth reiterating that our revised narrative finds strong support in all three of the case studies.

Having affirmed the chronology of one sectarian narrative (i.e., the Imāmīs) and revised that of another (i.e., the Zaydīs), the final part of this study focuses on the actual mechanisms for identity formation. It first examines accounts that deal with the probity of early *ḥadīth* transmitters. Much of this material emphasizes the importance of ritual practice in the determination of a figure's sectarian loyalties. The manner of prayer was particularly significant as a shorthand for assessing the reliability of transmitters, but this assessment also included other ritual acts (e.g., ablution, the times for breaking the fast, pilgrimage). In many cases, the "proper" performance of rituals effectively outweighed adherence to (or advocacy of) problematic theological tenets. Such was the case with Sulaymān al-Aʿmash whose eventual classification as a Sunnī was predicated on his ritual positions as opposed to his theological views that (apparently) included an affirmation of ʿAlī's intercession on the Day of Judgment. The importance of ritual was ultimately institutionalized through a demarcation of sacred space that accompanied the transformation of tribal mosques into sectarian mosques. The process culminated in the 3rd/9th and 4th/10th centuries with a growth in the importance of the pilgrimage, an act perceived as a clear and very public affirmation of sectarian identity.

Bibliography

Note on Alphabetization: Names that begin with articles such as al, von, and van are alphabetized according to the main part of the name (al-Baghawī, for example, appears as Baghawī, al-).

Journal Abbreviations

BSOAS	*Bulletin of the School of Oriental and African Studies*
EI²	*The Encyclopaedia of Islam* (New Edition)
EIʳ	*Encyclopaedia Iranica*
IJMES	*International Journal of Middle Eastern Studies*
ILS	*Islamic Law and Society*
JAL	*Journal of Arabic Literature*
JAOS	*Journal of the American Oriental Society*
JNES	*Journal of Near Eastern Studies*
JIS	*Journal of Islamic Studies*
JSAI	*Jerusalem Studies in Arabic and Islam*
JSS	*Journal of Semitic Studies*

Abbott, Nabia, *Studies in Literary Papyri* (Chicago: University of Chicago Press, 1957–72).

Abū Dāwūd Sulaymān b. al-Ash‘ath (d. 275/889), *Sunan* (Beirut: Dār Ibn Ḥazm, 1998).

Abū Ḥayyān al-Andalūsī, Muḥammad b. Yūsuf (d. 745/1344), *al-Baḥr al-muḥīṭ*, ed. ‘Ādil Aḥmad ‘Abd al-Mawjūd and ‘Alī Muḥammad Mu‘awwaḍ, 8 vols. (Beirut: Dār al-Kutub al-‘Ilmiyya, 1993).

Abū Nu‘aym, Aḥmad b. ‘Abd Allāh (d. 429/1038), *Ḥilyat al-awliyā’*, 10 vols. (Cairo: Maktabat al-Khānjī, 1932–8).

Abū Ya‘lā ibn al-Farrā’, Muḥammad b. al-Ḥusayn b. Khalaf (d. 458/1066), *al-Jāmi‘ al-ṣaghīr fi’l-fiqh*, ed. Nāṣir b. Sa‘ūd b. ‘Abd Allāh al-Salāma (Riyadh: Dār Aṭlas, 2000).

Aḥmad b. Ibrāhīm (d. 353/864), *al-Maṣābīḥ*, ed. ʿAbd Allāh b. ʿAbd Allāh b. Aḥmad al-Ḥūthī (Amman: Muʾassasat al-Imām Zayd b. ʿAlī al-Thaqafiyya, 2002). Aḥmad b. Ibrāhīm authored the first half of this work ending with (or after) the entry on Yaḥyā b. Zayd (d. 125/743).

Aḥmad b. ʿĪsā b. Zayd (d. 248/862), *Amālī*, preserved in ʿAlī b. Ismāʿīl b. ʿAbd Allāh al-Muʾayyad al-Ṣanʿānī, *Kitāb raʾb al-ṣadʿ*, ed. ʿAlī b. Ismāʿīl b. ʿAbd Allāh al-Muʾayyad, 3 vols. (Beirut: Dār al-Nafāʾis, 1999).

ʿAlawī, Muḥammad b. ʿAlī al- (d. 445/1053), *al-Jāmiʿ al-kāfī*, (Ṣanʿāʾ: Muʾassasat al-Imām Zayd b. ʿAlī al-Thaqafiyya, forthcoming).

ʿAlī b. Bilāl (fl. 5th/11th century), *al-Maṣābīḥ*, ed. ʿAbd Allāh b. ʿAbd Allāh b. Aḥmad al-Ḥūthī (Amman: Muʾassasat al-Imām Zayd b. ʿAlī al-Thaqafiyya, 2002). ʿAlī b. Bilāl authored the second half of this work beginning with (or after) the entry on Yaḥyā b. Zayd (d. 125/743).

Amir-Moezzi, Muḥammad ʿAlī, *The Divine Guide in Early Shīʿism*, trans. David Streight (Albany: State University of New York Press, 1994).

Arendonk, Cornelius van, *Les débuts de l'imāmat zaidite au Yémen*, trans. Jacques Ryckmans (Leiden: Brill, 1960).

Ashʿarī, Abū al-Ḥasan ʿAlī b. Ismāʿīl al- (d. 324/935), *Maqālāt al-islāmiyyīn*, ed. Muḥammad Muḥyī al-Dīn (Cairo: Maktabat al-Nahḍa al-Miṣriyya, 1969).

ʿAyyāshī, Muḥammad b. Masʿūd al- (d. early 4th/10th century), *Tafsīr*, ed. Hāshim al-Rasūlī al-Maḥallātī, 2 vols. (Qumm: Chāpkhānah-i ʿIlmiyyah, 1961–2).

ʿAyyāshī, Muḥammad b. Masʿūd al-, *Tafsīr*, 3 vols. (Qumm: Muʾassasat al-Biʿtha, 2000).

Azmi, Mohammad Mustafa, *Studies in Early Ḥadīth Literature* (Indianapolis: American Trust Publications, 1978).

Baghawī, Ḥusayn b. Masʿūd al- (d. 516/1123), *Sharḥ al-sunna*, ed. Saʿīd Muḥammad al-Laḥḥām, 8 vols. (Beirut: Dār al-Fikr, 1994).

Bājī, Sulaymān b. Khalaf b. Saʿd al- (d. 474/1081), *al-Taʿdīl waʾl-tajrīḥ*, ed. Aḥmad Labzār, 3 vols. (Rabat: Wizārat al-Awqāf waʾl-Shuʾūn al-Islāmiyya, 1991).

Balādhurī, Aḥmad b. Yaḥyā al- (d. 278/892), *Ansāb al-ashrāf*, ed. Maḥmūd al-Fardūs al-ʿAẓm, 25 vols. (Damascus: Dār al-Yaqẓa, 1996–).

Barqī, Aḥmad b. Muḥammad al- (d. 273/887–8), *al-Maḥāsin*, ed. al-Sayyid Mahdī al-Rajjāʾī, 2 vols. (Qumm: al-Muʿāwiniyya al-Thaqafiyya, 1992).

Bayhaqī, Aḥmad b. al-Ḥusayn al- (d. 438/1066), *al-Sunan al-kubrā*, ed. Muḥammad ʿAbd al-Qādir ʿAṭā, 11 vols. (Beirut: Dār al-Kutub al-ʿIlmiyya, 1994).

Bayhoum-Daou, Tamima, "Hishām b. al-Ḥakam and His Doctrine of the Imām's Knowledge," *JSS*, 48 (2003) 71–108.

Bishr b. Ghānim (d. 199/815?), *al-Mudawwana al-kubrā*, ed. Muḥammad b. Yūsuf Aṭfayyish, 2 vols. (Syria: Dār al-Yaqẓa al-ʿArabiyya, 1974?).

Bourdieu, Pierre, *Distinction*, trans. Richard Nice (Cambridge, MA: Harvard University Press, 1984).

Brown, Jonathan, *The Canonization of al-Bukhārī and Muslim* (Leiden: Brill, 2007).

"The Canonization of Ibn Mājah," *Ecriture de l'histoire et processus de canonisation dans les premiers siècles de l'islam* in *Revue des Mondes Musulmans et de la Méditerranée*, 129 (2011).

Buckley, Ron, "Ja'far al-Ṣādiq as a Source of Shī'ī Traditions," *The Islamic Quarterly*, 43 (1999) 37–58.

"On the Origins of Shī'ī Ḥadīth," *Muslim World*, 88 (1998) 165–84.

Bukhārī, Muḥammad b. Ismā'īl al- (d. 256/870), *Jāmi' al-ṣaḥīḥ*, ed. Abū Suhayb al-Karmī (Riyadh: Bayt al-Afkār, 1998).

Burāqī, al-Ḥusayn b. Aḥmad al- (d. 1332/1914), *Tārīkh Kūfa*, ed. Mājid b. Aḥmad al-'Aṭiyya (Qumm(?): Intishārāt al-Maktaba al-Ḥaydariyya, 2003).

Calder, Norman, "The Significance of the Term Imām in Early Islamic Jurisprudence," *Zeitschrift fur Geschichte der Arabisch-Islamischen Wissenschaften*, 1 (1984) 253–64.

Studies in Early Muslim Jurisprudence (Oxford: Clarendon, 1993).

Cook, Michael, *Commanding Right and Forbidding Wrong in Islamic Thought* (Cambridge: Cambridge University Press, 2000).

Early Muslim Dogma (Cambridge: Cambridge University Press, 1981).

"Eschatology and the Dating of Traditions," *Princeton Papers in Near Eastern Studies*, 1 (1992) 23–47.

"The Opponents of the Writing of Tradition in Early Islam," *Arabica*, 44 (1997) 437–530.

Crone, Patricia, *God's Rule* (New York: Columbia University Press, 2004).

Meccan Trade and the Rise of Islam (Princeton: Princeton University Press, 1987).

"Serjeant and Meccan Trade," *Arabica*, 39 (1992) 216–40.

Crone, Patricia and Martin Hinds, *God's Caliph* (Cambridge and New York: Cambridge University Press, 1986).

Dakake, Maria, *The Charismatic Community* (Albany: State University of New York Press, 2007).

Dānī, 'Uthmān b. Sa'īd al- (d. 444/1053), *al-Bayān fī 'add āy al-Qur'ān*, ed. Ghānim Qaddūrī al-Ḥamad (Kuwait: Markaz al-Makhṭūṭat wa'l-Turāth wa'l-Wathā'iq, 1994).

Dārimī, 'Abd Allāh b. 'Abd al-Raḥmān al- (d. 255/869), *Sunan*, ed. Ḥusayn Salīm Asad Darānī, 4 vols. (Riyadh: Dār al-Mughnī, 2000).

Sunan, ed. Muṣṭafā Dīb al-Bughā (Damascus: Dār al-Qalam, 1991).

Dhahabī, Muḥammad b. Aḥmad al- (d. 748/1348), *Kitāb al-jarḥ wa'l-ta'dīl*, ed. Khalīl b. Muḥammad al-'Arabī, 2 vols. (Cairo: al-Fārūq al-Ḥadītha, 2003).

Mīzān al-i'tidāl fī naqd al-rijāl, ed. Ṣidqī Jamīl al-'Aṭṭār, 4 vols. (Beirut: Dār al-Fikr, 1990).

Tārīkh al-islām, 70 vols., ed. 'Umar 'Abd al-Salam Tadmurī, 70 vols. (Beirut: Dār al-Kitāb al-'Arabī, 1987–).

Djait, Hichem, *al-Kūfa: naissance de la ville islamique* (Paris: Editions G.P. Maisonneuve et Larose, 1986).

Donaldson, Dwight, *The Shi'ite Religion* (London: Luzak, 1933).

Donner, Fred, *The Early Islamic Conquests* (Princeton: Princeton University Press, 1981).

Narratives of Islamic Origins (Princeton: Darwin, 1998).

Dutton, Yasin, *The Origins of Islamic Law* (Surrey: Curzon, 1999).

Original Islam (New York: Routledge, 2007).

"Sunna, Ḥadīth, and Madinan 'Amal," *JIS*, 4 (1993) 1–31.
El Shamsy, Ahmed, *From Tradition to Law* (Harvard University Ph.D, 2009).
Eliash, Joseph, "On the Genesis and Development of the Twelver-Shīʿī Three-tenet *Shahādah*," *Der Islam*, 47 (1971) 265–77.
Encyclopaedia Iranica, ed. Ehsan Yarshater (London: Routledge, 1982–).
Encyclopaedia of Islam, 12 vols., 2nd edition (Leiden: Brill, 1960–2004).
Ess, Josef van, "The Kāmilīya: On the Genesis of a Heresiographical Tradition," in Etan Kohlberg (ed.), *Shīʿism* (Burlington: Ashgate, 2003), 209–19.
Theologie und Gesellschaft im 2. und 3. Jahrhundert Hidschra, 5 vols. (Berlin: de Gruyter, 1991–7).
Goldziher, Ignaz, *Muslim Studies*, trans. C. R. Barber and S. M. Stern, 2 vols. (Chicago: Aldine, 1971).
Gunther, Sebastian, "*Maqātil* Literature in Medieval Islam," *JAL*, 25 (1994) 192–212.
Hādī ilā'l-Ḥaqq, Yaḥyā b. al-Ḥusayn al- (d. 298/911), *Kitāb al-aḥkām*, ed. Abū al-Ḥasan 'Alī b. Aḥmad b. Abī Ḥarīsa (Yemen(?): n.p., 1990).
Haider, Najam, *The Birth of Sectarian Identity in 2nd/8th century Kūfa* (Princeton University Ph.D., 2007).
"A Community Divided," *JAOS*, 128 (2008) 459–76.
"The Contested Life of 'Īsā b. Zayd," in Farhad Daftary and Gurdofarid Miskinzoda (eds.), *The Study of Shīʿī Islam* (London, forthcoming 2012).
"Prayer, Mosque and Pilgrimage," *ILS*, 16 (2009) 151–74.
Ḥalabī, Abū al-Ṣalāḥ Taqī al-Dīn b. Najm al-Dīn al- (d. 447/1055), *al-Kāfī fi'l-fiqh*, ed. Riḍā Ustādī (Iṣfahān: Maktabat al-Imām 'Amīr al-Mu'minīn 'Alī, 1980).
Halevi, Leor, *Muhammad's Grave* (New York: Columbia University Press, 2007).
Hallaq, Wael, "The Authenticity of Prophetic *Ḥadīth*," *Studia Islamica*, 89 (1999) 75–90.
"On Dating Mālik's *Muwaṭṭa'*," *UCLA Journal of Islamic and Near Eastern Law*, 1 (2001) 47–65.
The Origins and Evolution of Islamic Law (Cambridge: Cambridge University Press, 2005).
Hattox, Ralph, *Coffee and Coffeehouses* (Seattle: University of Washington Press, 1985).
Haykel, Bernard, *Revival and Reform in Islam* (Cambridge: Cambridge University Press, 2003).
Hetherington, Kevin, *Expressions of Identity* (London: Sage, 1998).
Hinds, Martin, "Kūfan Political Alignments and Their Background in the Mid 7th Century A.D.," *IJMES*, 2 (1972) 346–67.
"The Murder of the Caliph 'Uthmān," *IJMES*, 3 (1972) 450–69.
"The Ṣiffīn Arbitration Agreement," *JSS*, 17 (1972) 93–113.
Hodgson, Marshall, "How did the early Shī'a become sectarian?" *JAOS*, 75 (1955) 1–13.
The Venture of Islam, 3 vols. (Chicago: University of Chicago Press, 1974).
Ḥurr al-'Āmilī, Muḥammad b. al-Ḥasan al- (d. 1104/1693), *Wasā'il al-shīʿa*, 30 vols. (Qumm: Mu'assasat Āl al-Bayt, 1990).

Ibn 'Abd al-Barr, Yūsuf b. 'Abd Allāh (d. 463/1071), *al-Inṣāf fī mā bayna al-'ulamā' fī qirā'at bismillāh al-raḥmān al-raḥīm min al-ikhtilāf*, ed. 'Abd al-Laṭīf b. Muḥammad (Riyadh: n.p., 1997).
al-Istidhkār, ed. 'Alī al-Najdī Nāsif (Cairo: n.p., 1971–3).
al-Tamhīd, ed. Muṣṭafā b. Aḥmad al-'Alawī and Muḥammad 'Abd al-Kabīr al-Bakrī, 10 vols. (Lahore: al-Maktabat al-Qudūsiyya, 1983).
Ibn Abī Ḥātim, 'Abd al-Raḥmān b. Muḥammad (d. 327/938), *Kitāb al-jarḥ wa'l-ta'dīl*, 4 vols. (Ḥaydarabad: Maṭba'at Majlis Dā'irat al-Ma'arif al-'Uthmāniyya, 1941–53).
Ibn Abī Shayba, 'Abd Allāh b. Muḥammad (d. 235/849), *Muṣannaf*, ed. Sa'īd al-Laḥḥām, 9 vols. (Beirut: Dār al-Fikr, 1989).
Ibn Abī Ya'lā, Muḥammad b. Muḥammad b. al-Ḥusayn (d. 526/1132), *Kitāb al-tamām*, ed. 'Abd Allāh b. Muḥammad b. Aḥmad al-Ṭayyār *et al.*, 2 vols. (Riyadh: Dār al-'Āṣima, 1993).
Ibn Abī Zayd, al-Qayrawānī (d. 386/996), *Kitāb al-nawādir wa'l-ziyādāt*, ed. 'Abd al-Fattāḥ Muḥammad al-Ḥulw, 15 vols. (Beirut: Dār al-Gharb al-Islāmī, 1999).
Ibn al-'Arabī, Abū Bakr Muḥammad b. 'Abd Allāh (d. 543/1148), *Aḥkām al-Qur'ān*, ed. Muḥammad Bakr Ismā'īl, 4 vols. (Cairo: Dar al-Manār, 2002).
Ibn Bābawayh, Muḥammad b. 'Alī al-Qummī (d. 381/991), *Hidāya* (Qumm: Mu'assasat al-Imām al-Hādī, 1997).
Kitāb al-khiṣāl, ed. 'Alī Akbar al-Ghaffārī (Tehran: Maktabat al-Ṣadūq, 1969).
Man lā yaḥḍuruhu al-faqīh, ed. 'Alī Akbar al-Ghaffārī, 4 vols. (Qumm: Jamā'at al-Mudarrisīn, 1983).
Muqni' (Qum: Mu'assasat al-Imām al-Hādī, 1994).
Ibn Dāwūd al-Ḥillī, al-Ḥasan b. 'Alī (d. 740/1340), *Kitāb al-rijāl*, (Tehran: Dānishgāh, 1963).
Ibn Furāt al-Kūfī (fl. 4th/10th century), *Tafsīr*, ed. Muḥammad al-Kāẓim (Tehran: Mu'assasat al-Ṭab' wa'l-Nashr, 1990).
Ibn Ḥanbal, Aḥmad b. Muḥammad (d. 241/855), *Kitāb al-ashriba*, ed. Ṣubḥī Jāsim (Baghdad: Maṭba'at al-'Ānī, 1976).
Masā'il al-imām Aḥmad ibn Ḥanbal (riwāyat ibnihī Abī Faḍl Ṣāliḥ), ed. Faḍl al-Raḥmān Dīn Muḥammad, 3 vols. (Delhi: Dār al-'Ilmiyya, 1988).
Masā'il al-imām Aḥmad ibn Ḥanbal (riwāyat ibnihī Abī Faḍl Ṣāliḥ), ed. Ṭāriq b. 'Awaḍ Allāh b. Muḥammad (Riyadh: Dār al-Waṭan, 1999).
Masā'il al-imām Aḥmad ibn Ḥanbal (riwāyat Isḥāq b. Manṣūr), ed. Khālid b. Maḥmūd al-Rabāṭ, 2 vols. (Riyadh: Dār al-Hijra, 2004).
Masā'il al-imām Aḥmad ibn Ḥanbal (riwāyat Isḥāq b. Manṣūr), ed. Muḥammad b. 'Abd Allāh al-Zāḥim, 10 vols. (Medina: Wizārat al-Ta'līm al-'Ālī, 2004).
Ibn Ḥazm, 'Alī b. Aḥmad (d. 456/1064), *al-Muḥallā bi-'l-āthār*, ed. 'Abd al-Ghaffār Sulaymān al-Bundārī, 12 vols. (Beirut: Dār al-Kutub al-'Ilmiyya, 1988).
Ibn al-Humām, Muḥammad b. 'Abd al-Wāḥid (d. 863/1459), *Fatḥ al-qadīr*, ed. Muḥammad Maḥbūb al-Ḥalabī, 10 vols. (Cairo: Maktabat Muṣṭafā al-Bābī al-Ḥalabī, 1970).
Ibn Idrīs al-Ḥillī, Muḥammad b. Manṣūr (d. 598/1202), *Kitāb al-sarā'ir*, 3 vols. (Qumm: Mu'assasat al-Nashr al-Islāmī, 1990).

Ibn al-Jawzī, Abū al-Faraj 'Abd al-Raḥmān b. 'Alī (d. 597/1201), *al-Muntaẓam fī tārīkh al-mulūk wa'l-umam*, ed. Muḥammad 'Abd al-Qādir 'Aṭā and Muṣṭafā 'Abd al-Qādir 'Aṭā, 20 vols. (Beirut: Dār al-Kutub al-'Ilmiyya, 1992).
Ibn Kathīr, Ismā'īl b. 'Umar (d. 774/1373), *Tafsīr*, ed. Muṣṭafā al-Sayyid Muḥammad *et al.*, 15 vols. (Jīza: Mu'assasat Qurṭuba, 2000).
Tafsīr al-Qur'ān al-'aẓīm, 7 vols. (Beirut: Dār al-Andalus, 1966).
Ibn Ma'īn, Yaḥyā (d. 233/848), *Min kalām Abī Zakariyya Yaḥyā b. Ma'īn fī rijāl*, ed. Abū 'Umar Muḥammad b. 'Alī al-Azharī (Cairo: al-Fārūq al-Ḥadītha, 2008).
Ibn Māja, Muḥammad b. Yazīd (d. 273/887), *Sunan* (Karachi: n.p., 1952–3).
Ibn al-Mashhadī, Muḥammad b. Ja'far (d. 594/1198), *al-Mazār al-kabīr*, ed. Jawād al-Qayyūmī al-Iṣfahānī (Qumm: Mu'assasat al-Āfāq, 1998).
Ibn Miftāḥ, 'Abd Allāh b. Abī al-Qāsim (d. 877/1472), *Sharḥ al-Azhār*, 10 vols. (Ṣan'a': Wizārat al-'Adl, 2003).
Ibn al-Muqaffa', 'Abd Allāh (d. 142/760), *Risālat ibn al-Muqaffa' fī'l-ṣaḥāba* in *Āthār Ibn Muqaffa'* (Beirut: al-Kutub al-'Ilmiyya, 1989).
Ibn al-Murtaḍā, Aḥmad b. Yaḥyā (d. 840/1437), *al-Baḥr al-zakhkhār*, ed. 'Abd Allāh b. 'Abd al-Karīm al-Jarāfī, 6 vols. (Beirut: Mu'assasat al-Risāla, 1975).
Kitāb al-azhār (Beirut: Dār al-Maktabat al-Ḥayā, 1973).
Ibn al-Murtaḍā, Ibrāhīm b. al-Qāsim (d. 547/1152) *Ṭabaqāt al-Zaydiyya*, (mss Yemen).
Ibn al-Muṭahhar, Ḥasan b. Yūsuf al-'Allāma al-Ḥillī (d. 726/1325), *Mukhtalaf al-shī'a*, 10 vols. (Qumm: Markaz al-Abḥāth wa'l-Darasāt al-Islāmiyya, 1991).
Muntahā al-maṭlab fī taḥqīq al-madhhab, 15 vols. (Mashhad: n.p., 1991).
Tadhkirat al-fuqahā', 20 vols. (Qumm: Mu'assasat Āl al-Bayt, 1993–4).
Ibn Qudāma, Muwaffaq al-Dīn 'Abd Allāh b. Aḥmad (d. 620/1223), *al-Mughnī*, ed. 'Abd Allāh b. 'Abd al-Muḥsin al-Turkī and 'Abd al-Fattāḥ Muḥammad al-Ḥulw, 15 vols. (Cairo: Hajr, 1986).
al-Mughnī, ed. Muḥammad Sharaf al-Dīn al-Khaṭṭāb *et al.*, 16 vols. (Cairo: Dār al-Ḥadīth, 1996).
Ibn Qulūyah, Ja'far b. Muḥammad (d. 367/978–9), *Kāmil al-ziyārāt*, ed. Bihrād al-Ja'farī (Tehran: Nashr Ṣadūq, 1996).
Ibn Qutayba (d. 276/889?), 'Abd Allāh b. Muslim, *Ma'ārif*, ed. Tharwat Ukāshah (Cairo: Dār al-Ma'ārif, 1969).
Ibn Rushd al-Ḥafīd, Muḥammad b. Aḥmad (d. 595/1199), *Bidāyat al-mujtahid*, ed. Muḥammad 'Alī al-Sayyid Muḥammad (Qumm: Mu'assasat al-Nashr al-Islāmī 1999–).
Ibn Rushd al-Jadd, Muḥammad b. Aḥmad (d. 520/1126), *al-Muqaddamāt*, ed. Muḥammad Ḥujjī, 3 vols. (Beirut: Dār al-Gharb al-Islāmī, 1988).
Ibn Sa'd, Muḥammad (d. 230/9845), *Kitāb al-ṭabaqāt al-kabīr*, ed. 'Alī Muḥammad 'Umar, 11 vols. (Cairo: Maktabat al-Khānjī, 2001).
al-Ṭabaqāt al-kubrā, ed. Muḥammad 'Abd al-Qādir 'Aṭā, 9 vols. (Beirut: Dār al-Kutub al-'Ilmiyya, 1991).
Ibn Ṭāhir al-Baghdādī, 'Abd al-Qāhir (d. 428/1037), *al-Farq bayn al-firaq*, ed. Muḥammad 'Uthmān al-Khusht (Cairo: Maktabat Ibn Sīnā, 1988).
'Ijlī, Aḥmad b. Abd Allāh al- (d. 261/875), *Tārīkh al-thiqāt* (Beirut: Dār al-Kutub al-'Ilmiyya, 1984).

Iṣbahānī, 'Alī b. al-Ḥusayn Abū al-Faraj al- (d. 356/967), *Kitāb al-aghānī*, ed. Ibrāhīm Abyārī, 31 vols. (Cairo: Dār al-Sha'b, 1969–).
Maqātil al-ṭālibiyyīn, ed. Sayyid Aḥmad Ṣaqr (Beirut: Mu'assasat al-'Ālamī, 1998).
'Izzī, Abd Allāh al-, *'Ulūm al-ḥadīth 'inda al-Zaydiyya* (Amman: Mu'assasat al-Imām Zayd b. 'Alī al-Thaqafiyya, 2001).
Jarrar, Maher, "Arba'u rasā'il Zaydiyya mubakkira" in Ibrāhīm al-Sa'āfīn (ed.), *Fī miḥrāb al-ma'rifa* (Beirut: Dār Ṣādir, 1997), 267–304.
"Ibn Abī Yaḥyā," in Kees Versteegh *et al.* (eds.), *Transmission and Dynamics of the Textual Sources of Islam* (Leiden: Brill, forthcoming 2011).
"Some Aspects of Imāmī Influence on Early Zaydite Theology," in Rainer Brunner *et al.* (eds.), *Islamstudien Ohne Ende*, ed. Rainer Brunner (Würzburg: Deutsche Morgenländische Gesellschaft, 2002), 201–23.
"*Tafsīr Abī l-Jārūd an al-Imām al-Bāqir*," *Abhath*, 50–1 (2002–3) 37–9.
Jaṣṣāṣ, Aḥmad b. 'Alī al- (d. 370/981), *Aḥkām al-Qur'ān*, 3 vols. (Beirut: Dār al-Kitāb al-'Arabī, 1978?).
Jeffery, Arthur, *Materials for the History of the Text of the Qur'ān* (New York: AMS Press, 1975).
Juynboll, G. H. A., "Early Islamic Society as Reflected in Its Use of *Isnāds*," *Le Meseon*, 107 (1994) 151–94.
"Muslim's Introduction to His *Ṣaḥīḥ*," *JSAI*, 5 (1984) 263–311.
"Some *Isnād*-Analytic Methods Illustrated on the Basis of Several Woman-Demeaning Sayings from *Ḥadīth* Literature," *al-Qantara*, 10 (1989) 343–83.
"Some Notes on Islam's First *Fuqahā'* Distilled From Early *Ḥadīth* Literature," *Arabica*, 39 (1992) 287–314.
Kāsānī, 'Alā' al-Dīn Abū Bakr b. Mas'ūd al- (d. 587/1191), *Badā'i' al-ṣanā'i'*, ed. Zakariyya 'Alī Yūsuf, 10 vols. (Cairo: Zakariyya 'Alī Yūsuf, 1968).
Kennedy, Hugh, *The Prophet and the Age of the Caliphates* (New York: Longman, 1986).
Khaṭīb al-Baghdādī, Aḥmad b. 'Alī (d. 463/1071) *al-Jāmi' li-akhlāq al-rāwī*, ed. Maḥmūd al-Ṭaḥḥān, 2 vols. (Riyadh: Maktabat al-Ma'ārif, 1983).
Kitāb al-kifāya fī 'ilm al-riwāya (Hyderabad: Idārat Jam'īyat Dā'irāt al-Ma'ārif al-'Uthmāniyya, 1938).
Tārīkh madīnat al-salām. ed. Bashār Ma'rūf, 17 vols. (Beirut: Dār al-Gharb al-Islāmī, 2001).
Khiraqī, 'Umar b. al-Ḥusayn al- (d. 334/945), *Mukhtaṣar* (Damascus: Mu'assasat Dār al-Salām, 1959).
Kindī, Muḥammad b. Yūsuf al- (d. 349/961), *Wulāt Miṣr*, ed. Ḥusayn Naṣṣār (Beirut: Dār Ṣādir, 1959).
Kister, M. J., "The Expedition of Bi'r Ma'ūna," in George Makdisi (ed.), *Arabic and Islamic studies in honor of Hamilton A.R. Gibb* (Leiden: Brill, 1965), 337–57.
Kohlberg, Etan, "Early Attestations of the term 'Ithnā 'Ashariyya," *JSAI*, 24 (2000) 343–57.
"From Imāmiyya to Ithnā-'Ashariyya," *BSOAS*, 39 (1976) 521–34.
"Imām and Community in the Pre-*Ghayba* Period," in Said Amir Arjomand (ed.), *Authority and Political Culture in Shī'ism* (Albany: State University of New York Press, 1988), 25–53.

"Some Imāmī Shī'ī Views on the Ṣaḥāba," *JSAI*, 5 (1984) 143–75.
"Some Zaydī Views on the Companions of the Prophet," *BSOAS*, 39 (1976) 91–8.
"The Term *Rāfiḍa* in Imāmī Shī'ī Usage," *JAOS*, 99 (1979) 677–9.
"*Al-Uṣūl al-arba'umi'a*," *JSAI*, 10 (1987) 128–66.

Kūfī, Abū Isḥāq Ibrāhīm b. Muḥammad al- (d. 283/896), *al-Ghārāt*, ed. J. Muḥaddith Urmawī, 2 vols. (Tehran: Anjuman-i Āthār-i Millī, 1975).

Kūfī, Muḥammad b. Sulaymān al- (d. after 309/921), *Kitāb al-muntakhab* (Ṣan'ā': Dār al-Ḥikma al-Yamāniyya, 1993).

Kulaynī, Muḥammad b. Ya'qūb al- (d. 329/941), *Uṣūl min al-Kāfī*, ed. 'Alī Akbar al-Ghaffārī, 8 vols. (Tehran: Dār al-Kutub al-Islāmiyya, 1983).

Lalani, Arzina, *Early Shī'ī Thought* (London: I. B. Taurus, 2000).

Lucas, Scott, *Constructive Critics, Ḥadīth Literature, and the Articulation of Sunnī Islam* (Leiden: Brill, 2004).
"Divorce, *Ḥadīth*-Scholar Style," *JIS*, 19 (2008) 325–68.
"The Legal Principles of Muḥammad b. Ismā'īl al-Bukhārī and Their Relationship to Classical Salafi Islam," *ILS*, 13 (2006) 289–324.
"Where Are the Legal *Ḥadīth*," *ILS*, 15 (2008) 283–314.

Madelung, Wilferd, "Imām al-Qāsim b. Ibrāhīm," in *On both sides of al-Mandab: Ethiopia. South-Arabic and Islamic studies presented to Oscar Löfgren on his ninetieth birthday* (Stockholm, n.p., 1989).
Der Imam al-Qāsim ibn Ibrāhīm und die Glaubenslehre der Zaiditen (Berlin: de Gruyter, 1965).
"Some Remarks on the Imāmī *Firaq* Literature," in Etan Kohlberg (ed.), *Shī'ism*, (Burlington: Ashgate, 2003), 153–67.
The Succession to Muḥammad (Cambridge: Cambridge University Press, 1997).

Maḥbūbī, 'Ubayd Allāh b. Mas'ūd al- (d. 747/1346), *Mukhtaṣar al-Wiqāyāh*, 2 vols. (Beirut: Dār al-Kutub al-'Ilmiyya, 2005).

Majlisī, Muḥammad Bāqir (d. 1110/1699), *Biḥār al-anwār*, ed. Muḥammad Bāqir al-Maḥmūdī, 110 vols. (Tehran: Wizārat al-Irshād al-Islāmī, 1986–).

Mālik b. Anas (d. 179/795), *al-Muwaṭṭa'*, ed. Muḥammad Fu'ād 'Abd al-Bāqī, 2 vols. (Cairo: Dār Iḥyā' al-Kutub al-'Arabiyya, 1951).
Muwaṭṭa' (riwāyat 'Abd Allāh al-Qa'nabī), ed. 'Abd al-Majīd Turkī (Beirut: Dār al-Gharb al-Islāmī, 1999).
al-Muwaṭṭa' (riwāyat Muḥammad al-Shaybānī) ed. 'Abd al-Wahhāb 'Abd al-Laṭīf (Beirut: al-Maktabat al-'Ilmiyya, 2003).
Muwaṭṭa' (riwāyat Muḥammad al-Shaybānī), ed. 'Abd al-Wahhāb 'Abd al-Laṭīf (Cairo: Jumhūriyya al-'Arabiyya al-Muttaḥida, 1967).
al-Muwaṭṭa' (riwāyat Suwayd b. Sa'īd), ed. 'Abd al-Majīd Turkī (Beirut: Dār al-Gharb al-Islāmī, 1994).
al-Muwaṭṭa' (riwāyat Yaḥyā b. Yaḥyā al-Laythī), ed. Bashshār 'Awwād Ma'rūf, 2 vols. (Beirut: Dār al-Gharb al-Islāmī, 1996).

Marghīnānī, 'Alī b. Abī Bakr al- (d. 593/1197), *al-Hidāya*, ed. Muḥammad Tāmir and Ḥāfiẓ 'Āshūr Ḥāfiẓ (Cairo: Dār al-Salam, 2000).

Mas'ūdī, 'Alī b. al-Ḥusayn al- (d. 344/956?), *Kitāb al-tanbīh wa'l-ishrāf*, ed. De Goeje (Leiden: Brill, 1893).

al-Murūj al-dhahab, 4 vols. (Beirut: Dār al-Andalus, 1965).

Māwardī, 'Alī b. Muḥammad al- (d. 450/1058), *al-Ḥāwī al-kabīr*, ed. 'Ādil Aḥmad 'Abd al-Mawjūd and 'Alī Muḥammad Mu'awwaḍ, 24 vols. (Beirut: Dār al-Fikr, 1994).

Melchert, Christopher, *The Formation of the Sunnī Schools of Law* (Leiden: Brill, 1997).

"How Ḥanafism Came to Originate in Kūfa and Traditionism in Medina," *ILS*, 6 (1999) 318–47.

"The Life and Works of Abū Dāwūd al-Sijistānī," *Al-Qantara*, 29 (2008) 9–44.

"The *Musnad* of Aḥmad ibn Ḥanbal," *Der Islam*, 82 (2005) 32–51.

"Sectaries in the Six Books," *Muslim World*, 82(1992) 291.

Mizzī, Yūsuf b. al-Zakī 'Abd al-Raḥmān al- (d. 742/1341), *Tahdhīb al-kamāl fī asmā' al-rijāl*, ed. Bashshār 'Awwād Ma'rūf (Beirut: Mu'assasat al-Risāla, 1992).

Modarressi, Hossein, *An Introduction to Shī'ī Law* (London: Ithaca Press, 1984).

Crisis and Consolidation (Princeton: Darwin Press, 1993).

Tradition and Survival, vol. 1 (Oxford: One World, 2003).

Sanadīyāt (New Jersey: n.p., 2008).

Motzki, Harold, "The Author and His Work in Islamic Literature of the First Centuries," *JSAI*, 28 (2003) 171–201.

The Biography of Muhammad (Leiden: Brill, 2000).

"Dating Muslim Traditions," *Arabica*, 52 (2005) 204–53.

Ḥadīth, ed. Harald Motzki (Burlington: Ashgate, 2004).

"The *Muṣannaf* of 'Abd al-Razzāq al-Ṣan'ānī as a source of Authentic *Aḥādīth* of the First Century A.H.," *JNES*, 60 (1991) 1–21.

The Origins of Islamic Jurisprudence, trans. Marion Katz (Leiden: Brill, 2002).

"The Prophet and the Cat," *JSAI*, 22 (1998) 18–83.

"The Question of the Authenticity of Muslim Traditions Reconsidered," in Herbert Berg (ed.), *Method and Theory in the Study of Islamic Origins* (Leiden: Brill, 2003), 211–58.

Mu'ayyad bi-Allāh Aḥmad b. al-Ḥusayn al- (d. 411/1020), *al-Tajrīd*, ed. 'Abd Allāh Ḥamūd al-'Izzī (Amman: Mu'assasat al-Imām Zayd b. 'Alī al-Thaqafiyya, 2002).

Mu'ayyad bi-Allāh, Yaḥyā b. Ḥamza b. 'Alī al- (d. 749/1348), *al-Intiṣār 'alā 'ulamā' al-amṣār*, ed. 'Abd al-Wahhāb b. 'Alī al-Mu'ayyad and 'Alī b. Aḥmad Mufaḍḍal, 3 vols. (Amman: Mu'assasat al-Imām Zayd b. 'Alī al-Thaqafiyya, 2002).

Mufīd, Muḥammad b. Muḥammad al-, *Kitāb al-mazār* (Qumm: Madrasat al-Imām al-Mahdī, 1988).

al-Muqni'a (Qumm: Mu'assasat al-Nashr al-Islāmī, 1990).

Muḥaqqiq al-Ḥillī, Ja'far b. al-Ḥasan al- (d. 676/1277), *Sharā'i' al-islām*, 4 vols. (Tehran: Intishārāt Istiqlāl, 1994).

Sharā'i' al-islām, ed. 'Abd al-Ḥusayn Muḥammad 'Alī Baqqāl, 4 vols. (Qumm: Mu'assasat al-Ma'ārif al-Islāmiyya, 1994).

Muslim b. al-Ḥajjāj al-Qushayrī (d. 261/875), *Jāmi' al-ṣaḥīḥ*, ed. Muḥammad Fu'ād 'Abd al-Bāqī, 5 vols. (Cairo: Dār Iḥyā' al-Kutub al-'Arabiyya, 1955–6).

Muzanī, Ismāʿīl b. Yaḥyā al- (d. 264/878), *Mukhtaṣar* published as vol. 9 of al-Shāfiʿī, *Mukhtaṣar kitāb al-ʿUmm*, 9 vols., ed. Ḥusayn ʿAbd al-Ḥamīd Nīl (Beirut: Dār al-Arqam, 1993).
Najāshī, Aḥmad b. ʿAlī al- (d. 449/1058), *Rijāl al-Najāshī*, ed. Muḥammad Jawād al-Nāʾīnī, 2 vols. (Beirut: Dār al-Aḍwāʾ 1988).
Nasāʾī, Aḥmad b. Shuʿayb al- (d. 303/915), *Kitāb al-sunan al-kubrā*, ed. Ḥasan ʿAbd al-Munʿim Shalabī, 12 vols. (Beirut: Muʾassasat al-Risāla, 2001).
Sunan, 8 vols. (Cairo: n.p., 1930).
Sunan al-Nasāʾī, 9 vols. (Beirut: Dār al-Maʿrifa, 1991).
Nāshiʾ al-Akbar (Pseudo), ʿAbd Allāh b. Muḥammad al- (d. 293/906), *Masāʾil al-imāma* in Josef van Ess (ed.), *Frühe muʿtazilitsche Haresiographie* (Wiesbaden: In Kommission bei F. Steiner, 1971).
Nāṭiq biʾl-Ḥaqq, Abū Ṭālib Yaḥyā b. al-Ḥusayn al- (d. 424/1033), *Amālī* preserved in Jaʿfar b. Aḥmad's *Taysīr al-maṭālib*, ed. ʿAbd Allāh Ḥamūd al-ʿIzzī (Amman: Muʾassasat al-Imām Zayd b. ʿAlī al-Thaqafiyya, 2002).
al-Ifāda, ed. Muḥammad Yaḥyā Ṣāliḥ ʿIzzān (Yemen: Dār al-Ḥikma al-Yamāniyya, 1996).
Kitāb al-taḥrīr, ed. Muḥammad Yaḥyā Sālim ʿAzzān, 2 vols. (Ṣanʿāʾ: Maktabat Badr, 1997).
Nawawī, Yaḥyā b. Sharīf al- (d. 676/1277), *Majmūʿ sharḥ al-Muhadhdhab*, ed. Zakariyyā ʿAlī Yūsuf, 18 vols. (Cairo: Maṭbaʿat al-Imām bi-Miṣr, 1966–9).
Nawbakhtī, Ḥasan b. Mūsā al- (d. after 300/912), *Firaq al-shīʿa*, ed. Muḥammad Ṣādiq Āl Baḥr al-ʿUlūm (Najaf: n.p., 1936).
Newman, Andrew, *The Formative Period of Twelver Shīʿism* (Richmond: Curzon, 2000).
Noth, Albrecht, *The Early Arabic Historical Tradition*, in collaboration with Lawrence Conrad, trans. Michael Bonner (Princeton: Darwin, 1994).
Nuwayrī, Aḥmad b. ʿAbd al-Wahhāb al- (d. 732/1332?), *Nihāyat al-arab fī funūn al-adab*, 33 vols. (Cairo: Maṭbaʿat Dār al-Kutub al-Miṣriyya, 1923–).
Qāḍī Nuʿmān b. Muḥammad b. Manṣūr (d. 363/974), *Daʿāʾim al-islām*, ed. Āṣaf ʿAlī Aṣghar Fayḍī, 2 vols. (Cairo: Dār al-Maʿārif, 1951–60).
Qaffāl, Muḥammad b. Aḥmad al-Shāshī al- (d. 507/1114), *Ḥilyat al-ʿulamāʾ fī maʿrifat madhāhib al-fuqahāʾ*, ed. Yāsīn Aḥmad Ibrāhīm Darādikah, 8 vols. (Amman: Dār al-Bāz, 1988).
Qalahjī, Muḥammad Rawwās al-, *Muʿjam lughat al-fuqahāʾ* (Karachi: Idārat al-Qurʾān, 1989).
Qudūrī, Aḥmad b. Muḥammad al- (d. 428/1037), *Mukhtaṣar*, ed. Kāmil Muḥammad Muḥammad ʿUwayda (Beirut: Dār al-Kutub al-ʿIlmiyya, 1997).
Qummī, ʿAlī b. Ibrāhīm al- (d. 4th/10th century) (attrib.), *Tafsīr*, ed. Ṭayyib al-Mūsawī al-Jazāʾirī, 2 vols. (Najaf: Maktabat al-Hudaʾ, 1966–7).
Qummī, Saʿd b. ʿAbd Allāh al- (d. 300/913), *Kitāb al-maqālāt waʾl-firaq*, ed. Muḥammad Jawād Mashkūr (Tehran: Muʾassasat Maṭbūʿātī ʿAṭāʾī, 1963).
Qurṭubī, Muḥammad b. Aḥmad al- (d. 671/1273), *al-Jāmiʿ li-aḥkām al-Qurʾān*, 20 vols. (Cairo: Dār al-Kātib al-ʿArabī, 1967).
Rabīʿ b. Ḥabīb (d. 170/786?) (attrib.), *al-Jāmiʿ al-ṣaḥīḥ*, ed. ʿĀshūr b. Yūsuf (Beirut: Dār al-Ḥikma, 1995).

Rāfi'ī, 'Abd al-Karīm b. Muḥammad al- (d. 623/1226), *al-'Azīz*, ed. 'Ādil Aḥmad 'Abd al-Mawjūd and 'Alī Muḥammad Mu'awwaḍ, 14 vols. (Beirut: Dār al-Kutub al-'Ilmiyya, 1997).

Rahman, Sayeed, *The Legal and Theological Thought of Ibn Abi Zayd al-Qayrawani* (Yale University Ph.D., 2009).

Rāzī, Aḥmad b. Sahl al- (d. late 3rd/9th century), *Akhbār Fakhkh*, ed. Maher Jarrar (Beirut: Dār al-Gharb al-Islāmī, 1995).

Rāzī, Fakhr al-Dīn al- (d. 606/1209), *al-Tafsīr al-kabīr*, 32 vol. (Tehran: n.p., 198–).

Robinson, Chase, *Islamic Historiography* (New York: Cambridge University Press, 2003).

Rubin, Uri, "Exegesis and Ḥadīth: The Case of the Seven Mathānī," in G. R. Hawting and A. A. Shareef (eds.), *Approaches to the Qur'ān* (New York: Routledge, 1993).

Rustāqī, Khamīs b. Sa'īd al-, *Manhaj al-tālibīn*, ed. Sālim b. Ḥamad b. Sulaymān al-Ḥārithī, 16 vols. (Oman: Wizārat al-Turāth al-Qawmī, 1979).

Sadeghi, Behnam, "The Authenticity of Two 2nd/8th Century Legal Texts," *ILS*, 17 (2010) 291–319.

"The Chronology of the Qur'ān: A Stylometric Research Program," *Arabica*, 58 (2011) 210–99.

"The Traveling Tradition Test," *Der Islam*, 85 (2010) 203–42.

Sadeghi, Behnam and Uwe Bergmann, "The Codex of a Companion of the Prophet and the Qur'ān of the Prophet," *Arabica*, 57 (2010) 343–436.

Saḥnūn al-Tanūkhī, 'Abd al-Salām b. Sa'īd (d. 240/854), *al-Mudawwana al-kubrā*, ed. Ḥamdī al-Damirdāsh Muḥammad, 9 vols. (Beirut: al-Maktabat al-'Aṣriyya, 1999).

Samarqandī, Naṣr b. Muḥammad Abū Layth al- (d. 373/893), *Tafsīr*, ed. 'Alī Muḥammad Mu'awwad *et al.*, 3 vols. (Beirut: Dār al-Kutub al-'Ilmiyya, 1993).

Ṣan'ānī, 'Abd al-Razzāq b. Hammām al- (d. 211/827), *Muṣannaf fī 'l-ḥadīth*, ed. Ayman Naṣr al-Dīn al-Azharī, 12 vols. (Beirut: Dār al-Kutub al-'Ilmiyya, 2000).

Ṣan'ānī, 'Alī b. Ismā'īl b. 'Abd Allāh al-, *Kitāb ra'b al-ṣad'*, ed. 'Alī b. Ismā'īl b. 'Abd Allāh al-Mu'ayyad, 3 vols. (Beirut: Dār al-Nafā'is, 1999).

Sarakhsī, Muḥammad b. Aḥmad al- (d. 5th/11th century), ed. Muḥammad Rāḍī, 30 vols. (Cairo: Maṭba'at al-Sa'āda, 1906).

Schacht, Joseph, *The Origins of Muhammadan Jurisprudence* (Oxford: Clarendon, 1975).

Schoeler, Gregor, *The Biography of Muhammad*, trans. Uwe Vagelpohl (New York: Routledge 2011).

The Genesis of Literature in Islam, trans. Shawkat Toorawa (Edinburgh: Edinburgh University Press, 2009).

The Oral and the Written in Early Islam, trans. Uwe Vagelpohl (New York: Routledge, 2006).

Serjeant, R. B., "Meccan Trade and the Rise of Islam: Misconceptions and Flawed Polemics," *JAOS*, 110 (1990) 472–86.

Sezgin, Fuat, *Buhârî'nin Kaynaklari* (Istanbul, Ibrahim Horoz Basimevi, 1956).
Geschichte des arabischen Schrifttums, 15 vols. (Leiden: Brill, 1967).
Shāfiʿī, Muḥammad b. Idrīs al- (d. 204/820), *al-Umm*, ed. Maḥmūd Maṭarajī, 9 vols. (Beirut: Dār al-Kutub al-ʿIlmiyya, 1993).
Shahristānī, Muḥammad b. ʿAbd al-Karīm al- (d. 548/1153), *al-Milal wa'l-niḥal*, ed. Aḥmad Sayyid al-Kīlānī, 2 vols. (Cairo: Maktabat Muṣṭafā al-Bābī al-Ḥalabī, 1961).
Shalmaghānī, Muḥammad b. ʿAlī al- (d. 322/934), *Fiqh al-Riḍā* (Mashhad: al-Mu'tamar al-ʿĀlāmī li-l-Imām al-Riḍā, 1985).
Shammākhī, ʿĀmir b. ʿAlī al- (d. 792/1389), *Kitāb al-īḍāḥ*, 4 vols. (Beirut: Maṭbaʿat al-Waṭan, 1970).
Sharaf al-Dīn al-Ḥusayn b. Muḥammad (d. 661/1223), *Shifā' al-uwām*, 3 vols. (Ṣanʿā': n.p., 1996).
Sharafī, ʿAbd Allāh b. Aḥmad b. Ibrāhīm al- (d. 1062/1652), *al-Maṣābīḥ al-sāṭiʿat al-anwār*, ed. Muḥammad Qāsim al-Hāshimī and ʿAbd al-Salām ʿAbbās al-Wajīh, 3 vols. (Ṣaʿda: Maktabat al-Turāth al-Islāmī, 1998).
Sharīf al-Murtaḍā, ʿAlī b. Ḥusayn al- (d. 436/1045), *al-Intiṣār* (Najaf: al-Maṭbaʿat al-Ḥaydariyya, 1971).
Masā'il al-nāṣiriyyāt (Tehran: Rābiṭat al-Thaqāfa wa'l-ʿĀlāqa al-Islāmiyya, 1997).
Shawkānī, Muḥammad b. ʿAlī al- (d. 1255/1839), *Wabl al-ghamām*, ed. Muḥammad Ṣubḥī, 2 vols. (Cairo: Maktabat Ibn Taymiyya, 1995–6).
Shaybānī, Muḥammad b. al-Ḥasan al- (d. 189/805), *al-Āthār* (Karachi: Idārat al-Qur'ān, 1998).
Kitāb al-āthār, ed. Abū Wafā' al-Afghānī (Karachi: al-Majlis al-ʿIlmī, 1965–).
Shaybānī, Muḥammad b. al-Ḥasan al- (fl. 7th/13th century), *Nahj al-bayān*, ed. Ḥusayn Dargāhī, 5 vols. (Qumm: Nashr al-Hādī, 1998).
Shīrāzī, Ibrāhīm b. ʿAlī Abū Isḥāq al- (d. 475/1083), *al-Muhadhdhab fī fiqh al-imām al-Shāfiʿī*, ed. Muḥammad al-Zuhaylī, 6 vols. (Beirut: al-Dār al-Shāmiyya, 1992–6).
Spitaler, Anton, *Die Verszählung des Koran* (Munich: Verlag der Bayerischen Akademie der Wissenschaften, 1935).
Syed, Mairaj, *Classical Islamic Legal and Moral Thought* (Princeton University Ph.D., 2011 forthcoming).
Ṭabarī, Muḥammad b. al-Jarīr al- (d. 310/923), *Tafsīr*, ed. Ṣalāḥ ʿAbd al-Fattāḥ al-Khālidī, 7 vols. (Beirut: al-Dār al-Shāmiyya, 1997).
Tārīkh al-umam wa'l-mulūk, 8 vols. (Cairo: Maṭbaʿat al-Istiqāma, 1939–).
Ṭabāṭabā'ī, ʿAbd al-ʿAzīz, *Muʿjam ʿalām al-shīʿa* (Qumm: Mu'assasat Āl al-Bayt, 1996–7).
Tabbarah, Afif, *The Spirit of Islam*, trans. Hasan Shoucair and rev. Rohi Baalbaki (Beirut: Dār al-ʿIlm, 1978).
Ṭabrisī, Faḍl b. al-Ḥasan al- (d. 548/1153) *Jawāmiʿ al-jāmiʿ*, 2 vols. (Beirut: Dār al-Aḍwā', 1985).
Majmaʿ al-bayān, 8 vols. (Cairo: Dār al-Taqrīb Bayn al-Madhāhib al-Islāmiyya, 1958).
Majmaʿ al-bayān, 10 vols. (Cairo: Dār al-Taqrīb Bayn al-Madhāhib al-Islāmiyya, 1997).

Ṭabrisī, Ḥusayn Taqī al- (d. 1320/1902), *Mustadrak Wasā'il al-shī'a*, 27 vols. (Qumm: Mu'assasat Āl al-Bayt, 1986–2000).
Ṭahāwī, Aḥmad b. Muḥammad al- (d. 321/933), *Mukhtaṣar*, ed. Abū al-Wafā' al-Afghānī (Cairo: Dār al-Kitāb al-'Arabī, 1951).
Sharḥ ma'ānī al-āthār, ed. Muḥammad Zuhrī al-Najjār and Muḥammad Sayyid Jād al-Ḥaqq, 5 vols. (Beirut: 'Ālam al-Kutub, 1994).
Takim, Liyakat, "From *Bid'a* to *Sunna*: The *Wilāya* of 'Alī in the Shī'ī *Adhān*," *JAOS*, 120 (2000) 166–77.
Ṭayālisī, Sulaymān b. Dāwūd al- (d. 204/820), *Musnad*, ed. Muḥammad b. 'Abd al-Muḥsin al-Turkī, 4 vols. (Hajar: n.p., 1999).
Tirmidhī, Muḥammad b. 'Īsā al- (d. 279/892), *Sunan*, ed. 'Abd al-Wahhāb 'Abd al-Laṭīf, 5 vols. (Medina: al-Maktabat al-Salafiyya, 1965–7).
Tsafrir, Nurit, *The History of an Islamic School of Law* (Cambridge, MA: Islamic Legal Studies Program of Harvard Law School, 2004).
Tucker, William, *Mahdis and Millenarians* (New York: Cambridge University Press, 2008).
Ṭūsī, Muḥammad b. al-Ḥasan al- (d. 460/1067), *al-Amālī* (Qumm: Dār al-Thaqāfa, 1993).
al-Istibṣār, ed. 'Alī Akbar al-Ghaffārī (Qumm: Dār al-Ḥadīth, 2001).
Kitāb al-khilāf, 6 vols. (Qumm: Mu'assasat al-Nashr al-Islāmī, 1995).
al-Mabsūṭ fī fiqh al-imāmiyya, ed. Muḥammad Bāqir al-Bihbūdī, 8 vols. (Tehran: al-Maktabat al-Murtaḍawiyya, 1967).
al-Nihāya, 3 vols. (Qumm: Mu'assasat al-Nashr al-Islāmī, 1991).
Rijāl al-Ṭūsī, ed. Jawād al-Qayyūmī al-Iṣfahānī (Qumm: al-Mu'assasat al-Nashr al-Islāmī, 1994).
Tahdhīb al-aḥkām, ed. Ḥasan al-Mūsawī, 10 vols. (Najaf: Dār al-Kutub al-Islāmiyya, 1959).
Tustarī, Muḥammad Taqī al-, *Qāmūs al-rijāl*, 12 vols. (Qumm: Mu'assasat al-Nashr al-Islāmī, 1989–).
Walwālijīya, 'Abd al-Rashīd b. Abī Ḥanīfa al- (d. 540/1145), *al-Fatāwā al-walwālijīya*, ed. Miqdād b. Mūsā al-Furaywī, 5 vols. (Beirut: Dār al-Kutub al-'Ilmiyya, 2003).
Wansbrough, John, *The Sectarian Milieu* (London: Oxford University Press, 1978).
Warrām b. Abī Farrās (d. 605/1208), *Tanbīh al-khawāṭir*, ed. Muḥammad al-Akhūndī, 2 vols. (Tehran: Dār al-Kutub al-Islāmiyya, 1956–7).
Watt, Montgomery, *Muhammad: Prophet and Statesman* (London: Oxford University Press, 1967).
Yaḥyā b. Sa'īd (fl. 5th/11th century), *Kitāb al-īḍāḥ fi'l-aḥkām*, ed. Muḥammad Maḥmūd Ismā'īl, 3 vols. (Muscat: Wizārat al-Turāth, 1984).
Ya'qūbī, Aḥmad b. Abī Ya'qūb al- (d. 284/897), *Tārīkh al-Ya'qūbī*, ed. 'Abd al-Amīr 'Alī Muhannā, 2 vols. (Beirut: Mu'assasat al-'Ālamī, 1980?).
Yāqūt b. 'Abd Allāh al-Ḥamawī (d. 626/1229), *Mu'jam al-buldān*, ed. Farīd 'Abd al-Azīz al-Jundī, 7 vols. (Beirut: Dār al-Kutub al-'Ilmiyya, 1990).
Zamakhsharī, Maḥmūd b. 'Umar al- (d. 538/1144), *al-Kashshāf*, 4 vols. (Cairo: Maktabat Muṣṭafā al-Bābī al-Ḥalabī, 1966–8).
Zaman, Iftikhar, *The Evolution of a Ḥadīth* (University of Chicago Ph.D., 1989).

"The Science of *Rijāl* as a Method in the Study of Ḥadīths," *JIS*, 5 (1994) 1–34.
Zayd b. 'Alī (d. 122/740), *Musnad* (Beirut: Dār al-Maktabat al-Ḥayāt, 1966).
Musnad, ed. 'Abd al-'Azīz b. Isḥāq al-Baghdādī (Ṣan'ā': Maktabat al-Irshād, 1990).

Index

'Abbāsids, 6–10, 13, 200, 204, 205, 206, 208, 209–10
'Abd Allāh b. 'Abbās
  on *basmala*, 49, 74–5
  on prohibition, 154
  on *qunūt*, 105
'Abd Allāh b. al-Ḥasan, 201–2
'Abd Allāh b. Ma'qil, 123–6
'Abd Allāh b. Mu'āwiya, 6
'Abd Allāh b. 'Umar
  on prohibition, 49, 155–6
  on *qunūt*, 100, 102, 105
'Abd al-Malik b. Marwān, 5
'Abd al-Raḥmān b. Abzā, 90
'Abd al-Raḥmān b. Ma'qil b. Muqarrin, 50
Abū al-'Āliya Rufay' b. Mihrān, 219
Abū Bakr (1st caliph)
  appointment of 'Umar b. al-Khaṭṭāb, 195
  Batrī belief regarding, 19
  early-comers and policies of, 3–4
  Jārūdī belief regarding, 18
  Sulaymānī belief regarding, 20
Abū Ḥanīfa
  on *basmala*, 72–3
  on prohibition, 142–3, 153, 155
  and Sulaymān b. Mihrān al-A'mash, 226
Abū Ḥayyān al-Andalūsī, Muḥammad b. Yūsuf, 102, 112
Abū Hurayra, 74–5
Abū al-Jārūd Ziyād b. al-Mundhir, 18, 49
Abū Muslim, 200
Abū Ya'lā Muḥammad b. al-Ḥusayn, 69–70
Abū Yūsuf, Ya'qūb b. Ibrāhīm, 142–3
ahl al-ra'y
  accommodation with 'Abbāsids, 209–10
  overview of, 10
  use of written texts, 33
Aḥmad b. Ibrāhīm, 198
Aḥmad b. 'Īsā, 33, 36–8
  Jārūdization of Zaydism, 213
  on *qunūt*, 116–17, 126
'Ā'isha, 18, 19
'Alawī, Muḥammad b. 'Alī al-, 38, 116
'Alī (4th caliph and 1st Imām), 4–5, 194
  development of Zaydī Shī'ism, 17–21
  importance of pilgrimages to grave of, 244–5
  on prohibition, 154
  on *qunūt*, 50, 108, 123–6
  and unity of Kūfan Shī'a, 13–14
'Alī b. Muḥammad b. Sulaymān, 50
'Alids
  and 'Abbāsid dynasty, 6–10
  in *basmala* traditions, 84
  development of Imāmī Shī'ism, 14–16
  Jārūdī belief regarding, 18–19
  reasons for prominence of, 5
  uprisings, 13
alternative sources for history, 11
A'mash, Sulaymān b. Mihrān al-, 190
  evaluation of, 221, 225–7
  as transmitter of *qunūt* traditions, 127
'Āmir b. Sharāḥīl, 190
Amir-Moezzi, Muḥammad 'Alī, 15–16
'Amr b. 'Abd Allāh b. 'Alī, 85
Ash'arī, Abū al-Ḥasan al-, 194
ashrāf (tribal elites), 3–4

'Askarī, Ḥasan al- (11th Imām), 246–7
aṣl. *See uṣūl*
'Aṭā' b. Abī Rabāḥ, 31, 85
'Ayyāshī, Muḥammad b. Mas'ūd al-, 73

bādhiq, defined, 141. *See also* prohibition
Bajalī, Jarīr b. 'Abd Allāh b. Jābir al-, 240
Balādhurī, Aḥmad b. Yaḥyā al-, 199
Bāqir, Muḥammad al- (5th Imām)
  on *basmala*, 50, 84
  citation of in Sunnī and Imāmī collections, 45
  Masjid Suhayl, 235
  pilgrimages to Karbalā', 245–6
  on prohibition, 47–8
  on *qunūt*, 49, 123–6
  role in development of Imāmī Shī'ism, 13, 14–16
  taqiyya, 21
  as transmitter of *basmala* traditions, 87–90
Barqī, Aḥmad b. Muḥammad al-, 243
basmala, 57–94
  chains of transmission, 44–5, 86–90, 250
  Ḥanafī stance on, 59–61
  Ḥanbalī stance on, 68–71
  Imāmī stance on, 71–4
  legal authorities, 82–6
  Mālikī stance on, 61–6
  narrative style, 91–3
  Shāfi'ī stance on, 66–8
  Zaydī stance on, 74–7
  Baṣra
  Ḥanafīs and *basmala*, 60
  Mālikīs and *basmala*, 63–4
  Qur'ānic reading of, 63
  Sunnism and *basmala*, 85
Baṣrī, al-Ḥasan al-, 218–19
Batriyya (Zaydī), 251–2
  alternative origin narrative of Zaydism, 192
  and *basmala*, 86, 93, 94–0
  classical origin narrative of Zaydism, 191–2
  consolidation of, 200–4
  and prohibition, 175–6, 180, 185
  and *qunūt*, 126, 133, 136
  theological doctrines of, 17–21
Battle of Fakhkh, 208–9, 210, 211
Battle of Uḥud, 96, 98, 113, 117–18
Bayhaqī, Aḥmad b. al-Ḥusayn al-, 35
biblical stories, 52, 181, 182–4
Bi'r Ma'ūna, 97–8, 101, 104, 106, 113–14, 117–18
Bukayr b. Māhān, 200
Bukhārī, Muḥammad b. Ismā'īl al-, 10, 31

cautionary dissimulation (*taqiyya*), 21
chain of transmission. *See isnād*
common link method for dating traditions, 26–7
Cook, Michael, 27, 28, 40

Dakake, Maria, 15–16
Dārimī, 'Abd Allāh b. 'Abd al-Raḥmān al-, 24–34, 39–41, 217, 218
dating of literacy period, controversy over, 27
da'wa ('Abbāsid missionary network), 13, 200
Dhahabī, Muḥammad b. Aḥmad al-, 222, 223, 224
Dharr b. 'Abd Allāh b. Zurārā, 90
direct quotes of legal opinions, 49
  in *basmala* traditions, 92
  in prohibition traditions, 181, 182–4
  in *qunūt* traditions, 134, 135–6
Djait, Hichem, 231–4, 235–6

early-comers (social group in 1st/7th and 2nd/8th centuries)
  defined, 3
  and tensions between tribal-elites and late-comers, 3–4
evaluation of transmitters, 216–20
exegesis, 51–2
  in *basmala* traditions, 92, 94–0
  in prohibition traditions, 181, 182–4
  in *qunūt* traditions, 135–6
exemplary statements, 50
  in *basmala* traditions, 91–3
  in prohibition traditions, 181, 182–4
  in *qunūt* traditions, 134–6
extremist (*ghulāt*) ideas, 15
eyewitness accounts, 48–9
  in *basmala* traditions, 91, 92
  in prohibition traditions, 182–4
  in *qunūt* traditions, 134, 135–6

fajr qunūt. *See qunūt*
Fāṭima (daughter of the Prophet), 18
Fuḍayl b. Yasār, 47–8

ghulāt (extremist) ideas, 15
Goldziher, Ignaz, 24–5

Ḥabīb b. Qays, 127–33
Hādawī Zaydīs, 114, 116–17, 118, 119
Hādī, ʿAlī b. Muḥammad al- (10th Imām), 50
Hādī ilā'l-Ḥaqq, Yāḥyā b. al-Ḥusayn al- (Zaydī Imām)
  on *basmala*, 75–7
  on prohibition, 160–1
  on *qunūt*, 114–16
  rebellion of al-Ḥusayn b. ʿAlī, 207
ḥadīth (tradition) collections
  defined, 12
  re-examination of, 12
al-Ḥakam b. ʿUtayba, 227
Ḥanafis, 10–11
  and *basmala*, 59–61, 78, 79
  and prohibition, 141–6, 152, 163, 164–5, 169–70
  and *qunūt*, 97–100, 118–19
Ḥanbalīs
  and *basmala*, 68–71, 78, 79
  and prohibition, 153–6, 164–5
  and *qunūt*, 106–9, 119
Hārūn b. Saʿd al-ʿIjlī, 198, 202–3
al-Ḥasan b. ʿAlī b. Abī Ṭālib (2nd Imām), 17–18, 115
al-Ḥasan b. Muḥammad b. ʿAbd Allāh b. al-Ḥasan b. al-Ḥasan b. ʿAlī b. Abī Ṭālib, 207
al-Ḥasan b. Ṣāliḥ, 205–6, 227
Ḥasan b. Yaḥyā, 116–18
Hāshimī movement. *See da'wa* (ʿAbbāsid missionary network)
heresiographies
  and the revolt of Zayd b. ʿAlī, 193–7
  shortcomings of genre, 12, 24
Hibat Allāh Aḥmad b. Muḥammad b. al-Kātib. *See* Ibn Barniyya
Ḥillī, Ḥasan b. Yūsuf al-ʿAllāma al-. *See* Ibn al-Muṭahhar
Hishām b. ʿAbd al-Malik, 226
Hodgson, Marshall, 15–16, 206
Ḥurr al-ʿAmilī, Muḥammad b. al-Ḥasan al-, 35–6
al-Ḥusayn b. ʿAlī b. Abī Ṭalib (3rd Imām)
  rebellion of, 207
  and tribal elites, 5
  in Zaydī Shīʿism, 17–18
Ibāḍiyya
  and *basmala*, 78
  and prohibition, 163
Ibn ʿAbd al-Barr, Yūsuf b. ʿAbd Allāh
  on *basmala*, 63
  on *qunūt*, 101–2
Ibn Abī Layla, 126, 226
Ibn Abī Najīḥ, 47
Ibn Abī Zayd al-Qayrawānī
  on *basmala*, 64–5
  on prohibition, 146–9
  on *qunūt*, 101
Ibn al-ʿArabī, Abū Bakr, 65
Ibn Bābawayh, 109
Ibn Barniyya (Hibat Allāh Aḥmad b. Muḥammad b. al-Kātib), 245
Ibn Ḥanbal
  on *basmala*, 69
  exclusion from analysis, 35
  on *qunūt*, 107
  and Sulaymān b. Mihrān al-Aʿmash, 222
Ibn Hishām, 24
Ibn Isḥāq, 24
Ibn Jurayj, 30
Ibn Kathīr, Ismāʿīl, 112
Ibn al-Mashhadī, Muḥammad b. Jaʿfar, 244
Ibn al-Muṭahhar (Ḥasan b. Yūsuf al-ʿAllāma al-Ḥillī)
  on prohibition, 159
  on *qunūt*, 110–12
Ibn Qudāma, Muwaffaq al-Dīn ʿAbd Allāh b. Aḥmad
  on *basmala*, 70
  on prohibition, 154–6
  on *qunūt*, 107–9
Ibn Saʿd, Muḥammad, 221–2
Ibn Ṭāhir al-Baghdādī, ʿAbd al-Qāhir, 194–6
Ibrāhīm b. ʿAbd Allāh b. al-Ḥasan b. al-Ḥasan b. ʿAlī b. Abī Ṭālib, 6, 202–4
Ibrāhīm b. Muḥammad, 126
Idrīs b. ʿAbd Allāh b. al-Ḥasan b. al-Ḥasan b. ʿAlī b. Abī Ṭālib, 20, 208–9, 212
al-ʿIjlī, Aḥmad b. ʿAbd Allāḥ al-, 222, 223–4
Imāmate (*imāma*)
  divisions produced by doctrine of, 13–14
  significance in Shīʿism, 11
Imāmī Shīʿism, 249
  analysis of traditions, 80–2, 120–1, 122–3, 166–8, 169

Imāmī Shī'ism (*cont.*)
and *basmala*, 71–4, 79, 83, 84, 86, 87–92, 93, 94–0
common transmitters with Sunnism, 45
development of, 14–17
independence of, 189–90
legal authorities, 37, 42–3
and prohibition, 156–9, 164–5, 170, 171–2, 174–6, 177–8, 180, 181, 182–4, 185
and *qunūt*, 109–14, 119, 123–6, 127–33, 134, 135–6
research into written collections, 32–3
ritual practice and sectarian identity, 215–16
sources for traditions, 35–6
'Īsā b. Zayd b. 'Alī b. al-Ḥusayn b. 'Alī b. Abī Ṭālib, 202–3, 204–5
Iṣbahānī, Abū al-Faraj al-, 197–9, 202–3, 205
Islamic precedence (*sābiqa*), 3–4
Ismā'īl b. Ja'far al-Ṣādiq, 21
Ismā'īliyya
and *basmala*, 78
emergence of, 15
and prohibition, 163
isnād (chain of transmission), 108
basmala, 86–90, 250
and controversy over written sources, 24–34
geographical analysis, 39–41
prohibition, 176–80, 251
qunūt, 127–33, 251
single common transmitters and shared links, 43–6
skepticism regarding, 26
Isrā'īl b. Yūnus, 205

Jābir b. Yazīd b. Ḥārith, 127–33
Ja'far b. Aḥmad, 38
Jārūdiyya (Zaydī), 251–2
alternative origin narrative of Zaydism, 192
and *basmala*, 86, 93, 94–0
classical origin narrative of Zaydism, 191–2
emergence of, 207–10
marginality and the triumph of, 210–13
and prohibition, 175–6, 180, 185
and *qunūt*, 126, 133, 136
theological doctrines of, 17–21
Jaṣṣāṣ, Aḥmad b. 'Alī al-, 59–60
Ju'fī, 'Amr b. Shimr al-, 87–90
Ju'fī, Jābir b. Yazīd al-, 86–7
Juynboll, G. H. A., 26–7

Karbalā', pilgrimages to, 245–6
Karkhī, 'Ubayd Allāh b. al-Ḥusayn al-, 72–3
Kāsānī, 'Alā' al-Dīn Abū Bakr b. Mas'ūd al-, 146
Kāẓim, Mūsā al- (7th Imām), 16, 244
khamr, dispute over meaning of, 139. *See also* prohibition
Kindī, 'Abd al-Raḥmān b. Muḥammad b. al-Ash'ath b. Qays al-, 6
Kindī, al-Ash'ath b. Qays al-, 240
Kindī, Muḥammad b. Yūsuf al-, 219–20
Kohlberg, Etan, 15–16, 32–3, 225
Kūfa
founding of, 3
geography of, 233
governors of, 7–9
mosques of, 236
Qur'ānic reading of, 63
timeline of, 7–9
urban development of, 231–4
Kūfī, Muḥammad b. Sulaymān al-, 75, 76–7
Kulaynī, Muḥammad b. Ya'qūb al-, 35–6, 243

late-comers (*rawādif*), 3–4
legal authorities, 42–3
in *basmala* traditions, 82–6
in prohibition traditions, 170–6
in *qunūt* traditions, 121–7
list/sign traditions, 51
literary period, controversy over dating of, 27

Madelung, Wilferd, 15–16
Maḥbūbī, 'Ubayd Allāh b. Mas'ūd al-, 146
al-Mahdī ('Abbāsid caliph), 204
Majlisī, Muḥammad Bāqir al-, 33, 35–6, 51
Mālik b. Anas
on *basmala*, 62
and *Muwaṭṭa'*, 31
on *qunūt*, 100–1
Mālikīs
and *basmala*, 61–6, 78, 79
and prohibition, 146–50, 163–5
and *qunūt*, 100–3, 118–19
Ma'mar b. Rāshid, 30
al-Manṣūr ('Abbāsid caliph), 6, 204

Marghīnānī, 'Alī b. Abī Bakr al-, 145–6
masjid (mosques)
  accursed/hostile, 236, 240–2
  appropriation of sacred spaces, 235–42
  al-Ash'ath, 240
  Bāhila, 237
  Banī Jadhīma b. Mālik, 238
  Banī Kāhil, 237
  Banī Ẓafar, 238
  blessed/friendly, 236, 237–40
  demarcation of by sectarian groups, 231–5
  Ghanī, 237
  al-Ḥamrā', 237, 241–2
  al-Ḥannāna, 238
  Jarīr, 240
  Ju'fī, 237, 242
  al-Kūfa, 238–9
  al-Sahla, 238–9
  Ṣa'ṣa'a b. Ṣūḥān b. Ḥujr al-'Abdī, 237
  Shabath, 241
  Simāk, 240–1
  Suhayl, 237
  Taym, 241–2
  Thaqīf, 241–2
  Zayd b. Ṣūḥān, 237
Mas'ūdī, 'Alī b. al-Ḥusayn al-, 198
mawālī (non-Arab Muslim) population
  coalition with early-comers, 5
  defined, 5
Māwardī, 'Alī b. Muḥammad al-
  on *basmala*, 66–8
  on prohibition, 150–2
  on *qunūt*, 104–6
Mecca
  Qur'ānic reading of, 63
  Sunnism and *basmala*, 85
Medina
  basmala, 63, 64–5, 85
  qunūt, 101–3
Mizzī, Yūsuf b. Zakī 'Abd al-Raḥmān al-, 222, 224
Modarressi, Hossein, 15–16, 32–3
mosques. *See masjid*
Motzki, Harald, 28–32
Mu'āwiya b. Abī Sufyān
  death of, 5
  early-comers and, 4
Mu'āwiya b. 'Ammār, 47
Mufīd, Muḥammad b. Muḥammad al-Shaykh al-, 243
al-Mughīra b. Miqsam, 223
Muḥammad b. al-'Alā' b. Kurayb, 133
Muḥammad b. Sīrīn, 217
Mujāhid b. Jabr
  on *basmala*, 85
  on *qunūt*, 126
Mukhtār b. Abī 'Ubayd, 5
munaṣṣaf, defined, 141. *See also* prohibition
Murādī, Muḥammad b. Manṣūr al-, 38, 116–18
muthallath, defined, 141. *See also* prohibition
Muzani, Ismā'īl b. Yaḥyā al-, 66

nabīdh, defined, 140. *See also* prohibition
al-Nafs al-Zakiyya Muḥammad b. 'Abd Allāh b. al-Ḥasan b. al-Ḥasan b. 'Alī b. Abī Ṭālib, 91, 201–2, 203–4
Nakha'ī, Ibrāhīm al-
  on *basmala*, 51
  evaluation of transmitters, 218
  on *qunūt*, 108, 126
naqī', defined, 140. *See also* prohibition
narrative style, 46–52
  basmala, 91–3
  biblical stories, 52
  direct quotes of legal opinions, 49
  exegesis, 51–2
  exemplary statements, 50
  eyewitness accounts, 48–9
  prohibition, 181–5
  question-and-answer dialogue, 47–8
  qunūt , 134–6
  sign/list traditions, 51
  written correspondence, 50
Nāshi' al-Akbar, 'Abd Allāh b. Muḥammad al-, 193
Nāṣiriyya (Zaydī), 119, 120–1
Naṣr b. Sayyār, 200
Nāṭiq bi'l-Ḥaqq Yaḥyā b. al-Ḥusayn al-, 36–8
Nawbakhtī, Ḥasan b. Mūsā al-, 193–4
Nāwūsiyya (Imāmī), 15
non-Arab Muslim population. *See mawālī* population
Nu'mān b. Bashīr, 190

piety-minded/pietist groups
  accommodation, 206
  defined, 5, 10
  emergence of, 5–6

pilgrimages, 243–7
prohibition, 138–86
  chains of transmission, 176–80, 251
  definitions and explanations, 139–41
  Ḥanafī stance on, 141–6
  Ḥanbalī stance on, 153–6
  Imāmī stance on, 156–9
  legal authorities, 170–6
  Mālikī stance on, 146–50
  narrative style, 181–5
  Shāfiʿī stance on, 150–3
  Zaydī stance on, 159–62
Prophet
  on *basmala*, 50, 59–60, 62–3, 66–8, 70, 73, 75, 76–7, 80–2, 86
  on prohibition, 48–9, 51–2, 141, 143–4, 147–8, 151–2, 154–6, 157, 159, 163
  on *qunūt*, 95, 97–9, 104, 106, 110, 113–14, 117–18, 123–6
proto-Sunnī, defined, 10

Qasrī, Khālid b. ʿAbd Allāh al-, 6
Qudāma b. Maẓʿūn, 154, 160
question-and-answer dialogue, 47–8
  in *basmala* traditions, 92, 94–0
  in prohibition traditions, 181, 182–4
  in *qunūt* traditions, 134, 135–6
Qummī, Saʿd b. ʿAbd Allāh al-, 193–4
qunūt , 95–137
  chains of transmission, 127–33, 251
  Ḥanafī stance on, 97–100
  Ḥanbalī stance on, 106–9
  Imāmī stance on, 109–14
  legal authorities, 121–7
  Mālikī stance on, 100–3
  narrative style, 134–6
  Shāfiʿī stance on, 103–6
  Zaydī stance on, 114–18
Qurṭubī, Muḥammad b. Aḥmad al-, 65, 102, 112

Rāfiʿī, Abd al-Karīm b. Muḥammad al-, 153
rajʿa (return from the dead), divisions over, 20–1
rakʿa, defined, 96
Rassī, al-Qāsim b. Ibrāhīm al-, 116, 117, 126
rawādif (late-comers), 3–4
Rāzī, Fakhr al-Dīn al-, 112
Razzāq, ʿAbd al-. *See* Ṣanʿānī, ʿAbd al-Razzāq b. Hammām al-
ritual practice, 215–30
  and ambiguous transmitters, 220–8
  in evaluation of transmitters, 216–20

Ṣabbāḥ al-Zaʿfarānī, 205–6
sābiqa (Islamic precedence), 3–4
sacred spaces, 231–48
  appropriation of by sectarian groups, 231–5
  in Imāmī literature, 235–42
  pilgrimages to, 243–7
Saʿd b. Abī Waqqāṣ, 3
Sadeghi, Behnam, 29
Ṣādiq, Jaʿfar b. Muḥammad al- (6th Imām), 13
  on *basmala*, 47, 87–90
  development of Imāmī Shīʿism, 14–16
  pilgrimages, 244, 245–6
  on *qunūt*, 48
al-Saffāḥ (ʿAbbāsid caliph), 6
Ṣāḥib Fakhkh al-Ḥusayn b. ʿAlī b. al-Ḥasan b. al-Ḥasan b. al-Ḥasan b. ʿAlī b. Abī Ṭālib, 207–9
Saḥnūn al-Tanūkhī, ʿAbd al-Salām b. Saʿīd, 62
Saʿīd b. ʿAbd al-Raḥmān b. Abzā, 48, 90
Saʿīd b. Jubayr, 43
  on *basmala*, 49
  on *qunūt*, 126
Saʿīd b. al-Musayyab, 105, 126
Sajjād, Zayn al-ʿAbidīn ʿAlī b. al-Ḥusayn al- (4th Imām), 14
Sālim b. ʿAbd Allāh b. ʿUmar, 47
Sālim b. Abī Ḥafṣa, 227
Samarqandī, Naṣr b. Muḥammad Abū al-Layth al-, 60–1, 99
Ṣanʿānī, ʿAbd al-Razzāq b. Hammām al-, 29–31
Ṣanʿānī, ʿAlī b. Ismāʿīl b. ʿAbd Allāh al-, 36–8
Sarakhsī, Mūḥammad b. Aḥmad al-, 145
Ṣaʿṣaʿa b. Sūḥān b. Ḥujr al- ʿAbdī, Abū Ṭalḥa, 237
Schacht, Joseph, 26
Schoeler, Gregor, 25, 28–9, 31–2
sectarian identity, 189–214
  re-interpretation of Zaydism and, 213–14
  and ritual practice, 215–30
  and sacred spaces, 231–48
  Zaydism origin narrative, 192–213
Sezgin, Fuat, 28, 29

Shabath b. Rib'ī al-Tamīmī, 241
Shāfi'ī, Muḥammad b. Idrīs al-, 10, 65, 66, 103
Shāfi'īs
and *basmala*, 66–8, 78–9
and prohibition, 150–3, 163–5
and *qunūt*, 103–6, 118–19
Shahristānī, Muḥammad b. 'Abd al-Karīm al-, 194–6
Shalmaghanī, Muḥammad b. 'Alī al-, 109
Shammākh al-Yamāmī, 212–13
Sharaf al-Dīn Ḥusayn b. Muḥammad
on prohibition, 161–2
Shifā' al-uwām, 38
Zaydī Shī'ism and *basmala*, 74–5
shared links, 43–6. *See also isnād*; transmitters and shared links
basmala, 86–90
prohibition, 176–80
qunūt , 127–33
Sharīk b. 'Abd Allāh, 234–5
Shaybānī, al-Ḥarīsh b. 'Amr b. Dāwūd al-, 200
Shaybānī, Muḥammad b. al-Ḥasan al- (Ḥanafī)
on prohibition, 142–3
on *qunūt*, 97–8
Shaybānī, Muḥammad b. al-Ḥasan al- (Imāmī)
on *basmala*, 73
on *qunūt*, 114
Shī'ism, 3–22. *See also* Imāmī Shī'ism; Zaydī Shī'ism
early development of, 13–21
Shīrāzī, Ibrāhīm b. 'Alī Abū Isḥāq al-, 152–3
sign/list traditions, 51
Simāk b. Makhrama b. Ḥumayn al-Asadī, 240–1
structural analysis of traditions, 41–52
and *basmala*, 79–93
biblical stories, 52
direct quotes of legal opinions, 49
exegesis, 51–2
exemplary statements, 50
eyewitness accounts, 48–9
legal authorities, 42–3
narrative style, 46–52
and prohibition, 165–85
question-and-answer dialogue, 47–8
and *qunūt* , 120–36
sign/list traditions, 51
transmitters and shared links, 43–6
written correspondence, 50
Sufyān b. 'Uyayna, 30
Sulaymān b. Jarīr, 20, 212–13
Sulaymāniyya (Zaydī), 20–1
Sunnism, 51. *See also* Ḥanafīs; Ḥanbalīs; Mālikīs; Shāfi'īs
analysis of traditions, 80–2, 120–1, 122–3, 166–8, 169–70
and *basmala*, 83, 84, 85, 86, 87–93
and prohibition, 170, 171–2, 174, 175–80, 181–5
and *qunūt*, 123–6, 127–33, 134–6
research into written texts, 31–2
sources for traditions of, 35
Syria
support for caliphs, 4
Qur'ānic reading of, 63
reliance on soldiers from, 6

Ṭabarī, Muḥammad b. Jarīr al- , 61, 202, 207, 209, 211
Ṭabrisī, Faḍl b. al-Ḥasan al-, 35–6
on *basmala*, 73
on *qunūt*, 113–14
Ṭaḥāwī, Aḥmad b. Muḥammad al-
on prohibition, 142–5
on *qunūt*, 97, 98–9
Ṭalḥa b. 'Ubayd Allāh, 18, 19
Ṭālibiyya (Shī'ī), 18
taqiyya (cautionary dissimulation), 21
Ṭawūs b. Kaysān, 85
Thaqafī, al-Ḥajjāj b. Yūsuf al-, 6
Thaqafī, Yūsuf b. 'Umar al-
fighting between Zayd b. 'Alī and, 195, 197
governorship of, 6
Thawrī, Sufyān al-, 30, 205
on *basmala*, 78
on *qunūt*, 118
ṭilā, defined, 141. *See also* prohibition
tradition collections. *See ḥadīth* (tradition) collections
traditions, debate over authenticity of, 24–34, 39–41
traditionist movement/traditionists, 10
transmitters and shared links. *See also isnād*
and ambiguous sectarian affiliations, 220–8
basmala, 86–90
categorizations of, 216–17

transmitters and shared links (*cont.*)
evaluation of, 216–20
overview, 43–6
prohibition, 176–80
qunūt , 127–33
relevant factors in evaluation process, 218
tribal elites (*ashrāf*), 3–4
Ṭūsī, Mūḥammad b. al-Ḥasan al-, 35–6
discussion of prohibition, 156–9
opinion on *basmala*, 71–3
pilgrimages, 243–4
Tustarī, Muḥammad b. ʿAlī al-, 225–6

ʿUmar (2nd caliph)
on *basmala*, 48, 90
Batrī belief regarding, 19
early-comers and policies of, 3–4
Jārūdī belief regarding, 18
on prohibition, 144, 154, 160
ʿUmar b. Dharr b. ʿAbd Allāh, 90
ʿUmarī, ʿUmar b. ʿAbd al-ʿAzīz b. ʿAbd Allāh al-, 207–8
Umayyads, 4–6, 13, 200
Umm Salama, 72, 74–5
ʿUqba b. Thaʿlaba b. ʿAmr, 48–9
uṣūl (sing: *aṣl*), 32–3, 34, 35–6
ʿUtbī, Muḥammad al-Qurṭubī al-, 101
ʿUthmān (caliph)
Batrī belief regarding, 19
and early-comers, 4
Jārūdī belief regarding, 18
Sulaymānī belief regarding, 20

Vaglieri, Veccia, 203

Wakīʾ b. Jarrāḥ, 223
walāya, centrality of, 15–16
Walīd II b. Yazīd, 200
Walwālijīya, ʿAbd al-Rashīd b. Abī Ḥanīfa al-, 146
Wāqifiyya (Imāmī), emergence of, 15
Wāṣil b. ʿAṭāʾ, 194
witr qunūt . *See qunūt*
written correspondence, 50
in *basmala* traditions, 92
in prohibition traditions, 181, 182–4
in *qunūt* traditions, 135–6

Yaḥyā b. ʿAbd Allāh b. al-Ḥasan b. al-Ḥasan b. ʿAlī b. Abī Ṭālib, 208–9, 210–12
Yaḥyā b. Maʿīn, 151
Yaḥyā b. Zayd, 200–1
Yaʿqūbī, Aḥmad b. Abī Yaʿqūb al-, 198
Yūnus b. Bukayr, 44–5

Ẓāhirīs, 163
Zamakhsharī, Maḥmūd d. ʿUmar al-, 61, 99–100
Zayd b. ʿAlī, 33
on *basmala*, 91
Musnad, 36–8
on *qunūt*, 126
revolt of, 6, 13, 17, 192, 193–9
Zaydī Shīʿism, 249–50, 251–2
alternative origin narrative, 192–213
analysis of traditions, 80–2, 120–1, 122–3, 166–8, 169
and *basmala*, 74–7, 79, 83, 84, 85, 86, 87–93, 94–0
classical origin narrative, 189–92
common transmitters with Sunnism, 44–5
development of, 17–21
impetus for creation of, 13
legal authorities, 37–6, 42–3
and prohibition, 159–62, 164–5, 171–2, 174–80, 181–5
and *qunūt*, 114–18, 119, 124, 126, 127–33, 134–6
re-interpretation of, 213–14
research into written collections, 33–4
shared links with Sunnism, 45–6
sources for traditions, 36–8
Zayn al-ʿAbidīn. *See* Sajjād, Zayn al-ʿAbidīn ʿAlī b. al-Ḥusayn al- (4th Imām)
Zubayr, ʿUrwa b. al-, 126
al-Zubayr b. ʿAwwām, 18, 19, 100
Zuhrī, Muḥammad b. Muslim al-, 221–2

Cambridge Studies in Islamic Civilization

Titles in the Series

POPULAR CULTURE IN MEDIEVAL CAIRO *Boaz Shoshan*

EARLY PHILOSOPHICAL SHIISM: THE ISMAILI NEOPLATONISM OF ABŪ YA'QŪB AL-SIJISTĀNI *Paul E. Walker*

INDIAN MERCHANTS IN EURASIAN TRADE, 1600–1750 *Stephen Frederic Dale*

PALESTINIAN PEASANTS AND OTTOMAN OFFICIALS: RURAL ADMINISTRATION AROUND SIXTEENTH-CENTURY JERUSALEM *Amy Singer*

ARABIC HISTORICAL THOUGHT IN THE CLASSICAL PERIOD *Tarif Khalidi*

MONGOLS AND MAMLUKS: THE MAMLUK–ĪLKHĀNID WAR, 1260–1281 *Reuven Amitai-Preiss*

HIERARCHY AND EGALITARIANISM IN ISLAMIC THOUGHT *Louise Marlow*

THE POLITICS OF HOUSEHOLDS IN OTTOMAN EGYPT: THE RISE OF THE QAZDAĞLIS *Jane Hathaway*

COMMODITY AND EXCHANGE IN THE MONGOL EMPIRE: A CULTURAL HISTORY OF ISLAMIC TEXTILES *Thomas T. Allsen*

STATE AND PROVINCIAL SOCIETY IN THE OTTOMAN EMPIRE: MOSUL, 1540–1834 *Dina Rizk Khoury*

THE MAMLUKS IN EGYPTIAN POLITICS AND SOCIETY *Thomas Philipp* and *Ulrich Haarmann* (eds.)

THE DELHI SULTANATE: A POLITICAL AND MILITARY HISTORY *Peter Jackson*

EUROPEAN AND ISLAMIC TRADE IN THE EARLY OTTOMAN STATE: THE MERCHANTS OF GENOA AND TURKEY *Kate Fleet*

REINTERPRETING ISLAMIC HISTORIOGRAPHY: HARUN AL-RASHID AND THE NARRATIVE OF THE 'ABBĀSID CALIPHATE *Tayeb El-Hibri*

THE OTTOMAN CITY BETWEEN EAST AND WEST: ALEPPO, IZMIR, AND ISTANBUL *Edhem Eldem*, *Daniel Goffman*, and *Bruce Masters*

A MONETARY HISTORY OF THE OTTOMAN EMPIRE *Sevket Pamuk*

THE POLITICS OF TRADE IN SAFAVID IRAN: SILK FOR SILVER, 1600–1730 *Rudolph P. Matthee*

THE IDEA OF IDOLATRY AND THE EMERGENCE OF ISLAM: FROM POLEMIC TO HISTORY *G. R. Hawting*

CLASSICAL ARABIC BIOGRAPHY: THE HEIRS OF THE PROPHETS IN THE AGE OF AL-MA'MŪN *Michael Cooperson*

EMPIRE AND ELITES AFTER THE MUSLIM CONQUEST: THE TRANSFORMATION OF NORTHERN MESOPOTAMIA *Chase F. Robinson*

POVERTY AND CHARITY IN MEDIEVAL ISLAM: MAMLUK EGYPT, 1250–1517 *Adam Sabra*

CHRISTIANS AND JEWS IN THE OTTOMAN ARAB WORLD: THE ROOTS OF SECTARIANISM *Bruce Masters*

CULTURE AND CONQUEST IN MONGOL EURASIA *Thomas T. Allsen*

REVIVAL AND REFORM IN ISLAM: THE LEGACY OF MUHAMMAD AL-SHAWKANI *Bernard Haykel*

TOLERANCE AND COERCION IN ISLAM: INTERFAITH RELATIONS IN THE MUSLIM TRADITION *Yohanan Friedmann*

GUNS FOR THE SULTAN: MILITARY POWER AND THE WEAPONS INDUSTRY IN THE OTTOMAN EMPIRE *Gábor Ágoston*

MARRIAGE, MONEY AND DIVORCE IN MEDIEVAL ISLAMIC SOCIETY *Yossef Rapoport*

THE EMPIRE OF THE QARA KHITAI IN EURASIAN HISTORY: BETWEEN CHINA AND THE ISLAMIC WORLD *Michal Biran*

DOMESTICITY AND POWER IN THE EARLY MUGHAL WORLD *Ruby Lal*

POWER, POLITICS AND RELIGION IN TIMURID IRAN *Beatrice Forbes Manz*

POSTAL SYSTEMS IN THE PRE-MODERN ISLAMIC WORLD *Adam J. Silverstein*

KINGSHIP AND IDEOLOGY IN THE ISLAMIC AND MONGOL WORLDS *Anne F. Broadbridge*

JUSTICE, PUNISHMENT, AND THE MEDIEVAL MUSLIM IMAGINATION *Christian Lange*

THE SHIITES OF LEBANON UNDER OTTOMAN RULE *Stefan Winter*

WOMEN AND SLAVERY IN THE LATE OTTOMAN EMPIRE *Madeline Zilfi*

THE SECOND OTTOMAN EMPIRE: POLITICAL AND SOCIAL TRANSFORMATION IN THE EARLY MODERN WORLD *Baki Tezcan*

NON-MUSLIMS IN THE EARLY ISLAMIC EMPIRE: FROM SURRENDER TO COEXISTENCE *Milka Levy-Rubin*

RITUAL AND PIETY IN MEDIEVAL ISLAMIC LAW *Megan Reid*

24801214R00168

Printed in Poland
by Amazon Fulfillment
Poland Sp. z o.o., Wrocław